Paul Theroux was born in Medford, Massachusetts, in 1941, and published his first novel, *Waldo*, in 1967. He wrote his next three novels, *Fong and the Indians*, *Girls at Play* and *Jungle Lovers*, after a five-year stay in Africa. He subsequently taught at the University of Singapore, and during his three years there produced a collection of short stories, *Sinning with Annie*, and his highly praised novel *Saint Jack*. His other publications include *The Black House* (1974), a novel; *The Great Railway Bazaar: By Train Through Asia* (1975), an account of his adventurous journey by train from London to Tokyo and back; *The Family Arsenal* (1976); *The Consul's File* (1977); *Picture Palace* (1978; winner of the Whitbread Literary Award); *A Christmas Card* (1978); *The Old Patagonian Express: By Train Through the Americas* (1979); *World's End and Other Stories* (1980); *London Snow* (1980); *The Mosquito Coast*, which was the *Yorkshire Post* Novel of the Year for 1981 and the joint winner of the James Tait Black Memorial Prize; *The London Embassy* (1982), *Doctor Slaughter* (1985) and *Sunrise With Seamonsters: Travels and Discoveries 1964–1984* (1985).

Paul Theroux divides his time between Cape Cod and London.

PAUL THEROUX

The Kingdom by the Sea

A JOURNEY AROUND THE COAST OF GREAT BRITAIN

PENGUIN BOOKS

Penguin Books Ltd, Harmondsworth, Middlesex, England
Viking Penguin Inc., 40 West 23rd Street, New York, New York 10010, U.S.A.
Penguin Books Australia Ltd, Ringwood, Victoria, Australia
Penguin Books Canada Ltd, 2801 John Street, Markham, Ontario, Canada L3R 1B4
Penguin Books (N.Z.) Ltd, 182–190 Wairau Road, Auckland 10, New Zealand

First published by Hamish Hamilton 1983
Published in Penguin Books 1984
Reprinted 1985 (twice), 1986 (twice), 1987 (twice)

Made and printed in Great Britain by
Richard Clay Ltd, Bungay, Suffolk
Filmset in Monophoto Plantin

I dedicate this Book to those friends of mine in Britain who, giving me a welcome I must ever gratefully and proudly remember, left my judgment free; and who, loving their country, can bear the truth, when it is told good-humouredly and in a kind spirit.

Adapted from Charles Dickens's dedication
to *American Notes*, 1842

Contents

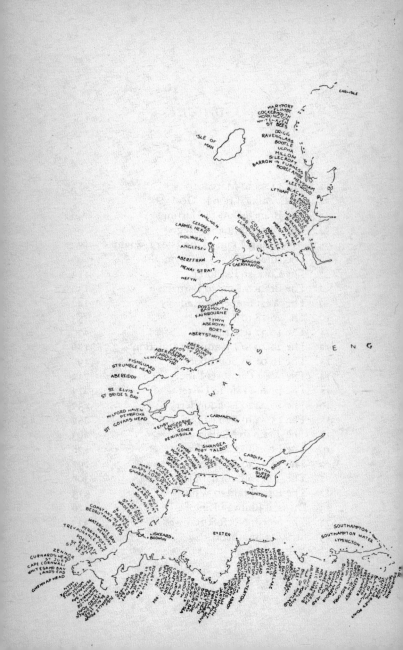

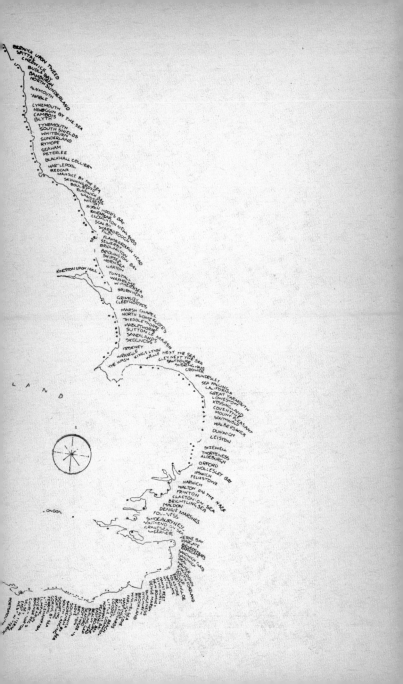

NORTH UIST

BENBECULA

SOUTH
UIST

BARRA

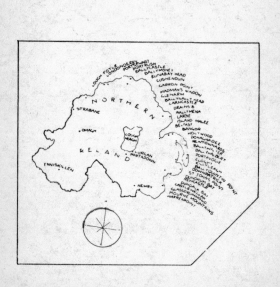

LOUGH FOYLE LONDONDERRY PORTRUSH PORTSTEWART BUSH BALLYCASTLE BALLYMONEY RUNABAY HEAD CUSHENDUN GARRON POINT MADMAN'S WINDOW GLENARM BALLYGALLY HEAD CARNCASTLE DRAINS B BALLYMENA LARNE ISLAND MAGEE BELFAST BANGOR HOLYWOOD DONAGHADEE NEWTOWNARDS BALLYWALTER BALLYHALBERT PORTAVOGIE CLOUGHY BALLYQUINTIN POINT PORTAFERRY STRANGFORD LOUGH ST JOHN'S POINT DUNDRUM BAY DUNDRUM DUNCARA BAY CASTLEWELLAN ANNALONG MOURNE MOUNTAINS WARRENPOINT

N O R T H E R N

I R E L A N D

STRABANE

OMAGH

LOUGH NEAGH

LURGAN PORTADOWN

ENNISKILLEN

NEWRY

'... it takes passionate pilgrims, vague aliens and other disinherited persons to appreciate the "points" of this admirable country'

– Henry James, *English Hours*

'This is one of the lessons of travel – that some of the strangest races dwell next door to you at home'

– Robert Louis Stevenson, *Across the Plains*

I

The 11.33 to Margate

Everyone seemed to be going to China that year, or else writing rude things about the Arabs, or being frank about Africa. I had other things on my mind. After eleven years in London I still had not been much in Britain. I had not set foot in Wales or even East Anglia. People joked about Bognor Regis. I had never been to Bognor Regis. But I joked about it too! And where was Porlock? And was Northern Ireland a nightmare and Scotland breathtaking? And what exactly were the Lincolnshire Wolds? What I knew of Britain I had got from books. Britain was the most written-about country in the world. That was the problem, really. You read one book about China and you think you've got a good idea of the place; you read twenty books about Britain, even *English Traits* and *Rural Rides*, and you know you haven't got the slightest.

I lived in London for half the year, and the rest of the time went away. I had come to dislike the city. 'A man who is tired of London is tired of life' – no, I was tired of hunting for parking places, tired of the crowds and the scribbled-on walls, the dirty old buildings and the ugly new ones. I was sick of London traffic and London presumptions and London smugness. And the grey underwear on London clothes-lines hanging limply under baggy clouds made me sad. London did not regard itself as a city but rather as an independent republic. Sometimes it seemed as big as Belgium; it could take a whole day to cross it by car. I was also bored with London books, which had titles like *Britain: What Went Wrong?* and *Is Britain Dying?* London people said that what was wrong with Britain was wrong with the western hemisphere. Like many other London people I had never really been in Britain This floating kingdom was a foreign country.

Britain was nearby, but 'nearby' was misleading. Distances in Britain were meaningless – so many places were so hard to get to, or else hated outsiders, or were names of villages that no longer existed: so much of Britain lay buried. I knew a little bit about some parts because in Britain there was an oral tradition that took the place of travel, like the Bognor jokes and Scotland was breathtaking and Cornwall was creepy and South Wales was awful and Rye was ever so lovely. Everyone appeared to know everything. It was word of mouth. Scotland had the Highlands, Cambridgeshire the Fens, and Norfolk the Broads – the words called up peaks and thickets and puddles. Northerners sounded to me as though they had learned English in language labs. In London, I had once mistaken a Welshman for a Dutchman – something in his inquiring voice. As for the Irish, I had never personally known anyone in London who took an Irishman seriously unless the Irishman was armed. 'Bogtrotters,' people usually said. 'Micks are friendly!' I had never met a soul in London who had been to Northern Ireland.

I did not know anything, and I was beginning to think that I was as bad and lazy as everyone else.

Once, from behind a closed door, I heard an English woman exclaim with real pleasure, 'They are *funny*, the Yanks!' And I crept away and laughed to think that an English person was saying such a thing. And I thought: They wallpaper their ceilings! They put little knitted bobble-hats on their soft-boiled eggs to keep them warm! They don't give you bags in supermarkets! They say sorry when you step on their toes! Their government makes them get a hundred dollar licence every year for watching television! They issue driving licences that are valid for thirty or forty years – mine expires in the year 2011! They charge you for matches when you buy cigarettes! They smoke on buses! They drive on the left! They spy for the Russians! They say 'nigger' and 'Jewboy' without flinching! They call their houses 'Holm-leigh' and 'Sparrow View'! They sunbathe in their underwear! They don't say 'You're welcome'! They still have milk bottles and milkmen, and junk-dealers with horse-drawn wagons! They love candy and Lucozade and leftovers called bubble-and-squeak! They live in Barking and Dorking and Shellow Bowells! They have amazing names, like Mr Eatwell, and Lady

Inkpen, and Major Twaddle and Miss Tosh! And they think *we're* funny?

The longer I lived in London the more I came to see how much of Englishness was bluff, and what wet blankets they could be. You told an Englishman you were planning a trip around Britain and he said, 'It sounds about as much fun as chasing a mouse around a pisspot.' They could be deeply dismissive and self-critical. 'We're awful,' they said. 'This country is hopeless. We're never prepared for anything. Nothing works properly.' But being self-critical in this way was also a tactic for remaining ineffectual. It was surrender.

And when an English person said 'we' he did not mean himself – he meant the classes above and below him, the people he thought should be taking decisions, and the people who should be following. 'We' meant everyone else.

'Mustn't grumble' was the most English of expressions. English patience was mingled inertia and despair. What was the use? But Americans did nothing but grumble! Americans also boasted. 'I do some pretty incredible things,' was not an English expression. 'I'm fairly keen,' was not American. Americans were show-offs – it was part of our innocence – we often fell on our faces; the English seldom showed off, so they seldom looked like fools. The English liked especially to mock the qualities in other people they admitted they didn't have themselves. And sometimes they found us truly maddening. In America you were admired for getting ahead, elbowing forward, rising, pushing in. In England this behaviour was hated – it was the way the wops acted, it was 'Chinese fire-drill', it was disorder. But making a quick buck was also a form of queue-jumping, and getting ahead was a form of rudeness – a 'bounder' was a person who had moved out of his class. It was not a question of forgiving such things; it was, simply, that they were never forgotten. The English had long, merciless memories.

There were no blank spaces on the map of Great Britain, the best-known, most fastidiously mapped and most widely trampled piece of geography on earth. No country was easier to travel in – the British invented public transport. And yet I had seen practically nothing of it. I felt ashamed and ignorant, but when

I began to think about travelling around Britain, I became excited
– because I knew so little. I wanted to write about it.

Writing about a country in its own language was a great
advantage, because in other places one was always interpreting
and simplifying. Translation created a muffled obliqueness – one
was always seeing the country sideways. But language grew out
of the landscape – English out of England, and it seemed logical
that the country could only be accurately portrayed in its own
language. So what was I waiting for?

The problem was one of perspective: How and where to go
to get the best view of the place? It was also a problem in tone
– after all, I was an alien.

The British had invented their own solution to travel writing.
They went to places like Gabon and Paraguay and joked about
the discomforts, the natives, the weather, the food, the entertainments. It was necessary to be an outsider, which was why they
had never written about Britain in this way. But it was a mystery
to me why no one had ever come to Britain and written about
its discomforts and natives and entertainments and unintelligible
dialects. The British, who had devised a kind of envious mockery
of other cultures, and who had virtually invented the concept
of funny foreigners, had never regarded themselves as fair game
for the travel writer. They did not encourage aliens to observe
them closely. They were like a tribe that plundered abroad and
were secretive and inhospitable at home. The British did not make
me think of Shakespeare but rather of head-hunters – their travel
writing a literary version of head-shrinking that had never been
used on them. I was eager to try.

But it was also a problem of itinerary. In a place that was criss-
crossed with ant-trails, a kingdom of bottlenecks and private
property and high fences, my route was a problem, because there
were too many routes. To take all the trains would be no more
than a mediocre stunt. The buses did not go to enough places.
A bicycle was out – too dangerous, too difficult – another stunt
A car was too simple, and anyway I had lived in London long
enough to know that driving on English roads was no fun. My
route was crucial. It was the most important aspect of travel.
In choosing a route one was choosing a subject. But every mile
of Britain had a road through it, there was a track across every

field, a footpath in every acre of woods. Perhaps this was why I had never travelled in Britain: I had been unable to decide on the route.

And then I had my way: narrowly, around the entire coast. It answered every need. There was only one coast, it was one undeviating route, and this way I could see the whole of Britain. In many respects, Britain *was* its coast – nowhere in Britain was more than sixty-five miles from the sea. Nearly the whole of the coast was unknown to me. And so as soon as I decided on this coastal route for my itinerary I had my justification for the trip – the journey had the right shape; it had logic; it had a beginning and an end; and what better way was there to see an island than circumambulating its coast?

The greatest advantage in this tour was that a country tended to seep to its coast; it was concentrated there, deposited against its beaches like the tide-wrack from the sea. People naturally gravitated to the coast, and they wore fewer clothes there – it was normal on the coast to be semi-naked, exposed.

The best trains – the slow, sweet branch lines – plied the coast. Many of these branch lines were doomed. Some people said that none would be left in ten years, and most people agreed that the impending railway strike, planned for the early summer, would kill the branch lines. There were also the green buses – I had sometimes seen them filling a country lane, but I had never ridden on one. And there were footpaths.

I had an impression that there was a continuous footpath that went around the whole coastline of Great Britain. Every part of the coast I had seen so far had had such a footpath. Usually it was a muddy twelve-inch path, with a brisk figure approaching in plus-fours and thick-soled shoes and a crackling plastic mackintosh, and carrying a bag of sandwiches and an Ordnance Survey map. I imagined this person to be just another feature of the British coast, like the old gun emplacements, and the iron piers, and the wooden groynes, and the continuous and circling footpath. But if there was not a footpath around the kingdom there was certainly a beach, and I could walk along the beach – from Fishguard to Aberystwyth, for example, where there was no connecting train. I would try to walk as much as possible; I would take trains if they were interesting lines, or if the weather was bad; and if I had to, I would take buses. It was so easy to speed through this country I would have to make strict rules in order to slow myself down.

'England resembles a ship in its shape,' wrote Ralph Waldo Emerson in *English Traits*. He was wrong: books by pious aliens were full of kindnesses of this sort. England, of course, resembles a pig, with something on its back. Look at it. It is a hurrying pig; its snout is the south-west in Wales, and its reaching trotters are Cornwall, and its rump is East Anglia. The whole of Britain looks like a witch riding on a pig, and these contours – rump and snout and bonnet, and the scowling face of Western Scotland – were my route.

No British journey could be original. Defoe had done the whole of Britain by road, Daniell and Ayton had sailed around it, Cobbett had gone throughout the south of England on horseback, and more recently H. V. Morton and J. B. Priestley had gone in search of England, banging up and down in the thirties and forties. There were Britain-by-train books and Britain-by-bus books, and books about cycling around. Some people had walked around Britain and written about it. The most impressive recent hike was that of a man who had walked every inch of the coastline. It was seven thousand miles, but he had been in a hurry. He had done it in ten months and practically walked his legs off - given himself two severe pressure fractures in his leg bones. I read his book. The trouble with travel stunts was that the trick was the thing; it was all a form of tight-rope walking and the performer never took his eyes off his own feet.

I wanted to look around and see Britain for myself. I did not intend a stunt, or a test of strength, or a public display. In fact, quite the opposite; and later, tramping the coastal path or riding the slow trains, I sometimes felt like the prince in the old story, who because he distrusts everything he has been told and every-thing he has read, disguises himself in old clothes and, with a bag slung over his back, hikes the muddy roads talking to every-one and looking closely at things, to find out what his kingdom is really like.

And I wanted to see the future. Travel is so often an experiment with time. In Third World countries I felt I had dropped into the past, and I had never accepted the notion of timelessness anywhere. Most countries had specific years. In Turkey it was always 1952, in Malaysia 1937; Afghanistan was 1910 and Bolivia 1949. It is twenty years ago in the Soviet Union, ten in Norway, five in France. It is always last year in Australia and next week in Japan. Britain and the United States were the present – but the present contains the future. A season of travelling with my eyes open in Great Britain, I thought, could not fail to show me what was to come. I was a little impatient with distant countries and past decades, but I was not looking for progress or invention necessarily. There was a deterioration and decay that seemed to me more futuristic than utopian cities of steel and glass.

And then an English friend of mine – just yapping – said, 'The seaside belongs to everyone.'

I knew this was exactly right and that I wanted to leave immediately.

I chose to travel on May Day. It was London's Labour Day, celebrated by marching union men and speeches in Trafalgar Square. But in some English villages a May Queen was chosen and crowned with a garland, and there was dancing around a maypole while a watching know-it-all, Major Uprichard, leered at fifteen-year-old Tracey Rivett in her garland and said, 'It's all phallic symbols, of course. Years ago, when we ran around painted with woad, these jollities turned into orgies. You see, the maypole has a desperately obvious significance ...'

Recently, May Day had been renamed and politically neutral-ized as Spring Bank Holiday. In the south of England it was associated with a day-trip to a coastal resort. It was traditionally a time when people headed for the beach, and since the fifties it had been the day when gangs of youths fought each other with clubs and chains, in Southend and Margate. The English were creatures of habit. And that was the reason I chose Margate.

I left Waterloo East on the 11.33, and at Gravesend I put down my newspaper. Pocahontas – Mrs John Rolfe – was buried at St George's church. The town bore the name Gravesend because, east of it, the dead had to be buried at sea. We approached the River Medway, the joined towns of Rochester and Chatham. My carriage was less than a third full – perhaps because it was a late train – or was it the low grey sky and the uncertain light? It was cool and damp; the weather forecast was 'scattered showers' – it was the forecast for Britain nearly every day of the year. It was no day for the beach.

There were four elderly people in the carriage. One was reading a paper with a headline that said, 'My Battle With Drugs'. Another old person had been saying as I passed, 'It was one of those merciful releases –' There were three families, parents and children, neatly dressed for their outing. A bang outside brought a young woman squinting to the window and her expression said: It sounded like a car backfiring – but that was what they always said about dangerous explosions these days. A little girl was laughing and gasping, and holding a bottle of Tizer: 'It went down the wrong way!'

An Englishman across the aisle did an extraordinary thing, for an Englishman. He asked me a question.

He said, 'Walking?'

I was dressed for it – knapsack, all-purpose leather jacket, oily hiking shoes, and (because we were approaching the coast) I had my map unfolded. I was obviously a foreigner, which made his question a safe one. Class-consciousness tended to keep the English rather watchful and buttoned-up. But this was a Bank Holiday train to Margate. Class was hardly an issue here.

Yes, I said, I was walking and also riding – depending on the weather.

'The weather's been letting us down,' he said. The weather in England was not a neutral topic. It was full of personification; it involved struggle and conflict. It could be wayward, or spiteful, and then people said, 'It's been trying to rain all day.' Or it could be toiling on your behalf: 'The sun's been trying to come out.' Or, as the man said, it could be lazy and selfish; it could let you down. People imagined British weather to be something like the British character: it was a British-like miasma up there hovering and doing things to you.

We talked about the weather, this miasma. The man shared the English relief that spring had come. It had been a hard snowy winter, the country had seized up. So this was the annual gift, but it was unimaginable. It was impossible to anticipate the beauty of spring-time in England. It was sudden, mild, fragrant, and full of colour – magic rising out of the mud.

Then he said, 'American?'

Yes, I said, but did not elaborate. I said, 'I've always wanted to go to Margate.'

'You should go to Canterbury instead.'

They always said that, the natives. They sent you to traipse around the sights – the ruins, the churches, the hot streets – and they went to a simple lovely place and had beer under a tree.

'Full of history,' he was saying. 'Lovely town, beautiful old cathedral. You could change at Sittingbourne.'

No, I thought: No sightseeing; no cathedrals, no castles, no churches, no museums. I wanted to examine the particularities of the present.

I said, 'Where are you going?'

I guessed that his name was Norman Mould. It was one of my small talents to be able to tell a person's name by looking at him. Those old people up front – they were the Touchmores. The little girl drinking the Tizer – Judith Memery. The man behind the *Express* – Roger Cockpole. And so forth.

Mr Mould said, 'Ramsgate,' and that was the first indication I had had – his flicker of satisfaction and his willingness with the word and the way he said it, 'Ramsgit' – that Ramsgate was probably posher than Margate. But I also thought: That's another reason I don't want to go to Canterbury, Norman. I want to go where everyone else is going.

'It's like this Falklands business,' Mr Mould was saying, but now he was talking to the woman next to him, his wife, Nancy Mould, who was reading a newspaper.

In the next few weeks that was to be a common phrase. Politics would come up, or sometimes it was race, or religion; and then someone would say, *It's like this Falklands business . . .*

The war had not yet started. The Falklands had been overrun by Argentine troops, and British ships had encircled the islands and had declared an exclusion zone for a radius of two hundred miles. No shots had been fired, no men had been killed; there was little news. Most people assumed this was bluster, and bluff, and counter-bluff, and that after a period of time the Argentines would climb down. Two nights before this, the American president had smiled at a British journalist on a BBC news programme and said, 'I don't see why there should be any fighting over that ice-cold bunch of rocks down there.'

Mr Mould, across the aisle, had turned away from me. Our conversation had ended, and now I saw why: he was eating. He had taken out a bag of sandwiches and a thermos jug and he and his wife had covered their laps with the newspaper (*British Convoy In War Readiness Off Falklands*) and were sharing lunch. The English became intensely private and rather silent when they ate; their gestures were guarded and economical and precise. They were tidy and self-conscious. Suddenly, eating, they were alone.

It was then that the door at the end of the car banged open and I heard the tramp of heavy boots, and laughter and shouts.

'I fucking will do 'im if he don't fank me next time!'

'You fucking won't, you wally!'

'Fuck off – I will!'

They were loud – ear-splitting – but the picnicking English people across the aisle, and the elderly people, and each young family in its own pew, did not hear a thing. The picnickers went on eating in their tidy way, and everyone else became silent and small.

'– because I fucking said I would!'

I had seen their heads at Chatham passing by the windows of the carriage. I had hoped they would move on to another carriage, and they had. But they were loud and violent and could not sit still, and now that we were past Gillingham ('... the head-quarters of the religious sect known as the Jezreelites, or the New and Latter House of Israel') they had entered this carriage. There were seven of them. They called themselves Skinheads.

Their heads were egg-like – completely hairless. But it was not baldness, there was no shine; they were pale grey shaved domes, with the bright white snail-tracks of scars tagged over them. It was the size of the heads that I found alarming. A head without any hair is a small thing. It can look like a knob with eyes and ears. A human being is changed remarkably by hairless-ness – the appearance is hardened and the person looks insectile and dangerous. They had tattoos on their heads, small symbols and words, and tattoos on their earlobes, and earrings. They were dressed identically in short leather bomber jackets, with T-shirts underneath. The backs of their hands were tattooed. The Union Jack was the commonest tattoo among them. They wore very tight jeans that were a bit too short, the cuffs reaching the tops of vicious high-laced boots. The boots were shiny, these boys were oddly clean, their faces were very white.

'Look at that fucking bloke out there – what a silly cunt –'

' 'ey, leave off, you fucking wally!'

They were frolicking on the seats, thumping each other, and still shouting. Mr and Mrs Mould were drinking tea out of plastic mugs.

'The long-range forecast called for fine weather,' one of the Touchmores whispered.

Then, behind me, I heard, 'Daddy –' It was a child's small voice: *Dud-day*.

'Please, darling, I'm reading.

'Daddy, why –'

'Yes, darling?'

'Daddy, why are those men saying "fuck off"?'

'I don't know, darling. Now do please let me read my paper.'

His voice was nervous, as if he had been holding his breath. I had certainly been holding mine. The seven Skinheads had disturbed the Sunday peace of this jogging train; they had brought uneasiness to the car. They were fooling, but their fooling was violent and their language was terrible and reckless. I am sure that everyone else in the car was paying close attention to our progress along the line. We had passed Sittingbourne and Faversham and were headed towards Whitstable.

'There, Daddy, they just said it again. "Fucking hell." '

'Hush, darling. There's a good girl.'

'And that one said fuck, too.'

'That's enough, darling.' The man's voice was very subdued. He did not want anyone to hear. But he was just behind me, and his daughter was next to him – she could not have been more than five or six. I caught a glimpse of her. Her name was probably Sharon.

'Daddy –'

Dud-day.

'– why don't they put them off the train?'

The man did not reply to this. He probably would not have been heard in any case. The Skinheads were screaming, and running in the aisle – one had the word *Skin* tattooed on his neck – and one little Skinhead, a boy of about thirteen, also tattooed and shaven, and wearing an earring, was yelling, 'You fucking cunt, I'll fucking kill you!' and kicking at another Skinhead, who was older and bigger and laughing at this little infuriated Skin.

Herne Bay had a reputation for riffraff, but the Skinheads did not get off at Herne Bay. They were still swearing and kicking the seats and pushing each other as we pulled out of Herne Bay. And at Birchington-on-Sea ('grave of D. G. Rossetti, d. 1882, memorial window in the church'), one Skinhead screamed, '*I'll fucking kill you right now for saying vat!*'

They had been an awful irruption, and they had brought a sense of terror to the carriage. Such language, such fighting! The day was damp-grey and peaceful, but these monkey-faced boys with their tattoos and their tiny heads had made it frightening. And all the while, the decent English people with lowered heads and mugs of tea were pretending that nothing was happening; and the Skinheads were behaving as if no one else existed – as if they were alone in the railway carriage. In that sense they were very English Skinheads.

We came to Margate. The Skinheads pushed to the door and fought their way out. Then we got out, politely – no, you first, I insist. None of us was harmed, but I think most of us would have said it was unsettling, the way you feel with drunks on board, or crazy people. We had felt threatened. I had meant to describe our progress to the coast, and when I had seen the mist over the Cooling Marshes I had wanted to recall the opening chapters of *Great Expectations*. It was too late for that. It was so hard to remember Dickens or Merrie England or 'this sceptr'd isle' or the darling buds of May so near to seven roaring Skinheads. All I could think was: 'We will fight them on the beaches . . .'

The Skinheads had come to the coast at Margate to fight. There was something nasty and purposeful about them. Everywhere, those tiny heads on big shoulders and the clumping of their jack-boots. Their enemies were the Mods. Mods wore knee-length army coats and crash helmets, and they rode motor scooters. They buzzed up and down the promenade. The Skinheads gathered across the promenade from the amusement arcade called 'Dreamland', in a little park, several hundred of them – all those shaven heads.

It was bleak and cold, and the wind pressed from the leaden-coloured Channel. I kept reminding myself that it was the first of May. But there was a holiday crowd at Margate, too, milling around, toting children, wearing hats that said *Kiss Me Quick – Squeeze Me Tight*.

On the Margate Sands I went for a stroll and then looked back at the town, at all the boarding houses jammed tightly on the terraces like plaster prizes on the shelf of the coconut shy, *Vacancies* signs in the empty windows, and canned laughter and real shrieks from 'Dreamland', and Indian families walking in groups of twelve on Marine Parade, and the Skinheads and seagulls and Mods in helmets, and the broken fingernails of their dirty hands, and scores of policemen, and the low sky and the dank foreshore and the dark corrugated water of the Channel, and a pop song playing – *Kick it – Kick it to death*: I could connect nothing with nothing.

Some people wore summer clothes in a hopeful goose-pimpled way, but most were warmly dressed. I saw a number of people wearing scarves and gloves. Mittens in May! There were about ten people standing on the sandy beach, but no one was swimming. They were peering at an oil slick that was a smooth puddle in the sea. On the sea wall there were scribbles saying WASTED YOUTH and ANARCHY and NAZIS ARE THE MASTER RACE. There were rain showers in the east, over the water, tall grey verticals hanging closely like wet towels on a line. It was no day for the seaside, and yet no one looked disappointed. Ten minutes later, when it started to drizzle, no one ran for cover.

Margate had never been fashionable. It had never even been nice. It had become a watering-place because doctors in the eighteenth century believed that sea water was healthful – not only sitting in it, or swimming, but also washing in it, and especially drinking it, preferably in the morning. It was the quest for good health that brought people to Margate and later to Brighton. It was the making of the British seaside resort, not only the notion that sea air was a sexual excitant – this may be true – but also that sea water was good for the bowels: 'A pint is commonly sufficient in grown persons to give them three or four sharp stools.'

The first bathing machine in the world appeared at Margate. It was a changing-room on wheels and, pushed a little distance into the sea, it preserved a prudish swimmer's modesty. Books about sea water and health became best sellers. In 1791, the Royal Sea-Bathing Infirmary was founded on the western cliffs of Margate. But nothing improved the tone of the place. In 1824, a traveller wrote, 'From an obscure fishing village, Margate, in the course of little more than half a century, has risen into a well-frequented, if not fashionable, watering-place.' A hundred years later, Baedeker's *Great Britain* described Margate as 'one of the most popular, though not one of the most fashionable watering-places in England'. So it had always been crummy and Cockneyfied, just like this, people down from London for the day shunting back and forth on the front in the cold rain, and walking their dogs and gloomily fishing and looking at each other.

I had thought of staying. I'll find a boarding house, I thought, and spend the rest of the day milling around and watching the progress of the gang-fight between the Skinheads and the Mods. I'll have fish and chips and a stick of Margate rock and a pint of beer. Tomorrow, after a big English breakfast, I'll sling on my knapsack and set off for Broadstairs and Ramsgate and Sandwich, along the coastal path.

The Skinheads had started scuffling, pulling Mods off their motor scooters. The policemen went after them with raised truncheons. I had no stomach for this. And did I have to spend the night here to confirm what I could easily predict? I was repelled by the tough ugly youths, the aimless people, the nasty music, the stink of frying, the gusts of violence. I decided not to stay. Why should I suffer a bad night in a dreary place just to report my suffering? I wanted to see the whole coast in a fairly good mood. So I kept walking, I strolled down Marine Parade past the ruined pier, and I climbed out of Margate in the rain that cold May afternoon, and started my tour around the kingdom's coast.

2

An Evening Train to Deal

When I had

> ... seen the hungry ocean gain
> Advantage on the kingdom of the shore,

and compared it to the way some bird-brains kicked the yellow chalk cliffs apart, broke them like crockery and threw the shards on to the promenade, I concluded that man did more damage than the tides. Outside Margate, the cliffs were broken, and initials and names and dates gouged into them; they had been hacked and scorched. This was the result of the boisterous spirits of the roaming gangs which visited the town and found there was not enough to do there. They also wrote with chalk: MADNESS, it said on the promenade – it was homage to a pop group; and PUNX and I WANT TO SKREW YOU.

I climbed some stairs that passed through a 'gate' – a cut – in the chalk cliffs and then walked along the path at the top to Cliftonville. This was a sedate suburb of Margate, full of small damp bungalows and ragged sparrows. A hawk flew slowly near the edge of the cliff, and gulls nagged nearer the sea. It was not quiet, what with the gulls and the surf sighing, and the wind scraping the hedges, but it was noisy in a peaceful way.

Many signs said DANGEROUS CLIFFS and warned walkers not to go too close to the edge. The chalk was collapsing, and I could see that large bluffs had toppled to the shore. It reminded me that in the few coastal parts of Britain where I had hiked there had been signs warning of breaking cliffs and unsafe paths. What I had seen of the Dorset coast was slipping into the Channel: portions of pasture-land and meadows had fallen, and the fences had gone with them in a tangle of posts and wire. These chalk

cliffs of Kent – so white and sturdy when seen from a distance
– were frail and friable, and this coast made Britain seem like
a country consisting of stale cake that softened and broke in the
rain.

The rain was patchy. I saw through its drapes two blind men
– one black, one white – being led along the path by two sighted
ladies. The black man said, 'Just how wide is it?' The white one
said, 'The dogs need a little space to play.' A pair of dogs trotted
behind this party, and the men tapped their canes as they went
past me. Farther on, I heard music. It was 'We'll Gather Lilacs
in the Spring Again', being played by a man seated at an organ
in an open-air amphitheatre. The wind whipped at the folding
chairs around him and made their canvas flutter and flap. There
were more than five hundred chairs, and all of them were empty.
The man went on playing and pulling out stops while the chairs
flapped under the grey sky. I continued down the path, along
the cloud-mottled water of the sea, and on this drab afternoon
I heard a nightingale singing in a hedge. 'The nightingale sings
of adulterous wrong.' T. S. Eliot was here having a mild nervous
breakdown in 1921, staying at the Albemarle Hotel right over
there in Cliftonville.

The sun came out as I walked along the North Foreland, past
Kingsgate with its small pretty cove and its modern castle on
one bluff, and a handsome lighthouse like a white pepper-mill
just behind it on a higher point of land. There were cooing doves
in the trees and the high box hedges of the big houses were like
fortifications.

Only four miles from Margate and it was the England of fresh
paint and flower gardens and tall chimneys. And there was a
clearer intimation of this area's respectability: this road smelled
of private schools – it was a certain kind of soap and a certain
kind of cooking, and the sound of young voices and laughter
coming from the open windows of large rooms. An hour ago it
had been Skinheads and chip-shops and rain on Margate Sands,
and now this breezy bourgeois headland in bright sunshine, as
I approached Broadstairs. I thought: Mexico is one landscape
– one visible thing – and all of Arabia is one thing; but I began
to suspect that every mile of England was different.

Broadstairs was full of flesh-coloured flowers. There were no

Skinheads here, no Nazi slogans, no signs saying *Anarchy!* – that was always a popular one in public toilets in England. There were about thirty Mods drinking cider on the front, passing half-gallon bottles back and forth. These boys had removed their jackets and crash helmets and shirts, and they sat in the sun on the green park benches. There was no loud music, no honky-tonk, at Broadstairs; the front was genteel – the iron ornateness of Victorian porches.

'Charles Dickens lived in this house', the sign said on a brick house, with a brick turret, that was smack on the coastal path at the edge of Broadstairs. Dickens had said that Broadstairs beat 'all watering-places into what the Americans call "sky-blue fits" '. This residence had been given the name 'Bleak House' and in its gift shop it was possible to buy pot-holders and tea towels and key chains stamped *Bleak House – Broadstairs*. Upstairs, the novelist's desk and wash basin were on view and could be seen for a small charge. It was of particular interest to me that Dickens had written most of *American Notes* in this house. He sat at this desk and looked out of that window and dipped this pen in that ink-pot and wrote, 'To represent me as viewing America with ill-nature, coldness or animosity, is merely to do a very foolish thing, which is always a very easy one.'

There was a fortune-teller's shop on the front at Broadstairs, with a sign saying *Olandah Clairvoyante*. She was said to be the wisest woman in Europe. A testimonial letter taped on to her window said, 'Dear Olandah, Whenever I feel depressed, which is every day, I take your letter out and read it and feel so much better –'

Which is every day? I went into the shop. Olandah was seated behind a curtain. She wore a scarf on her head and what looked like stage make-up and beads. Her expression was full of weary suspicion and she stared with such seriousness I thought she had terrible news for me.

She said, 'Do you want a reading?'

I said yes. She took my hand loosely, as if weighing it to bite. She said I was far from home – had my knapsack and muddy shoes given her a clue? She said I was doing a very difficult thing, but if she was referring to travelling around Britain perhaps she knew something I didn't, because I had not foreseen any difficulties. She said I was sensitive and artistic: perhaps a painter? 'Couldn't draw a rabbit,' I said. She said I was successful but that I tried to hide it. I was often in the company of strangers. Some of them would try to take advantage of me, but my character would overcome them.

All this she gathered by prodding the palm of my right hand and tracing her crimson fingernails on the lines I got from rowing a skiff in Cape Cod Bay.

'Do you see anything there about Northern Ireland?'

'Distant lands certainly. One of them might be Ulster.'

'Do I survive in the end?'

'Oh, yes. You lead a healthy life. You are not a smoker, for example.'

'Gave up a year ago. Pipe. I used to inhale it. I miss it sometimes like a dead friend.'

'You have many friends,' Olandah said, perhaps mishearing me. 'But you tend to keep away from them. You keep yourself to yourself. You are very independent.'

'Self-employed,' I said. 'One last query. Where am I going to sleep tonight?'

She stopped looking at my hand. She looked at my nose and said, 'Not at home.'

'What town – can you give me a hint?'

'I give character readings,' Olandah said. 'I don't give tourist information.'

This cost me seven pounds, which was about a pound more than it would have cost me to stay at a guest house, with bed and breakfast. Still, I was grateful for her encouragement and glad to have been reassured that I was going to survive.

Another sign in Broadstairs said, 'Seven miles out to sea from this point lie the dreaded Goodwin Sands – the great ship swallower – considered by a great many seafarers to be the most dangerous stretch of water in the world.' There were countless stories about the disasters and wrecks on the Goodwins. 'Their ingurgitating property is such, that a vessel of the largest size, driven upon them, would in a few days be swallowed up and seen no more.' What was not so well known was that at the turn of the century, at low water, the sands became very firm and cricket matches were played on them.

I passed the bundled-up old people on their benches, and the families with picnic baskets and balloons, the day-trippers waiting at the *Jugs of Tea for the Beach* sign, and I walked out of Broadstairs and through a gate to a narrow park dedicated to the memory of George VI. The land was higher here, and on this sea-cliff were magpies and dog-owners and kite-flyers. Down below were the original thirty-nine steps, leading to the sea.

On the other side of this park was Ramsgate.

The man on the train to Margate, Mr Mould, had seemed to me to be boasting when he told me he was going to Ramsgate. Anyway, these towns on the Kent coast a few hours from London were either described as Cockneyfied or not very Cockneyfied – the less of it the better, people said, since London influence on the coast was always seen as contamination. The coast represented an escape from every terrestrial ill. The worst was metropolitan oppression, and London was the epitome of that. When Baedeker described Ramsgate as 'a somewhat less Cockneyfied edition of Margate' it was intended as praise. That was in 1906, but even today such places were still measured by London, because London was the future and it was also pretty poisonous. When a coastal place was too big or too noisy or full of traffic – when it was inconvenient or ugly or it smelled – people said, 'Just like London,' in a helpless way, because now they were beside the sea and they couldn't go any further.

Ramsgate was larger but just as ugly as Margate, with a swimming pool on the front that looked like a Roman ruin painted blue. It was the 'Marine Bathing Pool' that had been neglected and now lay vandalized and full of smashed chairs and broken glass. 'The Council are at present discussing future development', the sign beside it said, but one could not read that without thinking of dynamite.

I had been hurrying. My hamstrings ached. I asked a man in a flat cap where the railway station was. He was grateful to me for asking directions and offered me three different routes – the station was some distance away.

His name was Len Shottery. He said, 'Are you walking it?'

I said yes.

'It's much too far to walk,' he said. 'Get in – I'll drive you.'

Mr Shottery climbed into the cab of his Department of Public Works truck. He had been out all day, putting out plastic cones to re-route traffic for tomorrow's ditch digging. He said he was a Londoner. 'I came down here five years ago and haven't been back once.' He was about fifty years old and he said this with the air of a man who has fled to the South Pacific.

'Watch them trains,' Mr Shottery said. 'They're not very clever on a holiday.'

I took the train nine miles to Sandwich and walked around the town. It was hardly bigger than Sandwich, Massachusetts, but it was a lovely place surrounded by flat green fields. It had survived and was still pretty and old-fangled because in the course of eight hundred years this coastal town had slipped inland and was no longer a great port. It had just closed up and now it was preserved, two miles from the sea, in its own rich silt. 'Queen Elizabeth visited the town in 1572, and the house is occupied in Strand Street,' and there I saw a man with a frightened face walking a tottering dog.

My idea was to walk to Deal, which was only five miles away. German prisoners of war had built the Sandwich to Deal road and cycle path, in 1946, before they were repatriated from their prison camp at Eythorne. I wanted to hike this road, but my legs ached from my hurrying, so I took an evening train.

I arrived in Deal in a glarey sunset. It was very quiet here, very empty, and I liked it for smelling of fish and seaweed. Everyone had gone home – into the house or back to London. The seafront was just rope and hauled-up fishing dinghies, and the wind was blowing along the stony shingly shore. Now the sea and the sky were blue. I sat down. The sun was like a carbuncle. I decided to stay.

At no point in three months of travel did I have a reservation in advance, at a hotel or a guest house. I wanted to come and go as I pleased and not be held to specific places and dates. I thought: If I can't get a room I'll move on to another place and look – but that was never necessary. I never found a hotel that was full, though I found many that were completely empty. I was never turned away. Some of the hotel owners or guest-house proprietors were embarrassed by their empty rooms. Some said it was too early in the season. 'We'll be packed in June,' they said in May. But in June they said, 'Things are quiet now, but it'll be a madhouse in July when the school holidays start.' In July they said, 'In August we're always fully booked.' But the season deepened and they were nearly always empty. Some of the owners said that people had stopped travelling in Britain – they went to Spain when they went at all. Some said, 'It's this recession. It's a world-wide problem.' Some people said, 'We're not a rich country any more. We're poor,' but that attitude made me wary, because those were the people who always overcharged me.

My method for finding a place to stay was to walk up and down the streets and to look for a clean or well-shaped building that had a view of the sea. I avoided the new hotel (too expensive) or the place in which I heard music playing (too noisy) or the damp tumble-down inn with the sway-backed roof that was usually buried in a back lane (stinks and hard beds). The tall semi-hotel I found in Deal after roaming around for twenty minutes looked all right – it had lovely windows; but after I gained entrance I saw it was no good. It smelled of bacon and beer, it was run by a fat dirty woman named Mrs Sneath, who smoked in my face.

'Cheapest single room I have is ten pounds,' Mrs Sneath said. 'That's bed and full breakfast.'

'Your sign says the room starts at seven pounds.'

'I don't have any left, do I,' she said.

'I'll take a ten pound one.'

'With tax that's eleven pounds fifty,' she said, writing out the bill, 'in advance. Make your cheque out to M. Sneath. You were well away,' she went on, speaking to another woman who was sitting lamely on a bar stool, with a small glass of lager.

'I was drinking gin,' this other woman said. Her name was Mrs Feeley. She was Irish and though she was speaking with Mrs Sneath, she kept looking at me in a friendly way, and seemed always to be on the verge of asking me where I was from, and then saying that she had wanted to go there her whole life.

'I was on shorts,' Mrs Sneath said. 'I thought that band were smashing, and all that food. Gillows did the catering. I stuffed myself with smoked salmon and those bits of ham rolled around the pineapple chunks with the toothpick through them. Rum don't give you a hangover, and I always drink lots of water. Don't gin make you cry?'

'Only sometimes,' Mrs Feeley said.

'I hadn't been to a wedding for ages,' Mrs Sneath said.

'They don't get married as much as they used to. They just seem to live together until they get sick of each other.' Mrs Feeley smiled at me, but she was still addressing Mrs Sneath. 'We had a marvellous wedding, Jerry and me. I was paralytic. They don't do that any more. It's the pill.'

Mrs Sneath did not reply. She was staring at me and compressing her cigarette in her yellow lips. 'You're in nineteen. Top of the stairs, last door on the right. The loo is down the hall. Breakfast's at nine.'

'I wanted to be away at eight,' I said.

'Bloody crack of dawn,' she said.

'I'm walking to Dover,' I said.

'Dover's lovely,' Mrs Feeley said in her friendly way. She was fleshy and full of encouragement. She said, 'But it used to be much prettier than it is now.'

'Breakfast's at nine,' Mrs Sneath said and wrung the sweat from her palms by clutching her filthy shift. She blinked the smoke out of her eyes and gave me an eskimo squint and said, 'If I made exceptions I'd be doing breakfasts all the morning. It's a proper cooked breakfast, see, that's why I'm not cheap.'

She handed me a baton – a stick of wood with a key wired to it.

'Nineteen. Top of the stairs.'

I walked through Deal that night. It was only a few streets but they were pleasant streets, and on the front I could hear the sea lifting the smooth stones on the beach and then draining through them with a swallowing sound. At a dark patch of sea-front a girl and boy stopped me. 'Hey.' I thought they were going to ask me directions. They were both about eighteen years old. The girl said, 'Give me forty-five pence, will you?'

I could not imagine why she was asking me for this exact sum, which was about a dollar. I said no.

'It's not much,' she said. 'It's nothing.'

They were neatly dressed and both of them were smoking cigarettes.

'He's a poof,' the girl said, and they both laughed.

They sat in the dark watching television with still blue faces: Mrs Sneath and her husband, Will, and Mrs Feeley and Jerry, and a deranged-looking drifter named Yerby, and Mrs Sneath's father, Charlie Wensum, from Skegness. 'Skeggy,' he called it. He loved the coast. Mr Wensum was a man of perhaps seventy-five, though it was hard to say for certain in that dark room. His skin was blue from the television. I had the impression from their silence and the way they sat, with their feet up, and squashing cushions, that they did this every night. A sign on the door said *TV Lounge – Residents Only*.

The news was on. I could hear Yerby breathing hard. No one spoke. The screen showed a map of the Falklands, two small rags of land.

Mrs Sneath said, 'What do you think of this Falklands business?'

I said it seemed reasonable to fight for what was yours.

'People say they can't see the point of it,' Jerry Feeley said. 'Can you see the point of it?'

I said I didn't know anything except that so far it was a war without any casualties, and if it stayed that way it would be easier to reach an agreement with Argentina.

'No casualties he says.' This from Yerby.

The news was terrible. An Argentine battleship had been sunk with 1200 men aboard. Most of the men were feared drowned. This ship was the *General Belgrano* and these were the first deaths of the war. This had been announced only a few minutes before I had entered the room.

No one said anything for a while, perhaps out of a fear of saying the wrong thing. What was said in the moments after a tragic announcement was always remembered.

But Mrs Sneath was agitated. Her voice was guilty and defiant.

'They say they're going to eat the sheep!'

'Who's going to eat the sheep?' I asked.

'The Argies – who else?' she said. 'When they run out of food.

When they haven't got anything left. That's not fair, eating the sheep. They have no right. The Falklands may belong to Argentina, but they're British sheep!'

'Those poor men.' It was Mrs Feeley, speaking sadly.

Jerry said, 'They won't have a chance in that water.'

I was sitting on the sofa with Mr Wensum. His feet were drawn up under him; he was seated cross-legged like an Indian fakir, staring with his blue face at the bad news on the blue television. Without any warning I felt a nudge, a hard poke against my arm, and there was still pressure on my elbow. I looked down quickly and saw that Mr Wensum had put his foot on my arm. I found this a disgusting thing for him to do.

'I can't see the telly!' he shouted, and showed me his bright false teeth, bluer than his face.

I hated his feet so much I left the room.

There was no one else at breakfast. There were no other guests at the hotel. All the rooms were empty. The people watching the television had been family and friends. So Mrs Sneath had lied to me about the 'residents' and not having a cheaper room and having to cook breakfast all morning. She was in the kitchen, smoking and coughing over the frying pan. She said if I stayed another night she might be able to find me a cheaper room.

'Some other time,' I said. 'I'll be back.'

Never, I thought.

'It's up to you,' Mrs Sneath said. 'Dover's pricey. We're a lot cheaper here.'

Sure you are.

She put my plate of bacon and eggs in front of me and went to another table and smoked and drank her tea and read her *Sun*. The headline was *SUNK!* It referred to the *General Belgrano* and the 1200 dead men. It was the first of many gloating headlines.

Then I was out of the door and free, breathing fresh air – it was lovely walking away in the morning. I closed the door and left for good. Cheerio, they said. Mind how you go. And I was off, taking long strides, glad I didn't have to stay a minute longer. And when I got sick of the slimy salty breakfasts I just got up and walked out of the door before anyone else was awake, and let the cat out, and hurried for the first hundred yards and then slowed to a stroll when I realized that I would never have to go back. It was a liberating fantasy of running away from home.

I had no one to wait for, no bus to catch, no tickets to buy, no appointments. And the next time I find out that a hotel is dirty and I don't like the people, I'll leave, I thought, I'll just push on and find a better one. I liked thinking that I was always making progress whenever I walked away. And if I had bad luck it did not matter, because there was always something better farther up the line, a beach, or cliffs, or a famous town, or woods, and sometimes just the weather was a pleasure, as I went clockwise around the coast.

I was happy, going to places I had never been, that had only been names to me, or descriptions in books that had falsely fixed the place in my imagination. In *Rural Rides*, William Cobbett had said, 'Deal is a most villainous place. It is full of filthy-looking people. Great desolation of abomination has been going on here ... Everything seems upon the perish ...' And I had assumed it was like that, the judgement was so strongly expressed. But it was a small mild town, without a sea-wall or much of a beach, and few trees, and open to the breezes from France. It was raggedly respectable. The boats on shore looked practical – slow, clumsy, and made for one purpose; they had numbers but no names; rusty ironwork: fishing boats. Men still went out every day from this old trampled coast and its crowded houses, and they made a living at the hard work of catching fish.

They were winching the fishing boats up when I set out from Deal that day in bright sunshine. Winches on shore always meant there was serious fishing being done in a small way; and more than the usual number of public houses also suggested a fishing population; and timbers and rope-hanks and a kind of tar-smeared and indestructible litter on the foreshore meant fishermen, too. Another thing about fishermen was they never looked as though they could swim.

I walked a half a mile south and found Walmer altogether different. The news-stands seemed especially gruesome that day, with the headlines gloating over the sinking of the Argentine battleship, and all the deaths. I crossed the grassy patch from Deal into Walmer, beside the low shore ('generally believed to have been the first landing place of Julius Caesar in Britain'). Walmer had the smack of a London suburb – flower gardens and elderly shoppers, and a whiff of the sick-room and a sight of people dressed a little too warmly. In some coastal places people were living, and in others they were dying. Deal and Walmer, side by side, illustrated each type. There was further proof in Walmer. After a certain age, English people did not buy new shoes, but just went on cleaning and buffing the cracks in their old ones, and making them look decent. They looked at them and thought: *These will see me out.*

The beach here was level, a continuation of the Sandwich Flats, but ahead were the white cliffs of Coney Point and Bockhill Farm, beyond the village of Kingsdown. As I approached the cliffs I saw a sign indicating that a Ministry of Defence Rifle Range lay under the cliff and '*Do Not Touch Anything – It May Kill You*'. Another sign warned walkers to 'ascertain high water to prevent being cut off by the tide'. Most beach paths were subjected to tides, and so a walker might find himself unable to go forward or back. The term for such a predicament was 'embayed': to be trapped and immobilized by the rising tide. 'Walkers should be careful to consult a tide-table so as to avoid the risk of being embayed.'

I heard gunfire and saw that a red flag had been raised to indicate danger, and the waves lapped near the base of the chalk cliffs. So I walked on the meadow above. The sun dissolved and then a heavy shower of rain swept towards me across the fields and drenched me. The sun came out a few minutes later and steamed me dry. I had not visited Deal Castle or Walmer Castle; I wasn't sightseeing – at least not that kind of sight. This was what I had come for – rain and sun and green meadows along the coast. And I wanted to take trains. The clay-coloured water rose and fell with a noise of bursting, and the gulls above it hung in the air like kites.

As soon as I had left Deal I saw a low flat cloud, iron grey and then blue, across the Channel, like a stubborn fog-bank. The closer I got to Dover the more clearly it was defined, now like a long battleship and now like a flotilla and now like an offshore island. I walked on and saw it was a series of headlands. It was France, looking like Brewster across Cape Cod Bay.

Ahead on the path a person was coming towards me, down a hill four hundred yards away; but whether it was a man or a woman I could not tell. Some minutes later I saw her scarf and her skirt, and for more minutes on those long slopes we strode towards each other under the big sky. We were the only people visible in the landscape – there was no one behind either of us. She was a real walker – arms swinging, flat shoes, no dog, no map. It was lovely, too: blue sky above, the sun in the south-east and a cloud-burst hanging like a broken bag in the west. I watched this woman, this fairly old woman, in her warm scarf and heavy coat, and a bunch of flowers in her hand – I watched her come on, and I thought: I am not going to say hello until she does.

She did not look at me. She drew level and didn't notice me. There was no other human being in sight on the coast, only a fishing boat out there like a black flatiron. Hetta Poumphrey – I could see that was the woman's name – was striding, lifting the hem of her coat with her knees. Now she was a fraction past me, and still stony-faced.

'Morning!' I said.

'Oh.' She twisted her head at me. 'Good morning!'

She gave me a good smile, because I had spoken first. But if I hadn't, we would have passed each other, Hetta and I, in the clifftop meadow – not another soul around – five feet apart, in the vibrant silence that was taken for safety here, without a word.

The whiteness of the Dover cliffs, the soft blaze of bright chalk, was a bearable beautiful glare – white could seem immaculate in nature. Dover was a harbour town in a narrow valley, with bluffs on either side, and on those bluffs were a castle and a citadel. You looked up in Dover and saw battlements and fortifications. I walked along the east cliff just under the castle, and down Marine Parade to the Esplanade. It was a highly mechanized and busy harbour, cars and trucks lining up to take the ferry to France. A French flavour had crept into the town. Dover had a slight continental tang – the atmosphere in the streets, the faces of the strollers, the merchandise in the shops, the language on some signs. I had not known how unusual a thing this was, for the English made no concessions at all to other nationalities. They were neither hostile nor friendly. In any case, talk or chat was not in itself a friendly gesture in England as it was in the United States. Speaking to strangers was regarded as challenging in England; it meant entering a minefield of verbal and social distinctions. Better to remain silent, even on a path through a meadow with no one else around. The English were tolerant in the sense that they were willing to turn a blind eye to almost anything that might embarrass them. They were humane but they were also shy. After nine hundred years they still did not have strong views about the French, which surprised me, because after eleven years I thought of the French as the most unprincipled people in Europe. In Dover the English had adopted a different posture. They were courting the foreigners in Dover; the town had a slightly garlicky flavour, almost a hybrid feel – it was a small cultural muddle. But the Dover cliffs contained this aberration. It was like being at the bottom of a quarry. None of this cosmopolitan atmosphere would ever seep out.

It was only seven miles from Dover to Folkestone, but the railway line had the magnificence that all lines do when they run beside the sea. It was not just the sight of cliffs, and the sea breezes; it was also the engineering, all the iron embedded in rock, and the inevitable tunnel, the roar of engines and the crashing of waves, the surf just below the tracks, the flecks of salt water on the train windows that faced the sea. The noise was greater because of the cliffs; and the light was stranger – land shadows on one side of the train, the luminous sea on the other; and the track was never straight, but always swinging around the bays and coves. It was man's best machine traversing earth's best feature – the train tracking in the narrow angle between vertical rock and horizontal water.

Above the racing train was Shakespeare Cliff, named from a passage in *King Lear* ('There is a cliff, whose high and bending head/Looks fearfully on the confined deep'). We went past various futile holes that represented efforts to build a Channel tunnel to France. It was a very old scheme and even at the turn of the century there was a long shaft and a tunnel excavated for seven thousand feet under the Channel. The latest attempt to tunnel to France was abandoned in the 1970s. I wanted to ask someone on the train about this Channel tunnel. I changed my seat and sat opposite a harmless-looking man who was reading the full page of Falklands news in the *Daily Telegraph*. Was it around here, I asked, that the Channel tunnel was started?

He said yes – hardly yes, just nodded.

I said it seemed such a good idea I could not understand why it had been abandoned.

'No money,' the man said, a little crossly. He was Wing Commander R. G. H. Wraggett (Ret'd). 'This isn't a rich country. We can't do things like that any more. The Japanese have all the money now, and the Germans, and these Arabs.'

I was going to say that the Japanese had just this year dug a thirty-six-mile tunnel under the Tsugaru Straits, from Honshu to Hokkaido. But if I had said, 'Courage can make you prosperous,' he would have replied, 'Nips!' The English hated the Japanese for being rich over-achievers, for being guiltless racialists, for eating raw fish, for working like dogs, and for torturing their prisoners during the war. 'They despised us for surrendering in Singapore. They thought we should have done the decent thing – cut our bowels out and committed mass suicide.' So I didn't mention the Japanese tunnel and I didn't say that the Channel tunnel seemed to me one of the most important engineering works of our century. Britain's future might depend on it. But the effort had collapsed.

Wing Commander Wraggett said, 'We've got to learn how to tighten our belts.'

His 'we' meant everyone else, of course.

He returned to his paper. I changed my seat again and saw that we were arriving in Folkestone. I thought: To talk to that man I had to go back to the person I was eleven years ago, when it seemed all right to ask a stranger here a serious question. But how could I take this trip with my mouth shut? On the days when I did not speak to anyone I felt I had lost thirty pounds, and if I did not talk for two days in a row I had the alarming impression that I was about to vanish. Silence made me feel invisible.

I had only seen Folkestone once before, on a cold September

afternoon, from the window of the boat-train to France. Now, in May sunshine, it looked elegant, with mansions and hotels like the most luxurious hospitals. There was a whisper of illness all over Folkestone, something about the white faces at the windows on this fine day, and you could not look at a flower-bed without thinking of a sick-room. The old people there did not seem to walk so much as pace. But it was a stately town, with a Victorian face of red-brick, and a mile of grassy lawns, called The Leas, on the flat cliff above the seashore.

From here France was close, and had the same kind of cliffs, like the far bank of a great river. I could see the fissures in the chalk cliffs of Point Cambertin and Audresselles above Boulogne; and Cap Gris Nez and Cap Blanc Nez. Calais was just around the corner. It was not an optical illusion; but there was not the slightest tincture of Frenchness here. Some people waterskied to France when the weather was pleasant.

In Folkestone I met old Walter Dudlow as I was crossing the Leas, heading west. He asked me the time but I could tell he wanted to talk. He was trembling to tell me things. He had once been a gardener up here on the Leas. That's why he was here now – he still liked looking at them. Most places in England had changed but Folkestone hadn't changed a bit. His wife had died, his dog was gone. He had fallen down, slipped on a patch of ice last winter, and hurt his knees. That was very bad. It had affected his dancing. Now he was only dancing two or three nights a week.

'How many nights did you dance before that?'

'Five or six,' Mr Dudlow said. 'There's never any dancing on a Sunday, and even if there was I wouldn't go in for it, as a practising Christian.'

I asked him what kind of dancing.

'Old Time and Modern Sequence,' he said. 'How old do you think I am? Go ahead and guess.'

Old people were forever asking me this – perhaps they asked everyone? I said about seventy.

'Seventy-nine, next birthday.'

'I wouldn't have believed it,' I said.

He said, 'And I can touch my toes.'

He tried. He couldn't touch them.

'It's my bally knees!' Mr Dudlow said. 'Usually I can touch my toes without any trouble. I didn't realize I couldn't until just then!'

I said, 'You got pretty close.'

'I always said I'm the fittest man in Folkestone.' He was smiling, but he believed it. He said, 'Are you married?'

'Yes,' I said, smartly.

He winced a little and his face stayed stiff with surprise. If I was married what was I doing on a weekday with a knapsack on my back and walking down the coast alone in these shoes?

'I mean to say if you weren't married you'd make a lot of new friends by dancing,' Mr Dudlow said.

'Anyway, I am married – so dancing's probably not for me.'

Mr Dudlow shook his head and said, 'You think walking down the coast is interesting but I'll tell you dancing is much better.'

I had told him I was walking down to Littlestone-on-Sea.

He said, 'I go into a dance hall alone and come out with six or seven new friends.'

'What kind of friends are we talking about, Mr Dudlow? Men or women?'

'All kinds,' he said. 'It's my dancing, see.'

Now I noticed that he had kept glancing at his feet. He had small feet and very smooth shoes, and his trouser cuffs were rolled up as if to draw attention to them. He was proud of his feet.

'I've always danced. You've got to be fit to dance. I've got a dance tonight here, and another tomorrow in Dover. I'll go up on the afternoon coach.'

He wanted me to exclaim about his effort so that he could smile and say that dancing kept him young. But I said I wasn't really much of a dancer.

'Even if you're a loner you'd like it,' he said. So that was it: he thought I was a crazy loner. 'I mean, it's better than being a loner.' He looked from his tidy feet to my brown knapsack.

I said, 'I never thought of dancing, except tap dancing.'

'In that case you might like Modern Sequence,' he said. 'And what I like about it is there's no rough element. Know what I mean by rough element? Skinheads. Punks. These tough boys. Oh, you never find them in a ballroom.'

We reached the last lawn in the Leas and there, at a stairway to the shore – the village of Sandgate at the bottom step – he said goodbye. But he kept on talking.

3

The Branch Line to Hastings

Sandgate was a pretty, Irish-looking village squeezed between green cliffs and the narrow shore. It was full of antique shops and cottages, and it smelled of furniture wax and hot bread. But it straddled the main coastal road and this curse meant that although it was a tiny village it was hard for any pedestrian to cross the street.

I walked along the beach. At the far end of the bay, to the south-west, on the tip of what looked like a great rusty sickle of seashore, was the ness – the nose – of the Denge Marsh. The new landscape feature at Dungeness was easily visible from where I was walking, because it was a nuclear power station, with an ugliness and a size peculiar to such constructions. It was not the gigantism that was nasty – the size alone could not be fearsome. But the unnatural look of nuclear power stations was daunting. They could not be prettified. Their horrific aspect, to someone staring at them across a calm bay, was their explosive shapeless-ness, the random swollen angles, and all those radiating power lines, like orbs of model shock waves. The nuclear power station at Dungeness from fifteen miles away was grotesque – there was nothing near it but the flat sea and the lip of Romney Marsh, which was a long green depression, below sea level.

There were eighteen nuclear power stations in Britain, and all of them stuck on the coast, perhaps for the same reason that they had shooting galleries and rocket ranges and minefields and dynamite factories on the same coast. If something went wrong, the surf and the sea would take the force of the blast. And it was easier to stand guard over such danger zones and prevent enemies from trespassing. But when one of these nuclear power stations blew up or melted down – and the chances were that one would – the map would be wrenched and a contour punched out of the coast, and Britain would not look like a witch riding on a pig any more, but probably like a dwarf sprawled on a pork chop.

There was no one on the beach, no one swimming, no one walking, and no boats; but there was something I had seen before – at Margate, at Broadstairs, at Ramsgate and Walmer, wherever a road came near the seaside: cars parked and piled up, and people in them, always very old people, the old croak named Rathbone in his toy Morris, and the Witherslacks, Donald and Maureen, both of them sitting in the back seat of their green Cortina, and everyone else. They sat in their cars and stared out at the sea. They were on every beach road. When I walked past they hardly looked at me – perhaps a glance at the bulge in my knapsack, but not more than that.

If there was a place to park near a beach or a cliff, or any shelf of shore having a clear shot at the sea, the elderly people gathered there, side by side, their tin cars a little tremulous in the wind. I saw them everywhere, eating sandwiches, drinking tea out of plastic cups, reading the paper, looking fuddled. They always faced the water. They were old couples mostly, but they never seemed to be holding conversations. Often the man was asleep, and sometimes the woman was in the back seat and the man in the front ('I've got to have somewhere to put my sandwiches'). They were not bird-watchers or ship-spotters. Indeed, they did not seem to be looking at anything in particular. Their expressions were a little sad and empty, as if they were expecting to see something beyond the horizon or under the surface of the waves.

It looked sombre enough to be an English recreation, but I wondered whether it had any other significance. It seemed to me to hold the possibility of the ultimate fright, an experience of nothingness. It was only on the coast where if you angled yourself properly, you could look at nothing. I never passed these old people in their parked cars – they did not stir from them – without thinking that, in their own way, they were waiting for Godot.

I walked in a high wind and its flying grit to Hythe, where I saw a policeman wheeling his pushbike. I asked him if the little railway was still running down the coast. He said yes and directed me across the town. 'It's a mile,' he said, 'a long mile, really.'

Down Pulsifer Road and across Albert Street to Saltwood Grove – or names like that – where I asked a lady taking in her wash: Which way to the station? And it seemed funny that this was travel, necessitating a knapsack, binoculars and a knife – and I had a plastic poncho, too! Not here, but sometimes, even on a small suburban road, with a man clipping a hedge and a girl in a school uniform and a whistling postman, it seemed as foreign and far-off as Gangtok, though often not so safe, since in Sikkim murder is unknown. But it was travel, perhaps in a new sense but in an old place; because I was looking hard at it for the first time, and making notes; and because I had no other business there.

The Romney, Hythe and Dymchurch Railway was one of the narrowest and smallest in Britain, running from Hythe to Dungeness on fifteen-inch tracks. A sign at the station said, *Next train at 17.10,* and it was just after five; but the station was locked.

Marjorie Gait at a tea-stall nearby said, 'That stationmaster is barmy. Sometimes he doesn't open at all. Sometimes he's there at midnight.'

But I waited a few more minutes, and the train pulled in, whistling – a steam train, which looked like a toy but had been built to last. A man unlocked the station and beckoned me to the ticket window. I waited there. I was the only traveller.

There was a little placard stuck to the ticket window:

Places of Interest Along the Line –
> *Dymchurch:* Bingo, small Gift Shop
> *New Romney:* Main Railway Station
> *Greatstone:* Sandy Beach
> *Romney Sands:* Holiday Camp
> *Lade:* Fish and Chip Shop
>   Public Conveniences
> *Dungeness:* Lighthouse

Then the shutter went up and I bought a one-way ticket to New Romney from a man with greasy hands – he was the engineer, as well. He seemed a little surprised that it wasn't a round-trip ticket, since this railway was used mainly by joyriders and was kept in business by tourists. The two other passengers that evening were merely returning to New Romney and had come here to Hythe for fun, which was why they had not got off the train.

From the dawdling open car, where I sat with my feet up, in the cool empty light that slowed everything it touched this spring evening, I saw sheep and horses, wheat fields with breezes swimming through them and small houses built close to the ground. At Dymchurch there were yellow fields, one of the pleasures of May in England, the brightest crop: a whole field brimful of vivid buttery rape flowers. And beyond it, on the right-hand side of the tracks, under the lowering haze of a dusty day, ten miles of Romney Marsh. It was a drained marsh, an expanse of flat, fertile pastures. Henry James, who lived just to the south-west, at Rye, wrote that its charms were 'revealed best to a slow cyclist', and he listed them: 'little lonely farms, red and grey; little mouse-coloured churches; little villages that seem made only for long shadows and summer afternoons. Brookland, Old Romney, Ivychurch, Dymchurch – they have positively the prettiest names.'

At New Romney, no longer a port, the evening sunlight made the sky slant like a pale lid, so I had time to walk east to the beach and village there, Littlestone-on-Sea. It was no more than some bungalows, and a dead tree full of crows, and two terraces of old tall houses on a beach where the tide made the pebbles rattle like marbles in a jar. There was no wind – unusual, the hotel manager told me. 'The wind never stops.' The absence of wind seemed to prolong the daylight, and Littlestone was as calm as a lakefront.

The lady from the front desk, Mrs Turgis, showed me to my room and hesitated and then sat on my bed and said, 'You'll want this switched off,' and moved her slender finger against a toggle on the wall. 'The intercom,' she explained, 'when it's on we can hear everything that happens.'

'Me talking to myself,' I said.

'Or you might have a young lady in here,' Mrs Turgis said.

'Is that likely?' I said.

'And then you wouldn't want anyone to hear,' she said, and smiled. She was sitting on my pillow.

All day I had been travelling on sore feet with the sun against my face, marvelling at the easy language, the strange shore. But Littlestone-on-Sea was not far from London. Being here – being anywhere in England after dark – was a little like being lost.

Mrs Turgis stood up quickly, as if she had just remembered something, and went to the door. 'If you need anything, just –' and she smiled.

'I sure will' – in those words, because travelling had turned me back into an American.

The hotel was not full – a dozen men, all of them middle-aged and hearty and full of chat, making a remark and then laughing at it too loudly. They had been beating up and down the coast with cases of samples, and business was terrible. You mentioned a town, any town – Dover – and they always said, 'Dover's shocking.' They had the harsh, kidding manner of travelling salesmen, a clumsy carelessness with the waitresses, a way of making the poor girls nervous, bullying them because they had had no luck with their own wives and daughters.

Mr Figham, motor spares and car accessories, down from Maidstone, said the whole of Kent was his parish – his territory, shocking place. He was balding and a little boastful and salesman-skittish; he asked for the sweets trolley and as the pretty waitress stopped, he looked at the way her uniform had tightened against her thigh and said, 'That chocolate cake tickles my fancy –'

The waitress removed the cake dish.

'– and it's about the only thing that does, at my age.'

Mr Figham was not much more than fifty, and the three other men at his table about the same age laughed in a sad agreeing way, acknowledging that they were impotent and being a little wry about their sorry cocks not working properly. To eavesdrop on middle-aged Englishmen was often to hear them boasting about their lack of sexual drive.

I sat with all the salesmen later that night watching the hotel's television, the Falklands news. There was some anticipation. 'I was listening to my car radio as I came down the M20 ... One of my people said ... A chap I supply in Ashford had heard ...' But no one was definite – no one dared. '... something about British casualties ...'

It was the sinking of the *Sheffield*. The news was announced on television. It silenced the room: the first British casualties, a brand new ship. Many men were dead and the ship was still burning.

As long as the Falklands war had been without British deaths it was an ingenious campaign, clever footwork, an adventure. That was admired here: a nimble reply, no blood, no deaths. But this was dreadful and incriminating; and it had to be answered. It committed Britain to a struggle that no one really seemed to want.

One of the salesmen said, 'That'll take the wind out of our sails.'

There was a Chinese man in the room. He began to speak – the others had been watching him, and when he spoke they looked sharply at him, as if expecting him to say something in Chinese. But he spoke in English.

He said, 'That's a serious blow for us.'

Everyone murmured, *Yes, that was a serious blow for us*, and *What next?*, but I didn't open my mouth because already I felt like an enemy agent and agreed with the Argentine writer J. L. Borges's assessment of the Falklands war: 'It is just like two bald men fighting over a comb.'

Walking south from Littlestone was drearier in sunshine than it would have been in fog or rain, because the bright light exposed every woeful bungalow and every dusty garden, and it showed how in places there was nothing at all but pebbles. A little bad weather would have made it all a little mysterious and interesting. The sunlight made it plainly awful. This strip of bungalows went all the way to Dungeness and seemed to turn the corner. I could see this through my binoculars. I did not know then that the strip of bungalows was continuous for hundreds of miles of coast, all the way along Southern England to Land's End.

I struck out for Dungeness. It was a long horizontal walk across a squashy surface. I took a short cut and soon wished that I had kept to the road. The dead marsh was sand and stones and no trees, and it was hard walking. At one time in the early nineteenth century the local people wore what they called 'shingle shoes' made out of wood, for walking on this pebbly surface.

They were 'of a convenient length and width, with a receptacle for the foot in the middle, like the snowshoes used in northern countries'. In this way, some people had shuffled across Dungeness.

I walked to Greatstone on the bungalow strip, and then to Lydd-on-Sea, on the same strip. These places were so dull I thought of getting out of there on a bus, but when I told a man I wanted to find a bus he said, 'You'll be lucky,' and turned away.

'I hope the weather holds for you, Stan,' he said to a man beating a broom against his paved garden: crazy paving, gnomes, a birdbath, a rectangle of cruelly pruned rose bushes – all the bungalows were ugly in the same way, all the gardens were ugly in different ways.

I kept walking. It was possible for me to look through the front windows of these bungalows and see people polishing a souvenir horse brass, or buffing a cruet, or crocheting a doll with a long dress as a container for hiding the toilet roll. And I saw a woman at the window of one bungalow carefully biting the tip of her tongue and ironing an antimacassar. No one at Lydd-on-Sea was staring out of the window at the hideous nuclear power station and whispering, 'God help us,' but rather the general activity had to do with tidying. I thought about this as I walked along, and it seemed hugely appropriate that people were ironing antimacassars in a spot where a nuclear melt-down could be occurring. This was England, after all.

There were places around Dungeness where it looked as though the catastrophe had already happened. The Denge Marsh had a bombed, broken look. It was craters and quarries and gravel pits; no trees, only scrub and weeds; much barbed wire and miles and miles of grey pebbles. The whole of this corner of Kent looked that way to me on this brilliantly sunny day. And yet in this place which both man and nature had contrived to make horrible were the most beautiful birds – the lapwing (or green plover) with its long plume, and herons, and seven kinds of duck. Most of the birds had chosen to roost or swim in the gravel pits, but the place was so joylesss and the path so flat that not even the sight of thirteen swans in flight over it gave me any pleasure.

I discovered that day that the uglier a place was the slower

I walked. I went flat-footed through the marsh and through Lydd itself which had shade, and then around Lydd Camp ('Dangerous' my map said) – and I could hear shells exploding – 'lyddite', the high explosive made of picric acid, had got its name here. Somewhere along that road I entered Sussex, but the landscape did not improve. The army camp – why did they let the army hog the coast? – prevented me from walking on the shore, and denied me access to the beach. The cars on these roads seemed to be moving much faster than they would have elsewhere; but of course it was only natural that a driver should hurry through this desolation. I was walking and so every bit of it was forced upon me.

At last I reached Camber, a grey-white expanse of sloping beach, which extended for seven or eight miles towards Rye – that little hill in the distance. Camber Sands was empty, the beach deserted and no boats offshore. It was a weekday, but even so one might have expected a car, or one dog lover, or one picnicker, or a jogger. But there was no one at all on this lovely sunlit strand. That was another version of the English surprise – Dungeness, and then this, its opposite.

And then it went bad again, with slapped-together bungalows, and parking lots and holiday camps called 'Silver Sands' and 'Pontins'. There were no people here, but the buildings made this part of Camber look blighted. The beach was undeniably lovely and unspoiled, but at this western end of it the peeling, collapsing huts and rusting caravans and weeds and even a dump full of twisted metal and yesterday's plastic – this disfigurement was reminiscent of a Third World country, where they did not know any better, and just let the detritus pile up as evidence that this rubbish was another aspect of civilization. It struck me that as time passed some countries with nothing in common but poverty would begin to resemble one another because, while great civilizations are often vastly different and each culture is unique, everyone's junk is just the same.

This walk seemed interminable and full of detours. I had walked sixteen miles and had four more to go. But it was an easy hike from here on, through a meadow full of cows and along Rye Harbour to the town itself on its pretty hill. Rye was the quaintest town in this corner of England, but so museum-like in its quaintness that I found myself walking along the cobblestone streets with my hands behind my back, treating the town in my monkish manner of subdued appreciation like a person in a gallery full of *Do Not Touch* signs. Rye was not a restful place. It had the atmosphere of a china shop. It urged you to remark on the pretty houses and the well-kept gardens and the self-conscious sign painting and then it demanded that you move on. But it was not just the quaint places in England that looked both pretty and inhospitable. Most villages and towns wore a pout of rejection – the shades drawn in what seemed an averted gaze – and there were few places I went in England that did not seem, as I stared, to be whispering at me all the while, *Move on! Go home!*

I took the train to Hastings. Hastings was eleven miles away. It was a branch-line train from Ashford and not many people on it. It drew out of Rye, heading towards Winchelsea and the valley of the River Brede, across meadows and with poplars all around, making a stately progress through the green May countryside.

'Nice train,' I said to the man across the aisle.

'And they want to scrap it,' he said.

The British Railways Board had been trying to close down the line for nineteen years. That was usually the case with the branch lines. They were useful but unprofitable. (But on the other hand, no more unprofitable than lamp-posts or motorways.) The only ones not threatened with closure were those ferrying radio-active trash to and from nuclear power stations. As for the others, it was possible to tell from the beauty of a line or the thrill of the ride that the line would soon close. With one or two exceptions, there was not a railway line in Britain that was making a profit. And so, in time, they would all go. The branch lines would go first. And one day when there was no more fuel for private cars, it would be too late to get the trains back and go anywhere except, in a supervised Chinese way, from one big city to another in a brown bus. By then the great trains would all have been melted down and made into barbed wire fences.

This was what we talked about, the man across the aisle, Geoffrey Crouch by name, and I, on the way to Hastings, through this green corner of East Sussex. It was a lovely train, and all the stations were small and green. There were sheep at Winchelsea, and a black windmill on a hill. It was the month of flowering cherry trees, and this week the best blossoms – Doleham was full of them, dropping petals on the children homeward bound from school with satchels of books. At Three Oaks and farther on at Ore there were pink wild-flowers, and more sheep browsing in the meadows, and ivy growing so thickly on the oaks it seemed to upholster them. And on much of the line there were lilies of the valley growing wild along the railway embankment.

'Oh, yes, they'll scrap it all right,' Mr Crouch said. He was a farm labourer up the line at Hamstreet. When I arrived in Britain in 1971, these workers were earning an average wage of £13 a week. Mr Crouch was getting four times that now, but he was old and did not own his house and did not have a car.

At Hastings, he said, 'I'm glad I won't be around to see it.'

English people of a certain class often said things like this, taking a satisfaction in the certainty of death, because dying was a way of avoiding the indignity of what they imagined would be a grim future for them. They seemed to say: If you're vain enough to wish for a long life, you deserve to suffer!

A man in Hastings said to me, 'Why did I come here to live? That's easy. Because it is one of the three cheapest places in England.' He told me the other two but in my enthusiasm to know more about Hastings I forgot to write the others down. This man was the painter John Bratby. He did the paintings for the movie *The Horse's Mouth* and his own life somewhat re-sembled that of Gully Jimson, the painter-hero of the Joyce Cary novel on which the movie was based.

Mr Bratby was speaking in a room full of paintings, some of them still wet. He said, 'I could never buy a house this large in London or anywhere else. I'd have a poky flat if I didn't live in Hastings.'

His house was called The Cupola and Tower of the Winds, and it matched its name. It was tall and crumbling, and it creaked when the wind blew, and there were stacks of paintings leaning against every wall. Mr Bratby was thick-set and had the listening expression of a forgetful man. He said he painted quickly. He sometimes referred to his famous riotous past – so riotous it had nearly killed him. He had been a so-called kitchen sink painter with a taste for drawing rooms. Now he lived in a quiet way. He said he believed that western society was doomed, but he said this as he looked out of his Cupola window at the rooftops and the sea of Hastings, a pleasant view.

'Our society is changing from one based on the concept of the individual and freedom,' Mr Bratby said, 'to one where the individual is non-existent – lost in a collectivist state.'

I said I didn't think it would be a collectivist state so much as a wilderness in which most people lived hand to mouth, and the rich would live like princes – better than the rich had ever lived, except that their lives would constantly be in danger from the hungry predatory poor. All the technology would serve the rich, but they would need it for their own protection and to assure their continued prosperity. The poor would live like dogs. They would be dangerous and pitiful, and the rich would probably hunt them for sport.

This vision of mine did not rouse Mr Bratby, who was at that moment painting my portrait. 'There is no commercial considera- tion to this at all.' He had said of my painting, 'This is for posterity to see, when our society has completely changed.' He did not reject my description of the future. He scratched his head and went on dreading a police state where everyone wore baggy blue suits and called each other 'Comrade' – the Orwell nightmare, which was a warning rather than a reasonable prediction. Anyway, it was almost 1984 and here was J. Bratby with a delightful wreck of a house, painting his heart out in Hastings, the bargain paradise of the south coast!

It seemed to me that his fear of the future was actually a hatred of the present, and yet he was an otherwise cheery soul and full of projects ('Guess what it is – the long one. It's all the Canterbury pilgrims. Chaucer, you see.'). He said he never travelled but that his wife was very keen on it – had always wanted to go to New Orleans, for some reason. Now, his wife Pam was very attentive. She wore red leather trousers and made me a bacon sandwich. Bratby said that he had met her through a lonely hearts column, one of those classifed ads that say *Lonely gent, 54, stout but not fat, a painter by profession, south coast, wishes to meet* ... In this way they had met, and had hit it off and got married.

Hastings was full of painters. 'It's the cheapness, and the big houses, and the light is super,' Mick Rooney told me. He painted pictures of restaurant interiors – waiters, people having tea, enormous meals. He had started on Indian restaurants, all the ones called 'The Taj Mahal' or 'Bengal Tandoori', black proprietors and orange meals. They were packed with people and decor and bright colours. But I bought 'Cafe', a skinny old man eating a fried egg behind a greasy window, because it looked like Margate. Rooney was one of those rare artists whose work it was possible to praise without telling bald-faced lies about the pictures having motion and a sort of nervous eloquence and a quality of leaky objectivity and, oh shoot!, a kind of brooding beauty.

Writers are painful friends, and they are seldom friendly with each other. They are insecure in the presence of other writers. Composers of certain kinds of music are the same – tormented and intolerant. Yet some arts not only made the artist social but required it for him to succeed. Painting was one. Painters struck me as having warm uncomplicated friendships and probably more natural generosity than the practitioners of any other art. Perhaps this was because painting was such a portable, flexible thing. Painters painted outdoors, or in rooms full of people; they painted their lovers, alone, naked; they painted and ate; they painted and listened to the radio. It was a soothing way of doing your job.

It seemed to me that this was how the painters passed the time on the steep streets of Hastings. Mick was painting Indian restaurant scenes, Bratby was doing portraits of the living in anticipation of Armageddon, Gus Cummins was doing green skulls, and his wife Angie was doing lovers reclining in front of mirrors; and others were doing the fishermen at Old Town and the sea-monsters at nearby Fairlight. They were all good friends and boon companions, living cheaply in large decaying houses with lots of children and cats. They had plenty of talent and some success, but this was England after all, where no one – least of all a good painter – was really rewarded or punished; in England, whatever your profession, you made your own life.

The painters brightened Hastings and it seemed to me full of energy and industry and good humour, just the sort of place to recommend to a sensitive friend or relation with an artistic bent. All this and salubrious air, from Cliff End to Bulverhythe!

I was eating two pigeons in a restaurant with Rooney and praising the town one night, when at the mention of a person I had found particularly good-natured, Rooney looked doubtful.

'You might be right,' Rooney said, implying that I was completely mistaken.

'Sarah Milverton – that lady you introduced me to – she seemed just the sort of secure fulfilled person –'

'Don't,' Rooney said. 'Her husband died a week ago. Cancer. And he had been manic for eight years.'

'How manic?'

'Doing his nut – that's how manic. He heard voices for eight years. That's a lot of voices. Sarah's had a terrible time.'

I said, 'What about that guy telling the jokes – Orlock?'

He said, 'You noticed no one laughed at the jokes?'

This was true, and now that I thought of it Orlock had seemed a trifle frenzied in his joke-telling. But it had been a drunken meal, confirming my impression of Hastings as an artists' colony full of optimistic romance and spirited intimacy.

'You noticed his bandage?'

No, I had not seen Orlock's bandage.

'It was on his arm – his whole arm. Seventeen stitches,' Rooney said. He looked at me as though at a child, pitying my innocence, smiling despairingly at what he had to tell me, regretting that the subject had come up. 'Orlock tried to kill himself this morning with a razor.'

But I still liked Hastings, and I would have stayed longer except that I had as yet seen very little of the British coast. There was so much of it ahead of me I sometimes had the urge to cut and run – simply get on an express train and make a dash for Wales, or fly to Scotland and forget Ulster. But I had vowed to make my way slowly around the whole coast, and so one rainy morning Rooney walked west with me along the promenade.

If Hastings had been richer, all these Victorian buildings would have been torn down. The town was too poor to be vulgar and it had enough friendly artists to avoid being philistine. And was I right in thinking that painters liked being near the sea – something to do with the light? Rooney thought there might be something in this. Painters and fishermen seemed to go together. At the fish market in Hastings, Rooney said, you could find fish that you wouldn't see anywhere else in Britain – squid, octopus, cuttlefish and guinet. And the sole was the best in the country. At the tall Scandinavian-looking net sheds, made out of black planks, the fishermen sat with basins of fish, mending nets, saying very little. Rooney said they were impenetrable men and had their own customs. For example, if they saw a priest or nun in the early morning they would not go out fishing that day.

'You can imagine what they'd do if they saw the pope!' he said.

As a matter of fact, the pope was expected in Britain within a month, the first papal visit ever.

At Queen Victoria's statue in Warrior Square, where Hastings flattened into St Leonards-on-Sea, Rooney said, 'This is as far as I go. It's all geriatrics from here to Land's End!'

St Leonards was dull and colourless, full of low forbidding houses in which plants with dusty leaves were arranged in waist-high windows. It began to rain hard, and though St Leonards was slightly improved by the blur of the downpour, I did not linger there, but instead took the coastal train two stops to Bexhill-on-Sea. When I got to Bexhill I realized that St Leonards had been seedy.

'Like all the larger English watering places, it is simply a little London *super mare*.' What Henry James wrote of Hastings and St Leonards was truer now of Bexhill-on-Sea. 'With their long, warm seafront and their multitude of small cheap comforts and conveniences, (they) offer a kind of résumé of middle-class English civilization and of advantages of which it would ill become an American to make light.'

A résumé of middle-class English civilization was a high street lined with shops selling sensible practical merchandise – plain food and brown clothes; not many restaurants but plenty of tea shops; a busy bus route; semi-detached houses, with hedges and pebbledash façades; a park bench every twenty yards; a bowling green; a severe seafront – no fun-fair visible, and few public houses; and a largely elderly population of shuffling Tories.

And there was the De la Warr Pavilion, where on the various decks and verandas, the very old people sat in chairs with blankets in their laps staring out to sea, like people on a cruise, resting between meals. They drank tea, rattling their china cups on trembling saucers. They read the latest Falklands news without blinking: they have been through two world wars and might well have been in this very place when Adolf Hitler stood gloating at them through binoculars from the heights of the French coast.

If Bexhill-on-Sea was a résumé of one English class, the De la Warr Pavilion – moored there on the seafront like an ocean liner – was a résumé of Bexhill-on-Sea. Its lounges smelled of sickness and liniment, it echoed with lilting organ music, its tea-drinkers looked anguished; and yet it was a good warm place where I could sit comfortably (I rented a deck chair) and write up the diary I had neglected since before Hastings. I bought a cup of tea, like the others, and a chocolate biscuit; I stared at the sea and, writing my diary, I felt eighty years old but very safe and dry. It seemed clear to me that once an English person had reached Bexhill-on-Sea he had no intention of going any farther. This was, so to speak, the edge of the cliff. That was why the town was filled with dull comforts and warm rooms and large windows and busy churches. No one raised his voice here. There was no need. It was a monotonous drone of voices, an unvarying buzz of sibilant whispers. Nothing was urgent. People came here and admitted they were old and spent the rest of their lives looking after each other. On the English coast, the geriatric communities like Bexhill were almost utopian in the way the oldies co-operated in the struggle against ageing.

Far from making light of Bexhill, as Henry James feared Americans might be prone to do in a watering place of this kind, I felt I was taking it too seriously. I wandered around the pavilion and saw that there was an entertainment every day – a show, a band concert, a ballet, or an exhibition. That day there was an Antiques Fair, and that night the East Sussex Keep Fit Rally, and the next day the Sussex Opera and Ballet Society Weekend. And I had just missed the Warbleton and Buxted Band on the De la Warr Terrace ('deck chairs 30 pence').

I struck up a conversation with one Albert Crapstone, a deaf retired gent who had come here from Tunbridge Wells to die. He had a *Daily Express* on his lap, full of Falklands action. We talked about this, and then he said, 'You're a Yank,' and stiffened.

'And you came in, late as usual,' he said, meaning that the United States had just announced her support for Britain in the military action against Argentina. 'Just like the Great War, and the Second World War. At the last possible moment! Typical!'

He leaned forward, crumpling his newspaper.

'You can go back and tell your president we don't need his bloody help,' Mr Crapstone said.

'Fine,' I said, because a man with a hearing aid always has a tactical advantage in an argument – and what was the point? 'I'll tell him the next time I see him. I think he's over at Cooden Beach having a swim.'

'What's that?' Mr Crapstone demanded, twisting his face at me.

Cooden Beach was a few miles west, but the rain had stopped and the walk took me through suburban streets rather than along the shore. The houses were large detached villas with privet hedges like fortress walls and densely planted flower-beds, another Surbiton-on-Sea, the solidest London suburb grafted on to the solidest stretch of the south coast, the best – at least for the Crapstones in those villas – of both worlds. There were no youths at all in sight; every human I saw there was elderly, and most of them were attached to a leash and being pulled along by a dog, and even the dogs looked senile.

I walked towards Pevensey ('Pevensey Bay being the spot where William landed his army in 1066') and decided that anyone who came ashore at Cooden Beach or Bexhill-on-Sea would find himself face to face with the quintessential England – not just coastal, seaside holiday, retirement England, but secretive, rose-growing, dog-loving, window-washing, church-going, law-abiding, grumpy, library-using, tea-drinking, fussy and inflexible England.

The rain started again, then stopped, and then turned into a steady drizzle. I found it tiring to walk through rain. From time to time I sat on a memorial bench ('In Memory of B. D. H. Walliswood 1902–1978 Who Loved This View'). Each time I sat down something odd happened: birds flocked in a friendly way and seemed to fuss near my feet, expecting to be fed. Then more would come and soon there were fifteen or twenty birds tweeting at me. It was another proof of the temperament of the English people here – they fed the birds, as many old people seemed to do, and so the birds were not afraid of human beings.

The rain drove me back on to the railway. I took the train across the flat meadowy marsh called Pevensey Levels, past the temporary looking cottage settlements at Norman's Bay. This was part of the holiday coast, the dwellings ugly and unpleasant, and only the place-names were memorable, like Wartling and The Crumbles. The train swung several miles around the flat meadow, making a wide circle, and then turned on a long meadow as flat and green as a billiard table and approached Eastbourne from the back. There was no coastal line here, because the original line went from Lewes to Hastings, and Eastbourne hardly existed then. The Eastbourne spur was not added until later, but it was decades before Eastbourne came into its own. It was a village until the turn of the century.

Eastbourne was planned and zoned in a calculated way, designed to be elegant and deliberately unreachable by day-trippers. It was meant to be high-class and it succeeded because it was just a bit too far from London to attract cheese-paring tourists. It did not have a harbour – so it was spared the high spirits of sailors and the taint of trade. The streets were laid out, the hotels inserted, the parks, the golf links, the bandstands, the pier, and the front – no shops were to be allowed on it – all of those were determined at the time of Eastbourne's building. And it worked. It had never been Cockneyfied. The town had a graspable size, and a sense of civic pride and a modest grandeur. Folkestone's elegance was its geriatric propriety. But Eastbourne was a thriving place and there was enough in it that was ordinary to give balance to its beauty.

I stayed in a village just outside Eastbourne, not far from Beachy Head. Mountain climbers often practised climbing the sheer wall of Beachy Head, and it was also a favourite spot for suicides – thirty in the past two years. There was a valley just west of where I was staying, in which ardent socialists had settled and become landowners and country squires. They were union men or politicians who, after a career of howling at the rich, had been awarded knighthoods and appointed to directorships and had become well-to-do themselves. They lived in manor houses or on large farms and some, amazingly, still espoused views which were in contradiction to the way they lived. It was a curious combination of secrecy, hypocrisy and the sort of muddle that enabled an Englishman to hold two opposing views in his head. And it demonstrated that the best way to become a baron or an earl or a knight of the Garter was to spend half a lifetime singing 'The Red Flag' and becoming a conspicuous irritation to the establishment. It was an easy transition from any smoke-filled room of whining conspirators to a seat in the House of Lords. The English aristocracy had nearly always been recruited from the ranks of flatterers, cut-throats, boyfriends, political pirates and people of very conceited ambition. So it was not so strange that this blue valley on the coast of East Sussex was populated by wine-bibbing lords who had formerly been Marxist union men named Jones and Brown.

I set off for Brighton on foot, starting at Birling Gap. The tide was high, so I could not walk along the beach. I was not sorry about this. In this way I was spared the possibility of being embayed or of the cliffs falling down and braining me – they were very crumbly cliffs. I walked in bright sunshine across the Seven Sisters to Seaford. The turf on these seven bluffs was very spongy and green. There were sheep in the meadows that lay parallel to this high part of the coast. Their bells clunked as they jerked their heads up to look at me. And there were gulls on the cliffs. Gulls squawk, but they also bark, scream, shriek, yap, whimper and crow. Sometimes, roosting, they whine. I also heard them mew like cats. They are stupid hungry birds and there was a common species on the British coast that had a head so black and hooded they looked like hangmen.

There were rabbits on the Seven Sisters. They were small cute creatures. They had burrowed into the seventh sister, eaten much of her grass and in this way had loosened the whole bluff by allowing the rain and erosion to take hold. The little beasts hippity-hopped all over the bluff, and they were in the process of destroying one of the most beautiful cliffs on the coast – the bunnies had just about brought it down.

I came to the Cuckmere river. That was a problem. The South Downs Way detours around it – there was no way of getting across the wide wet estuary. I walked along the east bank of the Cuckmere river, past World War Two pillboxes and gun emplacements, and herons and swans. Then over the bridge and across Seaford Head to Seaford proper, which was a nice town,

once full of prep schools. Most of the schools were now closed
and Seaford was regarded as something of a backwater, overshadowed by Newhaven on the green River Ouse. Virginia Woolf
had drowned herself a few miles upstream in 1941.

I walked on, through Newhaven and up the bluff to Peacehaven, until it started to rain. Peacehaven was solid with
bungalows on little plots with just room enough for a garden,
garden gnome and a square yard of crazy paving. I caught a bus
here. It swayed on the high cliff road, past the open space that
marks the Zero Meridian; past Telscombe Cliffs where, under
a sky of yapping gulls, all the sewage of Brighton and Hove
empties into the English Channel. And then into Rottingdean.

In Rottingdean 'in 1882 there had been but one daily bus from
Brighton, which took forty minutes,' Rudyard Kipling wrote in
his autobiography *Something of Myself*. 'And when a stranger
appeared on the village green the native young would stick out
their tongues at him.' It was, he said, an almost empty coast of
green fields and isolated houses. But it changed in Kipling's lifetime. Before he died in 1936, he wrote, 'Today, from Rottingdean
to Newhaven is almost fully developed suburb, of great horror.'
It was much worse now, so I stayed on the bus and did not get
off until we reached Brighton.

4

The 18.11 to Bognor Regis

People in Brighton were imagined to be perpetually on the razzle, their days spent prowling The Lanes or Marine Parade, and their nights full of ramping sexuality. Think I'll go down and have a dirty weekend, people said. Brighton had a great reputation. You were supposed to have fun in Brighton, but Brighton had the face of an old tart and a very brief appeal.

It was an hour from London. It was one of London's resorts. It was two hours from Dieppe by ferry. It was one of France's resorts. The scowling foreigners gave it a crassly cosmopolitan air, but no one knew what to make of it. Greeks and Indians opened restaurants and cheap shops, and then stood in front hardly believing that business could be so bad. The English were shrewder. They opened casinos and public houses. There were more pubs in Brighton than in any other seaside town in Great Britain, because there was little else to do but drink. Serious fishermen went down to Newhaven, and swimmers up the coast a little to Hove. Like many places that had a great reputation, Brighton was full of disappointed and bad-tempered visitors.

Brighton Rock contains the popular impression of Brighton: gangsters, hilarity, murder and Mortal Sin – all in sight of Palace Pier. But Graham Greene subsequently wrote in an introduction to the novel that while he had been fastidious about the detail in the novels set in Mexico and Indo-China, the setting of Brighton 'may in part belong to an imaginary geographic region'. He said he was writing about the past – already, in 1937, that Brighton had vanished and so 'I must plead guilty to manufacturing this Brighton of mine.'

Even so, the novel is very good in describing Brighton disappointment and the progress of the day-trippers: 'They had

stood all the way from Victoria in crowded carriages, they would
have to wait in queues for lunch, at midnight half asleep they
would rock back in trains to the cramped streets and the closed
pubs and the weary walks home. With immense labour and
immense patience they extricated from the long day the grain
of pleasure: this sun, this music, the rattle of the miniature cars,
the ghost train diving between the grinning skeletons under the
Aquarium promenade, the sticks of Brighton rock, the paper
sailors' hats.'

That was it, more or less. I had been to Brighton so many
times I had no desire to linger. Much better, I thought, to push
on to Bognor, where I had never been. But I had someone to
see in Brighton – Jonathan Raban was there on his boat, the
Gosfield Maid, moored at Brighton Marina, just beyond Kemp
Town and the nudist beach ('Bathing Costumes Are Not
Required To Be Worn Past This Sign'). Jonathan had said that
he was taking a trip around the British coast and was planning
to write a book about it. This interested me. All trips are different,
and even two people travelling together have vastly different
versions of their journey. Jonathan was doing his coastal tour
anti-clockwise, stopping at likely ports in his boat.

He seemed contented on his boat. He had framed prints and
engravings on the walls, and Kinglake's *Eothen* was open on a
table under a porthole. It was strange to see a typewriter and
a TV set on board, but that was the sort of boat it was, very
comfy and literary, with bookshelves and curios.

'This must be your log,' I said, glancing down. The entries
were sketchy ('. . light rain, wind ESE ...') – nothing very
literary here, no dialogue, no exclamation marks.

He said, 'I keep planning to make notes, but I never seem to
get round to it. What about you?'

'I fiddle around,' I said. It was a lie. I did nothing but make
notes, scribbling from the moment I arrived in a hotel or a guest
house and often missing my dinner. I hated doing it. It was a
burden. But if I had been in Afghanistan I would have kept a
detailed diary. Why should I travel differently in Britain?

I said, 'I hate Brighton. I think there's a kind of wisdom in
that – the British person, or even the foreigner, who says simply,
I hate Brighton. What's there to like here? It's a mess.'

'Yes, it's a mess,' Jonathan said. 'That's one of the things I like about it.'

'I've never seen so many dubious-looking people,' I said.

He said, 'It's full of tramps,' and he smiled again. Then he said that the most unexpected things happened in Brighton. He would be walking along and he would see someone dressed up as Cardinal Wolsey or Robin Hood, or musicians, or people singing and having a grand time.

I said I saw only bums and day-trippers and people trying to, um, extricate from the long day the grain of pleasure.

We decided to have lunch in the centre of Brighton, and so took the little train that rattled from the Marina, past the nudist beach, to the Aquarium. The nudist beach was mostly naked men staring hard at each other. This created heavy traffic on that part of the front. We were pestered by a man with a monkey when we got off the train. I kept wanting to say, 'See what I mean?'

'I had my parents on the boat for a week,' Jonathan said, in the restaurant.

Odd sort of voyage, I thought – Mum and Dad on his thirty-foot boat, hardly enough room to swing a cat in the galley, no privacy, rough seas, typewriter skittering sideways, all of them sleeping in the same small area, 'Are you sure you won't have another fish finger, son?' and 'I'm going to use the toilet, if no one has any objection.'

That was how I imagined it.

'Who was the captain?' I asked. I knew that Jonathan's father was a clergyman, and it seemed to me that a clergyman was apt to take command.

'I was in charge,' Jonathan said. 'After all, it's my boat.'

He said his book would be about all the places he had known and lived in on the British coast – a dozen or more.

I said that I wanted to write a book about all the places I had never seen before, which was most of the British coast.

At last, I said I had to be moving on.

'Where to?'

'Bognor,' I said.

'Good old Bognor,' he said. 'So you're headed down the promenade.'

'Right,' I said. It was a lovely afternoon.

He said he would be sailing towards Rye in a day or so, and then to Dover and up the east coast.

'Watch out for the Goodwin Sands,' I said. I told him what I had heard in Broadstairs, how they swallowed ships.

We shook hands and went our separate ways – Jonathan to fight the gales, and I to go down the prom towards Bognor. Some trip, I thought, as I sauntered along the promenade. But I was learning things and getting fresh air, and some day I would be too old for this and would be taken for a tramp if I tried it. Even now people sniffed and tried not to stare. A man of forty with a knapsack could easily be a serious crank.

As I strolled, I could see that Hove was low spirits and lawns, and the monotonous frenzy of Brighton gave way to clean old houses and rather spent pensioners. The front, which had been more or less continuous since Margate, was breezy, but now I knew – because I had left it and walked on – that Brighton's chief characteristic was the youthfulness of its visitors: the young had made it seem aimless and wasteful. Hove was not that way.

Hove, like many other places on the English coast, had chalets. The name was misleading. They were huts, and chalet was mis-pronounced to suit them – 'shally', the English said, an appropriate word made out of shanty and alley. There were hundreds of them shoulder to shoulder along the front. They had evolved from bathing machines, I guessed. The English were prudish about nakedness (and swimming for the Victorians had been regarded as the opposite of a sport – it was a sort of immersion cure, a cross between colonic irrigation and baptism). The bathing machine – a shed on a pair of wheels – had been turned into a stationary changing room, and then arranged in rows on the beachfront; and at last they had become miniature houses – shallys.

Hove's shallys were the size of English garden sheds. I looked into them fully expecting to see rusty lawnmowers and rakes and watering cans. Sometimes they held bicycles, but more often these one-room shallys were furnished like doll-houses or toy bungalows. You could see what the English considered essential to their comfort for a day at the beach. They were painted, they had framed prints (cats, horses, sailboats) on the wall, and plastic roses in jamjar vases. All had folding deck chairs inside, and a shelf at the rear on which there was a hotplate and a dented kettle and some china cups. They were fitted out for tea and naps – many had camp cots, plastic cushions and blankets; some had fishing tackle; a few held toys. It was not unusual to see half a fruitcake, an umbrella, and an Agatha Christie inside, and most held an old person, looking flustered.

All the shallys had numbers, some very high numbers, testifying to their multitude. But the numbers did not distinguish them, for they all had names: *Seaview, The Waves, Sunny Hours, Bide-a-Wee*, picked out on their doors or else lettered on plaques. They had double-doors – some looked more like horse boxes than cottages. They had curtains. They had folding panels to keep out the wind. Many had a transistor buzzing, but the shally people were old-fashioned – they actually were the inheritors of the bathing-machine mentality – and they called their radios 'the wireless' or even 'my steam radio'.

They were rented by the year, or leased for several years, or owned outright – again, like bathing machines. But they were thoroughly colonized. They had small framed photographs of children and grandchildren. When it rained, their occupiers sat inside with their knees together, one person reading, the other knitting or snoozing, always bumping elbows. In better weather they did these things just outside, a foot or so from the front door. I never saw a can of beer or a bottle of whisky in a shally. The shally people had lived through the war. They had no money but plenty of time. They read newspapers, and that day everyone looked as if he was boning up for an exam on the Falklands campaign. It was becoming a very popular war.

The shallys were very close together, but paradoxically they were very private. In England, proximity creates invisible barriers. Each shally seemed to stand alone, no one taking any notice of the activity next door. *Seaview* was having tea while *The Waves* pondered the *Daily Express*; *Sunny Hours* was taking a siesta, and the pair at *Bide-a-Wee* were brooding over their mail. All conversation was in whispers. The shallys were not a community. Each shally was separate and isolated, nothing neighbourly about it. Each had its own English atmosphere of hectic calm. A by-law stipulated that no one was allowed to spend a night in a shally, so that shally was a daylight refuge, and it was used with the intense preoccupation and the sort of all-excluding privacy that the English bring to anything they own – not creating any disturbance, nor encroaching on anyone else's shally, and not sharing. Anyone who wished to know how the English lived would get a good idea by walking past the miles of these shallys, for while the average English home was closed to strangers – and was closed to friends, too: nothing personal, it just isn't done – the shally was completely open to the stranger's gaze, like the doll-houses they somewhat resembled, that had one wall missing. It was easy to look inside. That's why no one ever did.

I walked out of Hove and on to Portslade and Southwick, which had a handsome power station on a neck of land just offshore, so that with its two tall chimneys it looked like a steamship moored on the coast.

At Southwick I met Mrs Ralph Stonier. She was standing in the sunshine in her old overcoat, waiting for a bus. She said the buses never came. She was a native of Southwick. She hated it: overbuilt, she said. It used to be very quiet here, but no more. Of course, it was much worse in Brighton. You couldn't live on the coast these days. She didn't know what was going to happen except that things would surely get worse. She stood stiffly, facing the oncoming traffic. The English could look so tired and so determined at the same time! She was taking the bus because the train was too expensive, even though as a pensioner she travelled for half fare. She had a country accent, as all the older natives seemed to on the south coast.

'I'm going to Bognor,' I said to Mrs Stonier, not that she had asked.

She said, 'That's miles away!'

It was twenty miles. I took the train to Worthing.

Irby and Vitchitt, two schoolboys, were talking behind me in low serious voices, on the train. They were both about fifteen years old.

Vitchitt said, 'If you could change any feature of your body,' and he paused, 'what would you change?'

'Me fice,' Irby said. He had not hesitated.

Vitchitt said, 'Your '*ole* fice?'

'Yeah.'

Vitchitt stared at him.

Irby said, 'Me 'ole fice.'

'What about your oys?'

'Me oys,' Irby said. 'I dunno.'

'What about your 'air?'

'Me 'air.' Irby looked stumped. 'I dunno.'

'What about ya rears?'

'Me years,' Irby said. 'Smaller anyway.'

'What about teef?' Vitchitt said.

'Dunno. I have to fink about vat,' Irby said.

And then, as they pushed through the door at Worthing, they began to talk about contraceptive devices.

Signs near Worthing said 'Pleasure Park' and 'Leisure Centre' and 'Fun Palace'. In England, such signs spelled gloom. And yet Worthing, with its proud hotels and guest houses, did not look bad. It was a breezy, villagey place, with tree-lined streets, and like the folks who lived in it, Worthing was a little old, and a little lame, and a little stout, but it still had sparkle. It had the restful friendliness of a favourite uncle or aunt – lots of dignity but no airs, and a great deal of salty gentility and decent fatigue.

These south coast towns could look terribly *visited*. It gave them a hackneyed, worn-down appearance; then they were a bit frayed and exposed, and there were many more cars than people, and plenty of shows and always a sign saying *Coaches Welcome*, and that too-loud heartiness and relentless querying to which the English were prone on holidays: Sleep all right? Enjoying yourself? Have a nice trip down? Find your friends from last year? Fancy a cup of tea? Like the show? and Hope the weather holds – isn't it glorious? The visited towns were stale with this chat, and at certain times of the day and every Sunday morning they looked very dusty and very empty.

Worthing was somewhat like that, but with an overlay of charm; Bognor Regis was this way to the core, and its look was that of a fairground – frenzied when it was busy and desolate when empty. I got there by walking to Goring-on-Sea, where the houses were bigger and smugger than Worthing's, and a pretty girl on the pier was selling a plump Dover sole to a man for a reasonable price. I walked another two miles to Ferring, then sat down on the village green because I had sore feet. Rather than turn the simple trip to Bognor into an ordeal, I took the train the rest of the way. Littlehampton was plain and semi-detached and flinty, the sort of place in which the people did little but water their plants. Then across the River Arun (Arundel was upstream, but I had vowed: No castles) to Climping and pretty farms and a bright field deep with yellow mustard; and then Elmer and a Butlin's camp that served as a kind of warning that Bognor was around the bend.

Bognor was empty. They could look awful when they were empty. The wind came off the Channel, stirring the suds at the shore, and it blew through the town. Nothing moved, there were no trees, and anything loose had been blown away in the winter. There was just the sound of the wind sawing at the edges of houses and swelling under the eaves. And the emptiness was exaggerated by the presence of Butlin's holiday camp, on the shore road into town. Butlin's was full and busy – shouts, the struggle of excitement, the sound of bugles – and so, in this empty town, it had the feel of a concentration camp. Everyone in Bognor was at Butlin's, but it was not easy to explain, because the camp was barrack-like buildings fenced in like a prison, and the bright paint on its old-fashioned shapes only served to make it look more sinister. And this full camp in empty Bognor made Bognor seem lopsided.

I thought: One of these days I'll have a look inside a holiday camp when it is in full swing. Most of these places were on the coast, so I would be able to take my pick.

'Oh, yes, it's very quiet,' Miriam Pottage said, as she showed me to my room in the Camelot Guest House. Miss Pottage was in her sixties and had candy in a pocket of her apron, toffees and caramels, which she peeled – depositing the cellophane in another crinkling pocket – and ate continuously the way a chain-smoker smokes. 'Mind you,' she said, turning on the stairs and still sucking – the caramels gave her mouth a monkey jut – 'it's always quiet this time of the year.'

It was what everyone said, but it never quite accounted for such great emptiness. I was the only person here at Camelot.

It was a cold house, full of damp carpets. Miss Pottage explained that they turned the heating off at Easter, and then turned it on again, the downstairs rads, in October. It was a habit, like. And you could always put on a cardigan if you were feeling the cold – better that than running up an enormous bill at the electricity board. And even if it was uncomfortably cold what was the point in heating a whole house in order to heat one person?

'But when the season's on,' Miss Pottage said, 'I'll be run off me feet.'

She was one of those people who when she spoke seemed to be saying the thing for the third or fourth time, although I am sure that was not the case and it was only that she enunciated slowly and was brutally dull. She made me seem clairvoyant, because whenever she opened her mouth I knew what was going to come out. She was a humourless soul, and she had infuriating patience. She was very kind to me and did not charge much for the room.

I liked the quiet here. It was the opposite of Brighton, nor was it elderly like Worthing. Bognor was not at all bad – that was a pleasant discovery, like finding a virtue in a person no one liked. Bognor was restful, the front was windswept and bare, the pier was shut, it had no pretensions, practically everyone was at Butlin's holiday camp, beyond the big fence.

Night fell on Bognor and turned the town into a village. The wind was still strong but there was no sound of the sea and nothing salty in the air. I had dinner at the only chip shop in Bognor that was open – I was becoming knowledgeable about fish and chips and English breakfasts, and starting to dislike them.

'I wrote a book about women because I am a woman and I know women and understand them,' a woman said on a radio that was playing behind a bar in a public house. There was more. 'We have different bodies and different options. We are completely different from men. I actually quite like being a woman, and I think –'

'*Claptrap!*' Mr Love, the barman said and switched it off and made a face at me. 'Makes me want to spew.' He was washing glasses, angrily polishing them with a cloth wrapped around his wrist. 'Load of bloody cobblers.' I thought he was going to smash a glass. 'Ever hear such rubbish?'

I agreed with him. I was always reassured when someone felt his intelligence had been insulted by a radio or television programme.

In another public house there was a television set. I drank and waited until the news came on. It was Falklands news but nothing specific.

At the bar, Mrs Hykeham, with an old scarf yanked on her head, and puffy, smoker's eyes, said, 'It's stupid for Britain to be killing fourteen-year-old boys in the Falklands. That's how old they are. There was this letter smuggled out, see. It was in the paper. It told how the little Argies were cold and scared and homesick.'

She went on in this vein and soon everyone in the bar was shouting at her. But it made her more contrary and she wouldn't budge. She seemed secretly pleased to be disagreeing with everyone and she repeated the letter she had read and looked at the rest of them with contempt.

There was another woman in the bar. This was Mrs Wackerfield. She had dog teeth and a way of staring. She said flatly that she was planning to go to the United States with her husband and children. She wanted to find work. Her husband knew everything about motors, and she knew about catering. Mrs Wackerfield was not more than forty. Her husband Richard just sat there. He seemed to be thinking: Should Birdie be telling this bloke all these things?

'We'll go and stay for about five or six years,' she said.

Her voice was London-stuffy. She was drinking Pimm's.

'We'll make some money and then come home,' she said.

She was very certain about everything.

'I want to go to California,' she said. 'It's lovely there, we've been twice. I don't want anything to do with New York, and Florida's getting spoiled. We'll sell up here and go, and start a business of some kind. We're not going to work for anyone else. We never do that. We'll save our money and then come home. I'd never think of staying there. We don't want that.'

Mrs Wackerfield continued to describe how she and Richard were going to settle in California for a while, because England was useless as far as work went, but it was her home, she said; she would come back. Richard said nothing. Now he was looking at me, perhaps wondering whether I objected to their presuming in this way. 'We'll use your country for a few years and then ditch it when we've made our pile' – that was what they were saying. I did object to their presumption, but I kept my mouth shut.

I stayed in Bognor longer than I had planned. I grew to like Miss Pottage at Camelot. The beach was fine in the sunshine, and there was always an old man selling huge horrible whelks out of a wooden box on the front. He said he caught them himself. It was sunny but the shops were closed and the front was deserted. The season hadn't started, people said.

I began to think that Bognor had been misrepresented. The oral tradition of travel in Britain was a shared experience of received opinion. Britain seemed small enough and discussed enough to be known at second-hand. Dickens was known that way: it was an English trait to know about Dickens and Dickens's characters without ever having read him. Places were known in this same way. That was why Brighton had a great reputation and why Margate was avoided. Dover, people said, the white cliffs of Dover. And Eastbourne's lovely. And the Sink Ports, they're lovely, too. It was Dickens all over again, and with the same sort of distortions, the same prejudices, and some places they had all wrong.

'I don't know as much as I should about Dungeness,' a man said to me, who didn't know anything about it at all. I went away laughing.

Broadstairs was serious, but Bognor was a joke. I was told, 'It's like Edward the Seventh said' – it was George the Fifth – 'his last words before he died. "Bugger Bognor!" That's what I say.' Bognor had an unfortunate name. Any English place-name with *bog* or *bottom* in it was doomed. ('The bowdlerization of English place-names has been a steady development since the late eighteenth century. In Northamptonshire alone, Buttocks Booth became Boothville, Pisford became Pitsford and Shitlanger was turned into Shutlanger.') Camber Sands had a nice rhythmical lilt and was seen as idyllic – but it wasn't; Bognor contained a lavatorial echo, and so it was seen as scruffy – but it wasn't.

All English people had opinions on which seaside places in England were pleasant and which ones were a waste of time. This was in the oral tradition. The English seldom travelled at random. They took well-organized vacations and held very strong views on places to which they had never been.

5

A Morning Train to the Isle of Wight

The coast for the fifty miles west of Bognor was full of pleats and tucks – harbours, channels, inlets; and Southampton Water, and the bays of Spithead. The coastal footpath around Selsey Bill gave out at one of the two Witterings. Beyond it were inconvenient islands and not enough causeways, and a path made impossible by the scoops and cuts of all this water. There were no walkers here. This territory was for sailors – full of fine bays, friendly harbours and the waterlogged geography of the Solent; all the blowing boats.

Just under the irregular coast was the Isle of Wight – shaped like the loose puzzle-piece that most offshore islands resemble. I could reach it by train, taking the ferry from Portsmouth, and there was another train that went down the right-hand side of the island, from Ryde to Shanklin. I wanted to see what Henry James had called 'that detestable little railway'. This was the best way of skipping across the crumbs of land that made that part of the English coast from Bognor to Bournemouth so hard for the walker. I would simply take the morning train to the Isle of Wight.

I thought I might be the only passenger to Portsmouth, and was still convinced of it as we crossed the green fields to Chichester ('. . . a handsome Market Cross, erected in 1500, but much damaged by the Puritans'), and Fishbourne, which was full of new mauve lilacs and booing children; but at Bosham, a middle-aged couple – the Lucketts – got on and seemed eager to tell me, but without appearing to boast, that they were going to Southampton to see the *Queen Elizabeth II* set sail for the Falklands.

'And of course we'll pop in and see my sister at the same time,' Mrs Luckett said, embarrassed by my lack of response. The Lucketts were off to wave plastic Union Jacks at a departing troopship – what was I supposed to do? Sing a chorus of 'There'll Always Be An England?' 'She's out at Hedge End in a maisonette. Her husband's in the transport business.'

'By "transport business" she means he's a lorry driver,' Mr Luckett said maliciously. He was not close to his brother-in-law. 'Mad about CB radios,' Mr Luckett went on. ' "A big ten-four to that rig, Rubber Duck." It's the most awful cobblers.'

'He travels all over the country,' Mrs Luckett said.

I said, 'And you live in Bosham?'

'Bozzam,' Mr Luckett said, and I believed at the time that it was a different place.

I said, 'I hope nothing happens to the *Q.E. II*.' The Lucketts looked up, a little startled. 'I mean, in the war.' They looked even more alarmed. 'This Falklands business.'

They seemed a little calmer when I said that. You weren't supposed to say *the war*, but rather *this Falklands business*.

'She'll be fine,' Mr Luckett said.

'Oh, yes,' Mrs Luckett said.

They were very proud, but it also occurred to me that they were going all the way to Southampton mainly because it was a beautiful sunny day, and because Mrs Luckett's sister was nearby. They told themselves they were going to cheer the *Q.E. II*, but I had the impression that if it had been raining they would not have gone.

There were apple blossoms all along this pretty line, and they looked like a brilliant form of knitting – bright blown-open stitches of white yarn fastened to rain-blackened boughs. I thought, at Emsworth: What a nice old-fashioned station platform, freshly painted wood and a small fireplace in the waiting room.

Warblington was no more than a short platform – a halt behind a town, no station – and there was a man in a little narrow box selling tickets, and another man with a flag. Whenever I saw too many railwaymen and not many passengers, I thought: They're going to axe this train. The car was soon empty. The Lucketts changed at Havant for Southampton. I could have got off at Havant, too, and waited ten minutes and been back in Clapham Junction in time for lunch. That was another hard thing about travelling in England – the short distances, the fast trains, the easy access – always a clear shot to London – and the sad gravitational pull of home.

But I stuck to the train and went in search of some more Lucketts. Anyone else planning a send-off for British troops? I did not find anyone, but scratched on the train door was a recent message: '*The Argentines are Wankers – Bomb the Barstards.*'

After spending two hours in the city in 1879, Henry James concluded, 'Portsmouth is dirty, but it is also dull.' He had been there trying to confirm the 'familiar theory that seaport towns abound in local colour, in curious types, in the quaint and the strange'. He found Portsmouth 'sordid', and he did not soften towards the town until he saw the harbour.

History had not altered Portsmouth, much less enhanced it. Passing from Portsmouth and Southsea Station to Portsmouth Harbour Station, the train crossed Commercial Road. Charles Dickens was born on this road in 1812. But Dickens's birthplace was just a torrent of traffic on a thoroughfare that looked like the Balls Pond Road. This was the coast on which you saw a plaque saying, *In a House On This Spot, The Poet Percy Bysshe Shelley wrote 'Grant, O Darkling Woods, My Sweet Repose'*, and you looked up and saw a petrol station.

Portsmouth was associated with *Nicholas Nickleby*, H. G. Wells and Captain Marryat. Charles II was married here, Conan Doyle invented Sherlock Holmes here, and Rudyard Kipling was so unhappy here that, at the age of five, he told the hag who was looking after him that he wanted to strangle her, and for the rest of his life referred to that woman's residence as 'The House of Desolation'. But none of this made the town of Portsmouth visibly interesting, because nothing could. Like most British sea-port towns, Portsmouth was its harbour. It was wrong to look behind the harbour for anything better.

This harbour was choppy with the criss-crossed wakes of gun-boats coming and going, their flags flying and their sailors scrambling over their decks. I identified this activity with the Falklands news and I assumed these boats were setting out that day for the South Atlantic. Portsmouth harbour contained a flotilla of Royal Navy ships, giving solemn hoots on their horns. Looking north towards the Royal Dockyard I could see the topmost sections of the masts of H.M.S. *Victory*, but it was the gunboats in the harbour that were bucking the waves. These days, many harbours I saw looked self-important and purposeful and over-cautious: they were battle-ready. The Falklands war depended almost entirely on the strength of the British fleet and it had brought the cold excitement of patriotism to these harbours.

South of the harbour mouth, the Isle of Wight was a long flat shadow in the morning mist. I bought a ticket to Shanklin and boarded the ferry *Southsea*. It was a windy crossing of Spithead, the waves were blue-black and the sea froth was being whipped from their peaks. We sailed towards Ryde, which even at this distance I could tell was an old-fashioned place, for its skyline was church spires. And that was always a good sign, the steeples and spires; the most heartening aspect of any of these coastal towns was a skyline in which spires predominated – I liked walking into these places. I was always happier seeing church spires, even though I did not regard myself as religious and seldom entered a church. I was sometimes betrayed by this impression. In some towns the church had been sold and was now a craft centre or a movie theatre. What to do with a defunct church was always a problem in England. Muslims occasionally petitioned for the church to be sold to them so that they could turn it into a mosque, but the request was always turned down. It seemed too much like defilement to worship Allah at St Cuthbert's. Instead the church was made into a bingo hall, or else torn down and a petrol station built in its place.

The Isle of Wight was too far from the mainland to be commercially useful. It was picturesque, it received visitors, old folks went there to retire. It was to be stared at and admired. Before I went there I imagined that it was like a table-top, with a simple beauty – flat, and plenty of grass, a park planted in the ocean. I was surprised to see that Ryde was fairly large. It was Victorian brown brick, redder where it was more recent, stacked against the hillside – I had been wrong in imagining it flat – and Ryde had the coiled streets that were peculiar to the coastal towns on the Isle of Wight.

Henry James loathed the train here, calling it '... a gross impertinence ... an objectionable conveyance'. The railway was so ugly and the island so pretty that the sight of this 'obtrusive' thing was 'as painful as it would be to see a pedlar's pack on the shoulders of a lovely woman'.

It is an odd image, especially as there were many lovely women on the Isle of Wight when I was there, and as they were Ramblers most of them were wearing the sort of knapsacks that James found so painfully inappropriate. In fact, it singled them out as hearty and independent and easy-going. As for the detestable train, it was a great deal more comfortable, and cheaper, and less noisy, than the numerous clumsy buses that crowded the island's roads. A hundred years ago the train looked like a foolish novelty, but now the narrow unimproved carriage roads were no more than dangerous chutes down which tourist buses, and swaying double-deckers, and plump long-distance coaches went much too fast, and on many roads only one vehicle could pass at a time. One of the most popular topics of conversation on the Isle of Wight was the dreadful traffic and the slow progress on the bad roads. People had come here intending to escape these terrors.

The train was a hand-me-down, or more properly another retiree: it had served its time on the London Underground and been taken out of service, and now it was in active retirement, plying back and forth from Ryde to Shanklin. It was from the thirties, it had that look, very plain and rather dark and full of handles and belts for strap-hangers; it was rattly and had a London smell of cigarettes and brake dust. But it was still very serviceable. There were eighty girls in my carriage, heading for Sandown, a school outing from Hampshire: they were small fat-faced girls, flushed from shouting, with damp hair, and steamy glasses. They had been yelling all the way across Spithead on the ferry. They were being watched with disapproval by exhausted-looking holiday people, the arriving couples on their way to Ventnor, and by middle-aged men carrying hand-bags. It hardly mattered that we were crossing the Isle of Wight. This train might have been going from Clapham to Waterloo on the

Northern Line in London, the passengers were so shabby and unenthusiastic. The schoolgirls were schoolgirls. The English could appear to bring no joy at all to a vacation, and so they looked appropriate here on this old underground train.

But now the metropolitan train was in the sticks, crossing fields that were bounded by low woods, and at the foot of a high down was Brading ('a decayed town', the guidebook said). There were real hills and real valleys near Sandown – who would have thought this small island could contain the best kind of English landscape? Shanklin was a large and breezy town, built on sloping streets. It was the last stop. I bought an apple and a sandwich – my usual lunch – and took them down to the beach to eat. The beach was some distance below the town. It was sunny enough today for me to sit on the sand and, like the elderly people on the benches behind me, and the old folks on the esplanade, read the Falklands news in the paper. These days it was bombing missions and aerial dog-fights, just the sort of thing to gladden the hearts of the army veterans on the park benches of Shanklin.

There were deep rural valleys all the way to Ventnor. I had decided to treat the Isle of Wight in the same way as England, and to make my way around the island's coast. Ventnor was an English resort in an Italian setting, the town tucked into bluffs and straggling along terraces and dropping from ledges. The way it cascaded from cliffs was Italian, and the balconies were Italian, and the tall windows, too.

I kept looking for the wilder, woodier stretches of coast or smaller settlements, but all I saw were piled-up towns and congested harbours and, on remote clifftops, sprawling hotels and stairways hacked into the sea-wall. The Isle of Wight's southern coast was entirely high cliffs and so it had been civilized with stairs. But this built-upon coast was interesting, and whatever else one could say about the appalling traffic it was also interesting, as the shallys in Hove were, and the people staring seaward from their cars, and the gatherings of old folks in their seaside settlements.

'The roads here are horrible,' Alf Doggett said. He had come down from London, Hither Green actually – *Ivver Grain* was what he said – and had expected Ventnor to be different. 'It's a blooming disgrace.'

Rose Doggett wondered whether they wouldn't have been better off in Cornwall. She had liked Newquay, on that one visit.

'You can't move here. It's all buses. They're fifty years behind the times,' Alf said. 'You don't think it's serious.'

I had been smiling. I cultivated complainers.

I said, 'No, no, I do think it's serious! Please go on.'

'And there's the caravans,' Rose said.

'Don't mention caravans,' Alf said, and tapped his chest. 'Me blood pressure.'

We were on a bench, on one of the Ventnor ledges, facing down at the surfy beach. Because of its position in the steep notch, Ventnor seemed both smaller and cosier than sprawling Shanklin. But the Doggetts, Alf and Rose, had become glum, talking about the traffic. And now they were talking about 'the mainland', as if we were far at sea and not twenty minutes by ferry to Portsmouth.

The Thackwoods were on an adjacent bench, sharing a Mars bar as they had done most afternoons since retiring to Ventnor from Bolton in Lancashire four years ago. I had seen Mr Thackwood – Herbert – prick up his ears at Alf's 'blooming disgrace'. He knew we were talking about traffic. Anyway, it was the usual topic.

'It's the Council,' Mr Thackwood said.

Alf Doggett uncrossed his legs and smiled at Mr Thackwood, who did not smile back. He was not being unfriendly, he was merely preparing to say, 'I've had it up to here,' and he could not do that smiling.

'The Council's stupid,' Mr Thackwood said.

The Doggetts nodded. Alf said, 'I couldn't agree more.'

'I used to roon a big one – bigger than this blewdy council, I can tell you,' Mr Thackwood said. 'They don't know what they're doing.'

'They're flipping useless,' Alf said.

Mr Thackwood said, 'They don't give a booger.'

Now Marion Thackwood spoke to Rose Doggett, confidentially, woman to woman. She said, 'They don't give a ding.'

They settled down to a long pleasant afternoon of complaining, and I was sure a friendship would emerge from it, and then there would be tea at the Doggetts' and Scrabble at the Thackwoods',

Marion would encourage Rose to join the Women's Institute, and Alf and Herbert would take the coach into Ryde to watch football. At Christmas, there might be a glass of sherry for the Thackwoods when the Doggetts had them over to meet their son Ted and his wife and the two grandchildren, Keith and Amanda, and then they'd all look at Ventnor and say, 'It's not half bad here, really. Bit of sunshine, no frost. And it's snowing in London!'

That was how I left them – making friends and tearing into the County Council. And I thought: This is better than castles.

I went via St Catherine's – more English cottages, another Italian setting – and across the cliffs to Blackgang.

Blackgang was associated with smugglers – few places on the British coast did not claim to be the haunts of wreckers or mooncussers. The thievery was boasted about and romanticized until it seemed a kind of heroism. It did not have any taint of criminality, and the whole of the south coast had pockets vying with one another over whose smugglers were the darkest or most daring. *The Smugglers' Inn* was one of the commonest names for a bar on the coast. Smuggling was fun, smuggling was blameless, smuggling was British.

There was a 'Fantasy Theme Park' at Blackgang, with statues and murals and tableaux of smuggling; there were books about it and signs showing the way to smugglers' caves and, of course, there were inns and public houses associated with this activity.

'Look, Ron,' Penny Battley said. She was on a Blue Sky Tour from Yorkshire. 'Smooglers.'

The statues depicted cut-throats in black eye-patches, with tattoos on their arms, carrying casks of brandy.

Daniel Defoe was near here in 1724. He wrote, 'I do not find they have any foreign commerce, except it be what we call smuggling, and roguing; which I may say, is the reigning commerce of all this part of the English coast, from the mouth of the Thames to the Land's End in Cornwall.' A hundred years later, Richard Ayton in *A Journey Around Great Britain* wrote how he would fall into conversation with men on the coast and then, after talking about fishing, they 'reverted with pride to those days when a little honest smuggling cheered a man's heart ... with a drop of unadulterated gin. "But these are cruel times," they observed, "and the Lord only knows how we shall be obliged to give up next." '

Where there was smuggling there was usually the plundering of wrecks, another piece of thievery that was regarded as having simple manly virtues, and needing no more justification than the ethic of finders-keepers. When wrecks were few, ships were lured on to rocks with false lights, and then the wreckers, village hearties, would swarm from the coast and pick it clean. Ayton met these men, too. He wrote, 'Amongst themselves, a man who had robbed a vessel of property to the amount of fifty pounds might pass for a very honest fellow; but if he were known to have stolen a pocket handkerchief on shore, he would be shunned as a thief. They talk of a good wreck season as they do a good mackerel season, and thank Providence for both.'

I grew a little tired of being asked to enjoy the romance of smuggling. Like smugglers today, they were vicious cheats and bullies, who sneaked at night and squealed when they were caught. I could not see them as harmless, and at the very least they were grubby and mendacious. But they were praised for their recklessness and their courage. Meanwhile, back at the South Goodwin lightship, and on the Sussex coast, and through-out the tight bays and coves of south Cornwall, men were still smuggling for a living. Illegal immigrants, seasick Pakistanis and puking Bangladeshis were being sneaked ashore near Deal, and cigarettes into Broadstairs, and bootleg brandy into Cornwall from Brittany, 'but don't tell anyone I told you,' my source, Arthur Tulley, said.

It was twenty miles from Ventnor to Freshwater Bay, but it was an empty path. The fields were open and very wide and the long hills had views for miles, so that approaching I could see the high wind from the Channel giving the wheat the look of a rip-tide and, when it lessened to a breeze, silken currents were stirred in the tassels.

I walked to Freshwater Bay and kept walking, across Tennyson Down (the poet once lived nearby and so had the photographer Julia Margaret Cameron) to Needle Down and West High Down, the westernmost point of the Isle of Wight. There, a series of chalk columns rose out of the sea and were known to sailors as the Needles. There were parts of those downs that were nearly five hundred feet high and I could easily see the sun setting behind Swanage, seventeen miles away. Then I walked back to Freshwater Bay, and there I stayed the night.

'I work about ten hours a day,' Daphne Wrennell said at the Albion Hotel, 'and I get an hour off in the morning and about three hours in the afternoon. Wednesdays are free. I'm from Wales – me mum's Welsh – we're all from somewhere different here at the Albion. I've been coming back here every year for the past four years to work. It's quite nice, really. I know it's not a real job, but you get two months off a year when the hotel's closed – no, we don't get paid for that. That's in the winter. I have a bit of a rest then. I was thinking of doing some travelling next winter. I might go to Turkey. I always fancied Turkey. I got some brochures – it's not very expensive, is it? I was thinking of going alone. Think I should?'

I urged her to take a friend and gave her the usual cautions.

The sun was shining the next morning, so I decided to walk the back roads to Yarmouth. It seemed to me that there was little traffic on the island, but that the roads were so crooked and narrow the few cars were often held up, and the buses were so large they went slowly, causing obstructions. I was told that it was possible to whip around the island in an hour and a half, but that the buses prevented this.

'In my youth, we used to call those "sharabangs",' a man told me. We had stopped to watch a bus that had become jammed against a curve in order to let a horse and buggy go past. Querying faces with white noses and eyeglasses appeared at the windows of the bus.

'Sharabangs,' the man repeated. This was Francis Pitchford, an accountant from Surrey. He had a cottage here and would be retiring to it soon. Listening to him on the road that morning, it struck me that many people who appeared to be reminiscing were actually gloating or boasting, or even lying.

'I can remember,' Mr Pitchford said, 'the two-tier buses, very big ones, drawn by horses. Now that shows you how old I am.'

But he was not very old, certainly not much over sixty – and that was nothing to boast about. I did not believe him, but I kept my mouth shut, and I let him say, 'Oh, this was way before your time, young fellow.'

There was a kind of hostility in this, something like *I've been here longer than you*, a very English way of putting down a stranger, telling you that he was older than you were. I had heard Englishmen pretend to be older than they were in order to score a point. It was only the old in England who were allowed to be opinionated.

He was still grinning at the stranded bus when I walked on.

I saw a card in the window of a general store farther up the road. It said,

> *Catholics – Remember These Words?*
> IN NOMINE PATRIS ET FILII ET SPIRITU SANCTU
> ... followed by HOLY MASS, which until a few years
> ago could be heard in every Catholic church in the land.
> The same HOLY MASS is still celebrated privately in
> Newport on the 3rd Sunday of the month.
> *Telephone: Newport 4220*

It made the Latin mass seem like a secret ceremony and indeed the tone of the note hinted at a clandestine service, calling up images of early Christians and whispered consecrations. I wondered if on the Isle of Wight there were not an old-style unreformed Catholicism taking hold, and I longed to know more. I found a public phone box and dialled the number, but I got no reply. It was perhaps an example of my aimlessness that I would gladly have changed my plans and walked to Newport to find out about the secret Catholics if I had been able to raise anyone with the phone call.

The path through the woods to Yarmouth was straight and level; once it had been a railway line, and now it was a cinder track, used mostly by hackers. A large bird alighted on the path. I took out my binoculars and saw it was an English jay, *Garrulus glandarius*, large, beautifully coloured, noisy and very shy. It flew up suddenly, as if propelled by its harsh squawk. It had been startled by a young woman coming down the path towards me.

I knew she would be frightened of me. Two women had been murdered ('savagely') in some woods near Aldershot the day before. It had been reported in the papers and on the television news. These days everyone watched the news, because of the Falklands war, and so there was an unusual consciousness of public events. It was not explained what 'savagely' meant, but anyone could guess: a razor or a knife, probably; and the woman-hating slasher was almost certainly a solitary man with a plausible face, and wearing old clothes, with his weapon in his knapsack, and oily hiker's shoes on his feet – probably a man like me, on a path like this.

She saw me and froze. I wanted to go another way, but there was a marsh beside the path, so I had to stick to this route and walk right past her. I tried to be jaunty, but that brought a look of terror to her face. She looked away, but there was an intensity in her alert movements which was like panic – she was not breathing, she was listening. She was about twenty-two and her fear had made her features very plain. I wanted to say, 'It's not me!'

I said, 'Good morning,' as I passed her.

She mumbled something in a frightened voice. I felt sorry for her, and did her the favour of hurrying away. I looked back: she was running down the path towards Freshwater.

Yarmouth was a fine place, very small and solid, made of large stones the damp had turned green on the low pretty buildings, with proud streets and a little compact ruin of a castle. ('The *Arbella* sailed from Yarmouth for Massachusetts in 1630.') It was a very private town on a cosy harbour and it had a long slender pier. It was an ancient place, almost as old as the island itself; it faced north. The ferry was just about to leave, so I jumped aboard.

It was here, on the Solent, that Tennyson wrote 'Crossing the Bar', but in the morning it was hard to imagine 'Sunset and evening star,/And one clear call for me!' and the poet recommending his soul to Heaven. The sun was sparkling on the water behind the yachts tipping towards Yarmouth – a Force Eight was blowing, and I could see the collapsed Hurst Castle to the west, jutting on a spit of land from Hampshire, its arches like a set of broken dentures. There was a lovely lighthouse beside it, a white pawn on the water.

In this way I left the Isle of Wight, and sailed on the ferry to Lymington, with its clusters of masts and the grass growing around the harbour. It reminded me of a Cape Cod town, a village on the sea, like Barnstaple or Sandwich. It had a little round harbour and the train went right down to the pier, where the ferry docked.

Travelling to Brockenhurst from Lymington – only five of us boarded this little train: its days were numbered, surely – I thought how easy it was for me to travel around Britain. When the path ran out there were trains or buses, and they left on time. This reflection was prompted by the arrival of the train immediately after the ferry docked in this fairly insignificant place. Money was easy – I could use personal cheques or get money at any bank, even in a village such as Lymington. People were generally efficient and helpful, and some were friendly; everyone spoke English; I was never in danger; it was impossible for me to get lost. Was it any wonder that England was the most widely explored country on earth? In a sense, nothing was unknown in England – it was just variously interpreted. But I knew that I needed this ease – the language, the money, the safety – because it was the subtlest culture on earth to explain. The English found foreigners funny because foreigners weren't English, and because it was impossible for anyone to become English. To an American, this attitude was itself funny and puzzling. But even after eleven years of groping for explanations I was still groping, and I was in unfamiliar places, on the coast. What a relief that everything worked so well and I was never afraid!

We were at the edge of the New Forest, and the heather and gorse and its flatness gave it the look of a moor. The wild ponies were not much higher than the new ferns ('Adders and lizards are not uncommon'). At Brockenhurst, a convenient railway junction, because it was in the middle of nowhere, I changed for the Bournemouth train. The train did not hurtle towards Bournemouth, but rather dawdled pleasantly – at the pretty village of Sway, with an old-style railway platform which, in this spring heat, looked like a setting for the opening of a story by Saki; at Hinton Admiral, which sounded like the name of a butterfly or a dahlia, and was as lovely as its name; at Christchurch, after crossing the broad pastures and wheatfields; and Pokesdown, which was densely settled, a suburb of Bournemouth, the next stop. I got out at Central Station and walked to the front.

The chines, or ridges, of Bournemouth supported row upon

row of hotels and guest houses. Bournemouth's good weather – the best in Britain – had turned it into a resort, with pretty parks and ugly buildings, bistros and discos. It looked like a country town that became a city too quickly, but though it wore its newness awkwardly it had enough parks and promenades to justify its reputation for being a stroller's city. It was, heart and soul, a seaside resort, and so inevitably full of shufflers and people staring and vaguely smiling. And all those hotels – thousands, it seemed, on the toast-coloured crumbling cliffs. It did not have the tone of Eastbourne, which it resembled in some ways, but it was undeniably prosperous. It was crowded, and yet its heights and the winding streets of its hills made it bearable. Viewed from West Cliff it looked the epitome of a south coast resort, occupying about fifteen miles of shore-line. Bournemouth was also famous for its golf courses. Golf was a coastal sport, not to say passion, but that was not so surprising, since 'links' was an old word that described the kind of sandy and turfy seashore we associate with a golf course.

People sat silently in cars, eating bananas, chewing sandwiches, and reading the gutter press: ARGIES LOSE TWO! was the head-line today – two planes, or two ships. All the headlines exulted when Argentina suffered casualties, but British losses were some-what understated, and most of the time it was reported in the language of British sports reporting. It was sunny but windy on the front at Bournemouth, and people were variously dressed. I saw Ivy in her old overcoat and gloves and woolly scarf walking past Susan, supine in her bikini. Russell was a black boy with red hair and four earrings in each ear and a futile and obscure tattoo on his dusky arm; he was shadowing Kim, fifteen years old, with *Billy* very clearly tattooed on the side of her neck. The retired and the unemployed, the very old and the very young – Bournemouth had them in common with all the other seaside places I had seen. Middle-aged people wearing knapsacks were rather rare, which was perhaps the reason I received so many stares.

I lingered at the shallys to look inside and examine the furnishings (here a toaster, there a potted plant). It was too windy to read the newspaper outside. Most of the shally people were drinking tea, and some were sunbathing with all their clothes on, their hands stuck in their pockets, and their faces pinched at the glaring sun.

I walked along West Cliff and down a zigzag path to the promenade. I was not quite sure where I was headed, but this was the right direction – west: I had been going west for weeks. I walked past Alum Chine, where Stevenson wrote *Dr Jekyll* (Bournemouth was the most literary place, with the ghosts of Henry James, Paul Verlaine, Tess Darbeyfield and Mary Shelley and a half a dozen others haunting its chines) and then, looking west, and seeing the two standing rocks on the headland across the bay, called Old Harry and Old Harry's Wife, I decided to walk to Swanage, about fourteen miles along the coast.

My map showed a ferry at a place called Sandbanks, the entrance to Poole Harbour. I wondered whether it was running – the season had not started – so, not wishing to waste my time, I asked a man on the promenade.

'I don't know about any ferry,' he said.

He was an old man and had grey skin and he looked fireproof. His name was Desmond Bowles, and I expected him to be deaf. But his hearing was very good. He wore a black overcoat.

'What are those boys doing?' he demanded.

They were windsurfing, I explained.

'All they do is fall down,' he said.

One of the pleasures of the coast was watching windsurfers teetering and falling into the cold water, and trying to climb back and falling again. This sport was all useless struggle.

'I've just walked from Pokesdown –'

That was seven miles away.

'– and I'm eighty-six years old,' Mr Bowles said.

'What time did you leave Pokesdown?'

'I don't know.'

'Will you walk it again?'

'No,' Mr Bowles said. But he kept walking. He walked stiffly, without pleasure. His feet were huge, he wore old shiny bulging shoes, and his hat was crushed in his hand. He swung the hat for balance, and faced forward, panting at the promenade. 'You can walk faster than me – go on, don't let me hold you up.'

But I wanted to talk to him: eighty-six and he had just walked from Pokesdown! I asked him why.

'I was a stationmaster there, you see. Pokesdown and Boscombe – those were my stations. I was sitting in my house – I've got a bungalow over there' – he pointed to the cliff – 'and I said to myself, "I want to see them again." I took the train to Pokesdown and when I saw it was going to be sunny I reckoned I'd walk back. I retired from the railways twenty-five years ago. My father was on the railways. He was transferred from London to Portsmouth, and of course I went with him. I was just a boy. It was 1902.'

'Where were you born?'

'London,' he said.

'Where, in London?'

Mr Bowles stopped walking. He was a big man. He peered at me and said, 'I don't know where. But I used to know.'

'How do you like Bournemouth?'

'I don't like towns,' he said. He started to walk again. He said, 'I like this.'

'What do you mean?'

He motioned with his crumpled hat, swinging it outwards.

He said, 'The open sea.'

It was early in my trip but already I was curious about English people in their cars staring seawards, and elderly people in deck chairs all over the south coast watching waves, and now Mr Bowles, the old railwayman, saying, 'I like this . . . the open sea.' What was going on here? There was an answer in Elias Canetti's *Crowds and Power*, an unusual and brilliant – some critics have said eccentric – analysis of the world of men in terms of crowds. There are crowd symbols in nature, Canetti says – fire is one, and rain is another, and the sea is a distinct one. 'The sea is multiple, it moves, and it is dense and cohesive' – like a crowd – 'its multiplicity lies in its waves' – the waves are like men. The sea is strong, it has a voice, it is constant, it never sleeps, 'it can soothe or threaten or break out in storms. But it is always there.' Its mystery lies in what it covers: 'Its sublimity is enhanced by the thought of what it contains, the multitudes of plants and animals hidden within it.' It is universal and all-embracing, 'it is an image of stilled humanity; all life flows into it and it contains all life.'

Later in his book, when he is dealing with nations, Canetti

describes the crowd symbol of the English. It is the sea: all the triumphs and disasters of English history are bound up with the sea, and the sea has offered the Englishman transformation and danger. 'His life at home is complementary to life at sea: security and monotony are its essential characteristics.'

'The Englishman sees himself as a captain,' Canetti says: this is how his individualism relates to the sea.

So I came to see Mr Bowles, and all those old south coast folk staring seawards, as sad captains fixing their attention upon the waves. The sea murmured back at them. The sea was a solace. It contained all life, of course, but it was also the way out of England – and it was the way to the grave, seawards, out there, offshore. The sea had the voice and embrace of a crowd, but for this peculiar nation it was not only a comfort, representing vigour and strength. It was an end, too. Those people were looking in the direction of death.

Mr Bowles was still slogging along beside me. I asked him if he had fought in the First World War.

'First and Second,' he said. 'Both times in France.' He slowed down, remembering. He said, 'The Great War was awful ... it was terrible. But I wasn't wounded. I was in it for four years.'

'But you must have had leave,' I said.

'A fortnight,' he said, 'in the middle.'

Mr Bowles left me at Canford Cliffs and I walked on to Sandbanks. The ferry was running – they called it 'the floating bridge', and it resembled a barge shuttling on a pair of chains across the harbour mouth of Poole. I crossed and stepped on to an empty mile of sand dunes and scrub, called Studland Heath. It was an old wind-blown place. There were lovers on this heath, plainly copulating in the sandy craters. I walked on, past men standing up in waist-high heather. Some were naked and watchful. I took them to be perverts. Some stood on hillocks and just stared into the middle distance. The land was as flat as a floor. And it was littered with blowing paper – magazine pages, which I examined and found to be pornographic. In the remotest parts of this wild place there were girlie magazines and book pages, some of them torn into small pieces. I supposed that lonely men had taken them here, crept into the dunes by the sea and examined them, feeling safe and hidden.

I was uneasy on this part of the coast path. It was not only the violence of the magazines. It was the wind, the dry grass, the desolation, the solitary standing men. It was one of a number of places on the coast where I expected to happen upon a dead body – a torso, decomposed, with missing limbs.

It was better, greener as I climbed higher and walked over Ballard Down to Swanage, a small bright town on a sweep of bay.

'The trouble with Swanage is that it's not on the way to anywhere,' Sally Trubshaw said. Miss Trubshaw owned a public house. She had a Great Dane which she fed prawn-flavoured potato crisps. She had only recently come to Swanage, but she said that few people ever passed through it. 'That's why business is so bad.'

Places in which business was bad were often especially pleasant. Swanage had an atmosphere of convalescence, fresh air and fishing boats and wind-scoured streets. It had grown a little over the years but it had not been modernized. The train no longer ran from Wareham. It was the sort of small half-asleep seaside town that was perfect after a long walk.

That night, after I wrote my diary, I went into a pub and asked people: How far to Weymouth on the coastal path?

'It'll take you six days,' Ted Witchell said. 'It's all up and down.'

'Two weeks,' Lester Pride said, and wagged his head at me. 'You like it up and down, do you?'

'I like it straight,' I said.

This delighted Lester Pride.

'The path,' I said.

'Listen to him!' Lester Pride said, and ordered me a drink.

He was wearing a sweatshirt that said LIFEGUARD in large letters and, under it, 'Beach Boys Club'.

'It's the biggest faggots' club in California,' he explained. He took a little bow. 'You like it?'

I said it was very nice. An English person would wear a sweatshirt saying *Penn State* and regard it as the height of fashion that year. English style was full of back-handed compliments.

Lester Pride went to the window.

'There's a policeman outside. He's going to come in and arrest you for being drunk in charge of your leather jacket.'

I was wearing my all-purpose leather jacket and my oily hiker's shoes.

'Where did you get that jacket! I hate it! My wife used to wear leather things all the time. I couldn't stand it! Which reminds me' – and now he addressed everyone at the bar – 'celebration tomorrow, my *decree nisi*. Champagne for everyone!'

This was greeted with general approval, but Lester Pride just shrugged and stepped closer to me and said in a kind of mock-confidential way, 'I run a pub not far from here, right? Listen, no one in two hundred years has ever lost money running it – except me! I'm going broke – I hate it. Why not come over and have a drink right – oh, God –'

I had downed my drink and was preparing to go back to my hotel.

'– you're going to walk to bloody Weymouth. You're just about to say you've got to get to bed early, so you can bore everyone stiff with talk about rocks and interesting rock formations! Oh, Jesus, please forget it. Your leather jacket will get up and start without you – or those shoes, look at them, aren't they adorable – and you can catch up with them as they go hopping along the path. You Yanks are such –'

I left Swanage at nine the next morning, a lovely sunny day, and walked to Durlston Head. Below were the Tilly Whim Caves – more smuggler stories. I walked on, a little inland, so I would not have to go up and down the bluffs. The gorse bushes had bright yellow flowers and the land was open – it was like traipsing around the edge of a great country, on top of its sliced-off side. I went across Dancing Ledge and through Seacombe and up Winspit, and various notches in the coast with steep terraces, and valleys of sheep browsing under ivy-strangled hawthorns. These terraces, the ridges of the edge of the valley, were caused by ploughing six hundred years ago. At the village of Worth Matravers, I read that these furrows were called 'strip lychetts' and the tourist sign said, 'The need to plough such steep terraces was probably lessened after the dramatic population decline caused by the Black Death of 1348–9.' Most of these Dorset villages were a great deal smaller than they had once been, and they had never recovered from the plague of the fourteenth century – nor had they forgotten it. The plague burying grounds were still clearly marked.

After lunch at the Square and Compass – the inn-sign had something to do with the quarrying of local stone, a type of shelly limestone called Purbeck marble – I walked across a large headland called St Alban's Head and hiked to a pretty bay, Chapman's Pool. On my way there I met Joan and Reg Flanchford. They were crossing a pasture.

'She's got a plastic hip,' Reg Flanchford said.

They hurried behind me to the stile. I stepped aside and let the woman climb it.

'That's a plastic hip,' Reg said.

Joan Flanchford tried to look dauntless

'Put your best foot forward,' Reg said.

Then Joan was on the other side, and I was making tracks for Hounstout Cliff, which was almost vertical for 175 feet, but full of birds. The coast cut in and led me up and down and took me past a waterfall splashing into the sea and it foamed on the grey shale foreshore that was scored in straight squares, like great flat paving stones.

The sun and wind made the long grass flicker like fire on the Kimmeridge Ledges. I walked these cliffs through the hot afternoon and did not meet another soul. There were pastures on the cliffs, and just to the left of the overgrown path two hundred vertical feet of gull-clawed air to the sliding surf, and the whole ocean beyond. This was the most beautiful stretch of coast I had seen so far, and I was alone on it. My happiness was greatly increased by the thought that I did not have the slightest idea where I was going. I always felt I was safe – everything would be fine – if I stayed on the coast.

There was a tower at the edge of the cliff ahead. It stood on its own, it was attached to nothing, it looked like a ruined lighthouse. This was at Kimmeridge Bay. A man with a pamphlet, named Evercreech, told me that it was called the Clavel Tower and that it was almost two hundred years old. Clavel was a clergyman and also a stargazer. He used the tower for his astronomy. It was a delicate structure, and the steeps and headlands of this coast made it seem more delicate, because there was no other building near it.

Just inland there was a car park. Most of the people were in their cars, staring out to sea, but some others were tramping around and smiling and looking winded.

I sat down on the grass below the tower. That noise was not the sea – it was the booming of big guns. Just west of the bay my map labelled the next six miles *Danger Area*. It was another army firing range, and they were at it today – presumably practising for the Falklands. I walked into Gaulter Gap and saw that red flags were flying at the onward path: no entry.

My detour took me inland, via Corfe Castle and Wareham and some tiny Dorset villages. I found some friends. I ate spaghetti. I drank scrumpy. I listened to 'The Stranglers' – their current hit was about the pleasures of heroin. I made my way back to the coast, stepping on to it again at Lulworth Cove, on the other side of the firing range.

Then it was so steep and tedious I could not enjoy the odd landscape features – the circularity of the cove, the comic look of Durdle Door, the precipice at Bat's Head. I hurried on the path towards Weymouth, where I wanted to spend the night. But it was a long hike. I headed for the cliffs at White Nothe – flesh-pale, corpse-like stone – and then above Ringstead Bay to Burning Cliff, a ledge of combustible shale. John Miles, from the village of Loders, said the cliff had actually been on fire for many years and then mysteriously went out. There was still oil in Dorset. In places it seeped out of the ground. In the 1970s some of Dorset's most beautiful countryside was being eagerly offered to oil companies by local farmers. I once told a farmer that if they didn't watch out the peaceful valleys of Dorset would be covered with hideous oil rigs. This farmer, Lew Swineham, said, 'They be having lights on them, those oil wells,' and he smiled with satisfaction. 'Like Christmas trees.' Somehow, the oil boom missed Dorset, which made farmers like Lew Swineham very cross. For a brief period they thought they might have seen their last of muddy boots and wet silage.

'The bus just went,' Roger said at the Smuggler's Inn in Osmington Mills. 'That's the last one. Have a meat pie instead '

Weymouth and the Isle of Portland had been in view almost
since Lulworth, for ten miles or so. They lay in the distance,
through the haze, at sea level. But up here, above Weymouth
Bay, there were holiday camps on the bluffs, looking more than
ever like prisons. I decided that the posher they were the more
they looked like concentration camps. These were built for
strength, solid walls and concrete paths, and chainlink fences,
and barbed wire, and signs warning trespassers of guard dogs.
On this sunny day, fully clothed people slept on deck chairs.
They had scowling sunburned faces. I could hear them snoring
from forty yards away.

Now it seemed downhill, across some cliffs, and down a gully
to a sea-wall. I walked on top of the wall the last few miles into
Weymouth. I liked Weymouth immediately. It was grand without
being pompous. It had a real harbour. It was full of boats. All
its architecture was intact, the late-Georgian terraces facing the
esplanade and the sea, and cottages and old warehouses on the
harbour. I liked the look of the houses, their elegance, and the
smell of fish and beer among them. I walked around. There was
plenty of space. The weather was perfect. I thought: I could live
here. That thought made me happy, but the next day I left my
hotel and just kept walking.

6

The Inter-City 125 to Plymouth

On this part of the coast it was easy to get out of town – any town, even a large one like Weymouth. A ten-minute walk took me through the narrow outskirts; then there were no more shops. Ten more minutes: no houses. Five minutes: no signs. And then there were only chestnut trees with plumy blossoms, and the twelve-inch path, and the sound of waves.

But here at the hamlet of Fleet there were no waves. It was a silent shore for nine miles, for just offshore, and running from Portland to Abbotsbury, was one of the strangest coastal features of Britain, the Chesil Bank. It was a low ridge of pebbles banked in the sea, a wall of little stones that was perfectly straight and parallel to the shore. The beach was on the other side. On my side, where there was no sound of surf, the lagoon called the Fleet lay still and in places was sour green and stinking of dead eelgrass. Because of that wall of pebbles (it looked as geometric as a man-made reef, but in fact had been pushed there during the Ice Age) this was the quietest part of the English coast: no wind, no gulls, no sound of water; only the shimmer of sun on the stagnant flats.

I heard a sound – two sounds – a rapid sawing, a high muffled hee-haw, like the harsh hum of silk being woven in a clapping loom. It came closer, strengthened to a kind of breathing, though I could not place it. I listened and looked sharp, and I saw two huge swans flying low over the Fleet, beating their wings, tearing the air with them, and the sound was that of their urgent wing-beats, echoing in Gore Cove. When they were directly overhead they sounded like two lovers in a hammock.

I walked on. Past Herbury I counted fifty-seven swans swimming in the lagoon, and I took a path that led me a little

inland, through sunlit woods. I looked very closely at the birds
and flowers and trees in this place, and noted their names and
variety, and the way the sun slanted on the glade and glanced
from the sea. I tried to remember every detail, because someone
had told me that a nuclear power station was planned for this
place, that would wipe it out.

Cutting through a pasture I did not first see the bullocks, but
hearing their hooves I turned and saw them following me. I
walked faster. They did the same. I ran, and they ran after me,
about fifteen of them, making that curious rocking motion that
bullocks do when they try to hurry. When they were just behind
me I dived over a fence into a bank of stinging nettles and
brambles. The bullocks crowded to have a look at me. This was
near Wyke Wood. I felt like a jackass, because I was out of breath,
and scratched and stung, and the bullocks were snorting and
drooling. Behind them, down the field, there was a full-grown
bull. His feet were planted firmly into the turf and his head was
lowered at me.

I told the bullocks they were stupid and nosey. They moved
a few feet away, enough for me to disentangle myself from the
brambles. 'Don't bother me – stay there – you, too!' I said, and
backed down the pasture to the gate, while the big bull watched.
The animals obeyed me in a reluctant way, but stubbornly,
edging forward whenever I turned away.

Then I vaulted a fence and was safe. Perhaps I had never been
in danger, but I had felt threatened. They began pushing at the
fence as I walked on. And I thought how domestic animals are
a much greater nuisance than wild animals – they are dependent
and badly behaved and seem wilful and obtuse.

After a few more hills I saw St Catherine's, a lovely ruined
chapel on the summit of a hill in Abbotsbury. There was a
swannery in Abbotsbury, which was why I had seen so many
of the birds on the shore. The village had a monkish grey-
stone appearance – there was once a Benedictine monastery here
– and the tithe barn and the cottages all looked as though they
had been built by friars for the glory of God. In fact, it was
now a village of house-proud English people who, at great
expense, had restored the place and planted roses.

The path from here to West Bay and Bridport was straight

along the shore, and a lovely sunset haze hung over the thatched village of Burton Bradstock, where land and water met, green and grey.

That night at the Crown Inn of Uploders I saw a sign saying 'Rook Pie'. What did it mean?

Robin Upton, the landlord, said, 'Ask my wife.'

Shelley Upton was in her thirties and studious-looking, and she clearly enjoyed being asked about rook pie. She said, 'The boys around here shoot rooks, you see. I heard their guns. I asked them what they did with the birds. They said, "Oh, we throw them over the hedges." I said to myself, "If they're killing them anyway and throwing them over the hedges, one might as well find a way of cooking them and eating them." And then I remembered a recipe for rook pie, in my Castle's Dictionary of English Cooking. That goes back to 1880. It's rook and onions and a homemade crust. It's very good.'

I said I wanted to try some. She served it to me at the rear of the pub. The rook was dark meat, with a gamy grousey taste. I liked it very much, and her crunchy pastry, too, and the Dorset ale.

Not long after this there was a headline in the Bridport newspaper: *Poison-pen Attack on Rook Pie Couple*. Apparently, a mention of Mrs Upton's rook pie in the paper provoked a number of people to write abusive letters to the Uptons. Mr Upton described the letters as 'nasty' and the people as 'nutters'. He went on, 'One said they hoped we died of cancer, and the other that burning in hell was too good for us.' The letters were of course from English bird-lovers, and Shelley Upton – the cheery soul in the country pub – was reported by the paper as now a nervous wreck, afraid to answer the phone or open letters.

Had Shelley Upton been a dog or cat in distress, she could have counted on the support of a pet-loving English public.

Yesterday's *Daily Telegraph* reported that the unfortunate Hyland family, whose two daughters were tortured, tarred and feathered by the IRA, had hurriedly left their home, belongings and pet dog in the Falls Road area to go into hiding.

By lunch two people, a woman ringing on her own behalf

and a representative of the Ulster Society for the Prevention of Cruelty to Animals, had telephoned our correspondent at his hotel, expressing their concern for the welfare of the dog.

Daily Telegraph (16 May 1972)

More recently, in what became known as 'The Case of the Battered Budgie', a man was convicted in Bristol of causing unnecessary suffering to his pet budgerigar by placing it in a sink full of water. He was given a conditional discharge and ordered to pay £48 witness costs. The witness was a Mr John Bird. Mr Bird 'said that he saw the blue and white budgie called Sally, shivering with fright in George Brownless's ground floor flat'. The case gained a certain notoriety but at no point had anyone suggested that the prosecution of Mr Brownless for excessively wetting his pet budgie was a waste of public money. Rather, there was a kind of comic self-congratulation: 'You see how far we English are prepared to go in order to maintain our reputation for being eccentric and gentle?' But English animal-lovers could be violent, too. The Animal Liberation Front carried out destructive guerrilla raids on behalf of laboratory beagles and rabbits.

I walked a little farther down the coast and in a pub near Bridport I met a young man named Fuggle, who was twenty-four, and who told me, 'I once dyed my hair purple – aubergine, actually – and then I walked around. I wanted to call attention to myself. I mean, I wanted to stand out in a crowd. Funnily enough, no one seemed to care. Didn't take a blind bit of notice!'

I said, 'So your purple hair was a failure?'

'You might say so,' Fuggle said. Fuggle had an odd habit, but it was one I had seen in other people. Whenever he turned to look at me, he shut his eyes, and when he moved his head away he opened them again. 'Anyway, I put henna on my hair, and it all turned bright orange. A man said to me, "What's that all about then?" And I said, "Don't you see I'm trying to tell you something?"'

'What were you trying to tell him?'

'Obvious, isn't it?' Fuggle said.

I said it was not obvious to me.

Fuggle said, 'I was trying to tell him I was different. I'm not like other blokes.'

'Because your hair was orange?' I said.

'No, no, no,' Fuggle said, facing me and shutting his eyes. 'I mean different deep down. I'm just not like other blokes.'

'Give me an example,' I said.

'For example, I'm engaged to a girl. I don't know whether I'm going to marry her, but I'm engaged. She's four feet eight and I'm six feet two. She can't understand me. And for another example, I'm not jealous. I don't know what the word means. One night I wanted to go out for a drink. My best friend, Brian, was there. I said, "I just want to go out alone, for a drink." I'm like that. Sometimes I want to be alone. I said, "You two stay here." Emily wanted to come with me, but I said, no. Finally I said, "Stay here and watch the telly." Emily said there was nothing on telly. I said, "Then you can go to bed together." I didn't care. That's the way I am.'

I said, 'What was Brian's reaction when you told him he could go to bed with your girlfriend?'

Fuggle thought a moment, then said, 'He just smiled.' And Fuggle began to smile, too, though his eyes remained shut.

Bridport had no surprises for me. It was one of the few places on the British coast I actually knew. I had once lived up the road at South Bowood, which was a crossroads, four houses and a pub. The pub, called the Gollop Arms, was now closed for good and the owner – in England they were more like pharisees than publicans – in retirement.

The prettiest place on the coast near here was a hill called Golden Cap. I took a bus to Morcombelake and climbed the hill and then set off in the sunshine for Lyme Regis, making my way through the woods and along the cliffs to Charmouth. It was only two miles from Charmouth to Lyme Regis. The rocky shore was full of fossils, and it was much easier and quicker than along the high cliffs and through the back gardens of bungalows. But when the tide was up it was impossible to walk along the shore.

I asked a man selling tickets at the parking lot at Charmouth whether I had time to walk to Lyme on the beach. He said that the high tide was at ten to three.

'It's half-past eleven now,' I said, 'So the tide's only halfway up.'

'It's more than halfway at Lyme,' he said. His name was Warren Hawtree. 'You might get stuck.'

I said, 'What do you think I should do?'

'I'll have to ask,' Mr Hawtree said.

He returned a few minutes later and said, 'The old feller says you can just make it if you hurry. Otherwise you'll be caught by the tide.'

I began to speak, but he shooed me away saying, 'Don't hang about!'

I set off, jumping from rock to rock. The fossils were visible on the rock surfaces, petrified snails on one slab and fossilized fish on another. All these rocks had tumbled from the cliff and there was no law against hacking them to pieces, looking for an ichthyosaurus (the first one was found near here in 1811). But I did not pause. Lyme was shining gently above its stone pier. Behind me I could see where I had walked all the way from the Chesil Bank and Weymouth. The Isle of Portland was indistinct and blubberlike; it could have been a whale that had blundered against the Dorset coast to die.

Because of the tide, I was the only person on this stretch of beach. It was deserted and full of cracks and corners, another of the places where I expected to find a corpse, a murder victim, a suicide, or more likely someone who had accidentally drowned and been washed ashore. I had never had this spooky feeling in a wild country, in Africa or Asia, but on the British coast, whenever I was in a lonely place, I looked down and expected to see a dead man.

The tide was high near Lyme, washing against the cement slope of the sea-wall. There was room to walk, but the wall was covered in green sea-slime, and so it was very slippery. I crossed it on all fours and at Lyme I felt as if I had won a close race.

'That's where they made that film,' a shuffling gent named Beaver said, and he smiled at the Cobb, remembering the film he had seen up in Swindon, where he lived. He had motored down to Lyme with the wife. He was not sure where he was headed. At his age, he said, you lived one day at a time. He wasn't thinking of retirement yet and certainly did not want to move to an elephants' graveyard, as he called Bournemouth and Worthing and the other places where oldies were clinging to the coast. But the grandchildren were in the Midlands and the wife didn't drive.

Ellen Beaver said, 'She was ever so pretty,' thinking of the American actress who had stood on the Cobb in the movie.

'It looks just the same!' Tom Oscott said, also smiling at the stone pier. The Golatelys and the Frekes were also staring.

There was no glamour like the glamour of a movie, and this fairly tedious and pretentious romance set in Lyme Regis had succeeded where *Persuasion* had failed, and that year Lyme Regis was associated with an American actress named Meryl Streep rather than Jane Austen.

The town itself was a sort of Regency bottleneck, a continuous line of traffic being squeezed between tea shops and coaching inns. The town was one of the many on the British coast which, delicately made and seeming to defy gravity, seemed magnetized to its steep cliffs. I spent my time there walking along the Undercliff, a strange landscape feature caused by a great landslip in 1839 – twenty acres subsided and a seaside ravine opened, known as the Chasm. It was full of flowers and fossils, and it was protected: a little wooded preserve, between the cliffs and the sea. After a day scrambling along the slippery Undercliff, I found a house on the way to Yawl with a *Vacancies* sign in the window.

This was the Skeats'. 'We do bed and breakfast,' Margaret Skeat said.

Vesta Skeat was thirteen and sneaked lipstick when her mother was not looking. She had a loud laugh and marble-white skin and a T-shirt that said *Adam and the Ants*.

'Is that all the clobber you have?' she said, standing in the doorway of my room as I unslung my knapsack. Other guests had had sleeping bags, some had tents, one had about five pairs of shoes. Vesta picked her elbow and told me she hated school.

'You're the bed and breakfast man,' Vesta Skeat then said.

'That's me,' I said.

Vesta widened her eyes and said, 'Madness!'

Her mother screamed her name. Vesta said softly, 'Shut up, you silly cow,' and then winked at me and went obediently downstairs.

I locked the door. Bed and breakfast man? Madness? She
was referring to a pop song about a tramp who travelled from
house to house, sleeping on sofas, and it was sung by the group
who called themselves Madness.

The next day I took a country bus to Axminster. It was not
far, but I had a train to catch. A man getting off the bus offered
his newspaper to the driver. It was the *Sun*, with a Falklands
headline: THIS IS IT! – suggesting an invasion of the islands
by the British was imminent, and that it would soon result in
a recapture of the territory.

The bus driver said, 'That's a Tory paper.'

'I'm through with it,' Mr Lurley said.

Dan, the bus driver, said, 'I don't want it.'

'Why not?' Mr Lurley said.

'Tory paper!'

'They're all the same,' Mr Lurley said, and left it on the little
shelf under the windshield with Dan's lunch bag (two cheese
and chutney sandwiches, a small over-ripe tomato, and a Club
Biscuit).

Dan picked up the newspaper and threw it out of the bus door.

'They're not the bloody same,' he said. 'That's a Tory paper.'

This was up the road from Yawl on the way to Axminster,
in the middle of the English countryside, the conservative
passenger, and the socialist behind the wheel.

We travelled through the softly sloping meadows of Devon.
A sign on every seat in the bus said, *Lower your head when leaving
your seat*, because there was a danger of banging your head on
the luggage rack.

To get to what was formerly the Great Western Railway, I
bought a ticket at Axminster. This line had once been the London
and South Western Railway. All these railways had been trimmed
and made smaller and cheaper. I rode to Exeter ('The town was
stormed by the Danes in 876 ... It was wantonly attacked from
the air in 1942, when 40 acres, including many ancient buildings,
were destroyed') and then changed to a train from Dawlish, on
the line once known as the Great Way Round.

This track was laid by the engineering genius Brunel on the
very edge of the English coast. He had had to build stone embank-
ments and tunnels – he had reshaped the coast. The line was

a combination of slow curves and high-speed straights, surf on one side, cliffs on the other, five miles of excitement. And even along the river Exe it was an experience – the racing train and the river's tide slipping down, thunder and water, and then the bright light of the ocean bathing the train between tunnels.

Dawlish looked wonderful as the train drew in, with the rain falling softly on the station platform on the sea. The platform was like a pier. But when I got out and the train drew away I saw that Dawlish was small and dull. I asked a man about the hotels here and he said, 'I don't know as much as I should about Dawlish,' which was precisely what a man had said to me about Dungeness.

I walked down the wet road to Holcombe to look at the standing rocks at Holcombe Head called the Parson and Clerk, another set of dragon's teeth like Old Harry and His Wife and the Needles. I ambled along the sea-wall towards Teignmouth, and every so often a train would shoot past me, and wet me, and nearly blow me into the ocean. I thought that the train on the rocky shore, rolling through a storm, was one of the most beautiful sights in the world. I came to Teignmouth.

'You're alone?' Mrs Starling said at the Victory Guest House, glancing at my knapsack, my leather jacket, my oily shoes.

'So far,' I said.

'I'll show you to your room,' she said, a little rattled by my reply.

I was often warmed by a small thrill in following the younger landladies up four flights to the tiny room at the top of the house. We would enter, breathless from the climb, and stand next to the bed somewhat flustered, until she remembered to ask for the five pounds in advance – but even that was ambiguous and erotic.

Most of them said *You're alone?* or *Just a single, then?* I never explained why. I said I was in publishing. I said I had a week off. I said I liked to walk. I did not say that I had no choice but to travel alone, because I was taking notes and stopping everywhere to write them. I could only think clearly when I was alone, and then my imagination began to work, as my mind wandered. They might have asked: How can you bear your own company? I would have had to reply: Because I talk to myself – talking to myself has always been part of my writing and, by the way, I've just been walking along the sea-wall from Dawlish in the rain muttering, 'Wombwell ... warmwell ... nutwell ... cathole ...'

In quiet Teignmouth ('Keats stayed here in 1818, correcting the proofs of "Endymion"'), under the red cliffs, old people were bowling in the rain at the green on the seafront, though the promenade was empty and the pier was closed. At the Riviera Cinema, a turn-of-the-century theatre, there were posters for the Teignmouth Operatic Society's production of *The Pajama Game*. I wandered around the town and, finding nothing better, returned and bought a ticket.

The theatre was less than a third full, mostly old people talking too loud and humming to the music. In the course of the production, one of the actors accidentally sat on a telephone, and another almost brained himself by backing against a steel post, and a large piece of scenery fell over during the solemn scene that followed the company picnic. There were fluffed lines and sour notes, and the American accents were either Irish and adenoidal or else frank West Country burrs, the local accent. In a dance number one elderly hoofer fell down with a thud that startled some of the audience from their sleep.

But these were minor matters. The play was done with gusto and the audience enjoyed it – they found it funny, they laughed, and they were moved by the romantic parts. It was a comedy about a union. In Britain they needed a comedy about a union. The cast was numerous and, judging from the programme notes, they were all amateurs – clerks, shop assistants, accountants, teachers. The interpretation was shaky but there was a clear understanding of American culture among the players – far greater than any equivalent group would have shown in the United States.

Plays in England were seen to be a suitable outlet for the emotions. The English liked dressing up, they liked the clubby community of amateur dramatics, they enjoyed the pressure and team-work of play production. For the duration of the play they were released from their lives and their work; they could shout and sing, they could express misery or joy; there was no such thing as a class system. They were free. So it struck me that even *The Pajama Game* in Teignmouth fulfilled the oldest reason for having plays – it was cathartic and afterwards everyone, players and spectators alike, felt much better.

Back at the guest house Mrs Starling introduced me to George Windus, who had side-whiskers and baggy pants and a florid face. I suspected that Mrs Starling hoped that Mr Windus would ask the questions she was too timid to risk.

'What brings you to Teignmouth then?' Mr Windus said. His nose was swollen, the colour of the burgundy he was drinking.

I was in publishing, I said. I had a week off. I was travelling along the coast.

'What do you think?' Mr Windus said, and pinched his whiskers.

'Folkestone's nice,' I said.

'Folkestone!' he roared, and Mrs Starling blinked.

Now he spoke to Mrs Starling, whose hands were clasped at her throat. Her mouth was small and uncertain, and her dark eyes watchful. Her hair was rumpled – ringlets in disarray – and very attractive.

Mr Windus was still shouting: 'Twenty-five years ago I was in Folkestone! I wasn't above twenty-seven years old. I was there with my wife, staying on the top floor of a hotel – five flights up. On the day we left, I parked my Landrover at the front door, to make it easy for us to pack up. We were loading and then out of nowhere came a furious little woman! She said to me, "Parking that horrible motor out there at the entrance – you're lowering the tone of this hotel! Oh, you're lowering the tone!"'

This made Mrs Starling twitch.

Mr Windus turned to me and said, 'No, Folkestone is not nice!'

It was raining hard the next day – too wet for walking: I was no adventurer – so I bought a one-way ticket on the fast train to Plymouth. Once, this was called the Cornish Riviera Express, on the Great Western Railway; now it was the '125' Inter-City on British Rail. I sat in Second Class and looked at Devon. Most of the passengers were old people, starting vacations. They talked very loudly. I sometimes had the impression that the whole of southern England was full of deaf people talking much too loudly.

The rain came down. We went along the north bank of the

muddy Teign to Newton Abbot, which looked very ugly in the storm. We set off again at a good clip.

'There's none of that old-time noise,' Mr Purewell said. 'No whistles and bells and that. It can play tricks on you! You're saying goodbye to someone, and the train just pulls out and surprises you. There's no warning! But I've got a great appreciation for these One-Two-Fives and' – he paused, we went a mile, he resumed – 'I used to be a bit puzzled why they were called that. I asked a few people. And then I was told it was their maximum speed.'

We were in the tame and gentle hills of Devon, near Totnes ('It consists mainly of one long congested street with many old houses with interesting interiors ...'). Here the rain made the landscape mild, and sheep grazed near flowering hedgerows, and from the railway tracks to the horizon there were ten shades of green.

'I gave up smoking,' Mr Gussage said. 'The queer thing was it had never entered my head to do it! But it was Budget time, you see. I went into my tobacconist for my usual tin and he said, "We've been sold out for a fortnight." Then I thought of giving up. I'd nothing to smoke – they were out of Three Nuns. And I managed. Now if anyone smokes in my house I open the windows. It don't half make a house dirty – smoke. Sometimes, with people smoking, I can hardly see across the room.'

Lloyd Gifford was Mr Gussage's friend. They were bound for Plymouth and a guest house near the Hoe. They were in their seventies and carrying on a shouted conversation.

Mr Gifford said, 'My father smoked! He loved his pipe, my father. I remember what he smoked. It was called Ogden's. The tin was orange. There was a picture of an Indian on it. On his birthday, or at Christmas, we always gave him a tin of Ogden's. He loved his pipe.'

Mr Gifford, telling the story, had made himself sad. But Mr Gussage had heard 'Christmas' and was off.

'I've finished with all present-giving!' he shouted. 'And I don't want to get any. I said to myself, "I've decided now that I've moved permanently I don't want to get any presents." I wrote everyone a letter saying, "Please don't send me any gifts – just send me a suitable card."'

Mr Gifford was still damp-eyed with the memory of his father, the pipe, the tins of Ogden's. He said nothing to his companion.

'And do you know?' Mr Gussage said. 'They were relieved!'

Side by side on another seat were Mr Bleaberry and Mr Crake. They were also old, they were also shouting.

'First thing I do after we get settled in,' Mr Bleaberry said, 'and if it's not raining, we'll go to the station and get timetables. I like to be up to date with my timetables.'

This set Mr Crake thinking. At last he said, 'We used to go everywhere, my wife and I.' There was a silence. 'And that probably added fire to the fuel.'

Dartmoor was on the right – the high rounded hill called Ugborough Beacon standing near other sudden bulges. In the meadows on the left side of the tracks lambs were fleeing from the train.

Raymond Greasely had been talking ever since the train had pulled out of Newton Abbot. Now he was saying, '... and my daughter is the pastoral assistant. There's a pastor, so she's the pastoral assistant. When she gets through with her studies she'll be a reverend. And she's still doing her journalism. How she does it all I don't know. There's an abbey near her and the combined churches got together. I don't know about the Catholics. I think they stayed out. They always do, don't they? They call it a sin if they join up with anyone else. There was one big service at the abbey, everyone except the Catholics. My daughter's job, as pastoral assistant, was to read the lessons, two lessons. I'll bet she got a thrill out of that ...'

A small old hunched-over man named Cox had sat in a rear seat and said nothing. He was looking out of the window. What was it about train windows that made people remember? Train windows seemed to mirror the past. Mr Cox stared and saw his face. After a time, even this very silent man spoke up.

'It's funny,' he said, seeming to waken. 'I've never shouted before or since, but I said to him, "Stop picking on me – find someone else to pick on! I won't take any more of this from you!" It just came out. I was mad. He was a bully. Some people are never happier than when they're picking on someone. After that, when he came to check on my fire extinguisher' – what was that? – 'he was very nice to me, we always had a chat.'

This memory seemed to embarrass the others, but Mr Cox was happy and even seemed to be savouring it.

'I think it's a detestable thing, picking on someone,' he said. 'I tried to bottle it up, but it made me bad-tempered. Then I shouted at him. It was the only time in my life. It just came out.'

After the villages of Devon, Plymouth looked vast. It was scattered over several valleys, and farther in it was on the hills as well. It was only the larger towns and cities of England that covered hills like this. The Plymouth outskirts looked ugly and dull.

'Busy, built-up place,' Mr Gussage said. 'I remember my mother and father came to my wedding. They were country people, and this was Brighton. They said, "Look at all them slate roofs."'

Mr Gifford was staring at Plymouth. He said, 'Yes. Look at all them slate roofs.'

7

The Cornish Explorer

A special train ticket I bought in Plymouth called 'The Cornish Explorer' allowed me to go anywhere in Cornwall, on any train. I travelled into the low shaggy hills, which were full of tumbling walls and rough stone houses, and yellow explosions of gorse bushes. I had lunch for eight pounds, which was twice as much as my ticket. The dining car was set for eighteen people, but I was the only diner. Elsewhere on the train, the English sat eating their sandwiches out of bags, munching apples and salting hard-boiled eggs. Times were hard. I realized that my lunch was over-priced, yet in a very short time there would be no more four-course lunch on these trains, no more rattling silverware, and no waiter ladling soup. But it was also ridiculous for me to be the only person eating: soup, salad, roast chicken and bread sauce, apple crumble, cheese and biscuits, coffee. There were two waiters in the dining car, and a cook and his assistant in the kitchen. The meal that most long-distance railway passengers had once taken for granted had now become a luxury, and Major Uprichard would soon be telling his grandchildren, 'I can remember when there were waiters on trains – yes, *waiters!*'

There were rolling hills until Redruth, and then the land was bleak and bumpy. There was only one working tin mine left in Cornwall (near St Just) but the landscape was scattered with abandoned mineworks, which looked like ruined churches in ghost villages. Cornwall was peculiarly uneven, with trees growing sideways out of stony ground, and many solitary cottages. On a wet day, its granite was lit by a granite-coloured sky and the red roads gleamed in a lurid way; it looked to be the most haunted place in England, and then its reputation for goblins seemed justified. It was also one of those English places which constantly reminded the alien, with visual shocks like vast battered cliffs and china clay waste dumps and the evidence of desertion and ruin, that he was far from home. It looked in many places as if the wind had creamed it of all its trees.

'I love the red earth,' Mrs Mumby said, staring out of the train window at the drizzle, and reminiscing. 'During the war I lived at Ross-on-Wye, in an antiquated old cottage. These Cornish cottages remind me of that. I don't like the architecture of today. Concrete jungle, I call it.'

Appearing to reply to this, Vivian Greenup said sharply, 'I've looked everywhere for my husband's walking stick. My daughter brought it to the hospital, in case he might need it. After he died, I looked everywhere and couldn't find it.'

Mrs Mumby stared at Mrs Greenup and her expression seemed to say: *Why is Vivian running on like this about her dead husband's walking stick?*

'It's quite a weapon,' Mrs Greenup said. 'You could use it as a weapon.'

We came to Penzance ('somewhat ambitiously styled the "Cornish Riviera" . . . John Davison, the Scottish poet, drowned himself here'). I changed trains and went back up the line about seven miles to St Erth, and there I waited in the rain for the next train to St Ives.

There were few pleasures in England that could beat the small three-coach branch-line train, like this one from St Erth to St Ives. And there was never any question that I was on a branch-line train, for it was only on these trains that the windows were brushed by the branches of the trees that grew close to the tracks. Branch-line trains usually went through the woods. It was possible to tell from the sounds at the windows – the branches pushed at the glass like mops and brooms – what kind of a train it was. You knew a branch line with your eyes shut.

We went along the river Hayle and paused at the station called Leland Saltings, which faced green-speckled mud flats. Hayle was across the water, with a mist lying over it. There were two more stops – it was a short line – and then the semi-circle of St Ives. It was Cornish, unadorned, a grey huddled storm-lit town on several hills and a headland, with a beach in its sheltered harbour. Today, in the rain, it was quiet, except for the five species of gulls that were as numerous now as when W. H. Hudson was here and wrote about them.

All the great coastal towns of England were a mixture of the sublime and the ridiculous. Here was the sublime climate and the pearly light favoured by watercolourists, the sublime bay of St Ives and the sublime lighthouse that inspired Virginia Woolf to write one of her greatest novels, and the sublime charm of the twisty streets and stone cottages. And there was the ridiculous; the postcards with kittens in the foreground of harbour scenes, the candy shops with authentic local fudge, the bumper stickers, the sweatshirts with slogans printed on them, the souvenir pens and bookmarks and dish towels, and the shops full of bogus handicrafts, carved crosses and pendants. These carvings at St Ives advertised 'Our Celtic Heritage – The Celts were famous for their courage and fighting qualities, which carried them before the birth of Christ from their homeland north of the Alps, across the known world ...' Cornish pride was extraordinary, and it was more than pride. It had fuelled a nationalist movement, and though the last Cornish-speaking person died in 1777 (it was Dolly Pentreath of Mousehole), and Cornish culture today was little more than ghost stories and meat pies, there was a fairly vigorous campaign being fought for Cornwall to secede from England altogether. It was not for a vague alien like myself to say this was ridiculous, but it did seem to me very strange.

Across St Ives Bay were sandy cliffs and dunes, and I thought of walking along that shore to the village of Portreath – it was about twelve miles: I could do it before nightfall. But the rain was coming darkly down like a shower of smut, and I still had my Cornish Explorer ticket. So I walked to St Ives Head, where the Atlantic was riotous, then I returned to the station to wait for the little train to take me back to St Erth.

The graffiti at St Ives Station said, *Wogs ought to be hit about the head with the utmost severity*, and under this, *Niggers run amok in London – St Ives next!* and in a different hand: *Racism is a social disease – you should see a doctor.*

I went back to St Erth and changed for the main-line train to Liskeard, going back the way I had come, past the mining chimneys and the clay deposits and the great hard sweeps of stony

land and the green glades that each contained a large house –
one comfortable family – but no more.

The branch-line train to Looe was waiting at Liskeard. It ran
on a single track through a narrow ravine under the main-line
viaduct and made a big loop through the countryside, past ivy-
covered walls and steep hills to Coombe Junction, where a man
in a rubber raincoat yanked levers to change the points, nudging
the train down the branch line to Looe and the coast. There were
about twenty-five people on the three coaches of this train, and
the train went so slowly it did not even startle the horses cropping
grass by the side of the track.

The woods on this rainy day were deep green. The branches
bumped and brushed the windows. We came to St Keyne. There
was a famous well here. 'The reported virtue of the water is this,
that, whether husband or wife come first to drink thereof, they
get the mastery thereby.' There is a ballad by Southey in which
a man describes how, just after his wedding, he went to the 'gifted
Well' and had a drink, so that he would be 'master for life', but
his wife was quicker-witted.

> I hastened, as soon as the wedding was done,
> And left my Wife in the porch;
> But i' faith she had been wiser than me,
> For she took a bottle to church.

Even so slight a poem as this seemed to give the acre of woods
at St Keyne a curious importance. This was true all over England,
which was why England was so hard to describe: much of it had
been written about by great men, and the very mention of a
place in a literary work tended to distort the place, for literature
had the capacity to turn the plainest corner of England into a
shrine.

We came to Sandplace, and then Causeland. The Looe river
was hardly a river here. You could jump across it at Causeland,
but then it widened from a creek into something more substantial,
a waterway containing tussocky islands. On one of them there
was a swan sleeping in a nest, looking like the fragments of a failed
wedding cake, and the rocks of the shore looked nastily like dead
ferrets. At the confluence of the West Looe river we passed the
steep narrow harbour of Looe, another apparently magnetized

village and a sign saying, 'Headquarters of the Shark Angling Club of Great Britain'.

It was still light and I was stiff from my shuttling back and forth with my Cornish Explorer ticket. And the rain had finally stopped. So I oiled my hiking shoes and as night fell I walked along the coastal cliffs, past Hendersick and through the buttercups at the Warren above Talland Bay to Polperro. Just below Crumplehorn – I was muttering the names to myself as I went – I found a pleasant-looking pub and got a room for the night. Everything seemed very simple and there was always enough daylight to do anything I pleased.

Polperro was a village of whitewashed cottages tumbled together in a rocky ravine on the sea. The streets were as narrow as alleys and few of them could take motor vehicles. I saw a full-sized bus try to make it down one street – hopeless. At best, one small car could inch down a street knocking the petals off geraniums in the window boxes at either side. When two cars met head-on there was usually an argument over who was to reverse to let the other pass.

The loathing for tourists and outsiders in Cornwall was undisguised. I had a feeling that it was the tourists who had made the Cornish nationalistic, for no one adopted a funny native costume quicker or talked more intimidatingly of local tradition than the local person under siege by tourists. Polperro was a pretty funnel but with the narrowest neck, so there was nowhere to go but the tiny harbour. It was true that the Cornish derived most of their income from tourists; but there was no contradiction in the way they both welcomed and disliked us at the same time. Natives always had very sound reasons for disliking outsiders; the Cornish fishermen had nothing whatsoever to do with tourists, but the other Cornish were farming people and treated tourists like livestock – feeding them, fencing them in, and getting them to move to new pastures. We were cumbersome burdens, a great headache most of the time, but at the end of the day there was some profit in us.

Mr Tregeagle, the hotel-keeper I met in Polperro, had been a farmer for thirty years. He had had dairy cattle, between sixty and seventy head, and he had also grown vegetables. The month before I arrived in the village he had chucked his farm in Bodmin.

He had bought this little hotel in the hope of making a living, but he laughed when he admitted that he had never run a hotel before and knew practically nothing about it.

'I was losing thousands on my milk,' Mr Tregeagle said. 'I owed money to the bank. The price of feed increased and the price of milk dropped. Last year it was terrible. I was in debt and I was working eighteen hours a day. I said to myself, "What's the point?" I began selling my cows. I hated doing it, but I had no choice.'

'What about your vegetables?' I said. 'You could feed yourself, couldn't you?'

'The vegetables were useless. I had a garden full of lovely lettuces. One morning I brought three crates – about a hundred lettuces – down to the local greengrocer. He offered me a penny a piece for them. A bloody quid for three crates!'

'Did you sell them?'

'I took them home and buried them, and I ploughed the rest of them under. And then I said, "That's it – I'm selling." The Tregeagles have been farming here for generations, but we'll never go back to the land again.'

There was a South African couple at the hotel, Tony and Norah Swart. He was a fat and rather silent red-faced man in his mid-forties, and she was harder and younger, talkative and unsmiling, a girl with a grudge. Tony's silence was a kind of apology, for Norah was usually complaining, and she had that hypersensitivity that some South Africans have, the bristling suspicion that any moment she is going to be accused of being a bumpkin, and the justified fear that she *is* a bumpkin. She was proud of, and at the same time hated, her snarling accent and bad manners.

It had been a horrible trip from Capetown. They had wanted to stop in Nigeria and Zaire, but those African countries would not let them enter. Norah Swart said, 'It's bleddy unfair.'

I said this was probably because Africans were discriminated against in South Africa. They treated Africans like dogs, so African countries were disinclined to put out the red carpet for South Africans.

'The real trouble,' Mrs Swart said, 'is that we were too nice to them. When the Australians were shooting their Abos and you were killing your Indians, we were looking after our blacks.

'Of course,' I said. 'You're famous for looking after your blacks.'

'Kristy, my Australian friend, said to me, "If you'd shot yours like we did ours you wouldn't have these problems today."'

I said, 'What a pity you didn't exterminate them.'

'That's what I say,' Mrs Swart said. The thought of mass murder softened her features and for the first time she looked almost pretty.

But her husband saw I was being sarcastic. He kept his gaze on me and went very quiet.

They especially hated the Africans in Namibia. They called it 'Southwest', they said it belonged to them, they wanted to raise caraculs there, and Norah Swart made a noise at me when I asked her what a caracul was. They said they would never willingly turn it over to African rule, but when I said that African rule was inevitable in Namibia ('stop calling it Namibia,' she said) the Swarts said they would fight for it. It was an empty land, Tony Swart said – only 400,000 people in it. He swore this figure was correct, but later I checked and found the population to be almost two million, of whom 75,000 were white.

I asked them where they had travelled in England.

'Lyme Regis,' Mrs Swart said. 'Where they made that movie.'

'We're just motoring down the coast.'

'What was the name of that movie, Tone?'

Tony shook his head. He did not know.

Mrs Swart said, 'People around here keep telling us to read Daphne du Maurier. Have you read it?'

She thought Daphne du Maurier was the name of a novel. Instead of setting her straight I said that it was a very good novel indeed and that the author, Rebecca something, had written many others. I urged her to ask for *Daphne* at the local bookshop.

Polperro was in such a deep ravine the sun did not strike it in the morning. I walked through the damp dark village – straight overhead the sky was blue – and climbed out of the little harbour on to the cliffs, just as a bright mist descended. It hung lightly over the rocky shore and the purple sea, and created luminous effects of live creatures appearing and disappearing near the tumbledown cliffs, and dripped morning light on the waves. It whitened the surf and the foam sliding patchily back from the

rocks. Bright and indistinct with shadowy light, and softened
by mist, the whole coast that morning was like a Turner watercolour, or more than one, because it kept dripping and changing,
the greens and blues becoming sharper as the morning wore on.

I was setting out to have lunch at Fowey, and I planned to
walk on to Par, where there was a railway junction. The grass
on this path was wet with mist and dew and before I had gone
half a mile my shoes were soaked, in spite of the oil I had put
on them in Looe.

This was the softer side of Cornwall, damper and greener than
the north coast that was pounded by the Atlantic. The whole
cliff was green, from the top to the sea, full of ivy and meadow
grass and brambles. The cliffs of Cornwall were depicted always
as rocky, like ruined castles and castle walls. 'I like Cornwall
very much. It is not England,' D. H. Lawrence wrote. 'It is
bare and dark and elemental ... bare and sad under a level sky.'
He meant the other coast, the Cornish stereotype of black headlands on a choppy sea, and charming desolation. But here on
the path to Fowey the cliffs were like steep meadows. The
bramble bushes and the gorse made a mild reflection in the water;
the trailing ivy gave a delicacy to the sea, and the foliage muffled
the wind. The air was sweetened by all this greenery, and the
fragrance of the rain was partly its soft stutter on the grass. There
was nothing elemental here, thank God.

Two battered old ladies appeared on the path, tramping
towards me out of the gorse – Miss Brace and Miss Badcock.
They were half-naked, leathery and terrifying in halters and faded
shorts, and though it was cool on these cliffs they were perspiring.
Old ladies in skimpy clothes could look defenceless. These two
looked formidable – rather plump and plain and dauntless, with
lined faces, and varicose veins standing out on their calves like
thongs. They were very brown. They carried walking sticks with
spiked tips. One had a bright patch on her shorts saying
'Bad Gastein'. They were ramblers, they said, and then as if to
prove it said they had walked here from Land's End.

'And we 'aven't tooched pooblic transport,' Miss Brace said.

Northerners. Her rucksack must have weighed a hundred
pounds. She had the tent, Miss Badcock had the cooking gear
– you could hear the clink of the skillet.

Miss Badcock said, ''ow mooch does your knapsack weigh?'

I said not much. They plumped it with their hands, and weighed it, and laughed, taking me for a twinkie.

'We've got spare shoes,' Miss Badcock said.

'Let's go, Vera,' Miss Brace said. And she explained to me, 'We're in a hoora to find accommodation in Polperro.'

I said, 'Polperro is full of hotels.'

'We want a youth hostel,' Miss Brace said.

A youth hostel? They were each well over sixty – Miss Badcock looked closer to seventy. I could see Miss Badcock's navel.

They had walked a hundred and fifteen miles since last Thursday. Had they seen anything interesting?

Miss Brace said, 'We 'ad soom nice coves and bays. We 'ad soom nice villages. We joost walk by.'

Miss Badcock said, 'We don't stop mooch.'

They asked me where I was going. I said, to Fowey and then to Par today.

Miss Brace said, 'It's a canny little step.'

A canny little step was similar to *a fair old trot*. Why didn't the English ever use the word 'far'?

We went our separate ways, and now it began to rain. Miss Brace had said that was the reason they were so scantily dressed – because of the rain: fewer clothes to get wet, and they dried more quickly. I had been ashamed to say that I had a hooded plastic raincoat. I now put it on and walked around Lantivet Bay and on to Lantic Bay, where the water was wonderfully marbled with sea foam, the white veiny effect heightened by the luminous blue-green water that was flat and gleaming.

Towards lunch time I walked around Blackbottle Rock and into the village of Polruan. This village was so tiny, and its roads so narrow, a sign to the entrance of the village said: 'Vehicular Access to Village Prohibited for Day Visitors 10 a.m.–6 p.m.'

It was strange the way some of these villages were protected. Polruan was sealed off: no traffic. But people still lived there, taking refuge in their small houses and the distant past. And visitors parked up the road and wandered around, peering through cottage windows and remarking on the cobblestones.

There was a ferry from Polruan to Fowey, across Fowey Harbour. The ferry sign said:

Adults   25p
Children 25p
Dogs   12p
Pram   12p
Cycle   25p

All these villages looked better from the water, face-on like Fowey from its ferry, with all their watching windows and all the peeling paint and storm damage. Fowey was perpendicular, built around the rock shelves of the steep harbour, and the houses were faded and stately. At the head of the harbour was a green wedge of woods and the emptying Fowey river, and at the harbour mouth high battlements in ruins. Fowey had been a harbour from ancient times. It looked an excellent place to start a long voyage, because it was a beautiful settled place, like a serene lakeside village.

I had my lunch – a sandwich – on the cliff at the west side of the harbour and, startling the wrens in the hedges, set off again. I walked at the margins of pastures, on the cliff edges above the sea, and around coves to a headland called the Gribbin, where there was a candy-striped beacon – a marker for sailors. From this height I could see St Austell, and Par sprinkled at the head of St Austell Bay, and twenty miles of coast – mountainous heaps of china clay refuse, and Black Head, and the whole of dark blue Mevagissey Bay as far as Dodman Point. The distant rocks in the sea were called the Gwinges.

One of the pleasures of travelling this fractured coast was such a vista. The irregularity of the English coast offered unusually long views, and these heights helped. A vantage point like the Gribbin made this part of Cornwall look like a topographical map with raised features in bright colours – the best views were always like dazzling maps. And in contrast to the sea, there were the reassuring pastures: on one side the cows and bees and sheep, and slate walls and the smell of manure, and on the other side the gulls and cormorants and whiff of salt spray; and these mingled. The gulls crossed into the pastures, the crows strutted on the sand, and the smells of muck and salt mingled, too.

I walked on. Under the trees above Polkerris, which was a small harbour and beach, there was a cool shade and a rich aroma, a whole acre of wild garlic.

Par was small and ugly, a china clay factory wrapped around half its bay, and the other half a clutter of caravans and broken-down shallys. Rising behind this miserable beach were long terraces of hollow-eyed houses. Factory effluent had stained the water. I had been heading for Par all day, but instead of stopping I walked through the town to the station and caught the train that crossed the narrow part of Cornwall.

This branch-line train from Par to Newquay was a delight. We were heading west, and the bright sun was propped just above the horizon. I took the seat behind the driver, in the first carriage, and slipped my wet shoes off. There was nothing in the world more restful; the train seemed like the highest stage of civilization. Nothing was disturbed by it, or spoiled; it did not alter the landscape; it was the machine in the garden, but it was a gentle machine. It was fast and economical and as safe as a vehicle could possibly be.

Mr Kemp, the conductor, said, 'When I took over this train they said they were going to close the line. That was eighteen years ago! They're still saying it, but they haven't done it yet.'

But of course they would eventually, because they had closed down a hundred others just like it, all over the country. I suggested this to Mr Kemp.

He said, 'I'll be retired by then. But it'll be a shame if they close it. It's a beautiful line!'

We went through a green corridor of sunlit trees and sparkling leaves to Luxulyan. And then the landscape became stony, and rather bruised-looking, as the interior of Cornwall often appeared. The hills of rubbish from the china clay factories looked like pyramids – thick, broad-bottomed and sprawling across treeless plateaus – so that the effect was that of a lost city, as empty and geometric as any Aztec ruin. This was not far from the tiny village of Bugle.

The scars and eruptions – I supposed they were mines – showed clearly on the long low hills falling away from Roche. I heard someone referring to 'barrows', but didn't know whether he meant the china clay pyramids or the ancient burial mounds in the distance. The train passed under a number of small stone bridges. They were old and solid and symmetrical and looked both Chinese and ecclesiastical to me, but as I was thinking this a man behind me named R. T. Justice began explaining to his friend Maurice that this was Victorian railway architecture. It still looked Chinese and ecclesiastical.

Most of the people on this train – about sixty of them – were on what they called a 'whist holiday', having travelled most of the day from Wolverhampton. I asked what a whist holiday was. It was three days of whist in a hotel at Newquay – just cards, in the lounge, while the Atlantic smashed against the coast. It was quite nice, really, they said. It made a change. They did it every year, taking advantage of the low-season prices. They were old and rather sweet and softly talkative.

Then there came a loud, deaf lady's voice. It was one of the widows, Mrs Buttress. 'You see, they're Indian extracts!' she said. 'Yes, *extracts*! From Africa! But they're very refined! And as far as their English is concerned they could be dark-coloured English people. They come from a very well-to-do family. And they're so polite! They are very kind to me, always bringing me things – the loveliest shawl! Sometimes it's food. Well, the food is interesting but you wouldn't want to make a whole meal of it, would you? I never comment on the food, but their fabrics are really quite fine. Now their child is car-mad! Their first names are impossible, but their surname is easy. It's Baden. An Indian name. But it's easy to remember, because it's like Baden-Powell!'

The train swung around the back of Newquay, which was so thickly piled against the coast it had displaced the cliffs with three miles of hotels and boarding-houses.

About a half-hour after arriving in Newquay I was sitting in a front room, a dog chewing my shoe, and having a cup of tea with Florence Puttock ('I said leave that shoe alone!'), who was telling me about the operation on her knee. It was my mention of walking that brought up the subject of feet, legs, knees and her operation. And the television was on – there was a kind of disrespect these days in not turning it on for Falklands news. And Queenie, the other Peke, had a tummy upset. And Mrs Puttock's cousin Bill hadn't rung all day; he usually rang just after lunch. And Donald Puttock, who lisped and was sixty-one – he had taken early retirement because of his back – Donald was watching the moving arrows on the Falklands map, and listening to Florence talking about ligaments, and he said, 'I spent me 'ole life in 'ornchurch.'

Somehow, I was home.

But it was not my home. I had burrowed easily into this cosy privacy, and I could leave any time I wished. I had made the choice, for the alternatives in most seaside towns were either an hotel, or a guest house, or a bed-and-breakfast place. The latter alternative always tempted me, but I had to feel strong to do it right. A bed-and-breakfast place was a bungalow, usually on a suburban street some distance from the front and the promenade and the hotels. It was impossible to enter such a house and not feel you were interrupting a domestic routine – something about Florence's sewing and Donald's absurd slippers. The house always smelled of cooking and disinfectant, but most of all it smelled of in-laws.

It was like every other bungalow on the street, except for one thing. This one had a sign in the window, saying *Vacancies*. I had the impression that this was the only expense in starting such an establishment. You went over to Maynards and bought a *Vacancies* sign, and then it was simply a matter of airing out the spare bedroom. Soon, odd men would show up – knapsack, leather jacket, oily hiker's shoes – and spend an evening listening to the householders' stories of the cost of living, or the greatness of Bing Crosby, or a particularly painful operation. The English, the most obsessively secretive people in their day-to-day living, would admit you to the privacy of their homes, and sometimes even unburden themselves, for just five pounds. 'I've got an awful lot on my plate at the moment,' Mrs Spackle would say. 'There's Bert's teeth, the Hoover's packed up, and my Enid thinks she's in the family way ...' When it was late, and everyone else in bed, the woman you knew as Mrs Garlick would pour you a schooner of cream sherry, say 'Call me Ida', and begin to tell you about her amazing birthmark.

Bed and breakfast was always vaguely amateur, the woman of the house saying she did it because she liked to cook, and could use a little extra cash ('money for jam'), and she liked company, and their children were all grown up and the house was rather empty and echoey. The whole enterprise of bed and breakfast was carried on by the woman, but done with a will, because she was actually getting paid for doing her normal household chores. No special arrangements were required. At its best it was like a perfect marriage, at its worst it was like a night with terrible in-laws. Usually I was treated with a mixture of shyness and suspicion; but that was traditional English hospitality – wary curiosity and frugal kindness.

The English required guests to be uncomplaining, and most of the people who ran bed-and-breakfast places were intolerant of a guest's moaning, and they thought – with some justification – that they had in their lives suffered more than that guest. 'During the war,' they always began, and I knew I was about to lose the argument in the face of some evidence of terrible hardship. During the war, Donald Puttock was buzz-bombed by the Germans as he crouched under his small staircase in Hornchurch and, as he often said, he was lucky to be alive.

I told him I was travelling around the coast.

'Just what we did!' Mr Puttock said. He and Florence had driven from Kent to Cornwall in search of a good place to live. They had stopped in all the likely places. Newquay was the best. They would stay here until they died. If they moved at all (Florence wanted fewer bedrooms) it would be down the road.

'Course, the local people 'ere 'ate us,' Mr Puttock said, cheerfully.

'Donald got his nose bitten off the other day by a Cornishman,' Mrs Puttock said. 'Still hasn't got over it.'

'I don't give a monkey's,' Mr Puttock said.

Later, Mrs Puttock said that she had always wanted to do bed and breakfast. She wasn't like some of them, she said, who made their guests leave the house after breakfast and stay away all day – some of these people you saw in the bus shelter, they weren't waiting for the number fifteen, they were bed-and-breakfast people, killing time. It was bed and breakfast etiquette to stay quietly out of the house all day, even if it was raining.

Mrs Puttock gave me a card she had had printed. It listed the attractions of her house.

- TV Lounge
- Access to rooms at all times
- Interior-sprung mattresses
- Free parking space on premises

– Free shower available
– Separate tables

The lounge was the Puttocks' front room, the parking space was their drive, the shower was a shower, and the tables tables. This described their house, which was identical to every other bungalow in Newquay.

I was grateful for the bed-and-breakfast places. At ten-thirty, after the Falklands news (and now every night there was 'Falklands Special'), while we were all a bit dazed by the violence and the speculation and Mr Puttock was saying, 'The Falklands look like bloody Bodmin Moor, but I suppose we have to do something,' Mrs Puttock would say to me, 'Care for a hot drink?' When she was in the kitchen making Ovaltine, Mr Puttock and I were talking baloney about the state of the world. I was grateful, because to me this was virgin territory – a whole house open to my prying eyes: books, pictures, postcard messages, souvenirs and opinions. I especially relished looking at family photographs. 'That's us at the Fancy Dress Ball in Romford just after the war ... That's our cat, Monty ... That's me in a bathing costume ...' My intentions were honourable but my instincts were nosey, and I went sniffing from bungalow to bungalow to discover how those people lived.

It was either that – the Puttocks in their bungalow – or the opposite – vast bare cliffs of windswept stone that were blasted by the Atlantic. I used to leave the bungalow and laugh out loud at the difference. The town of Newquay in its charmless way was bleaker than the cliffs. It was dreary buildings and no trees. But the visitors were decent folks, mainly old people who were rather overdressed for such an ordinary place. The men wore hats and ties and jackets and the women dresses and pearls. It looked like church-going garb, but they were off to buy the *Express* or the *Telegraph*, or to walk to the bandstand and back. They seldom strayed out of the town and were never on the cliffs.

In a month or so, Mr Puttock said, it would all be roaring with yobbos, fat youths with moustaches and oafish girls, drinking themselves silly and doing damage, or at least leaving a trail of vomit along the promenade. Mr Puttock intimated that a population composed of the very old and the very young did not exactly make Newquay sparkle.

Dorothy, a half-Indian, half-English girl I met, said this was true. Newquay was slow, she said. Dorothy had spent the past two years sewing buttons on cardigans in a sweatshop in Leicester, so she certainly knew what slow meant. Otherwise, she was full of surprising answers.

Did she like her job at the Indian restaurant?

She said, 'I like the hours – six to midnight.'

What was her ambition in life?

'I'd like to own a factory.'

How had she prepared herself for factory-owning?

'I've got an O-Level in Needlework.'

What did she do for fun?

'Martial arts, you know? Tae-Kwon-Do. And I like making joompers.'

Most people agreed that Newquay was a hard place in which to make a living. The fish-and-chip shops would not open until June, and then it was a short season – two months or less. 'And the real problem with chip shops,' Mr Ramsay told me, 'is that you can't tell them apart. I can't tell the difference, and I run one! If they use fresh fish and fresh potatoes that's another story, but not many of them do.' Ramsay was on the dole. 'I'll re-open my shop in about a month.'

I was beginning to find the Puttocks a little trying. I had told them I was in publishing and they pestered me with dull questions about books. They regarded books as clumsy, pointless things, and Donald Puttock smiled in pity whenever he mentioned them. What was the use? he seemed to say. He had no objection to them, but what was the good of them? He was entirely ignorant; he had a few harmless opinions. Mrs Puttock had her dogs and her jigsaw puzzles. There was nothing more. Sometimes I imagined that they were terribly frightened.

One night after the news – an invasion of the Falklands was predicted – I asked Mr Puttock what he thought about the war.

He said, 'I don't know anything about it,' and left the room.

I wondered what his politics were, but when I asked him who his Member of Parliament was he said he did not know.

'We've been so busy for the past couple of years,' Mrs Puttock explained.

If they had secrets I never learned them, but in a superficial way they had made it possible for me to invade their privacy for a few days.

And then I was overcome with the in-law feeling of wanting to go – of stepping outside and never coming back. That morning I studied the weather forecast, because I would need fairly good weather for my walk along the cliffs to Padstow. The *Telegraph* said, 'Scattered clouds ... occasional showers.' But there was a large weather item on the front page:

CLOUDS BEGIN TO THIN OUT

Clouds from Wednesday's intense cold front began to thin out over the Falklands yesterday. Overcast low and broken high clouds still covered the islands and adjacent waters, but the heaviest weather was in the east and north.

The deepening low pressure area was centred at the southern tip of South America.

Fairly good weather meant there would be an invasion of the Falklands by British troops. On the other hand, I had no definite idea of what the weather would be like for me on the coastal path to Padstow.

I slipped away from the Puttocks' bungalow, feeling as if I had been sprung from prison, and I hurried to the path. It was cloudy and slightly rainy, but the visibility was good and the path was firm. I could see the black headlands in the distance, Berryl's Point, after the sweep of Watergate Bay, and Park Head, and in the smoky distance, the giant shadow of Trevose Head.

I walked on. There was no greenery here. It had been torn away. There was only a thin meadow on top of the rock cliffs. The coast was high, hard and grey, and the rocks split and wrinkled, some of them cleft open. The coves were great jagged hollows of slooshing surf and waves – what noises came out of the caverns under those cliffs! But it was familiar thunder, for this coast was like the coast of Maine.

The paths were steep and narrow, and by the time I walked the five miles to Mawgan Porth I was ready to stop for a coffee.

There was a detachment of US Marines guarding – what? – probably an atomic bomb on the cliffs here at Mawgan, but I did not meet them. I met the Wheekers, Marian and Bob, who had just rolled out of bed and were having tea, 'and I wouldn't mind a bowl of flakes,' Marian said. Her sparse hair was coppery with henna and she sucked smoke out of the cigarette she had pinched in her fingers.

'I'm tired,' Mr Wheeker said carefully, 'because I 'ave just woke up. Heh.'

He looked at me and grinned to signal that he had intended a joke.

I asked them whether they had heard the news on the radio – that an attack on the Falklands was expected.

'I never listen to the news,' Mr Wheeker said. 'Know why?'

No, I said, I didn't know why.

'Because there's nothing you can do about it. Right, my dear?'

Mrs Wheeker agreed, and then she narrowed her eyes at me and said, 'Course, you people 'ave been criticizing us.'

I said I had been under the impression that the United States had given material support to the British and, because of it, had alienated the whole of South America. I wanted to tell him about the Monroe Doctrine, but he was at me again.

'We're in this all alone,' he said. 'And the French are worse than the Americans.'

Mrs Wheeker said, 'My father always said, "I'd rather have the Germans over here than the French."'

I said, 'Do you mean the German army?'

'The German anything,' Mrs Wheeker said. 'It's them French I 'ate.'

A car drew up to the hotel and a family tumbled out, yelling.

'Too many tourists 'ere, that's the trouble,' Mr Wheeker said. 'That's why the Cornish are so unfriendly, like. They can't stick the tourists.'

'Course, that's where all their money comes from,' Mrs Wheeker said. 'Kick out the tourists and they wouldn't 'ave a penny.'

'You're walking, then?' Mr Wheeker said, his teacup shaking at his mouth.

I said yes, along the cliffs.

'How many miles you reckon on walking, then?' he asked.

I said I averaged between fifteen and twenty a day.

'We never walk,' Mr Wheeker said, and made it sound like self-abuse.

'We *have* walked,' Mrs Wheeker said.

I said, 'It's not much fun in this weather.'

'It's been trying to rain all morning,' Mrs Wheeker said.

I smiled. That was one of my favourite expressions.

'We never minded the weather,' Mr Wheeker said. 'We walked fifteen or twenty miles – *in an evening*. In rain, snow, wind, anything – anything except fog. Never in fog. We couldn't stick fog.'

'And another thing about the Cornish,' Mrs Wheeker said, suddenly bored by her husband, who was almost certainly lying about all the walking. 'The Cornish mispronounciate their words.'

This was wonderful. She mispronounced the word 'mispronounce'!

I remembered the Wheekers again later that day, because they were the only people I had met on the path, and when I arrived in Padstow I heard the news that the Falklands had been invaded; a British frigate, the *Ardent*, had been sunk and twenty-two men drowned, and a bridgehead established at San Carlos, and hundreds of Argentines killed. I especially remembered the Wheekers' bored silly faces and how little they cared.

The River Camel was black that afternoon. Instead of crossing it I went to Wadebridge. I decided to return to the main line and Exeter, and take the branch line to the North Devon coast. I set out the next day thinking: To be anonymous and travelling in an interesting place is an intoxication.

8

The Branch Line to Barnstaple

Among the quiet hills and meadows in the middle of Devon, this small train of three spruce coaches was the only moving object, and its harmless racket the only sound. It was one hour from end to end of the branch line, Exeter to Barnstaple, much of it along a stream called the River Taw which the train crossed and recrossed. It was the last rural branch line in the shire.

Because it was a remnant, soon to be swept away, it was greatly favoured by railway buffs. Their interest always seemed to me worse than indecent and their joy-riding a mild form of necrophilia. They were on board getting their last looks at the old stations, photographing the fluting and floriation, the pediments and barge-boards and pilasters, the valencing on the wooden awnings, the strapwork, and – in railway architecture every brick has a different name – the quoins. They knew that when the line was closed like the four others that had once been joined to it, every beautiful station would be sold to anyone who could raise a mortgage to turn it into a bungalow for a boasting family.

It seemed odd to be inland after so much coast. I missed the drenching light, the sea boiling under the cliffs, the sound of surf on sand which was like the sound of grieving. Here the landscape was motionless and silent, long low hills and withered villages – some were half-dead, like Copplestone, with its shut-down station and grass knee-deep on the platform. This branch line was old, finished in 1854, and it had always been useful. But it was faintly comic, as all country trains seemed as they jerked across meadows and made the cows stare. This one was full of Bertie Wooster touches, especially in the names. It went through the Creedy Valley, and on to Yeoford, Lapford, Eggesford and Kings Nympton; Portsmouth Arms Station was actually a public house with a funereal saloon bar, and Umberleigh was probably the setting of *Jeeves Lays an Egg*. Now we were in the valley of the Taw. We rattled into Barnstaple, which was a slightly frumpish, down-at-heel town on both banks of the muddy river.

It was raining. The train passengers looked bored. But it was not boredom, it was the habitual patience which stiffened the English like a kind of hard glaze.

Our arrival made them talkative. Few risked the subject of the Falklands war. It was only after the most violent incidents that people discussed it. They talked cautiously about the weather, their children, their health. 'It's the bugloss that gets me this time of year,' Mrs Badgworthy said. And her friend Joan said, 'I do hope they have a dry fortnight in Majorca' – worrying about someone else's weather.

Barnstaple had become a sorry town. Once it had been a large railway junction, with three stations. Now it had only one station, and the line stopped dead, miles from the coast, leaving Barnstaple nowhere. It had a damp, haunted look that was partly dereliction and partly the result of the demolishing or conversion of its best buildings. Queen Anne's Walk, an elegant colonnade and building that had served as a riverside quay and bustling office for merchants and seamen for three hundred years, was now the Barnstaple Old People's Rest Centre – a worthy but melancholy end. It was a silted-up sea-port at the end of a withering railway line.

For the first time in weeks I saw crowds of hikers. They were young, they looked healthy, they had orange rucksacks, many were Americans. They had no intention of lingering in Barnstaple; they were setting out for Clovelly and Hartland Point, and their numbers discouraged me from doing the same. I felt somewhat inhibited: I imagined many of them to be travel writers, with knapsacks full of notes. They asked me intelligent, probing questions. I ran into the hikers all over town – I was fair game, I had a knapsack, too, and oily shoes and a rain-spattered map. Where was I going? What was I doing? They asked for details I could not supply. I escaped to Ilfracombe, on the north coast.

The point about Ilfracombe, surely, was that it had not been designed for cars. It was a classic railway resort, with tall hotels and sloping streets. It had been built on a very steep hillside and was full of shifting perspectives of the Bristol Channel. There was a *Vacancies* sign in every window. I could imagine people pouring out of the now defunct Ilfracombe Station and heading for all those boarding houses. In the twenties and thirties, Welshmen came by the thousands on the steam packets from across the water, and roistered up and down Ilfracombe, squandering their return fare on beer. It was a town for the stroller, not the driver – it was hard for cars to negotiate the streets, which were very steep and narrow; there was nowhere to park; the hills made cars dangerous. Motor traffic had just about destroyed this dramatic seaside antique.

The dark clouds over Ilfracombe turned the grass on the great swollen headlands very green. Henry James tip-toed around the town in 1872 and found it over-planned and a little gimcrack. He usually objected to the settled and bricked-up look of the English watering places, but in Ilfracombe he sighed when he saw the handrails and signboards and the old ladies and sheep, and he wished with all his heart for 'something more pathless, more idle, more unreclaimed from ... deep-bosomed nature'. Of course, Ilfracombe now looked much more used and worn out than it had then; but not far from it, and on many parts of the North Devon coast, it was easy to find deep-bosomed nature – just that, in fact, because the headlands were magnificent and bosomy and between them was always a steepness that the locals called a cleave.

I walked to Hele Bay and Watermouth Cove. They were wooded and full of pink and blue wild-flowers. There were pale spring flowers everywhere. No one could tell me their names. I came to Big Meadow and saw a sign:

> Welcome to Big Meadow!
> Sorry: No motorcycles
>   No groups of Men
>   No Dogs

Combe Martin farther on was a small village on a rocky bay, in the shadow of two tall hills, the Little Hangman and the Great Hangman. As I walked into it I could see the whole of it at the head of the bay, the houses, the bars, the hotels, the church, and then I was on its only street, strolling past the cottages. Their windows were open. At one I heard '... *seven more Argentine aircraft have been shot down*,' from a radio, and further on, another radio saying that so far four hundred and fifty men had been killed in the Falklands fighting.

I found a place to sleep, by traipsing through the town in my usual fashion and sizing up the likely places. I had a shower and dinner – a pollack caught a few hours ago off this coast, and apple and bilberry pie. There were English people in the dining room, talking in whispers about food in a shy hungry way as they ate.

It was in little country villages like Combe Martin that I saw the wildest and scruffiest youths, motorcyclists mostly – the sort banned from Big Meadow – who modelled themselves on Hells Angels. I could not explain why they were most numerous in the prettiest villages in the countryside. They played pool in pubs with names like 'The Old Haymow' and 'The Ploughman's Inn' (these places now had jukeboxes and video machines) and they had tattoos and leather trousers and chains. They were the last people I expected to see in the depths of this countrified coast, and it was oddest of all to see them, as I did in Combe Martin, drinking the local ale beside grizzled shepherds and fishermen. The most common night-time sound in the English coastal village, apart from the endlessly grieving surf, was that of the motorcycles farting down the main road at midnight.

The hotel people in Ilfracombe and Combe Martin said business was terrible this year. Last year was terrible too. They had never known it to be so bad. They had very few firm reservations.

Mr Deedy at the Bull said, 'See, no one wants to make plans ahead. They go on working. It's not only the money. They don't like to go away, because they don't know whether they'll have jobs to go back to.'

Then 'Falklands Special' was on television and we dutifully trooped towards Mrs Deedy's shout of 'It's the news!' The news was very bad, more deaths, more ships sunk. But there was always great bewilderment among people watching the news, because there was never enough of it and it was sometimes contradictory. Why were there so few photographs of fighting? Usually it was reporters speaking of disasters over crackly telephones. The English seemed – in private – ashamed and confused, and regarded Argentina as pathetic, ramshackle and unlucky, with a conscript army of very young boys. They hated discussing it, but they could talk all night on the subject of how business was bad.

'You just reminded me,' Mrs Deedy said. 'The Smiths have cancelled. They had that September booking. Mr Smith rang this morning.'

'Knickers,' Mr Deedy said.

'His wife died,' Mrs Deedy said.

'Oh?' Mr Deedy was doubtful, sorry he had said knickers.

'She wasn't poorly,' Mrs Deedy said. 'It was a heart attack.'

Mr Deedy relaxed at the news of the heart attack. It was no one's fault, really, not like a sickness or a crime. It was more a kind of removal.

'That's another returned deposit,' Mrs Deedy said. She was cross.

'That makes two so far,' Mr Deedy said. 'Let's hope there aren't any more.'

The next day I heard two tattling ladies talking about the Falklands. It was being said that the British had become jingoistic because of the war, and that a certain swagger was now evident. It was true of the writing in many newspapers, but it was seldom true of the talk I heard. Most people were like Mrs Mullion and Miss Custis at the Britannia in Combe Martin, who, after some decent platitudes, wandered from talk of the Falklands to extensive reminiscing about the Second World War.

'After all, the Germans were occupying France, but life went on as normal,' Mrs Mullion said.

'Well, this is just it,' Miss Custis said. 'You've got to carry on. No sense packing up.'

'We were in Taunton then.'

'Were you? We were in Cullompton,' Miss Custis said. 'Mutterton, actually.'

'Rationing seemed to go on for ages!' Mrs Mullion said.

'I still remember when chocolate went off the ration. And then people bought it all. And then it went on the ration again!'

They had begun to cheer themselves up in this way

'More tea?' Mrs Mullion said.

'Lovely,' Miss Custis said.

That was the day I left Combe Martin. I walked out of the village and climbed a thousand feet to the top of the Great Hangman. Down below I could see a headland that looked like a dog crouching with his snout in a puddle – the puddle being the Bristol Channel. Across the water, South Wales was a faint foreign blue.

There were steep cleaves, beautiful and exhausting, all the way to Lynton. The hills rose plumply from the water's edge and the path circled the hollows, treeless here and with such a pitch that, descending them, I usually slid and lost my balance and, climbing, I found myself taking rapid stabbing steps that made my ankles sore. There was nothing to grasp, nothing to break my fall. In the middle of the cleave, way down and flowing from the head of the long valley there was always a creek or a river, looking sometimes like a snail-track and sometimes like a snake. It was this way for fifteen miles.

At the bottom of one winding path was the village of Trentishoe. In 1891 it had a population of ninety-seven; now it had been reduced to forty-five. The church ('the second smallest in Devon') was the size of a one-car garage. I had said I was not going to do any sightseeing, but the village was nowhere and the church was insignificant and very pretty, so I went in. It smelled of Bible bindings and brass polish. Its list of Rectors went back to the year 1260, seven hundred years accounted for. A notice said that a number of the graves in the churchyard were unknown people whose bodies had washed up on the shore in Elwill Bay, below this church, St Peter's.

I left the path near Heddon's Mouth and took the steepest way across the cut, on stony patches between the clumps of heather, and tugged back by thorns, and on all fours through the wild-flowers, and skidding on loose chippings of shale. I found it slow going, but I was in no particular hurry. After that high hill I came to Martinhoe, and then to a headland full of trees. These woods were wrecked and looked wonderful. It was called Woody Bay and was littered with fallen trees. They had blown down in the winter's hurricane-force winds, and blocked most of the paths, making this part of the coast tangled and wild, with great splintered tree trunks. It was a marvellous ruin – still-alive trees fractured all over the floor of the woods.

There was a motor road to the Valley of Rocks. I had seen very few people all day; but this place, on every map because Shelley had praised it and because it had a car park, had a hundred people clambering over the rocks and yelling. The rock formations had good names, such as 'Mother Meldrum's Cave' and 'The White Lady' and 'The Devil's Cheese Ring', but I skipped on to Lynton just the same.

There was once a railway to Lynton. It was not open long, about sixty years. There was still a club in the village called 'The Lynton and Barnstaple Railway Association'. Normally I had no interest in railway clubs and I avoided the company of railway buffs; but I liked the motto of this railway association in Lynton: 'Perchance it is not dead, but sleepeth . . .'

At about five-thirty in the afternoon, just after tea, everyone left Lynton. It became a deserted village and seemed to slumber there on the crest of the hill until the next morning, when it woke again with the hullabaloo of people. I thought the people must have gone to Lynmouth, four hundred feet down the cliff on a small harbour. Old guide books called Lynmouth 'one of the loveliest villages in England'. But the people had not gone to Lynmouth. That village was empty, too, full of *Vacancies* signs and very quiet saloon bars and dim whispers; the only full-throated sound was that of the tide battering the sea-wall. The light was strange in these sister-villages above and below the pinnacles of cliff; facing north and tucked into a cove, they lost the sun in the afternoon, so they were lit by the gleaming Channel and the near-mirage of Wales. But Lynmouth remained a cool glade, rather damp and sheltered on the banks of the two rivers that rose in Exmoor and converged among a battered and rather scoured-looking watercourse.

Lynmouth had a rearranged, half-put-away appearance, because thirty years ago much of it had been demolished by a torrent of water. Even now, people visited the village to examine the damage done by the Great Lynmouth Flood Disaster. But where did they go after tea?

A street-sweeper named Mr Bedge told me the people were from Butlin's holiday camp in Minehead, eighteen miles away.

I said, 'But there are thousands of people!'

'It's a big camp,' Mr Bedge said.

I liked the liquid evening light in Lynmouth, but the village was clammy and full of shadows. Lynton had a whiter light, more sky, and a breeze, and even deserted it looked rather dignified and old-fashioned on its cliff-top.

Next month there would be a movie one day a week in Lynton.

'But if there are thirty people at the film show the owner will be pleased, and if there's fifty it'll be a bloody miracle,' Sid Henry told me.

Mrs Henry said, 'We're dying on our feet.'

There was a great deal of talk, at the Henrys' and all over the village, of *Lorna Doone*, which was set just down the road towards Porlock. But it was another example of literature giving an area an importance that in time had displaced the book. No one here had read *Lorna Doone*, but it didn't matter because the district had already been hallowed by it, and now it was seen in a kind of blurred and respectful way. How could you possibly disparage a place that had inspired a famous novel?

But there was a greater source of interest at the Henrys'. This was the honeymoon couple, a frail young man and a big laughing woman who was about five years older than her new husband. A silence fell over the dining room when the couple came down to breakfast. The Campbells stared into their porridge (they were Australian – nervous and uncritical); the Hibberts, from London, became small and watchful; and I pretended to read the newspaper. B. and G. Chandler (that was how it went in the Guests' Register, always one of my favourite books at any overnight stop) were the honeymoon couple. They took their seats at breakfast, and she talked and he squinted. Mr Chandler looked terrible, pale and rather beaten; and Mrs Chandler was robust, rosy-cheeked, full of talk, as if perhaps she fed off him at night. She made the plans – 'Let's go to Clovelly today' – and he just sat there, grimacing.

We wanted to hear him say something. We wanted to know what he was thinking. Most of all we wanted him to assert himself ('I can't take much more of this!') but in two days he never spoke. He listened, he squinted, he grew a bit smaller; but that was all. And then the *Just Married* signs that had been stuck to their bumper and the *Honeymooners!* that had been scrawled in soap on the car doors vanished, and by the time they left Lynton the Chandlers looked as though they had been married for twenty years.

I left Lynton on the Cliff Railway, a cable car that descended to Lynmouth. I took a bus to Porlock, ten miles away. The road cut across the north of Exmoor, a rather brown forbidding place, and down the long Porlock Hill. The roads were so steep there were signs on ramps saying, 'Danger – escape for Runaway Vehicles – No Parking' and 'Warning to Pedestrians – Do Not Loiter Near This Bend – Danger from Vehicles Out of Control'.

Porlock, the home of the man who interrupted the writing of 'Kubla Khan', was one street of small cottages, with a continuous line of cars trailing through it. Below it, on the west side of the bay, was Porlock Weir, and there were hills on all sides that were partly wooded.

A hundred and seventy years ago a man came to Porlock and found it quiet. But he did not find fault. He wrote: 'There are periods of comparative stagnation, when we say, even in London, that there is nothing stirring; it is therefore not surprising that there should be some seasons of the year when things are rather quiet in West Porlock.'

I walked towards Allerford, and on the way fell into conversation with a woman feeding birds in her garden. She told me the way to Minehead – not the shortest way, but the prettiest way, she said. She had light hair and dark eyes. I said her house was beautiful. She said it was a guest house, then she laughed. 'Why don't you stay tonight?' She meant it and seemed eager, and then I was not sure what she was offering. I stood there and smiled back at her. The sun was shining gold on the grass and the birds were taking the crumbs in a frenzied way. It was not even one o'clock, and I had never stopped at a place this early in the day.

I said, 'Maybe I'll come back some time.'

'I'll still be here,' she said, laughing a bit sadly.

There was an ancient bridge at Allerford. I bypassed it and cut into the woods, climbing towards the hill called Selworthy Beacon. The woods were full of singing birds, warblers and thrushes; and then I heard the unmistakable sound of a cuckoo, which was as clear as a clock, striking fifteen. The sun was strong, the gradient was easy, the bees were buzzing, there was a soft breeze; and I thought: This was what I was looking for when I set out this morning – though I had no idea I would find it here.

All travellers are optimists, I thought. Travel itself is a sort of optimism in action. I always went along thinking: I'll be all right, I'll be interested, I'll discover something, I won't break a leg or get robbed, and at the end of the day I'll find a nice old place to sleep. Everything is going to be fine, and even if it isn't it will be worthy of note – worth leaving home for. Sometimes the weather, even the thin rain of Devon, made it worth it. Or else the bird song in sunlight, or the sound of my shoesoles on the pebbles of the downward path – here, for example, walking down North Hill through glades full of azaleas which were bright purple. I continued over the humpy hills to Minehead.

9

The West Somerset Railway

To the east, beyond the grey puddly foreshore – the tide was out half a mile – I saw the bright flags of Butlin's, Minehead, and vowed to make a visit. Ever since Bognor I had wanted to snoop inside a coastal holiday camp, but I had passed the fences and gates without going in. It was not possible to make a casual visit. Holiday camps were surrounded by prison fences, with coils of barbed wire at the top. There were dog patrols and *Beware* signs stencilled with skulls. The main entrances were guarded, and had turnstiles and a striped barrier that was raised to let certain vehicles through. Butlin's guests had to show passes in order to enter. The whole affair reminded me a little of Jonestown.

And these elaborate security measures fuelled my curiosity. What exactly was going on in there? It was no use my peering through the chainlink fence – all I could see at this Butlin's were the boating lake and the reception area and some snorers on deck chairs. Clearly, it was very large. Later I discovered that the camp was designed to accommodate 14,000 people. That was almost twice the population of Minehead! They called it 'Butlinland' and they said it had everything.

I registered as a Day Visitor. I paid a fee. I was given a brochure and a booklet and *Your Holiday Programme*, with a list of the day's events. The security staff seemed wary of me. I had ditched my knapsack in a boarding house, but I was still wearing my leather jacket and oily hiking shoes. My knees were muddy. So as not to alarm the gatekeepers I had pocketed my binoculars. Most of the Butlin's guests wore sandals and short sleeves, and some wore funny hats – holiday high spirits. The weather was overcast and cold and windy. The flags out front were as big as bedsheets and made a continual cracking. I was the only person at Butlin's dressed for this foul weather. I felt like a commando. I made some people there suspicious.

With its barracks-like buildings and its forbidding fences it had the prison look of the Butlin's at Bognor. A prison look was also an army camp look, and just as depressing. This one was the more scary for being brightly painted. It had been tacked together out of plywood and tin panels in primary colours. I had not seen flimsier buildings in England. They were so ugly they were not pictured anywhere in the Butlin's brochure, but instead shown as simplified floor plans in blue diagrams. They were called 'flatlets' and 'suites'. The acres of barracks were called 'The Accommodation Area'.

It really was like Jonestown! The Accommodation Area with the barracks was divided into camps – Green, Yellow, Blue and Red Camp. There was a central dining room and a Nursery Centre. There was a Camp Chapel. There was also a miniature railway and a chairlift and monorail – all of them useful: it was a large area to cover on foot. It was just the sort of place the insane preacher must have imagined when he brought his desperate people to Guyana. It was self-contained and self-sufficient. With a fence that high it had to be.

The Jonestown image was powerful, but Butlin's also had the features of a tinselly New Jerusalem. This, I felt, would be the English coastal town of the future if most English people had their way. It was already an English town of a sort – glamorized and less substantial than the real thing, but all the same recognizably an English town, with the usual landmarks, a cricket pitch, a football field, a launderette, a supermarket, a bank, a betting shop, and a number of take-away food joints. Of course, it was better organized and had more amenities than most English towns the same size. That was why it was popular. It was also a permanent fun-fair. One of Butlin's's boasts was: 'No dirty dishes to wash!' Another was: 'There is absolutely no need to queue!' No dishwashing, no queuing – it came near to parody, like a vacation in a Polish joke. But these promises were a sort of timid hype; England was a country of modest expectations and no dishes and no queues were part of the English dream.

It was not expensive, £178 a week for a family of four, and

that included two meals a day. They were mostly families, young parents with small children. They slept in numbered cubicles in the barracks at one of the four camps, and they ate at a numbered table in one of the dining rooms, and they spent the day amusing themselves.

The Windsor Sports Ground (most of the names had regal echoes, an attempt at respectability) and the Angling Lake were not being used by anyone the day I was there. But the two snooker and table tennis rooms were very busy – these rooms were about half the size of football fields and held scores of tables. No waiting! There was bingo in the Regency Building, in a massive room with a glass wall, which was the bottom half of the indoor swimming pool – fluttering legs and skinny feet in water the colour of chicken bouillon. There was no one on the boating lake and no one in the outdoor pool, and the chapel was empty. The crazy golf was not popular. So much for the free amusements.

'Yes, it *is* true, nearly everything at Butlin's is free!' the brochure said.

But what most of the people were doing was not free. They were feeding coins into fruit machines and one-armed bandits in the Fun Room. They were playing pinball. They were also shopping for stuffed toys and curios, or buying furs in the Fur Shop, or getting their hair done at the Hairdressing Salon. They were eating. The place had four fish and chip shops. There were tea shops, coffee bars, and sweet shops. They cost money, but people seemed to be spending fairly briskly. They were also drinking. There were about half a dozen bars. The Embassy Bar (Greek statues, fake chandeliers, red wallpaper) was quite full, although it was the size of a barn. The Exmoor Bar had a hundred and fifty-seven tables and probably held a thousand drinkers. It was the scale of the place that was impressive: the scale, and the shabbiness.

It was not Disneyland. Disneyland was a blend of technology and farce. It was mostly fantasy, a tame kind of surrealism, a comfortable cartoon in three dimensions. But the more I saw of Butlin's the more it resembled English life; it was very close to reality in its narrowness, its privacies and its pleasures. It was England without work. Leisure had been overtaken by fatigue and dull-wittedness: electronic games were easier than sports, and eating junk food had become another recreation. No one seemed to notice how plain the buildings were, how tussocky the grass was or that everywhere there was a pervasive sizzle and smell of food frying in hot fat.

In that sense, too, it was like a real town. People walked around believing that it was all free; but most pastimes there cost money, and some were very expensive, like a ticket to the cabaret show that night, 'Freddie and the Dreamers', a group of middle-aged musicians who were a warmed-up version of their sixties' selves.

If it had a futuristic feel it was the deadened imagination and the zombie-like attitude of the strolling people, condemned to a week or two of fun under cloudy skies. And it was also the arrangements for children. The kids were taken care of – they could be turned loose in Butlin's in perfect safety. They couldn't get hurt, or lost. There was a high fence around the camp. There was a Nursery Chalet Patrol and a Child Listening Service and a large Children's Playground. In the planned cities of the future, provisions like this would be made for children.

Most of the events were for children, apart from whist and bingo. As a Day Visitor, I had my choice of the Corona Junior Fancy Dress Competition, a Kids' Quiz Show, the Trampoline Test, the Donkey Derby, or the Beaver and Junior Talent Contest Auditions. The Donkey Derby was being held in a high wind on Gaiety Green, among screaming children and plodding animals. I went to the talent show auditions in the Gaiety Revue Theatre. A girl of eight did a suggestive dance to a lewd pop song; two sisters sang a song about Jesus; Amanda and Kelly sang 'Daisy' and Miranda recited a poem much too quickly. Most of the parents were elsewhere – playing one-armed bandits and drinking beer.

I wandered into the Camp Chapel ('A Padre is available in the Centre at all times'). There was a notice stuck to the chapel door: '*At all three services prayers are being said for our Forces in the Southern Atlantic.*' I scrutinized the Visitors' Book. It asked for nationality, and people listed 'Welsh' or 'Cornish' or 'English' or 'Scottish' next to their names. There was a scattering of Irish. But after the middle of April – after the Falklands war had begun – people had started to put 'British'.

I found three ladies having tea in the Regency Building

Daphne Bunsen, from Bradford, said, 'We don't talk about this Falklands business here, 'cause we're on holiday. It's a right depressing soobject.'

'Anyway,' Mavis Hattery said, 'there's only one thing to say.'

What was that?

'I say, "Get it over with! Stop playing cat and mouse!"'

Mrs Bunsen said they loved Butlin's. They had been here before and would certainly come back. Their sadness was they could not stay longer. 'And Mavis's room is right posh!'

'I paid a bit extra,' Mrs Hattery said. 'I have a fitted carpet in my shally.'

It was easy to mock Butlin's for its dreariness and its brainless pleasures. It was an inadequate answer to leisure, but there were scores of similar camps all around the coast, so there was no denying its popularity. It combined the security and equality of prison with the vulgarity of an amusement park. I asked children what their parents were doing. Usually the father was playing billiards and the mother was shopping, but many said their parents were sleeping – having a kip. Sleeping until noon, not having to cook or mind children, and being a few steps away from the chippy, the bar and the betting shop: it was a sleazy paradise in which people were treated more or less like animals in a zoo. In time to come, there would be more holiday camps on the British coast. 'Cheap and cheerful,' Daphne Bunsen said.

Butlin's was staffed by 'Redcoats' – young men and women who wore red blazers. It was a Redcoat named Rod Firsby who told me that the camp could accommodate fourteen thousand people ('but nine thousand is about average'). Where did the people come from? I asked. He said they came from all over. It was when I asked him what sort of jobs they did that he laughed.

'Are you joking, sunshine?' he said.

I said no, I wasn't.

He said, 'Half the men here are unemployed. That's the beauty of Butlin's – you can pay for it with your dole money.'

After Butlin's, my boarding house in the lower town seemed very tame. There were thirteen fragrant old ladies in residence for a week. They enthused about places like Wimbleball Reservoir, and Clatworthy, and Dunkery Beacon, and the castle at Dunster.

Sometimes they mentioned *Lorna Doone* in respectful tones. But they had read the novel. They were retired Welsh schoolteachers, very sweet-natured and precise and knowledgeable.

One night I watched *Damien – Omen II* with eight of them in the so-called 'TV Lounge' – the back room, with extra chairs. I was astonished at the silliness of the movie, but I looked around the room and saw that the Welsh ladies were squinting seriously at it. It was so preposterous I wanted to hoot. The Devil's son was somehow living with an American family, and the fact that they were obscenely rich and living like lords in Chicago was supposed to make it believable. The Devil's son had flinty eyes and went to a military academy where periodically he reverted to his devilish self, calling down Satan's wrath on the school bullies. There was often a shiny crow overhead, croaking and doing damage – wreaking havoc was how one was supposed to view it. Nothing in this plot made me regret that I had missed *Omen I*, but because I had missed it I had to ask questions of the Welsh ladies. I always got prompt replies.

'Who is that man?'

'One of the Devil's Disciples,' Miss Ellis said, with a slewed Welsh emphasis on the last syllable.

Some of the ladies were knitting. One read a newspaper during the commercial breaks. They chatted about Wimbleball and Dunster. But they were silent during the movie. Only I spoke up, because I was confused.

'What's that statue?'

'Oh, that will be the Whore of Babylon, I expect,' Miss Thomas said in her sweet Welsh voice.

The little brat had *666* inscribed on his scalp.

'That's the Number of the Beast,' Miss Ellis said.

But I hadn't asked.

'Revelations,' Miss Parry-Williams said.

Towards midnight, after most of the characters had been murdered by the Devil's son, the film ended. The back room was now filled with the syrupy smell of the Welsh ladies' cologne. They stifled yawns and stood up.

Miss Thomas said, 'I shouldn't be a bit surprised if we saw *Omen Three* before very long! Good night Gwyneth, good night Alice, good night –'

★

The schoolteachers made me impatient to see Wales. They looked English but their demeanour was amused and remote. They whispered at breakfast, they were very polite, even circumspect; they behaved as though in a foreign land.

There was no path on this stretch of coast to Bristol. I put my maps aside and took the West Somerset Railway. It was Britain's longest private line – twenty-five miles, operating between Minehead and Taunton. The British Rail service had ended in 1971. The West Somerset line was both a passion and a business for the people who ran it – some were volunteers. The station at Minehead had been preserved as a sort of usable antique, full of nostalgic signs advertising cigarettes and motor oil. That aspect – the backward-looking part of it – rather irritated me. The trouble with railway buffs was that they were not really interested in going anywhere. They were playing; taking photographs, posing on locomotives, collecting engine numbers. They relished the dusty aesthetics of railway lore.

They especially liked dressing up. That seemed to be part of the English character, entering into fantasy, putting on different clothes and setting the old dull personality aside. It was what made amateur dramatics in England so energetic; drag acts here were so humorous that they did not need the justification of being wholesome. And so much of English life required costumes: clothes represented freedom or power or a new self. The members of the House of Lords wore ermine, and Oxbridge students wore robes, and even milkmen wore a distinctive leather jerkin; and there was no more serious boast than a bowler hat. The railway buff crossed the thin line between dressing up and travesty; but the English seldom bothered to make much of a distinction between the two in any case. The reward for restarting a railway line was the chance to dress up as a Stationmaster, or a Conductor, or a Guard, or even a Sweeper, with a uniform and special buttons and a certain kind of hat.

The train was full of joyriders pretending to be passengers; there and back, that was always the railway buff's itinerary. They liked the atmospherics. They took pictures of each other, and of the woodwork and steam. We went along the shore to Dunster and its dark brown castle ('The Dutch embossed leather hangings are outstanding'), then on to Watchet, turning inland for Williton

Still the railway buffs snapped pictures and marvelled at the old signs: 'Woodbines' and 'Pratt's Motor Spirit' and 'Craven "A" – Will Not Affect Your Throat'. I gathered that these signs excited memories of the old days, when there were hundreds of trains like this rattling through the English hills. At just the point where the railway buff's excitement was at its most feverish ('Crikey, Ralph, don't it take you back?'), and they began unpacking sandwiches from their lunch boxes and setting up their thermos flasks of hot tea, the train stopped at Bishop's Lydeard and everyone was ordered out. We were put on a bus and taken in silence to Taunton. So the West Somerset Railway was something like Butlin's holiday camp – lots of razzmatazz but not much substance. Somehow it was not the answer to the transport needs in that part of Somerset.

On the 14.21 to Weston-super-Mare a man named Wilf pinched a piece of cigarette paper into a little gutter and then dropped strings of tobacco into it. He licked it, and rolled it, and twisted one end – it looked like a firecracker – and then turned to me and said, 'Any idea what time we get to Bristol?'

I said I didn't know. 'I'm going to Weston-super-Mare.'

He set his cigarette on fire and then took it out of his mouth and said *sheesh*, expelling the smoke. 'Better you than me.'

And then, perhaps because he knew I was going to Weston-super-Mare, Wilf avoided me and showed no interest in conversations. Or perhaps my knapsack had put him off? And yet I found that wearing a knapsack was a kind of advertisement of willingness and more than anything it stirred the English passion for giving directions. Giving directions here was a form of conversation. But Wilf just smoked and sulked, and when I got off the train he shook his head, as if indicating that I was making a big mistake.

Under a dark collapsing sky, Weston-super-Mare looked bleak and residential and rather funless. Like Bexhill and Worthing and some other places on the south coast it was a large town with the soul of a suburb. And it was in such places that I regretted the endless roads of flat housefronts and pined for a little vulgarity or something vicious. In Weston-super-Mare I was directed to the 'Waxworks'.

On the way there, down the promenade, I saw that the wind had whipped the water into troughs. Even in this poor light there was a wonderful view – of Wales, of the two black islands, Flat Holm and Steep Holm, and at the end of the beach a curved loaf-shaped landspit called Brean Down. The beach was long and mostly empty and very grey, and it was flatter than the water. Parked on the sand, as in a cartoon of desert mirages, were a red Punch and Judy booth, and two yellow huts, one labelled *Tea-Stall* and the other *Shellfish Bar*. A flapping pennant said *Donkey Rides – 20 pence*. The few people on the beach lay heavily bundled-up on the sand, like war wounded on a beach-head. Their faces were tight with discomfort. A fat old lady with wild hair, wearing a winter coat but barefoot, stood and howled, '*Arthur!*' The donkeys stamped and shuddered in a little group, looking thoroughly baffled. And here on the promenade, hunched-over ladies with big handbags tipped their stoutness into the wind and breathed loudly through their teeth. Across the street at the Winter Gardens people were buying tickets for tonight's show, 'Cavalcade of Song'. Beyond the donkeys, beyond the fat barefoot lady and the Punch and Judy booth, a new island surfaced and sprouted trees. Then I saw it was a ship going by.

I was so unaccustomed to a place like Weston-super-Mare that with a little concentration I saw it in a surrealistic way. What were all these different things doing there? They had accumulated over the years, slowly, piling up like the tide-wrack, and because it had happened so slowly, no one questioned it or found it strange. And this was also why I could spend days in the seaside resorts, fascinated by the way the natural coast had been deranged and cluttered. It did not matter much whether a town was pretty or ugly – although ugly ones were often the most telling. The image of the tide-wrack was accurate in some places. Other towns were like river mouths where, mounting like silt, a century of pulverized civilization had been deposited, often floating from the darker interior of England.

At the 'Waxworks' there were models of movie stars and sports figures on the first floor, and on the next floor there were murderers. The top floor showed various torture chambers. In his essay 'The Decline of the English Murder', George Orwell wrote, 'If one examines the murders which have given the greatest amount of pleasure to the British public, the murders whose stories are known in their general outline to almost everyone and which have been made into novels and rehashed over and over again by the Sunday papers, one finds a fairly strong family resemblance running through the greater number of them.' The 'family resemblance' is a quiet respectable man who reluctantly decides on murder because it seems less disgraceful than, for example, being caught in adultery. The crime is meticulously planned and carried out, but there is a tiny slip and the murderer is caught. 'With this kind of background, a crime can have dramatic and even tragic qualities which make it memorable and excite pity for both victim and murderer.'

The murderers shown at the Waxworks suited this analysis, and they also illustrated the decline. Here was 'The Yorkshire Ripper' (Peter Sutcliffe) and 'The Black Panther' (Donald Neilson). The Waxworks was popular partly because the English were law-abiding, and no one knows more inner turmoil or is so susceptible to the romance of wrong-doing than the law-abiding person. But it was also popular for a much more straight-forward reason: in British law the criminal's privacy – and very often his identity – is strenuously protected. A man may murder and be caught and be found guilty without the public ever seeing his face. No picture of 'The Black Panther' had ever been published. So the revelation of the wax figures excited the watcher like certain kinds of pornography, and the gory tableaux on the top floor – a whipping, a beheading, 'The Death of A Thousand Cuts', had a similar interest for a person secretly starved of a bit of raw cruelty. It was like breaking a taboo – even though most of the murderers looked silly in lopsided wigs, and the torture victims looked like big shattered steak-and-kidney pies.

Perhaps there was also a connection between murderers and seaside resorts. Typically, the murderer committed his crime – wife-poisoning was the stereotype – and then went to a watering place like Weston-super-Mare, because it was easy to blend in with the ill-assorted types who were found there. And he was caught on the promenade. It was one of the paradoxes of English life that the most respectable-looking places and the most innocent circumstances excited the strongest suspicions of crime.

The next day I took the train to Bristol. I tried to interest myself in the St Paul's district, where race riots had broken out the year before. There were gutted buildings and some still stank of burned mattresses, but otherwise it seemed an ordinary slum. I spoke to an Indian sociologist, Dr Barot, who said that the West Indian household had been very authoritarian. In the course of a generation or two the parents' authority had been weakened and the children had stopped submitting. In fact, the children had become British; but there was no work, there was anger and aimlessness, and very few bothered to study at the higher levels Only a handful of blacks attended Bristol University.

'I could introduce you to some really angry blacks,' a man named Fletcher said at my Bristol boarding house.

But then the weather turned fine again and I decided that, instructive though it would be to meet some really angry blacks in Bristol, it had not been my intention on this coastal jaunt to invite gloom. In a general sort of way, I knew why they were angry. So I declined the introduction and crossed the River Severn which at that point was also the sea.

10

The 16.28 to Tenby

'It's that bubble car over there,' Mr Crabb the guard said at
Temple Meads Station in Bristol. He pointed to a three-car train,
the sort I had been seeing on branch lines. I was now headed
for Cardiff. A man named Hicks on this train said that he could
remember the days when the Red Dragon Express ran to Cardiff
– and here we were, he said, on this manky little train! I did
not encourage him. I liked these trains, because it was possible
to sit behind the driver in the first coach and look straight out
of the front window at the tracks ahead. And it was always
interesting to watch the driver's busy hands on the controls.

'We're pushing towards Stanley,' Mr Hicks said.

He meant in the Falkland Islands. He was reading, over my
shoulder, the Falklands news in my *Times*. I asked his opinion
of the war.

He said, 'We have to do it. Our land's been taken. The Argies
have to be stopped. They can't get away with it.' He looked out
of the window and grunted. 'That's how Hitler got started!'

The train was rolling. On that line, you did not leave Bristol
until you left England, because its suburbs straggled all the way
to the Severn Tunnel, ten miles of housing estates and factories.
As in other parts of England, the newer industrial buildings
looked frail and temporary.

The tunnel lasted a minute or so and then we were travelling
in a deep ditch. But I knew from the brown stones of the ditch
walls and the way they were cut and pointed, that we must be
in Wales, although I could not see anything but a strip of blue
sky and these walls. This was confirmed at the next stop,
Cyfforded Twnel Hafren, Severn Tunnel Junction.

We surfaced in Wales and at once the landscape looked

different: meadows and crooked hills and all the hawthorns in bloom. The factories were distant smudges. I had travelled enough in the past month to know that it was possible to tell which part of England I was in by the way the fields were marked – whether by a wall or a hedge or a fence, and what kind. The white hawthorns had been planted at the boundaries of every field, in a way I had never seen before: we were in another country. It was in fact a nation of like-minded people. The bilingual signs (*Welcome Croeso*) were as unnecessary as the road signs in Canada, but like Canada's they served a political purpose – a cheap sop tossed to the nationalists.

We passed a tumble-down farm, a small wood-framed factory, a row of poplars, some sheep. Now I understood why the Welsh had taken to Patagonia. I saw more farms, small and poor, but rural poverty always looked to me more bearable than the forms that poverty took in a city. Poverty brought people low, and pushed them into the past. In the countryside this merely meant farming in a cruder way; poor city people had to go still farther back and become scavengers in order to survive.

Newport rose up on the left, a power station and the rolling mills and furnaces of the doomed Llanwern Steelworks. The Victorian house-fronts looked slightly foppish, with multi-coloured bricks and stripes. Sometimes Wales looked like another country, and at other times it seemed like an earlier version of England – upright and antique and dusty and church-going, with all the colour schemes wrong.

There were preparations afoot in Cardiff for the Pope's visit. He was due in three days: an altar had been erected and a 'mass site' prepared up at Pontcanna Park in Llandaff, near the old Cathedral ('Cromwell's soldiers used the nave as a tavern and post office, and the font as a pig trough, and burnt the cathedral's books at a formal ceremony at Cardiff Castle'). No Pope had ever visited Wales.

In Cardiff, on Queen Street, Mrs Prichard said, 'So the Pope's staying with you, Doris?'

'Yes? Oh, well, never mind,' Doris said. 'I'll make him comfortable.'

'He'll want looking after,' Mrs Prichard went on, still not smiling. 'He's got a healthy appetite, that one, all the travelling.'

'I'll tell the milkman to leave me an extra pint,' Doris said. 'The Pope's stopping upstairs, I'll say.'

'You'll want more than an extra pint of milk! I should buy some gammon and cabbage. He's Polish, Doris.'

As soon as I saw it, I wanted to leave Cardiff. In any case, it was seldom my intention to linger in the large cities. In Britain they were cavernous and intimidating, like the fortresses they had once been. They seemed to have heavy eyebrows. They were not for walkers. They were full of indoor miseries that made me impatient. Their buildings were blackened and their people wary of my questions. I never got lost in the countryside, but these cities could make me feel as if I was drowning. It could take a day or two to find out how to leave these places. They were always encumbered with ruins. Cardiff was no place for a pedestrian like me.

My remedy, walking to Barry Island, did not work. It was a peninsula, but even so it was unreachable on foot. There were no paths here, only the mazy roads of South Glamorgan, packed solid with houses. In Grangetown, I thought: They really do look like towns from years ago, living on in old-fashioned, semi-respectable decrepitude. I walked on to Cogan, an awful-looking place. Wales was visibly poorer than England but I found it to be much better-natured.

At Cadoxton I found a railway station and went the rest of the way on the branch line, sitting behind the driver. There were signs painted on the slates of house roofs. They were meant to be seen from the train and the letters were two-feet high. GOD IS LOVE, one said, and another one, CHRIST DIED FOR THE UNGODLY. We passed several acres of rusty locomotives – a sort of graveyard for steam engines – and then came to Barry Island. Half of it was a Butlin's camp, and the rest a small seafront with severe amusements.

I sat on the front, near a stall selling whelks and jellied eels, listening to the flap of the Butlin's flags and wondering what to do next. There were no hotels in this place! It was for day-trippers, miners mostly, who rode out of the valleys for one frantic day. But now miners earned good salaries and were able to go further afield. So Barry Island had its holiday camp and its deserted arcades. I made a note: *Not much like Weston-super-Mare*

– because Weston-super-Mare was twelve miles away, across the bay.

I studied my map and decided to go to Llanelli. My train took me past Bridgend and Port Talbot and Neath. The landscape was industrial and yet was motionless and might have been dead. It was also a pebbledash wilderness of two-storey houses, great chains and terraces of them, arranged on narrow streets, striping the hills. It was nineteenth-century order, the workers' barracks, with rougher hills one range away – the Vale of Glamorgan and then into West Glamorgan. I changed trains in Swansea. Swansea was a vast cankered valley of sorrowful houses and grey churches and shut-down factories. I thought: No wonder the Welsh are religious! In South Wales, industry had burned and cleared the landscape and stacked it with sooty buildings. But most of the industries had failed – or looked moribund – and I could not look out of the train window without thinking of gangrene.

Llanelli had looked promising on the map. It was in the south-west corner of Dyfed, on the estuary of the Loughor river. I walked from the station to the docks. The town was musty-smelling and dull, and made of decayed bricks. My map had misled me. I wanted to leave, but first I wanted to buy a guide-book to Wales in order to avoid such mistakes in the future.

I passed a store with textbooks in the window. Dead flies lay on their sides on the book covers; they had not been swatted, but had simply starved; they seemed asleep. There were shelves in this bookstore, but not many books. There was no sales person. A husky voice came from behind a beaded curtain.

'In here.'

I went in. A man was whispering into a telephone. He paid no attention to me. There were plenty of books in here. On the covers were pictures of naked people. The room smelled of cheap paper and ink. The magazines were in cellophane wrappers. They showed breasts and rubber underwear, and there were children on some of them. The titles suggested that the naked tots were violated inside. No guide-books here, but as this pornography shop was Welsh the door had a bell that went *bing-bong*! in a cheery way as I left.

Welsh politeness was soft-hearted and smiling. Even Llanelli's Skinheads were well-behaved, and the youths with swastikas on their leather jackets, and bleached hair and earrings, or green hair and T-shirts saying *Anarchy* – even they seemed sweet-natured. And how amazing that the millions of Welsh, who shared about a dozen surnames, were the opposite of anonymous. They were conspicuous individuals and at a personal level tried hard to please. 'You're a gentleman!' one man would cry to another, greeting him on the street.

At Jenkins the Bakers ('Every bite – pure delight') I saw a strawberry tart with clotted cream on top. Were they fresh strawberries?

'Oh, yes, fresh this morning,' Mrs Jenkins said.

I asked for one.

'But they're thirty pence, darling,' Mrs Jenkins said, warning me and not moving. She expected me to tell her to forget it. She was on my side in the most humane way, and gave me a commiserating smile, as if to say: It's a shocking amount of money for a strawberry tart!

When I bought two she seemed surprised. It must have been my knapsack and my vagabond demeanour. I went around the corner and stuffed them into my mouth.

'Good morning – I mean, good evening!' Mr Maddocks the Stationmaster said at Llanelli Station. 'I knew I'd get it right in the end. It's patience you want!'

The rest of the people on the platform were speaking Welsh, but on seeing the train draw in – perhaps it was the excitement – they lapsed into English.

This was the 16.28 to Tenby. We slid out of Llanelli, past the tiny cottages and the brick houses. The average price of these houses was £15,000 and quite a few cost less than £10,000. I got this information from the *Llanelli Star*. On another page some cars were being advertised for £7,000.

Across the yellow-brown puddles of the Llanrhidian Sands was the lovely Gower Peninsula. We passed Burry Port and Kidwelly – there were rolling hills on one side and the muddy foreshore of the Gwendraeth estuary on the other. Then up the Tywi river to Carmarthen, which had a mundane grandeur – it needed either more ruins, or fewer. After Carmarthen, the real countryside began, the first I had seen in South Wales since crossing the Severn. The hills were green and lumpish and the valleys tangled with short leafy trees, some standing as hedges and boundaries and others in jumbled woods. I always expected to see small ponies in this landscape, they would have suited it. The land pattern and the foliage were new to me and I liked the wildness. It looked wild from neglect, like a place that had once been neat but was now overgrown. It had an untrimmed charm – the grass too long, the boughs drooping, like the shaggy imagery in a Dylan Thomas poem. Thomas had lived four miles south of this railway line, at Laugharne on the River Taf.

Narberth was a small white iron-girt station in a green glade of whirling gnats, a beautiful place for the train to stop in the late afternoon sun, and I felt a bit sad when we pulled out; and then sunset at Saundersfoot – I kept saying that phrase to myself – and Tenby, a town on a high cliff with more cliffs around it and boulder islands in its bay. It looked perfect. It was the loveliest town I had seen so far. I found a boarding house with a view of the harbour and made no plans to leave.

The elegant houses of Tenby standing tall on the cliff reminded me of beautifully bound books arranged on a high shelf; their bow windows had the curvature of book spines. The town was elevated on a promontory, and so the sea on three sides gave its light a penetrating purity that reached the market square, and fortified the air with the tang of ocean-washed rocks. It was odd that a place so pretty should also be so restful, and yet that was the case. But Tenby was more than pretty. It was so picturesque it looked like a watercolour of itself.

It had not been preserved by the fastidious tyrants who so often took over British villages, the new class who moved in and gutted the houses, and then, after restoring the thatched roofs and mullioned windows, hid a chromium kitchen in the inglenook that ran on microchips. Such people could make a place so picturesque it was uninhabitable. Tenby had been maintained, and it had mellowed; it was still sturdy, and I was glad I had found it. But it was the sort of place which denied a sense of triumph to the person who secretly felt he had discovered it – because its gracefulness was well known, it had been painted and praised, it was old even in Tudor times, and it had produced Augustus John (who wrote about Tenby in his autobiography

Chiaroscuro) as well as the inventor of the equal sign (=) in mathematics, Robert Recorde. But, then, there were no secret places in Britain that I had seen, there were only forgotten places, and places that were being buried or changed by our harsh century.

Tenby had been spared, and it was the more pleasing for being rather quiet and empty. I walked around dreamily. For the first time since I had set out on this trip I felt that a watering place was fulfilling its purpose – calming me, soothing me, making me want to snore over a book on a veranda with a sea-view.

'This place is a madhouse in the summer,' a publican named Nuttgens told me. 'It's chock-a-block. Pavements full of tourists, roads full of cars. You can't move! And there's usually a tail-back all the way to Saundersfoot –'

It was hard to tell whether he was boasting or complaining, but in any case I did not want to imagine Tenby being trampled. I liked to think of it always like this, quietly lived in, with book-shelf terraces of houses and twisty streets and that marvellous gauzy light.

Nuttgens said, 'Every business here is owned by an Englishman.' He himself was from Birmingham. 'And all the employees are Welsh.'

I asked him why this was so.

He tapped the side of his nose with his finger, suggesting that the English were cleverer.

Other English people in Tenby also told me this, but it was not so. My landlady was Welsh, the pub across the street was owned by a Welshman, and there were Welsh names everywhere on shop signs. And yet it was true that part of Tenby's appeal was that its English elegance had been softened by Welsh charm, and it had the faintly asymmetrical look one often sees in the most dignified former colonies.

There was a coastal path which went from Tenby to St Dog-maels, a hundred and seventy miles, around the shore of Pembrokeshire. I walked the few miles to Old Castle Head – the rocks at the shore had the look of lions' paws – and because I hated retracing my steps, I walked on to the nearest railway station and took the branch line to Pembroke Dock. This station was

Manorbier Newton. We passed Hodgeston ('the church chancel contains a double piscina and mutilated triple sedilia') and then strange events overtook the train. Or perhaps not strange but merely old-fashioned.

The train came to a sign at a road, saying, *STOP: Open Crossing Gates Before Proceeding*, and it stopped. The uniformed man who was both guard and ticket-collector got out and swung the gates open wide enough so that they blocked the little motor road and unblocked the railway tracks. Then the train shuddered and the birds sang and the train moved across the road. The guard closed the gates, latched them, boarded the train, and we resumed our journey through meadows and farms and low woods.

There was another sign: *STOP: Whistle Before Proceeding* The train obeyed — its whistle was a two-note trumpet blast — and we crossed the road. It was a hot afternoon, and the country roads smelled of warm tar and looked like dusty liquorice; and we stopped at short platforms, halts in the middle of farms, and at Lamphey in a pasture, the cow parsley lazily brushing the sides of the train.

When most of the rural branch lines were closed in 1964, this line was spared, and it continued to be spared because it carried people to the ferry which travelled from Pembroke to Cork, in the Republic of Ireland, or 'Error' as some Welshmen called it.

We pulled quietly into Pembroke. There were only seven of us on the train — it was not a ferry day. Pembroke seemed a very ordinary town, but had a grand castle. Across the harbour was Milford Haven ('described by Lord Nelson as the best natural harbour in the world'), which was densely and blackly industrial, with its tanks and refineries and its oil-cracking plant. Why were the most prosperous places the ugliest?

I asked Mr Peevey the Stationmaster the way to Haverford-west. It seemed there was no train that day, but there was a bus As he explained where the bus stop was his voice grew faint, and then he said, 'Listen. What's that?'

He squinted across the railway platform and turned his head, inclining his ears and spreading out his fingers, listening in a tense sort of way.

'Yes,' Mr Peevey said after a moment. 'Look.'

I did not see anything. I had not heard anything Mr Peevey

was smiling, and he looked at his watch – a Stationmaster's instinctive reflex, I supposed. He nodded at the air.

Then I saw the specks, thousands of them, just above the ground, like a veil descending through the air. It made me slightly dizzy, their motion, their numbers; it was like seeing spots.

'Bugs,' I said.

'Bees,' Mr Peevey said. 'They're swarming.'

They were darkly gathering, a large fuzzy gust of them approaching the platform.

Mr Peevey was not worried. 'My grandfather kept bees,' he said calmly. 'He could stir them around and get the honey and what-not. He never got stung. You get immune to bee stings. Most bee keepers are immune.'

'I suppose they could be dangerous?' I indicated the swarm.

'Kill you,' Mr Peevey said. 'That's how dangerous.'

He smiled again, marvelling – as people do – at murderous Nature.

'If you start flaking around, look you, that lot will bite you.' He giggled a little, in amazement rather than malice. 'You could be stung to death!'

They were great Bible readers, these Welsh people, and I was sure he was thinking of the text, *O death, where is thy sting?*

'I'd take the long way to the bus stop if I were you,' Mr Peevey said.

On the bus to Haverfordwest – the bus went slowly, and always down country lanes – I decided what it was that bothered me about the Welsh villages and towns. There was only one kind of cottage in the villages, and it was not a particularly pretty style; there was only one kind of terrace in the towns, and it was mournfully flat. They were one note, one colour, one class, and in some places every house was identical, and equally ugly. This in itself was not remarkable – such towns had counterparts in the United States – but these Welsh ones were entirely surrounded by woods and hills and fields, and so they looked sullen, with faces averted from the green hills.

Some towns can be transformed and given a memorable character by a chance encounter. And then it is your secret – you alone are the witness. I had this experience in Haverfordwest. Three people stood in front of a fruit shop. An old woman was using sign language to speak – she was flapping her hands. A young woman was translating this sign language into spoken Welsh to an old man with a dog. The man replied to the gesticulating dumb woman in Welsh. It was all Welsh and flying hands, and finally the old man took out a beaded purse and squeezed it open. He removed a pound note that had been folded into the size of a postage stamp – he unfolded it (this was like origami) and handed it to the old woman. She thanked him in sign language: this was translated into Welsh. The man replied in Welsh. The woman kissed the pound note and went away with the younger woman.

I still lingered, wondering.

The old man jerked his dog's leash. He said, 'Come on, Jasper!'

After all that, he spoke to his dog in English!

This incident coloured my feelings for Haverfordwest much more than if I had spent my time scrutinizing the voided lozenges on the church crests or marching up to Wiston and reminiscing myself into a stupor over Wizo the Fleming.

From here to Fishguard the land was green and smooth, occasionally erupting into rocky heaps, like the great hill of boulders at Wolf's Castle. Looking north from the village of Letterston, the rocky heaps in the distance were like fortresses and castle ruins. The Welsh landscape was the landscape of legend slightly out of focus, full of blurred castles and giants, and dragons that were actually cliffs. The coast of Fishguard was like that, stonier and bleaker and more ragged than I had seen in South Pembrokeshire. The stonework on some cottages was as patchy and colourful as a quilted blanket.

It was twenty-eight miles from Fishguard to St Dogmaels on the coastal path. I thought it would be a hard day's walk, but it took almost two, because of the steepness and the river detours. As I approached the end of it I met two fishermen, both named Jones, who told me with a kind of urgency that most *nights* they went out fishing for *salmon*, which they caught with *nets* slung out from *coracles*, and what did I think of *that*? I asked them how big the salmon were and what they got a pound. They were ten pounders, worth two quid a pound.

These men directed me to a hotel in Cardigan, up the River Teifi, where they fished. Perhaps they did not like my face. It was a very bad hotel, and I had a very strange encounter there – and not just very strange, but . . .

First I had to face Cardigan. Cardigan was poor, a place of high unemployment and hard-up people. The poverty was not immediately obvious; but with a growing sense of unease I began to notice that something was wrong. It was a frailty and un-certainty: things were very quiet – and then I studied the clothes, the houses, the food, the signs, the faces; and I saw that it was simple, they were poor.

'And the trouble with these depressed areas in Wales,' a nationalist named Humphries told me, 'is that they get a lot of cranks.'

What did he mean by cranks?

'Food cranks, like,' he said.

I said I inclined towards vegetarianism myself, and had even stopped smoking.

'And lesbians,' he said, in a challenging way. 'They paint pictures and have exhibitions in the Cardigan Town Hall.'

I said that seemed fairly harmless.

'Pictures of,' he swallowed, 'things I wouldn't mention.'

I went to the town hall. It was an exhibition of feminist paintings – mainly scenes of childbirth done in a simple spattery way. The people running the exhibition were grave bearded men and cape-wearing women; they had an affected gypsyish look, and were rather young. But I saw what Humphries meant by cranks: he meant English people.

Cardigan was Welsh-speaking Wales, so was North Pembroke-shire, so was the west coast, parts of Dyfed and Gwynedd. The limits of Wales spoke Welsh. This was the Celtic fringe, spiritual home of the Plaid Cymru Party, the nationalists, and this was also where English-owned cottages were burned down. Sixty cottages had been put to the torch in the past three years.

I wondered whether the Welsh could be explained in terms of being bilingual, which is so often a form of schizophrenia, allowing a person to hold two contradictory opinions in his head at once, because his opinions remain untranslated. The Welsh had that mildly stunned and slap-happy personality that I associated with people for whom speaking two languages was a serious handicap. It made them profligate with language, it made them inexact, it had turned them into singers – well, that was no bad thing, they said. I did not think it was a question of good or bad, but only a kind of confusion.

The Welsh stared in a friendly way. It could be disconcerting. The English never stared unless they were very angry (an English stare is like the Evil Eye) or wanted to score a debating point. The Welsh were like members of a family, but a large suspicious family. They certainly did have common characteristics, and they were more a nation than I had ever imagined. Sometimes it seemed to me that there was no such thing as English culture in a definable way. But Welshness was palpable, it was chattery and backward-looking. It surprised me that the Welsh had not burned down more cottages, the family feeling ran so strong.

'And they killed the commander,' a Court Clerk named Davies told me, describing a Falklands battle that had just been fought. Then Davies winced and said, 'His name was Jones.'

He let this sink in. He was moved by it. The Argies had killed one of their own Joneses! I had the impression that if the soldier's name had been Brown it would have made less of an impression.

And Marion Lewis at a public house in St Dogmaels said, 'They burn these cottages, the Plaid Cymru,' and she smacked her lips. 'Some of the chaps are very tough, you know. That's what I don't understand – there are still so many English cottages! The chaps do try, but they haven't been successful.'

She seemed a bit sorry there hadn't been more arson attacks.

I was bemused by the Welsh intonation. It was a whining, West Indian lilt, and it could be very soft and lisping, with slushy throat-clearings. It was full of interesting words. Some like *toiledau* and *brecwyst*, meaning 'toilet' and 'breakfast', did not appear to be ancient. And some were grunts, like the place-names Plwmp and Mwnt. But *corn* was the Welsh for horn and was obviously from Latin, and so was *cwn* (dog) and *bont* (bridge), and the word for church was *eglwys*, the same word as the French *église* and with the same pronunciation. I wondered if it was my imagination that suggested that, given the whine and squeak, and the rising querying tone on most words, it was hard to express anger in Welsh. I wanted to see someone lose his temper in Welsh, but I never did.

*

My strange encounter took place at the Hotel Harlech, a dismal semi-ruin not far from the silted-up river. It had been closed for years, and it smelled that way, of mice and unwashed clothes. The smell of rags is like the smell of dead men anyway, but this was compounded with the smells of dirt and wood-smoke and the slow river. I knew as soon as I checked in that it was a mistake. I was shown to my room by a sulking girl of fifteen, who had a fat pouty face and a pot belly.

'It seems a little quiet,' I said.

Gwen said, 'You're the only guest.'

'In the whole hotel?'

'In the whole hotel.'

My bed smelled, too, as though it had been slept in – just slept in recently, someone having crawled out a little while ago, leaving it warm and disgusting.

The owner of the Harlech was a winking woman with a husky laugh, named Reeny. She kept a purse in the cleavage between her breasts, she smoked while she was eating, she talked about her boyfriend – 'My boyfriend's been all around the world on ships.' Reeny's boyfriend was a pale unshaven man of fifty who limped through the hotel, his shirt-tails out, groaning because he could never find his hairbrush. His name was Lloyd, and he was balding. Lloyd seldom spoke to me, but Reeny was irrepressible, always urging me to come down to the bar for a drink.

The bar was a darkened room with torn curtains and a simple table in the centre. There were usually two tattooed youths and two old men at the table, drinking beer with Lloyd. Reeny acted as barmaid, using a tin tray. It was she who changed the records: the music was loud and terrible, but the men had no conversation, and they looked haggard and even rather ill.

The unexpected thing was that Reeny was very cheerful and hospitable. The hotel was dirty and her food unspeakable and the dining room smelled of urine, but Reeny was kind, and she loved to talk, and she spoke of improving the hotel; and she knew that Lloyd was a complaining old fake. Relax, enjoy yourself, have another helping, Reeny said.

She had the right spirit, but the hotel was a mess. 'This is Paul – he's from America,' Reeny said, and winked at me. She was proud of me. That thought made me very gloomy.

One night she introduced me to Ellie. She was red-eyed and very fat and had a gravelly voice; she was somewhat toothless and freckled; she came from Swansea. 'Aye,' she said. 'Swansea's a bloody bog.' Ellie was drunk – and she was deaf in the way drunks often are. Reeny was talking about America, but Ellie was still mumbling about Swansea.

'At least we're not tight,' Ellie said. 'Aye, we're careful, but the Cardies are tight.'

'That's us,' Reeny said. 'Cardies, from Cardigan. Aye, we're tighter than the Scots.'

Ellie screwed up her face to show how tight the Cardies were, then she demanded to know why I was not drunk, and she appealed to the silent haggard men, who stared back at her with dull damp eyes. Ellie was wearing a baggy grey sweater. She finished her pint of beer and then wiped her hands on her sweater.

'What do you think of the Cardies?' she said.

'Delightful,' I said. But I thought: *Savages*.

At midnight they were still drinking.

'I'm going upstairs,' I said. 'But I don't have a key.'

'None of the rooms have locks,' Reeny said, 'that's why there are no keys. See?'

Ellie said, 'Aarrgh, it's a quiet place, Reen!'

'Too bloody quiet, I say,' Reeny said. 'We have to drive to Saundersfoot for a little night life.'

Saundersfoot was thirty-three miles away.

'What is it, Lloyd?' Reeny said.

Lloyd had been grinning.

He said, 'He looks worried,' meaning me.

'I'm not worried,' I said.

This always sounds to me a worried man's protest. I stood there trying to smile. The four local men at the table merely stared back with their haggard faces.

'There's no locks in this place,' Lloyd said, with pleasure.

Then Reeny screeched, 'We won't rob you or rape you!'

She said it so loudly it was a few seconds before I could take it in. She was vivacious but ugly.

I recovered and said, 'What a shame. I was looking forward to one or the other.'

Reeny howled at this.

In the sour bed, I could hear rock music coming from the bar, and sometimes shouts. But I was so tired I dropped off to sleep, and I dreamed of Cape Cod. I was with my cousin and saying to her, 'Why do people go home so early? This is the only good place in the world. I suppose they're worried about traffic. I'd never leave –'

Then something tore. It was a ripping sound in the room. I sat up and saw a tousled head. I thought it was a man. It was a man's rough face, a squashed nose, a crooked mouth. I recognized the freckles and the red eyes. It was Ellie.

I said, 'What are you doing?'

She was crouching so near to the bed I could not see her body. The ripping sound came again – a zipper on my knapsack. Ellie was slightly turned away from me. She did not move. When I saw that it was Ellie and not a man, I relaxed – and I knew that my wallet and money were in my leather jacket, hanging on a hook across the room.

She said, 'Where am I?'

'You're in my room.'

She said, turning to me, 'What are you doing here?'

'This is my room!'

Her questions had been drowsy in a theatrical way. She was still crouching near my knapsack. She was breathing hard.

I said, 'Leave that thing alone.'

'Aarrgh,' she groaned, and plumped her knees against the floor. I wanted her to go away.

I said, 'I'm trying to sleep.' Why was I being so polite?

She groaned again, a more convincing groan than the last one, and she said, 'Where have I left my clothes?'

And she stood up. She was a big woman with big jolting breasts, and freckles on them. She was, I saw, completely naked.

'Close your eyes,' she said, and stepped closer.

I said, 'It's five in the morning, for God's sake.'

The sun had just struck the curtains

'Aarrgh, I'm sick,' she said. 'Move over.'

I said, 'You don't have any clothes on.'

'You can close your eyes,' she said.

I said, 'What were you doing to my knapsack?'

'Looking for me clothes,' she said.

I said in a pleading way, 'Give me a break, will you?'

'Don't look at me nakedness,' she said.

'I'm going to close my eyes,' I said, 'and when I open them I don't want to see you in this room.'

Her naked flesh went flap-flap like a rubber raincoat as she tramped across the hard floor. I heard her go, she pulled the door shut, and then I checked to see my money was safe and my knapsack unviolated. The zippers were open, but nothing was gone. I remembered what Reeny had screamed at me: *We won't rob you or rape you!*

At breakfast, Reeny said, 'I've not been up at this hour for ten year! Look, it's almost half-eight!'

Reeny had a miserable cough and her eyes were sooty with mascara. Her Welsh accent was stronger this morning, too.

I told her about Ellie.

She said, 'Aye, is that so? I'll pull her leg about that! Aye, that is funny.'

An old woman came to the door. She was unsteady, she peered in. Reeny asked her what she wanted. She said she wanted a pint of beer.

'It's half-eight in the morning!' Reeny said.

'A half a pint, then,' the old woman said.

'And it's Sunday!' Reeny said. She turned to me and said, 'We're dry on a Sunday around here. That's why it's so quiet. But you can get a drink at St Dogmaels.'

The woman looked pathetic. She said that in the coming referendum she would certainly vote for a change in the licensing law. She was not angry, but had that aged beaten look that passes for patience.

'Oh, heavens,' Reeny said. 'What shall I do, Paul? You tell me.'

I said to the old woman, 'Have a cup of tea.'

'The police have been after me,' Reeny said. 'They're always looking in.' Reeny walked to the cupboard. 'I could lose my licence.' She took out a bottle of beer and poured it. 'These coppers have no bloody mercy.' The glass was full. 'Forty-five pence,' she said.

The woman drank that and then bought two more bottles. She paid and left, without another word. She had taken no pleasure in the drink and there was no satisfaction in having wheedled the beer out of Reeny on a dry day in Cardigan – in fact, she had not wheedled, but had merely stood there gaping in a paralysed way.

I said, 'It's a hell of a breakfast – beer.'

'She's an alcoholic,' Reeny said. 'She's thirty-seven. Doesn't look it, does she? Take me, I'm thirty-three and no one believes it. My boyfriend says I've got the figure of a girl of twenty. You're not going, are you?'

11

The 10.32 to Criccieth

There was no good coastal path north of Cardigan – all the farms and fields were jammed against the cliff edge – but by scaring cows and climbing stone walls I managed a few miles. Then I came to Aberporth and could go no farther. For the next five miles or more it was an army rocket range, and the rockets were booming. The British were fighting a war, after all – 'this Falklands business'. Over two hundred and fifty men had died just the day before in the battle for a small sheep station at Goose Green. Most of the dead were Argentines, killed by British paratroopers in fury after word got out that a mock surrender with a white flag by an Argentine patrol had in fact been an ambush. '*Never Trust an Argie!*' the headline in the *Sun* said. Was this why the rockets were exploding at Aberporth?

It was true that much of the British coast was empty and practically anybody's; yet the rest was impossible. Things that were dangerous (like nuclear power stations), or that stank (like sewage farms), were shoved on to the coast. They were safer that way and out of sight. The coast was regarded as a natural home for oil refineries and gas storage tanks, and there was more rubbish on the coast than in any inland dump. The coast was where you got rid of things: they were borne away and lost in the deep sinkhole of the sea. The coast had more than its fair share of car parks and junkyards; and out of an ancient islanders' fear of invasion – of alien peoples plaguing her shores – the British had over-fortified their coast with military installations, gun emplacements and radar dishes of the sort I had seen in Dungeness and Kimmeridge. And as if that weren't enough they also had American missile bases and squads of American marines in various coves. These places looked as though they were expecting another onslaught of rapacious Danes or shield-biting berserkers. Of course, the coast was perfect for practising with machine guns or even bombs and cannons. Traditionally, the sea was safe to shoot at. Here at Aberporth it was rockets, and the incautious walker risked being blown up or arrested as a spy.

I turned back and stumbled up the grassy hill to the coast road. The road was narrow and the speeding cars made it dangerous – just room enough for two lines of traffic. I had to lean against the nettles on the bank to let the cars pass. I walked to Synod Inn, and when I became bored with waiting for a bus, I hitched. With my knapsack and leather jacket and the Ordnance Survey map in my hand, and needing a haircut, I looked like a hitch-hiker – with an unhurried, money-saving, ready-for-anything expression. I got rides easily, with farmers who were only going a quarter of a mile, and with men making deliveries, or heading for work. They usually said, 'And how are you liking Wales?'

Emrys Morgan, a carpenter, with a ripsaw in his back seat, said, 'Aw, the Englishman is a very secretive man. His attitude is, "I look after myself and God looks after all."'

I remarked that the Welsh I had met were very polite.

'Very polite are the Welsh,' Mr Morgan said. 'And much more polite than the English. We're different stock, with a different tradition. We're European Celts and they're Saxons and Normans.'

Huw Jones took me to Aberaeron in his old grey Singer Gazelle.

'This is where the Welsh left for Patagonia,' he said.

'I've been there.'

'Aberaeron?'

'Patagonia,' I said.

Aberaeron was an unusually neat and orderly town of Nash terraces and plain brown houses, and on some streets there were lovely Georgian houses on the left and pebble-dash council houses on the right.

'Most people in Wales are Labour Party supporters, not Welsh Nationalists,' another Jones told me. This Jones was a lawyer – a barrister. He said the Labour Party had a stranglehold on South Wales especially. 'They could put a bloody donkey up for parliament in South Wales, and if they said he was Labour he'd get in.'

We were riding up to Aberystwyth. The coast here was very

sloping – the green cliffs slanted down towards the sea. In the little bays and near villages there were always acres of orange tents and caravans.

'These people come down from Birmingham and the Midlands,' the lawyer Jones said, 'and they pitch their little tents. They look around and decide they like it. So they see a farmer. Has he got a cottage for sale? He probably does – farmers are having a very tough time, not enough work for their labourers. He sells the cottage. They're very cheap. It's a second home for these people. They just come and go as they please. Those are the people whose cottages are burned by the nationalists.'

I said, 'Wouldn't it be simpler to burn the tents?'

He laughed at this. So far I had not met anyone in Wales who objected to the burning of English-owned cottages, and some people seemed to find it considerate and humane, since they were always burned when the owners were away.

Welshness was also a look of orderly clutter, and Aberystwyth typified it – houses everywhere, though always attached to streets; the cliffs obliterated with cottages, but tidy cottages; a canyon of flat-faced and barren buildings on the seafront, but green mountains just behind. I stayed in a guest-house, Eluned Williams, Prop. 'You're not going?' she would say each morning after breakfast. Business was bad. But I wasn't going. I was doing my laundry. I was off to the beach ('well adapted for bathing, and yields cornelians, agates and other pebbles') to look at the tar-stained stones. I was browsing and sometimes buying in the antique shops – I bought an old walking stick which had a tiger's tooth for a handle. I was looking at the book stores – the University College of Wales gave Aberystwyth its studious air, but the Act of Parliament (1967) had made Welsh equal in importance to English and meant that every municipal and university meeting was twice as long, since they were conducted in both languages. One day there was a Peace March in Aberystwyth. There were signs in Chinese characters, and Buddhist monks, and adults and children, protesting against the building of a nuclear installation in Wales at Brawdy. 'Join us,' a man said to me. I was wearing my knapsack. I shook my head. 'Can't,' I said, 'I'm an alien.' That was the day I was doing my laundry. I was in my bathing suit, and every other article of clothing I owned was in my knapsack, to be washed.

I took the narrow gauge railway to the Devil's Bridge, through the Rheidol Valley, and the deep gorge of the Mynach. It was a toy train, and full of pipe-stuffing railway buffs and day-trippers. And there were rowdies, boys 'in care', I was told, abandoned by their parents, patronized by the state; they were pale tattooed thirteen-year-olds smoking cigarettes and saying, 'It's fulla fucken trees,' where William Wordsworth in another mood had written,

> There I seem to stand,
> As in life's morn; permitted to behold
> From the dread chasm, woods climbing above woods,
> In pomp that fades not; everlasting snows;
> And skies that ne'er relinquish their repose . . .

And there were parents, too. I treasured their angry remarks:

'Oh, *God*, Roger, can't you see he's just desperately tired!'

The child in question was spitting and kicking and crying, a furious little weevil who did not know where he was and perhaps thought, in his animal way, that he was going to die here.

And one mother, looking at the tormented face of her wet baby, grew very cold and sarcastic.

'Someone's going to have a warm bottom in a minute!' she said.

The baby groaned like a starving monkey and tensed its fingers, indicating fear and frustration.

The Welsh people on the train stared at this behaviour and thought: The English!

Ever since Tenby I had noticed an alteration in the light, a softness and a clarity that came from a higher sky. It must have been the Atlantic: certainly I had the impression of an ocean of light, and it was not the harsh daytime sun of the tropics, or the usual greyness of the industrialized temperate zone. Daylight in England often lay dustily overhead like a shroud. The cool light in west Wales came steadily from every direction except from the sun. It was especially strong as a force rising out of the distance and reaching earth again in a purer way as a reflection from the sky. The sunsets in Aberystwyth were vast, full of battle flames, never seeming to move and yet always in motion. It was a severe shore, and those houses looked harsh, but the Welsh light – the immense cold mirror of the Atlantic – made it gleam, and made its sadness visible.

One evening strolling on the front at Aberystwyth I remembered that, just a year before, I had stopped smoking my pipe. I had not had a smoke of anything for a year. To celebrate I bought a cigar, but Mrs Williams wouldn't let me smoke it at her house ('No one has ever smoked at "Y Wyddfa"' – the name of her house – 'and I don't think I could stand it if they did'), so I took it out to the front and set it on fire and smoked it until there was only an inch of a butt left, which I chucked into Cardigan Bay.

I took a two-coach branch-line train out of Aberystwyth, up the west side of the Rheidol Valley and around the bushy hills. The countryside here was tumbledown and beautiful. Dolybont was an old village of rough stone cottages and a squat church and thick hedges, and with his head out of his bedroom window a white-haired man was reprimanding his dog in Welsh.

The train climbed and paused. There were fifteen of us on it, and two got off. Then it picked up speed on a slope, and soon it was racing out of the hills, doing sixty or more, quite a speed for a little country railway train with squeaky wheels. We went on, tearing past the buttercups. We entered the plain that lay between the sea and the mountains, and on the plain's edge was the small seaside town of Borth, a straggling beachfront with the shadow of the Cambrian Mountains behind it. We swung east at the lip of the River Dovey, past Taliesin ('the grave of the Welsh Homer ... Taliesin, the greatest of the bards, sixth century ...') and then along the riverbank. Aberdovey was under the hills at the far side of the estuary; this whole place was wonderful – the river valley about two miles wide and a great deal of it flat grassy marsh in which sheep were grazing, and the valley sides were grey hills and mountains.

It was muddy and majestic all the way to Dovey Junction, where the river and the valley were shrunken. Because of its steady level progress, a train was the perfect way to see a landscape – it was impossible to be closer to the ground. And it was ar excitement to travel up a contracting valley, from the broad river mouth to the creek at its narrow throat – it was like being swallowed.

We came to Machynlleth ('believed to be the Roman Maglona') where I saw a sign advertising the Centre for Alternative Technology. I asked directions and was told it was three to four miles up the road. I walked there through the woods and found it at Llwyngwern, at the southern edge of Snowdonia National Park, in an abandoned slate quarry. It was a settlement on a hillside and at first sight seemed no more than a jumble of ridiculous windmills and hand-cranked contraptions set among cabins and flapping plastic. The flapping plastic was part of the solar power units, but it was a dull day and no solar power was being generated. Here and there were signposts with homilies on little placards. I copied one into my notebook: 'Waste is really a human concept, for in nature nothing is wasted – everything is part of a continuous cycle.'

The Centre for Alternative Technology was an elaborate and messy reproach to middle-class tidiness, a kind of museum of compost heaps and enormous and unfamiliar-looking toilets. There were buckets everywhere. Nothing was thrown away, and it was boasted that shit could be turned into valuable gas, and eggshells into rich humus, and this tin funnel labelled 'Pee Can' was for collecting urine, 'another valuable fertilizer'.

All of this was true, and there was a great deal of earnest work being done at the Centre to make it monumental, the apotheosis of a dunghill. Their gardens flourished. They made bran cookies and sprout salad and chunky vegetable soup, and their children had rosy cheeks. Wales was said to be full of communes like this, but the Centre charged admission and offered bed and breakfast. It was a happy-looking place and if it seemed a trifle preoccupied with waste matter and a little passionate on the subject of bowel movements, it could be explained in terms of Welsh culture in which both evangelism and toilet training figured fairly strongly. In any case, I was treated with hospitality by the Alternative Technologists. They regarded my knapsack as an indicator that I was one of them, deep down – and having seen what the old technology had done to South Wales I think I was. Any alternative was better than the nuclear reactors on the coast, even the odd designs they were advocating, the harmless energy of solar panels and the superior, multi-purpose shithouse.

I walked back to Machynlleth. A grouchy guard at the station, Willy Bevan, said he didn't bloody know which was the next bloody train to Barmouth. He consulted his timetable.

'Two-thirteen. But there's an "E" on it. What does *that* bloody mean?'

He checked the footnote.

'Not on Sundays,' he said. 'Today's bloody Friday '

He consulted the timetable again.

'And one at two-forty-eight. But there's an "A" on it. What does *that* bloody mean?'

He checked that footnote.

'Saturdays only,' he said. 'So the next bloody train –'

I went down the line in a small train to Dovey Junction and I continued on a second train to Barmouth. The junction was in the middle of the river valley, just a halt in a marsh, but the other train was waiting for this one as we drew in. The remote branch lines of Wales were run with efficiency and pride. The services were frequent, even here, and I could easily have crossed the line and taken a train to Shrewsbury and been in London in time for dinner.

The train travelled seawards along the north bank of the river, and then westerly into the glare of the afternoon sun skipping through the marsh. Tracking around a hillside on a ledge, the train swung away from the wide estuary of the Dovey, and its shore of sand and broken slate, and then north to Aberdovey: houses on the steep hillside, tin caravans on the beach.

Caravans – it soon became obvious – were the curse of the Welsh coast. They were technically mobile homes, but they were not mobile. At best they were tin boxes, the shape of shoe boxes – including the lid – anchored in a field next to the sea, fifty or a hundred at a time, in various faded colours. Sometimes they were plunked down on slabs of concrete, and where there were more than a hundred – I counted over three hundred in some places – there was a fish-and-chip shop and a tin shower and another tin outhouse with a sign saying *Conveniences*. What fresh water there was came from a standpipe surrounded by squashy mud. The whole affair put me in mind of nomads or refugees, certain

Afghans or Somalis or Kurds, or the dizziest gypsies who had perhaps made a little money but refused to abandon their old ways, sending their womenfolk out for buckets of water. You wondered how they could stand it so close to each other in such tiny unsheltered quarters, and you also began to ask the questions that true savages inspired – not the civilized Afghans or Somalis, but those people in remote parts who looked so naked and uncomfortable you wondered how they washed and ate and kept dry and did their business. And there was something totally savage in the way they did not notice the incongruity of the settlement, how ugly it was, how beautiful the beach. The caravan settlements were always hideous and always in the loveliest coves.

They were English people, of course, encouraged by the Welsh to have a cheap holiday here. Some lived in orange tents at the margins of the caravan fields. It was always a lurid sight on a hot day, the pink people reading the *Sun* in front of the orange tents, making cups of tea on little flaming tin stoves.

It was like the nuclear power stations and the junkyards and the shallys and sewage farms: you could do anything you liked on the British coast, beside the uncomplaining sea. The seaside belonged to everyone.

After Tywyn and more caravan camps the train climbed to open cliffs and travelled through rocky sheep pastures, and then near Fairbourne passed the foot of Cader Idris ('the chair of the giant Idris'), a high ridge with a three-thousand-foot peak which was one of the most beautifully shaped mountains in England. Then across the bar of the Mawddach estuary, with the watering place of Barmouth lying under a hill. The river was wide and purple-blue in the lowering sun, with flat sandy banks rising to steep hillsides and more mountains. Barmouth looked to be a place of great refreshment, but closer it was excruciating, much too small to contain the mobs, not enough car parks or pavements. The sunburned people were milling around, and – unusual on the coast – the train cut right through the middle of town; everything was halted and tangled while the train made its stop, and Barmouth was suddenly full of pedestrians impatient to cross the line.

I had thought of getting off at Barmouth, but I changed my mind when I saw the numbers of people – in fact, I did get off, but I hurried back on, not wanting to be duffilled. And I had another reason: there was a note in the Cambrian Coast Railway timetable that said, under certain asterisked stations, '*Calls on request. Passengers wishing to alight must inform the guard, and those wishing to join must give a hand signal to the driver.*'

I decided on Llandanwg. I told the guard I wished to alight there. We continued along the coast, passing four or five tiny platforms, and then the train stopped at Llandanwg, for me alone. Llandanwg was lovely, which was why it was full of ugly caravans. I walked to Harlech.

Welsh mountains looked like mountains, and its cottages like cottages, and its castles like castles. Harlech Castle was the very image of the grey mass of round towers high on a cliff that children dream about after a bedtime story of kings and princesses and dragons. But I kept my vow against entering castles or cathedrals, and instead walked through the Royal St Davids golf course to the dunes and examined the caravans and tents. I did not really hate them. I was fascinated by them, as I had been by the shallys on the English coast. I made notes about the furnishings (camp cots, folding tables, transistor radios playing loud music) and about the food (tea, biscuits, soup, bread, beans). The people in these encampments were great readers of the gutter press – lots of cheap newspapers were in evidence.

Tony Henshaw had been a policeman in Liverpool for five years, Constable Henshaw people called him, and he had thought of making a career of it. 'But last year had finished it for me,' he said.

He was rather cautious with me at first. He claimed that being a policeman in Liverpool was like anything else. But I knew it was not – or else why had he come to Harlech in his caravan, intending to spend the rest of his life here, and him not even being Welsh!

'It's rather a foony business,' Mr Henshaw said, looking around policeman-fashion, no sudden movements.

'Funny in what way?' I asked.

'I was in Toxteth last soomer.'

'You mean the riots?'

'Riots and fighting, like. It woosen't easy. They was kids everywhere in the streets. Everywhere you looked, kids. All of them fighting. The fighting was bad. It was very bad.' He became silent.

I stared and waited, expecting more.

'I can tell you I was scared.'

I said in a patronizing way, 'That's nothing to be ashamed of. You could have been killed.'

'I could have been killed,' he said gratefully.

Then he said, 'You actually feel sorry for some of them. They have no chance, no chance at all. It's awpless, really. The kids, small kids, all in tatters. It's sad.'

'So you quit?'

'I was dead scared,' he said. 'But the situation hasn't changed. I think of them sometimes – all in tatters.'

The next day, without thinking, I walked out of Harlech, past the castle and down the road to Tygwyn. It was about a mile. And then I remembered the train; but now I could see whether flagging it down – giving a hand signal, as the timetable said – actually worked. I waited and at about ten-thirty I heard the train whistle. I stuck my hand out. The train stopped for me. I got on and rode up the coast. It was the 10.32 to Criccieth.

We came to a long tidal estuary, and I saw across the water a dome, a church spire, a campanile, some pink and blue cottages and some fake ruins: Portmeirion. It was a fantasy village, a large expensive folly, built by Sir Clough Williams-Ellis (1883–1978), a Welsh architect. Inspired by Portofino and liking this part of the Welsh coast he created this village from scratch – the colours and shapes were not at all Welsh, and it looked unusual even from two miles away on a moving train. But it was a steamy day and soon Portmeirion disappeared into the heat haze.

In Penrhyndeudraeth, the next stop, there was a large explosives factory. The local people called it 'Cooks', after the former owners, but its correct name was the Nobel Explosives Factory, a horrible conglomeration of vats, tubes, metal elbows and wired-up pipes, arranged on the hillside like an enormous home-made whisky still, and surrounded by prison fences and barbed wire. The interesting thing to me was not that this ugly explosives factory was in a pretty village, or that this grubby dangerous business gave us the Nobel Peace Prize. It was rather that, for fifteen years in that same village of Penrhyndeudraeth, with this dynamite under him, lived Bertrand Russell, the pacifist.

Eight more miles on this sunny day and we drew into Criccieth, where I hopped out of the train. I owned a guide-book which said, '*Criccieth*: For several years this small town was the home of James (now Jan) Morris, probably the finest living British travel writer.' The 'James (now Jan)' needed no explanation, since the story of how she changed from a man to a woman in a clinic in Casablanca was told in her book *Conundrum*, 1974. She still lived near Criccieth, outside the village of Llanystumdwy, in what were formerly the stables of the manor house, looking northwards to the mountains of Eryri and southwards to Cardigan Bay.

I seldom looked people up in foreign countries. I could never believe they really wanted to see me, I had an uncomfortable sense that I was interrupting something intimate; but I did look up Jan Morris. She had written a great deal about Wales, and I was here, and I knew her vaguely. Her house was built like an Inca fort, of large black rocks and heavy beams. She had written, 'It is built in the old Welsh way, with rough gigantic stones, piled one upon the other in an almost natural mass, with a white wooden cupola on top. Its architecture is of the variety known these days as "vernacular", meaning that no professional architect has ever had a hand in it.'

She was wearing a straw calypso hat tipped back on her bushy hair, and a knit jersey and white slacks. It was a very hot day and she was dressed for it. There is a certain educated English voice that is both correct and malicious. Jan Morris has such a voice. It was not deep but it was languid, and the maleness that still trembled in it made it sultry and attractive. There was nothing ponderous about her. She shrugged easily and was a good listener, and she laughed as a cat might – full-throated and with a little hiss of pleasure, stiffening her body. She was kind, reckless and intelligent.

Her house was very neat and full of books and pictures. 'I have filled it with *Cymreictod* – Welshness.' Yes, solid country artefacts and beamed ceilings and a *No Smoking* sign in Welsh – she did not allow smoking in the house. Her library was forty-two feet long and the corresponding room upstairs was her study, with a desk and a stereo.

Music mattered to her in an unusual way. She once wrote, 'Animists believe that the divine is to be found in every living thing, but I go one further; I am an inanimist, holding that even lifeless objects can contain immortal yearnings ... I maintain, for instance, that music can permanently influence a building, so I often leave the record player on when I am out of the house, allowing its themes and melodies to soak themselves into the fabric.'

Perhaps she was serious. Inanimate objects can seem to possess something resembling vitality, or a mood that answers your own. But melodies soaking into wood and stone? 'My kitchen adores Mozart,' the wise guy might say, or, 'The sitting room's into Gladys Knight and the Pips.' But I did not say anything, I just listened approvingly.

'I suppose it's very selfish, only one bedroom,' she said.

But it was the sort of house everyone wanted, on its own, at the edge of a meadow, solid as could be, well-lit, pretty, cosy, with an enormous library and study, and a four-poster: perfect for a solitary person and one cat. Hers was called Solomon.

Then she said, 'Want to see my grave?'

I said of course and we went down to a cool shaded wood by a riverside. Jan Morris was a nimble walker; she had climbed to twenty thousand feet with the first successful Everest Expedition in 1953. Welsh woods were full of small twisted oaks, and tangled boughs, and moist soil, and dark ferny corners. We entered a boggier area of straight green trees and speckled shade.

'I always think this is very Japanese,' she said.

It did look that way, the idealized bushy landscape of the woodblock print, the little riverside grotto.

She pointed across the river and said, 'That's my grave – right there, that little island.'

It was like a beaver's dam of tree trunks padded all around with moss, then more ferns, and the river slurping and gurgling among boulders.

'There's where I'm going to be buried – or rather scattered. It's nice, don't you think? Elizabeth's ashes are going to be scattered there, too' (Jan Morris was married to Elizabeth before the sex-change).

It seemed odd that someone so young should be thinking of death. She was fifty-six, and the hormones she took made her look a great deal younger – early forties perhaps But it was a very

Welsh thought, this plan for ashes and a grave-site. It was a nation accustomed to ghostliness, and sighing, and mourning. I was travelling on the Celtic fringe, where they still believed in giants.

What did I think of her grave? she asked.

I said the island looked as though it would wash away in a torrent and that her ashes would end up in Cardigan Bay. She laughed and said it did not matter.

At our first meeting about a year before, in London, she had said suddenly, 'I am thinking of taking up a life of crime,' and she had mentioned wanting to steal something from Woolworths. It had not seemed so criminal to me, but over lunch I asked her whether she had done anything about it.

'If I had taken up a life of crime I would hardly be likely to tell you, Paul!'

'I was just curious,' I said.

She said, 'These knives and forks. I stole them from Pan-American Airways. I told the stewardess I was stealing them. She said she didn't care.'

They were the sort of knives and forks you get with your little plastic tray of soggy meat and gravy.

Talk of crime led us to talk of arson by Welsh nationalists. I asked why only cottages were burned, when there were many tin caravans on the coast that would make a useful blaze. She said her son was very pro-Welsh and patriotic and would probably consider that.

I said that the Welsh seemed like one family.

'Oh, yes, that's what my son says. He thinks as long as he is in Wales he's safe. He'll always be taken care of. He can go to any house and he will be taken in and fed and given a place to sleep.'

'Like the travellers in Arabia who walk up to a Bedouin's tent and say, "I am a guest of God" in order to get hospitality. *Ana dheef Allah.*'

'Yes,' she said. 'It's probably true – it is like a family here in Wales.'

And like all families, I said, sentimental and suspicious and quarrelsome and secretive. But Welsh nationalism was at times like a certain kind of feminism, very monotonous and one-sided.

She said, 'I suppose it does look that way, if you're a man.'

I could have said: Didn't it look that way to you when you were a man?

She said, 'As for the caravans and tents, yes, they look awful. But the Welsh don't notice them particularly. They aren't noted for their visual sense. And those people, the tourists, are seeing Wales. I'm glad they're here, in a way, so they can see this beautiful country and understand the Welsh.'

Given the horror of the caravans, it was a very generous thought, and it certainly was not my sentiment. I always thought of Edmund Gosse saying, 'No one will see again on the shore of England what I saw in my early childhood.' The shore was fragile and breakable and easily poisoned.

Jan Morris was still speaking of the Welsh. 'Some people say that Welsh nationalism is a narrow movement, cutting Wales off from the world. But it is possible to see it as liberating Wales and giving it an importance – of bringing it into the world.'

We finished lunch and went outside. She said, 'If only you could see the mountains. I know it's boring when people say that – but they are really spectacular. What do you want to do?'

I said that I had had a glimpse of Portmeirion from the train and wanted a closer look, if there was time.

We drove there in her car, and parked under the pines. She had known Clough Williams-Ellis very well. 'He was a wonderful man,' she said. 'On his deathbed he was still chirping away merrily. But he was very worried about what people would say about him. Funny man! He wrote his own obituary! He had it there with him as he lay dying. When I visited him, he asked me to read it. Of course, there was nothing unflattering in it. I asked him why he had gone to all the trouble of writing his own obituary. He said, "Because I don't know what *The Times* will write in the obituary they do of me."'

We walked through the gateway and down the stairs to the little Italian fantasy town on the Welsh hillside.

'He was obsessed that they would get something wrong, or be critical. He had tried every way he could of getting hold of his *Times* obituary – but failed, of course. They're always secret.'

She laughed. It was that hearty malicious laugh.

'The funny thing was, I was the one who had written his

obituary for *The Times*. They're all written carefully beforehand, you know.'

I said, 'And you didn't tell him?'

'No.' Her face was blank. Was she smiling behind it? 'Do you think I should have?'

I said, 'But he was on his deathbed.'

She laughed again. She said, 'It doesn't matter.'

There was a sculpted bust of Williams-Ellis in a niche, and resting crookedly on its dome was a hand-scrawled sign saying, THE BAR UPSTAIRS IS OPEN.

Jan said, 'He would have liked that.'

We walked through the place, under arches, through gateways, past Siamese statuary and Greek columns, and gardens and pillars and colonnades; we walked around the piazza.

'The trouble with him was that he didn't know when to stop.'

It was a sunny day. We lingered at the blue Parthenon, the Chantry, the Hercules statue, the Town Hall. You think: What is it doing here? More cottages.

'Once, when we lost a child, we stayed up there in that white cottage' – this about herself and Elizabeth when they were husband and wife.

There was more. Another triumphal arch, the Prior's Lodge, pink and green walls.

Jan said, 'It's supposed to make you laugh.'

But instead it was making me very serious, for this folly had taken over forty years to put together, and yet it still had the look of a faded movie set.

'He even designed the cracks, and planned where the mossy parts should be. He was very meticulous and very flamboyant, too, always in one of these big, wide-brimmed antediluvian hats and yellow socks.'

I was relieved to get out of Portmeirion; I had been feeling guilty, with the uncomfortable suspicion that I had been sight-seeing – something I had vowed I would not do.

Jan said, 'Want to see my gravestone?'

It was the same sudden, proud, provocative, mirthful way that she had said, *Want to see my grave?*

I said of course.

The stone was propped against the wall of her library. I had

missed it before. The lettering was very well done, as graceful as
the engraving on a bank note. It was inscribed *Jan & Elizabeth
Morris*. In Welsh and English, above and below the names, it said,

Here Are Two Friends
At The End of One Life

I said it was as touching as Emily Dickinson's gravestone in
Amherst, Massachusetts, which said nothing more than *Called
Back*.

When I left, and we stood at the railway station at Porthmadog,
Jan said, 'If only these people knew who was getting on the train!'

I said, 'Why should they care?'

She grinned. She said, 'That knapsack – is that all you have?'

I said yes. We talked about travelling light. I said the great
thing was to have no more than you could carry comfortably and
never to carry formal clothes – suits, ties, shiny shoes, extra
sweaters: what sort of travel was that?

Jan Morris said, 'I just carry a few frocks. I squash them into a
ball – they don't weigh anything. It's much easier for a woman to
travel light than a man.'

There was no question that she knew what she was talking
about, for she had been both a man and a woman. She smiled at
me, looking like Tootsie, and I felt a queer thrill when I kissed
her goodbye.

12

The 20.20 to Llandudno Junction

'I love steam, don't you?' Stan Wigbeth said to me on the Ffestiniog Railway, and then leaned out of the window. He was not interested in my answer, which was, 'Up to a point.' Mr Wigbeth smiled and ground his teeth in pleasure when the whistle blew. He said there was nothing to him more beautiful than a steam 'loco'. He told me they were efficient and brilliantly made; but engine drivers had described to me how uncomfortable they could be, and how horrible on winter nights, because it was impossible to drive most steam engines without sticking your face out of the side window every few minutes.

I wanted Mr Wigbeth to admit that they were outdated and ox-like, dramatic looking but hell to drive; they were the choo-choo fantasies of lonely children; they were fun but filthy. Our train was pulled through the Welsh mountains by a 'Fairlie', known to the buffs as a 'double engine' – two boilers – 'the most uncomfortable engine I've ever driven,' a railwayman once told me. It was very hot for the driver, because of the position of the boilers. The footplate of the Fairlie was like an oriental oven for poaching ducks in their own sweat. Mr Wigbeth did not agree with any of this. Like many other railway buffs, he detested our century.

This had originally been a tram line, he told me; all the way from Porthmadog to Blaenau Ffestiniog – horse trams, hauling slate from the mountain quarries. Then it was named 'The Narrow Gauge Railway', and opened to passengers in 1869. It was closed in 1946 and eventually reopened in stages. The line was now – this month – completely open.

'We're lucky to be here,' Mr Wigbeth said, and checked his

watch, a fob watch, of course, the railway buff's timepiece. He was delighted by what he saw. 'Right on time!'

It was a beautiful trip to Blaenau, on the hairpin curves of the steep Snowdonia hills and through the thick evening green of the Dwyryd Valley. To the south-east, amid the lovely mountains, was the Trawsfynydd Nuclear Power Station, three or four gigantic grey slabs. An English architect, noted for his restrained taste, had been hired in 1959 to make it prettier, or at least bearable, but he had failed. Perhaps he should have planted vines. Yet this monstrosity emphasized the glory of these valleys. I found the ride restful, even with the talkative Mr Wigbeth beside me. Then he was silenced by a mile-long tunnel. The light at the end of the tunnel was Blaenau Ffestiniog, at the head of the valley.

'Where are you off to, then?' Mr Wigbeth asked.

'I'm catching the next train to Llandudno Junction.'

'It's a diesel,' he said, and made a sour face.

'So what?'

'I don't call that a train,' he said. 'I call that a tin box!'

He was disgusted and angry. He put on this engine driver's cap, and his jacket with the railway lapel pins, and after a last look at his conductor-type fob watch, he got into his Ford Cortina and drove twenty-seven stop-and-go miles back to Bangor.

I walked around Blaenau. I had thought of spending the night there, but it seemed a dull place and I felt negligent, being away from the coast. It was still like a bright afternoon when I took the 20.20 to Llandudno Junction, but moments after leaving Blaenau Station we plunged into a tunnel two miles long. When we emerged I began looking for the peak of Snowdon on the west, and imagined that I saw it at Dolwyddelan. The castle ('in 1281 Llewelyn the Last was here . . .') was solitary and high and looked like a bad molar. At Betws-y-Coed I searched for Ugly House ('once an overnight stop for Irish drovers'), but could not see it. The village was pretty but overcrowded this hot evening, and I had a happy truant-playing feeling as I left on the empty train rolling north through the Vale of Conway, stopping at Llanrwst and Dolgarrog. Now the light was golden, and the motion of the little train lulled me as we travelled along the river under the peaceful hills to the coast.

*

I was not frightened at the hotel in Llandudno until I was taken upstairs by the pock-marked clerk; and then I sat in the dusty room alone and listened. The only sound was my breathing from having climbed the four flights of stairs. The room was small, there were no lights in the corridor, the wallpaper had rust stains that could have been spatters of blood. The ceiling was high, the room narrow: it was like sitting at the bottom of a well. I went downstairs.

The clerk was watching television in the lounge (he called it a lounge). He did not speak to me. He was watching *Hill Street Blues*, a car chase, some shouting. I looked at the register and saw what I had missed before – that I was the only guest in this big dark forty-room hotel. I went outside and wondered how to escape. Of course I could have marched in and said, 'I'm not happy here – I'm checking out,' but the clerk might have made trouble and charged me. But I wanted to punish him for running such a scary place.

I walked inside and upstairs, grabbed my knapsack and hurried to the lounge rehearsing a story that began, 'This is my bird-watching gear. I'll be right back –' The clerk was still watching television. As I passed him (he did not look up) the hotel seemed to me the most sinister building I had ever been in. On my way downstairs I had had a moment of panic when, faced by three closed doors in a hallway, I imagined myself in one of those corridor labyrinths of the hotel in the nightmare, endlessly tramping torn carpets and opening doors to discover again and again that I was trapped.

I ran down the promenade to the bandstand and stood panting while the band played 'If You Were the Only Girl in the World'. I wondered if I had been followed by the clerk. I paid twenty pence for a deck chair, but feeling that I was being watched (perhaps it was my knapsack and oily shoes?) I abandoned the chair and continued down the promenade. Later, I checked into the Queens Hotel, which looked vulgar enough to be safe.

Llandudno was the sort of place that inspired old-fashioned fears of seaside crime. It made me think of poisoning and suffocation, screams behind varnished doors, creatures scratching at the wainscotting. I imagined constantly that I was hearing the gasps of adulterers from the dark windows of those stuccoed terraces that served as guest houses – naked people saying gloatingly, 'We shouldn't be doing this!' In all ways, Llandudno was a perfectly preserved Victorian town. It was so splendid-looking that it took me several days to find out that it was in fact very dull.

It had begun as a fashionable watering place and developed into a railway resort. It was still a railway resort, full of people strolling on the promenade and under the glass and iron canopies of the shop-fronts on Mostyn Street. It had a very old steamer ('Excursions to the Isle of Man') moored at its pier head, and very old hotels, and a choice of very old entertainments – 'Old Mother Riley' at the Pavilion, the Welsh National Opera at the Astra Theatre doing *Tosca*, or Yorkshire comedians in vast saloon bars telling very old jokes. 'We're going to have a loovely boom competition,' a toothy comedian was telling his drunken audience over near Happy Valley. A man was blind-folded and five girls selected, and the man had to judge – by touching them – which one's bum was the shapeliest. It caused hilarity and howls of laughter; the girls were shy – one simply walked offstage; and at one point some men were substituted and the blindfolded man crouched and began searching the men's bums as everyone jeered. And then the girl with the best bum was selected as the winner and awarded a bottle of car-bonated cider called 'Pomagne'.

I overheard two elderly ladies outside at the rail, looking above Llandudno Bay. They were Miss Maltby and Miss Thorn, from Glossop, near Manchester.

'It's a nice moon,' Miss Maltby said.

'Aye,' Miss Thorn said. 'It is.'

'But that's not what we saw earlier this evening.'

'No. That was the sun.'

Miss Maltby said, 'You told me it was the moon.'

'It was all that mist, you see,' Miss Thorn said. 'But I know now it was the sun.'

The town was dominated by two silver-grey headlands of swollen limestone, Great and Little Orme. From Llandudno's pier-head on a clear day it was possible to see the Lancashire coast, and from West Parade on the other side (where Lewis Carroll stayed with the Liddell family and wrote part of *Alice*),

Bangor and the shore of Anglesey were greenishly apparent across Conway Bay.

There were two Indians in my railway compartment trying to open a briefcase. It had a combination lock, and they had the combination, but still they could not open it. They quarrelled a little, taking turns sighing at the stubborn lock, and then one said, 'You would be so kind?' I took the briefcase into my lap and spanked it and it popped open. It contained some combs, a bottle of hair oil, a blue diary, a Bengali movie magazine and a plastic pouch that was zippered shut. While one Indian removed a comb from the briefcase the other Indian picked up a valise and left the train, muttering.

The remaining Indian combed his hair and said he had never seen the muttering one before in his life. They had met over the briefcase.

This Indian, Mr Amin, said, 'I am in catering business.' He smiled and added, 'That is to say, catering and restaurantooring.'

He owned a curry shop in Bangor.

'I like Bangor and I am liking Vales,' he said. 'And the Vellish I am speaking as vell.'

'Say something in Welsh,' I suggested.

'I can say some few vords for you,' Mr Amin said. 'You are helping me with my briefcase and making me so happy. I am thinking and that other man, too, perhaps ve are not unlocking my case! And – vhat you vanted?'

'Welsh,' I said.

He straightened his head and in a clacking voice said, '*Bore da*. Good marning. *Croeso*. Velcome. *Diolch yn fawr*. Oh, thank you very much. *Nos da*. Good evening. *Cymru am byth*. Vales for ever.'

I said, 'Are you going to stay in Bangor for ever?'

'Who knows about for ever?'

'Let's say five years.'

He said, 'Yes.'

'How many Bangladeshis are there in Bangor?'

'Not more than eight.'

'Do you have a mosque?'

'No,' he said. 'But sometimes ve use a certain floor in the Student Union building.'

'Do you have a mullah?'

He said, 'Ven five or six pray, vun can be mullah.'

I asked, 'How many children do you have?'

'Questions! Questions!' He seemed short of breath, his face was a tight fit, he probably took me for the tax man.

'Sorry, Mr Amin. I have two children. Boys.'

He relaxed and looked envious. 'You are lucky. I have three girls, and then I try again, and then I just get a boy last year.'

We entered a tunnel – silence – and then emerged, and Bangor lay before us, big and grey. Mr Amin gathered his briefcase and paper bags and made ready to get off the train.

I said, 'You could have settled anywhere in Britain, Mr Amin. Why did you choose to settle in Bangor?'

He said, 'Because it reminds me of my town in Bangladesh. Bangor is just very like Sylhet.'

Was Sylhet severe and monotonous like this? Perhaps so. In any case, Indians had often told me how Cheltenham reminded them of certain towns in the Punjab, and Scotland was reminiscent of Simla, and after the Sultan of Zanzibar was overthrown he took himself to Eastbourne, claiming that it somewhat resembled his fragrant but decrepit sultanate in the Indian Ocean.

I stayed on the train and crossed the Menai Strait to Anglesey. The island was flat, as if it had detached itself from the mainland and become waterlogged. Its meadows were no more than gentle swells, and small houses and broken cottages lay scattered at great distances. It possessed the haunted look that Cornwall had, its rocks like ruins, its stillness like suspense. It had been the Druids' last outpost and it looked it. In such a flat grassy place it was possible to see that there was nothing threatening, and yet this apparent openness was itself eerie and suggested invisible dangers. It was the sound of the wind, the pale light, the flat shadows on the low ground.

The first station was the famous but practically unsayable Llanfairpwllgwyngyllgogerychwyrndrobwllllantysiliogogogoch ('St Mary's Church in a hollow by the white hazel close to the rapid whirlpool by the red cave of St Tysilio'). It is usually called

Llanfair P.G. but the full name appeared on the station signboard, which was fifteen feet long. There was nothing else of interest at the station or in the town, and indeed it was indistinguishable from the other twenty-two places called Llanfair (St Mary's) in Wales. I was told that the long name had been concocted by the village tailor a century before so that the place would seem singular, much as Cross Keys, Pennsylvania, had been officially renamed Intercourse.

The stations and villages along the route to Holyhead looked worn down and depressing. It was as if all the millions of lonely Irish people who travelled this way – this was the principal route – had devoured the landscape with their eyes, looked upon it with such hunger, that there was little of it left to take hold of and examine. It sometimes seemed that way to me in Britain, in the busiest places, as if a castle's ramparts or a hillside or a village – supposedly so picturesque – had been eroded by two thousand years of admiring scrutiny, the penetration of people's eyes. No wonder they now stood on the shore and looked out to sea.

Bodorgan Station was empty, and nearby was an empty hotel; Ty Croes was one ruined cottage; and then the land grew stonier and harsher and looked the sort of place where only Druids could be happy – wind-flattened grass and pitted rocks, a few throaty crows and flocks of barking seagulls.

After the village of Valley there was a causeway to Holy Island. We passed a large factory, Anglesey Aluminium, and slowed as we approached the town of Holyhead.

Holyhead was one of a number of British towns that seemed to be dying – blackening like an extremity with gangrene. It was too far, too barren, too still. It had gone to sleep and would die without waking. The ferry business – boats to the Irish port of Dun Laoghaire – was so bad they were advertising free litre-bottles of whisky for anyone who made the trip. But the ferries remained empty: no one had any money here. In Anglesey, where the local accent was not Welsh but rather a jaw-twisting Birmingham neigh, I was told that the unemployment rate was thirty per cent. It was a meaningless statistic – most statistics struck me as sounding frivolous and hastily invented – but the fact remained that people in Holyhead were visibly idle. They did not work, nor did they do much else but sit and stare. The tennis courts and football fields were empty, the bowling greens were empty – no sports. There was little drinking because no one could afford it; no movies.

'I sleep late and watch TV,' a man named Gower told me. He had been on the dole for five years and was only thirty-two.

The streets were empty. I walked through the town and felt a sense of despair, because I could not imagine that things would ever improve here. No one I met believed that the future would be any brighter, and a number of them said casually that they had thought of emigrating. Whenever British people spoke of emigration they mentioned North America first. Europe was just as bad as Britain, they said, and Australia was too far.

The younger ones had some hope. I deliberately sought out youths in Anglesey and asked them what their plans were. One thirteen-year-old told me he wanted to be a plasterer. I guessed that his father was a plasterer, but I was wrong. A fourteen-year-old told me he wanted to join the Royal Navy, and another's ambition was to be a carpenter. They hated school and perhaps they were right to hate it; what job would school prepare them for? A sixteen-year-old told me that he was about to take an exam, and then he wanted to go to college. What would he study?

'Catering,' he said. His name was Brian Craster.

I asked him if he meant cooking – being a chef.

'Yeah,' he said in his neighing accent, 'it's a two-year course '

'Then you get a job.'

'If there's one going. There's not much work around here. Just British Rail or the Tinto factory' – Rio Tinto Zinc ran Anglesey Aluminium – 'but they've started to lay people off.'

'Do you do any cooking now, Brian?'

'A bit,' he said. 'I can make cakes. Shepherd's pie and that.'

'Where do you want to be a chef?'

'Maybe London. Maybe get a job at the Savoy.'

None of the youths I met in Holyhead had ever been to London. Brian Craster wanted to go, but he seemed a little fearful and that made him sound defiant.

It was all council flats and uncut grass, barking dogs and broken stone walls. I felt sorry for the children, kicking tin cans, their hands in their pockets and their hair blowing, dreaming of being plasterers.

I walked through most of the western part of Holy Island, around South Stack and then back to the harbour. In a bus shelter overlooking New Harbour I saw a poem written in black ink.

> Now it is 1984.
> Knock-knock at your front door
> It's the suede denim secret police
> They have come for your uncool niece
> Come quickly to the camp
> You'll look nice as a drawstring lamp
> Don't worry – it's only a shower
> For your clothes – here's a pretty flower
>
> DIE on organic poison gas
> Serpent's egg already hatched
> You will croak you little clown
> When you mess with President Brown!

As I stood copying this into my small notebook, a middle-aged couple approached the bus shelter. They were Owen and Esther Smallbone from the council estate just west of Holyhead. They had a small flat for which they paid £16 a week. Owen Smallbone had been an accounts clerk at the harbour, but had taken leave of absence for medical reasons – a bad back. When he had recovered sufficiently to return to his job, there was no job, and he had been on the dole ever since – four years. Esther sometimes earned a little money looking after the children of working mothers – the Smallbones had no children of their own – but there was not much child-minding these days, because the mothers were being laid off, weren't they? They were always the first to go. Recently, Owen's back had begun again to bother him, which was why they were taking the bus. They were on the way to the General Post Office on Boston Street to purchase a Television Broadcast Receiving Licence (Including Colour) – for an 'apparatus for wireless telegraphy'. They rented a Sony 'Trinitron', eighteen inch, for £12 a month. The licence for watching it would cost £46.

They were very suspicious of me. I wondered why, and then I saw the reason. I had put my notebook away, but I was still holding my pen. So I had probably written that crazy poem, or if not the poem then perhaps I had drawn the picture of the penis, or else set down my telephone number with the message *Ring Roger for a good time, guys,* or – and this was the most likely – I was the one going around Holyhead scribbling FREE WALES and FWA, one of the arsonists. My knapsack told a story.

The Smallbones glanced at my pen. They were very annoyed. They were decent people, but even decent people could not find work these days. They were law-abiding – masses of people never bothered to buy a TV licence and didn't give a tinker's cuss when the television-detector van parked in Mostyn Close and trained its radar on the flats, with them inside the flats watching *Championship Darts* or *The Dukes of Hazzard* without a licence. And the Smallbones respected public property. They hated graffiti, and this on the wall of the bus shelter had been written by perverts, lunatics and fanatics. Sometimes it made them ashamed to be Welsh. Sometimes they felt like just jacking it in and going to Nova Scotia like the Davises, but that was years ago, and who wanted to hire a man with a bad back?

Ten minutes passed. The bus did not come. I waited a few more minutes and then decided to walk. The Smallbones were still waiting, and after I had gone they examined the walls of the bus shelter trying to determine which scribbles were mine.

I returned to Llandudno Junction for the third time and then to Llandudno. Now I noticed that there were seagulls on the platform of Llandudno Station, thirty or forty of them, waiting the way pigeons waited at Waterloo.

At last I decided to leave Wales. I took another train to Llandudno Junction. Today was Friday and the train was full of people returning to their homes in industrial Lancashire and West Yorkshire. Some had been further afield than Rhos-on-Sea and Colwyn Bay.

'The people crowded round us,' Janet Hosegood said. She was a librarian in Runcorn. She loved to travel. She had spent last year's Easter vacation on a group tour of three Chinese cities, Canton, Suchow and Shanghai, as she was telling old Mr Bolus, who had never been east of Mablethorpe.

Mr Bolus said, 'Ee?'

'They'd never seen eyes like ours,' Miss Hosegood said. She was fifty-one and loved country walks. *Spinster*, she wrote when marital status was asked for. She hated the abbreviation 'Ms' – 'Miss!' she usually said, showing her teeth.

Mr Bolus said, 'Ee?'

'In Channah,' Miss Hosegood said.

'Ee?'

'People's Repooblic,' Miss Hosegood said.

'Aye,' Mr Bolus said.

'Cause their eyes are slanty-like,' Miss Hosegood said.

'Aye,' Mr Bolus said.

'Six 'oondred and fifty pound it cost us, all in,' Miss Hosegood said.

But Mr Bolus had been distracted from this talk of China by the bulldozers outside Colwyn Bay, preparing to build something. *It can only be something awful*, he thought, for here there was mile after mile of shallys and villas and caravans and tents, facing the Irish Sea.

At last Mr Bolus looked away and said, 'Ee?'

Although it was a pleasant, rattling two-coach train, it was rather full of people and belongings. But what was especially annoying to the others was the appearance of Roland Painter-Betty and his dog, Ollie, the pair of them pushing down the aisle and then taking the only empty seat – seats, rather, because Roland snagged the window and the dirty great Alsatian leaped on to the seat next to him.

'Wonder if he paid full fare?' a man named Garside muttered.

Janet Hosegood said, 'That dog should be on the flipping floor.'

And they also hated the sight of Roland Painter-Betty's earring and chunky bracelet and Liberty scarf and the kind of puce-coloured shoes no normal man would wear.

It was all caravans from Abergele eastwards, places with names like 'Golden Sands', just tin boxes, miles of them, on flat stretches of sand – no trees.

We crossed the River Clwyd and came to Rhyl, which was stained with soot and looked punished. Its fun-fair and amusement park were silent, and it looked truly terrible.

Verna and Doreen, neighbours from Wallasey, had turned away from Rhyl. This was the last day of their holiday and they didn't want it spoiled – Verna explained that the sight of grotty places could leave a bad taste in your mouth. They talked about a mutual friend, Rose, who had recently moved into Stanley Road.

How's she getting on, then?' Verna asked.

'Talks to everyone. She's got a word for everyone,' Doreen said.

'She's a Londoner.'

'Well, this is it, isn't it? Your Londoners are a very outgoing people, aren't they?'

Some of the caravans were on marshland, sinking badly, some of them broken-backed on Morfa Rhuddlan ('where in 759 the Welsh under Caradoc were routed by Offa of Mercia').

No one said a word to Roland Painter-Betty or Ollie, stinking and slavering on the seat next to him. Everyone knew Roland was getting away with murder. But strangers were not addressed on British trains: they might be maniacs, they might be rude, or worse they might come from the class above you. If it was certain the stranger were a foreigner, then it was just possible someone would say, 'I wish you wouldn't do that.' But Roland was a native, and probably a poofter, and they could be so touchy – worse than women, some of them.

We stopped and everyone looked out of the windows: Prestatyn. It was red-brick, once important to the lead industry, then a holiday resort that had never quite caught on. *Come to Sunny Prestatyn*, posters said, mocking the bleak place. The tide was down and sand mounted towards the shore, forming banks and low dunes. Behind Prestatyn lay the empty green hills of Denbighshire.

The River Dee was hopeless with sand – seven miles wide at this point but scarcely navigable, as the brown bubbly flats seemed to prove. And the land was flat, too; the sheep had cropped it so closely and so evenly it looked like the surface of stagnant water. The town of Flint had turned its back on the river. It had a sullen wintry look and the British industrial smells of foot-rot, dead mice and old socks. The junkyards outside Shotton were a warning, for Shotton's steelworks were shortly to close and become junkyards, leaving thousands without jobs.

The sky was yellow-grey, like some kinds of smoke. It was June and in the immense torpor of the steaming day the passengers had begun to doze off, only one person acknowledging the fact that, just a mile from Chester, we crossed the Welsh border. Mr Bolus said it had been the Welsh border for a thousand years.

Janet Hosegood was talking, still telling Mr Bolus – he was deaf, I had now decided – about the People's Republic of China, her last year's holiday.

13

The 16.01 to Southport

Now I saw British people lying stiffly on the beach like dead insects, or huddled against the canvas windbreaks they hammered into the sand with rented mallets, or standing on cliffs and kicking stones roly-poly into the sea – and I thought: They are symbolic-ally leaving the country.

Going to the coast was as far as they could comfortably go. It was the poor person's way of going abroad – standing at the seaside and staring at the ocean. It took a little imagination. I believed that these people were fantasizing that they were over there on the watery horizon, at sea. Most people on the promenade walked with their faces averted from the land. Perhaps another of their coastal pleasures was being able to turn their backs on Britain. I seldom saw anyone with his back turned to the sea. Most people looked seawards with anxious hopeful faces, as if they had just left their native land.

I was in New Brighton ('Here Sibelius's music, conducted by the composer, was first publicly heard in England') strolling past the green-haired punks and the Rockers, who carried booming transistor radios as big as suitcases and listened to the pop group 'Raw Sewage' howl their hit *Kick It To Death*. I had skipped Chester, considering it too far inland for my coastal purposes, and I had taken a train to Birkenhead.

Five miles down the west bank of the River Mersey was Rock Ferry, a yellow and green ferry station made of wood and girders. It was the sort of grand Victorian structure the British were eager to demolish and replace with a building that did not need repainting – something made of corrugated plastic sheets bolted to iron pipes. That very day, the Kensington Town Hall in London had been pulled down, because although it was a fine example of a mid-Victorian baroque façade, the Tory council said it was worth only half a million pounds. The site, they claimed, was worth eight times that to a property developer for a bomb-proof high-density Manhattan-style block. So much for the Victorian baroque. Kensington needed cash, the councillors said. 'We can't afford to be sentimental.' It seemed only a matter of time before such a lovely building as this ferry landing was bulldozed into the river.

Liverpool, it was obvious from the ferry, was full of elegant old buildings. They were heavy but graceful. The city had three cathedrals and many church spires, and just as many open spaces from the blasts of German bombs. (We live in a time of short memories. A German tourist in Liverpool told me that he found the city rather wrecked and depressing – he much preferred Scotland.) Liverpool was not pleasant – no city was – but it was not bad. It was elderly, venerable, tough, somewhat neglected, and it had a very exposed look, because it was a city on the sea, one of the few large cities in Britain that was subjected to ocean gales. That was the Liverpool look: weatherbeaten.

I had expected it to be frightening: it was known as a city of riots. But it struck me as good-humoured, and inhabited by many people as alien as I was, living more or less as they pleased in what had once been extremely fine houses: the 'Somali Social Centre' was in a cracked Georgian house. It was the most Irish city in Britain, and so the most Catholic. The Pope had just visited and been wildly welcomed. The papal flags, yellow and white, were still fluttering from the beer signs on public houses and on streets down which the 'popemobile' (it was bulletproof, in spite of its silly name) had passed.

Emboldened by the apparent calm, I decided to walk from the Pierhead to the black district of Toxteth, which everyone called 'Liverpool Eight'. The previous summer at about this time the district had been in flames. Most of Liverpool's 40,000 blacks lived in Liverpool Eight.

I met a lady tramp. She was more grey than white, about sixty-odd and had the self-indulgent look of the drunken duchesses who were pictured in the society pages of the *Tatler*. She wore a woolly hat. She was pulling a loaded cart and had a dog on a leash. I had never met a lady tramp with a dog. I had the impression that this was her whole household on the cart – all her clothes and furnishings. There was a stink in the cart that might have been food. Her name was Mary Wilson. She quickly pointed out that she was not the same Mary Wilson who was married to a former British prime minister.

She said she would show me the way to Toxteth if I pulled her cart for a spell. I did so and nearly wrenched my arm, the thing was so heavy. She said she had picked up some bottles. There was money in bottles if you knew where to flog them.

She took a blackened pipe from under her rags and puffed it.

'Like Harold,' she said, elaborating the political connection. 'I enjoy my pipe.'

Mary's uncle and aunt had gone to the United States. They had intended to settle, but they had returned to Liverpool.

'There was a depression on at the time,' she said. 'Like this one.' She puffed her pipe. It smelled of burning rags. 'We'll never see the end of this one.'

She had the Liverpool knack of being able to speak without moving her lips.

'What do you want in Toxteth?' she asked.

'Just looking.'

'They had riots there,' she said. 'They bayned the place.'

'Who did?'

'The kids!' She didn't say blacks.

Liverpool used to be peaceable, she said. It wasn't peaceable any more. It was a blewdy disgrace. It was dangerous.

But it did not look disgraceful to me. It was better than the corresponding part of New York City, near the docks in Brooklyn, although it had the same bricks, and the same pong of dirt and oil and old iron.

Mary Wilson finally shuffled away. Her little dog's claws scratched on the sidewalk like matches being struck as he trotted beside her.

Mr Duddy, a street-sweeper I met at the corner of Windsor Street, said, 'Toxteth. Go to the cinema that's bayned to the ground, and when you coom to Princes Road tayn right.'

But I was still smiling at him.

He became shifty. 'What is it?'

As a street-sweeper, what was it like to sweep up after the riots?
I asked.

'Shocking,' Mr Duddy said.

'Give me an example.'

'They baynt a car,' he said.

'A lot of property was burned, I understand.'

'They tried to bayn a skule,' he said.

'But the whole place was in flames.'

'They was poodles of petrol,' he said.

'You must have seen some amazing things.'

Mr Duddy thought a moment, then said, 'I saw a pule of
blood.'

I walked on, down Princes Road. There was shabby gentility
mixed with unobtrusive ruin. There was something gothic about
lovely old buildings half burned to the ground, or turned into
brothels (surely door-bells labelled *Fiona* and *Janine* and *Miss
Tress* meant that?). Loud music came from the open windows of
the 'Nigeria Social Club' and at the 'Sierra Leone Social Club'
there were fat blacks in bowler hats and shabby business suits on
the steps, drinking beer out of cans. I assumed that the 'social
club' was a way of evading Britain's strict drinking hours, and the
names suggested not racism but rather nationalism or even
tribalism – I could not imagine anyone from Upper Volta or
Nigeria being welcome in the 'Ghana Social Club'.

Princes Road was a wide boulevard lined with trees. I followed
it down to Granby, counting policemen – eight in a matter of
minutes. They walked in pairs carrying steel-tipped canes about
a yard long, the sort of weapon that usually has a poetic name, like
'wog-basher'. The policemen gave the impression of friendliness
and deliberately chatted to bystanders and small children,
seeming to ignore the graffiti which said PIGS OUT and *Why are
coppers like bananas – coz they yellow, they bent, and they come in
bunches*.

The shops on side streets had either boarded-up windows or
else steel mesh grates, and the same grates sheathed the public
phone-boxes. I stepped into one of these phone-boxes and called
the Central Police Station and asked the information officer how
many black policemen there were in Liverpool.

'Who wants to know?' he asked.

'Just a curious American,' I said.

'I should have known,' he said. 'I'll tell you something – Liverpool is nothing like America. I know about the trouble you've got over there, and compared to that this is nothing. I could give you figures –'

'For starters, how many black policemen?'

'Twelve coloured officers,' he said. And the entire force was 4600.

'*Twelve!*' I laughed and hung up.

And the 'coloured' was interesting, too. Policemen were 'coloured', convicted criminals were 'West Indian', and purse-snatchers were 'nig-nogs'. But when a black runner came first in a race against foreigners he was 'English'. If he came second he was 'British'. If he lost he was 'coloured'. If he cheated he was 'West Indian'.

I kept walking. The riots had left marks on Liverpool Eight that were visible a year later: the broken windows had not been fixed, there were signs of scorching on walls and doors, and temporary barricades had been left in place. And there were posters advertising lectures by members of the Communist Party and the Socialist Workers Party – very angry lectures, judging by the titles ('Fight Back!', 'We Demand Action!' and so forth). And yet this area was not the ruin I had expected. I had been promised a wasteland, but it was no more than fine decaying houses and rotting odours.

In a ploy to gain entrance to a house I asked a shopkeeper (Manubhai Patel, formerly of Kampala, Uganda; drygoods and sundries) if he knew of a person who might sew a button on my leather jacket. Yes, he knew a *karia* – Gujerati for black – just around the corner.

'Thanks very much,' I said.

'*Kwaheri, bwana.*'

God, I thought, that feels good. It had been years since anyone had called me *bwana*.

Mrs Luster was from Barbados. She had lived in England since 1953, when West Indians were encouraged to leave their homes and emigrate to Britain by the Conservative government – it was thought there would be a severe labour shortage very soon. Mrs

Luster worked for about twenty years in a shirt factory, and then it closed ('all these imports from Hong Kong'). She was fifty-seven and been married twice; both husbands had died. Every night she said a prayer for God to send her another husband: it was no fun living alone. In her council flat, four upstairs rooms of an Edwardian terrace house (rent: nine pounds a week), she had pictures of the Queen, the Pope, Prince Andrew, the wedding of Prince Charles and Lady Diana, and Jesus Christ showing his heart in flames. Most of the pictures she had cut from magazines, but she also had postcards stuck to the wall, and five calendars, and there was so much furniture I had to walk very slowly, sliding between heavily upholstered chairs.

I asked her what she thought of Britain.

Mrs Luster said, 'It ain't what it was.'

Not far from Mrs Luster's house I saw three young men standing on the pavement. Their names were Pitt, Oliver and Peery. They had all been born in Liverpool and were out of work. They were all about twenty years old. When I approached them they were discussing the fortunes of a man who rejoiced in the name Funso Banjo. They claimed I knew him, but I said I had never before heard the wonderful name of Funso Banjo.

I asked them whether they thought there would be riots this year in Liverpool Eight.

Peery said, 'We already had a riot!'

'April,' Oliver said. 'Pretty big one, too.'

This was news to me. It had not been in any newspapers that I had seen.

They said that there was often trouble but that it was seldom reported by the national newspapers.

'They can't report everything,' I said. 'How big was the riot?'

They said that hundreds of people had taken part and that three cars had been burned. It had happened after the arrest of a black boy by the police – rumours had spread that the boy had been shot or beaten up by the police. The rumours were not true, but the riot had taken place just the same, and no one was sorry, because (Oliver told me) the police were always stopping black people and searching them.

I said, 'Do you think there will be more riots?'

'Depends on the police, don't it,' Pitt said.

I said, 'Then why not join the police?'

They reacted like scalded cats, and then they laughed, as if I had suggested the most improbable thing in the world.

'Just give me one reason,' I said.

'No one would talk to you,' Oliver said.

Peery said, 'You wouldn't have a friend left!'

I said that I had expected to find a devastated area, but instead this part of Liverpool seemed to me rather pleasant, with a good bus service and plenty of shops, even if they did have boarded-up windows.

Oliver said, 'It's not bad now.' And he smiled. 'But it's different when it gets dark.'

Sunset found me walking rapidly out of Liverpool Eight.

The train to Southport was a busy branch line, because the whole nineteen miles of coast that was designated Merseyside was inhabited by Liverpool's commuters. The first few miles were taken up with warehouses and the cranes of the dockyards. It was grimy and Brooklynesque, especially in the dark brick of the railway cut at Bank Hall, and again at the two Bootle Stations, the first with a black brimful canal and an old factory sign saying *Treacle For Health*, the second Bootle Station, New Strand, with its flattened buildings and vacant lots.

Even after six miles it seemed to me that we had never really left Liverpool – an unbroken line of dirty buildings continued up the coast, the same age as the buildings in Liverpool proper but, because they were darker and lower, very dreary. Waterloo ('founded in 1815') was a decrepit place, and it was nine miles before I saw any grass growing beside the line. At last the stations had a countrified look, and a lighter, leafier aspect. They had names like Hightown and Freshfields, but they were rather fine – places in Britain with names like Freshfields I had found almost invariably to be slums.

We came to a grassy duney heath, with hundreds of low burial mounds – tumuli. Perhaps they were bunkers from the war, though they might well have been bunkers from the golf courses that proliferated here – six so far and we were not even in Southport. The land continued flat, the commuters got off the little train and walked home through the pink and purple lupins, and then, forty minutes after leaving Liverpool, we arrived at the back end of Southport.

It seemed odd for a seaside resort to be built in one of the rainiest areas of Britain, but that was not the oddest feature of Southport. Odder still was its promenade, which was a quarter of a mile from the beach; and at low tide it was a mile along the beach to the water on the hard brown sand. When the tide was down the beach was a long ludicrous desert, but flatter than any desert I had seen. Cars drove across it. The pier was high and dry. The sun at 9:30 p.m. seemed to be setting at the far end of Egypt. There was no watery shimmer, no indication that it was setting in the ocean. It bumped the planet and was gone. Southport was a cluttered seaside resort without much sea, at the edge of seemingly limitless sands.

Because swimming had always been so hard to manage in Southport, the town had erected saltwater swimming pools, and a large mosaic on a bathhouse on the front advertised '*Victorian Seawater Baths – Entirely New Turkish, Russian and Swimming Baths – Finest in District.*' That was an old red-brick place, but there was a new one not far away with an Olympic-size pool, or 'pule', as they described it.

I stayed in a Southport bed-and-breakfast place, with a family, the Bertrams: Herb – out of work and suspicious and always eyeing me nervously when Trish – 'I find I can really relax with Americans' – got down on all fours on the front-room carpet to retrieve Jason's 'Happy Family' playing cards from under the sofa, or to sweep, or to shampoo the carpet. Trish was frequently on her hands and knees when I was sitting in the room. It was a posture that unnerved Herb. It was as if, in ape terms, she was 'presenting' to me – the bum-show that matters so much in baboon society. Was she symbolically submitting to me as she sponged the carpet? Herb picked his teeth and narrowed his eyes, daring me to look.

They were a young couple, they had always lived in Southport, and they hated it. Two days with the Bertrams made me gloomy and sometimes in the evening I felt we were three baboons in the room – no conversation but a great deal of meaningful posturing. They had pawned their best wedding present, a silver 'After Eight Mints' dispenser in the shape of an old English coach and horses (the box of mints went into the coach). Twenty-eight pounds it was worth, but the pawnbroker would only give them eleven. They often grumbled about this, using it as a personal illustration of their hard times. Their hopelessness and depression were infectious. They believed that nothing would ever happen to them to change their lives for the better. I had always imagined that people in this plight would become curious about the world and its possibilities; but they were indifferent to it.

Even Jason, who was twelve, was lacking in hope. He was a bright boy but he said he was in the 'B' class. 'All the posh woons are in the "A" class. Teacher's pets and that.' He said he was planning to leave school when he was sixteen.

'What would your mother say about that?'

'Me moom don't care.'

The dislike of school was not unusual, but the widespread distrust of education was another matter. Perhaps it was justified. Everyone said the schools were bad – the only good ones were private ones – and it was a fact that many well educated people were on the dole. And yet it depressed me to think of this young family dying of indifference.

Lord Street in Southport was a grand boulevard with arcades and Victorian iron canopies. This was gritty northern splendour, wide streets and big draughty buildings. But there were a great number of elderly people in it, and they added to Southport's atmosphere of feebleness and senility. Herb explained that this was June, the low season, and old age pensioners had special rates at hotels all over the Lancashire coast. I would see masses of mentally defective people, too, he promised; mental defectives also got special rates in the low season.

The day I left, I walked up to Marshside Sands, where Merseyside meets Lancashire, and then walked back again. A car followed me along the beach, passed me, and then stopped. The driver got out and sat on a bench, staring at me. I thought it might have been Herbert Bertram having another apeish fit of jealousy. But no, it was a youth in a leather jacket. I kept walking. I reached Marine Drive. He had got back into his car and followed me again. He drew up beside me.

'Want a lift?'

I said no.

'Pity,' he said, and drove away.

Love on all fours. It wasn't passion, it was just more pathetic sex.

On the branch line to Wigan, I opened the local Southport newspaper and read an advertisement for pornographic films. *Two big screens – Live strip-tease – only £2 – This Week 'The Hot One' – Reduced admission for unemployed, students and Old Age Pensioners.*

That, surely, was a sign of the times, and a vision of the world to come: discounts on pornography if we were unemployed or a student or very old, for the chances were much greater that if you were one or the other you would have enough spare time to turn porn shows into a habit.

Blackpool was only ten miles from Southport, but there was no direct road or train – the River Ribble was in the way – so I went via Burscough Bridge and Parbold and through flat green vegetable fields to Wigan, to change trains. Almost fifty years before, George Orwell had come here and used this manufacturing town to examine English working life and the class structure. He had found 'labyrinths of little brick houses blackened by smoke, festering in planless chaos round miry alleys and little cindered yards where there are stinking dustbins and lines of grimy washing and half-ruinous w.c.s.'

But Wigan today, on a cold overcast morning in June, had a somewhat countrified look, like a market town, its winding main street on a little hill, with red-brick hotels and two railway stations and many public houses fitted with bright mirrors and brasswork. I walked out of the centre of the town and it seemed to me that Crook Street, with its cobblestones, and hemmed in between the railway embankment and the Collier's Arms, could not have changed for a hundred years. The dark red terraced houses had flat fronts and leaded windows and soot on the pointing of the brick that emphasized the bricks' redness. This was what Orwell had seen.

It was now lifeless. The town had once been a centre of coal mining and cotton mills. Both industries were gone. Orwell had thought Wigan illustrated the evils of industry and the miseries of workers' lives. But he would have found that unthinkable today, because the only industry left was a canning factory. There

was a kind of grubby vitality in *The Road to Wigan Pier* (the title
was a lame joke – there was no pier), and a ferocious indignation
that working people were treated so badly. But now there was very
little work. This was an area of desperately high unemployment,
of a deadly calm – which was also like panic – and of an over-
whelming emptiness. Orwell's anger had made the suffering
Wigan of his book still seem a place of possibility. Better labour
laws, compassionate management, conscientious government and
more self-awareness ('the working classes *do* smell!') would, he
suggested, enable Wigan to be resurrected.

What Orwell had not reckoned on – no one had – was that the
bottom would fall out, and that in this post-industrial slump, with
little hope of recovery, Wigan would be as bereft of energy and as
empty a ruin as Stonehenge. So there was a terrible poignancy in
his complaints about dark satanic mills and the working
conditions in the factories and the mines, for when the mills did
not run and the factories were shut, and the pits were closed, the
effect was more terrible than the worst industrial defilement.

The real nightmare of northern England today was not the
blackened factory chimneys and the smoke and the slag-heaps and
the racket of machines; it was the empty chimneys and the clear
air and the grass growing on slag-heaps, and the great silence. No
one talked about working conditions now; there was no work.
Industry had come and gone. It was as if a wicked witch had heard
Orwell's carping ('factory whistles . . . smoke and filth') and said,
'Then you shall have nothing!' and swept it all away.

One of the most famous passages of Orwell's book described a
young woman he saw from a train near Wigan. She was kneeling
on stones and poking a stick into a waste-pipe to unblock it.
'She looked up as the train passed' and her face wore 'the most
desolate, hopeless expression I have ever seen.' Hers was not 'the
ignorant suffering of an animal. She knew well enough what was
happening to her.' And Orwell closed with the thought that she
understood all the implications of her filthy job and realized what
a 'dreadful destiny' she faced.

That vivid description made me watchful in Wigan. I was
walking back to Wigan North-Western Station when, passing a
row of 'little grey slum houses at right angles to the embankment'
– a train was just passing – I saw an old woman hanging out her

washing. A light rain had begun to fall. It seemed sad for an old woman to be hanging grey laundry on a line in the rain, but it made a peculiarly Wiganesque image. And she could have been the same woman who had been kneeling on the cobbles and unblocking the waste-pipe in 1936, now grown older and still enduring her destiny.

I was overcome with curiosity and wanted to talk to her. It meant climbing a fence, but she was not startled. She asked me if I was lost.

I said no, I just happened to be passing by – and she smiled, because she had seen me eagerly climbing the fence by the railway embankment.

Her name was Mrs Midgeley, she was a widow, she was 71. Her age was interesting. The woman Orwell had seen from the train was about 25, and that was in 1936; so she would be 71 today.

At the age of 15, in 1926, Margaret Midgeley began working in a factory, sewing shirts. She worked from eight in the morning until nine-thirty at night, with slightly fewer hours on Saturdays; her Sundays were free.

'They wouldn't do that today, would they?' she said with pride, and she added, 'No, they'd rather go on the dole!'

She was in Wigan, working, when Orwell came. She thought she had heard the name before, but she had never read the book. She said that outsiders seldom had a good word to say about Wigan, but she had been very happy there. She worked for fifteen years in the factory and then got married. Now her husband was dead, her children had moved away; she was alone. She said she often thought about her working days.

'How much did I earn? I *had* to earn thirty-two shillings.'

I said, 'What do you mean "*had* to"?'

'I was on piece work,' Mrs Midgeley said. 'If I didn't earn thirty-two bob it meant I was slacking. Oh, the foreman used to talk to us about that! You got shouted at! Maybe you'd only earn a pound, and then you'd be in lumber.'

'In lumber' meant in trouble, Mrs Midgeley said, but when I checked it in a dictionary of slang it was described as an obsolescent phrase for being in detention or in prison.

Mrs Midgeley did not see herself as having been exploited. Her memory of Wigan in the 1930s was of a kind of prosperity, with coal and cotton and a sense of community, and work for anyone who was willing.

'And you could better yourself if you wanted to,' she said.

But Wigan was hopeless now, she said. It was laziness and the dole and no prospects. Mrs Midgeley was nostalgic for the smoke ('Mind you, it could play merry hell with your washing!') and remembered with pleasure her workmates at the factory and their annual outing to Blackpool.

She said it frightened her to think of all the young people with nothing to do. It made her feel unsafe. It was a world without work – and that was a terrible thing to her, who had worked her whole life.

'And where are you off to, then?'

I said Blackpool.

'Lucky old you,' she said, and laughed.

On my way out of Wigan on the train I looked out of the window and saw a group of white-faced children. The rain had plastered their hair against their tiny heads, and their clothes were soaked, and their bare legs were dirty. They were struggling to pull a fence down at the back of a ruined house. They were busy and violent, they hammered at the pickets, they looked like small dangerous men. When they saw the train they spat at it and then they went on breaking the old fence.

14

The West Cumbria Line

Most of the horror cities of northern England were surrounded by smooth hills and cow pastures and the hopeful contours of green space; and so it was painful to see how Blackpool sprawled along the eastward bulge of Lancashire, displacing the grassy coastline with a fourteen mile funfair, from Lytham St Annes to Fleetwood. There was a no relief. And now I began to reassess Southport – it is only hindsight that gives travel any meaning – and, looking back, I realized that Southport had been modestly elegant. I had called it cluttered, but Blackpool was real clutter: the buildings that were not only ugly but also foolish and flimsy, the vacationers sitting under a dark sky with their shirts off, sleeping with their mouths open, emitting hog whimpers. They were waiting for the sun to shine, but the forecast was rain for the next five months.

The Falklands war had entered a new phase. British troops were creeping across the main island, preparing to retake Port Stanley. The headlines of the gutter press were QUEEN LASHES ARGIES and THREE BRITISH SHIPS HIT and THE MARCH TOWARDS STANLEY. This harsh news certainly coloured my feelings towards Blackpool, because one of the sights of seaside Britain that I knew would stick firmly in my mind was the long promenade and the three piers at Blackpool: the people sleeping in deck chairs, clutching copies of the daily paper, news of the bloody war. They woke snorting and vengeful-looking, with pink sleep-welts on their cheeks; and then they slapped their papers and went on reading. Tomorrow they would be using it for wrapping the fish and chips.

There was no landscape here. The mass of cheap buildings that had risen up and displaced the land had in its bellying way displaced the sea, too. Blackpool was perfectly reflected in the swollen guts and unhealthy fat of its beer-guzzling visitors – eight million in the summer, when Lancashire closed to come here and belch. This was northern gusto! This hideous promenade was 'The Golden Mile'! This bad weather was 'bracing'!

But it was just swagger and sandwiches. 'Bracing' was the northern euphemism for stinging cold and it always justified the sadism in the English seaside taunt, 'Let's get some colour in those cheeks.' It was another way of making a freezing wind compensate for the lack of sunshine. And yet not everyone in Blackpool was deceived. Beneath mountainous storm clouds, seventeen people on North Pier paid forty pence each to sit in the 'Sun Lounge' – a sort of greenhouse on the pier with salt-spattered windows – and listen to Raymond Wallbank ('Your Musical Host') play 'I'll Be Seeing You' on his console organ until the windows trembled. They sat and listened and read the *Daily Mail* – FIVE ARGIES DIE IN EXPLOSION – and when Raymond Wallbank took a breather, they chatted. Once again I noticed that the Falklands news made the English nostalgic about rationing and the blitz.

Mr Gummer wanted the Argentine mainland to be bombed – why not flatten Buenos Aires? After all, the Argies had captured a British sheep station. Those bloody bean-eaters had to be taught a lesson. Mr Gummer liked to say that he had been a socialist his whole life, but he had a lot of respect for the prime minister. She had guts, and he agreed that it was a good idea to call the British troops 'our boys'.

He had come to Blackpool to fish. He was retiring this year and lived with his wife Viv in a cottage in Swillbrook, just off the motorway. He had paid a pound to stand on the pier with his fishing rod, and after a morning of it he was almost out of the live worms he used as bait. Mr Gummer wondered: Should I have a longer rod?

'Hae ye caught owt?' This was Ernie Fudge. The Fudges said they would be stopping a week in Blackpool. Ernie had known Harry Gummer for donkey's years. They were both in wholesale decorating equipment, supplying do-it-yourself shops in this part of Lancashire.

'Nay,' Mr Gummer said. 'I want more tackle.' He was thinking of the longer rod.

'Got tackle there in hand!' Mr Fudge cried. 'Too bloody mooch tackle in fishing.'

Harry Gummer said, 'That's true of every 'obby tha takes oop. Me soon 'as a bloody bamboo pole can reach to bloody flagpole yonder.'

Ernie shrugged. He did not want to argue. Fishermen always looked helpless to him, dangling hooks blindly in the sea. But Harry was his friend.

'Hae ye seen 'odges?' Ernie said.

'Aye,' Harry said. 'He waar at t'oother end. I boomped into 'im. He waar wi' scroofy booger – a big thick bloke.' Harry showed with a gesture that the man had a big pot belly. 'Union bloke, 'odges says, and I says "Oh, aye," and he gives me 'is union bloody card. And then I says –'

I took a tram to Fleetwood, but there was no footpath to Lancaster that way. I returned to Blackpool and realized that the tram system made this part of the coast bearable. I had enjoyed the ride, even if I had used it to list all the features of Blackpool I disliked. And when I asked local people to tell me Blackpool's virtues I was confirmed in my dislike.

'But it's quaat naas soomtimes,' Murine Mudditch said. 'We've been living here ever since Ian was made redoondant.'

I asked her how she spent her time.

'Drinking and bingo,' she said.

'Every day?'

'Most days.'

'What if you don't like drinking and bingo?'

Mrs Mudditch had a bubbling bronchitic laugh.

She said, 'Then you've 'ad it!'

I wanted to leave Blackpool, and I was annoyed that it was not possible to walk away. I went to the bus station and bought a ticket to Morecambe. Five of us boarded the bus, and the bus went everywhere, stopping every quarter of a mile, at villages and at isolated public houses where sad-faced women waited with string bags.

Mrs Buglass was from Lancaster, but she hated the Lancashire type. She had lived too long in the south of England, she said – it had spoiled her.

'They're dead nosey up here,' Mrs Buglass said. 'They want to know all your business – always talking, always asking questions. The people in the south are very polite. They don't go on and on, they don't ask you about your private affairs. That's the big problem up here – no privacy.'

She smiled at me. We were on the top deck, front seat, Garstang up ahead.

'I like to keep meself to meself.'

And she winked at me.

What was there about an English wink that made me so uncomfortable?

Mrs Buglass said, 'I'd give anything to go back to Southend!'

'I'm on my way to Southend,' I said.

She winked agan. 'You're going in the wrong direction, darling.'

No, I said, I would get there eventually: I was going clockwise.

Morecambe was wrapped around the edge of a dirty sea, scowling, its blackened terraces and hotels reminiscent of certain fierce churches – all spikes and shadows. Much of the foreshore was stony, but where there was sand there were naked children kneeling and fat ladies holding their skirts against their thighs.

'Aye! This is good for you! Yer mightn't feel any bennyfit for ages and ages. Boot –'

And there were ponies, too, and heaps of pony shit, and on the front a joyless Pleasure Park and Fun City and Giftarama and a gypsy fortune teller named Annie Lee who looked at my knapsack and announced in a voice full of dramatic clairvoyance that I was a traveller and that I had never been to Morecambe before – nor was I likely to come here again, she added, which was incontestable.

But I liked Morecambe for its being sedate and dull and unapologetic. Its stateliness had been eroded by the blasts of wind, and it was the dampest place I had seen since Cornwall, but this lugubrious mood seemed to suit it. It astonished me that anyone would come here for a vacation and to have fun, since it seemed the sort of place that would fill even the cheeriest visitor – me, for example – with thoughts of woe. I imagined day-trippers getting off the train and taking one look and bursting into tears. But of course most people at Morecambe were enjoying themselves in the drizzle, and the fault was mine, not theirs. This was just another cultural barrier I was incapable of surmounting.

Nothing is more bewildering to a foreigner than a nation's pleasures, and I never felt more alien in Britain than when I was watching people enjoying their sort of seaside vacation.

On the branch-line train that travelled around Morecambe Bay in a wide swing to Barrow-in-Furness I thought: This is the first part of the north coast that doesn't look blighted. Perhaps it was because we were leaving Lancashire and entering Cumbria, crossing from county to county at Silverdale, where there were daisies growing on the platform, and the ringing stench of cow manure – a smell that sang like rotten ozone. It was hilly, green, misty, and the bay was so sandy it was possible on a good day to walk the nine miles across to Grange-over-Sands. I remarked on the lovely bay, but a schoolgirl named Gina (straw boater, necktie, blazer) said that the water was so filthy it was impossible to swim in, and there was also quicksand out there that sucked you under.

There were more wide wet patches on Cartmel Sands, and small black islands just offshore. We came to Ulverston ('Here Stan Laurel the film comedian was born'). It was a day's walk to the Lake District, up the River Crake and through the Furness Fells to Grizedale Forest and the long lakes of Windermere and Coniston Water. But I had vowed to stick to the coast. I was not in search of natural wonders. And not far away there was a great branch line that went from Barrow to Carlisle, much of it along the coast: the West Cumbria Line.

This part of the English coast had everything. It had fishing villages and mountains and coal mines that went under the sea. It had footpaths and a good train and several industrial towns; it had a soft duney shore; it had the scariest-looking nuclear reactor I had ever seen.

The Cumbrian Mountains rose up on the other side of Duddon Sands, the bare summit of Black Combe, and from Foxfield to Bootle the foothills of these mountains had forced the railway directly on to the coast. After Bootle the land became flatter; I was looking for a likely place to get off the train, and almost did at Ravenglass ('the junction of the Esk, the Mite, and the Irt'), but I was not quick enough.

To see Britain I had had to think of ways of slowing myself down. It was a small kingdom, and even the great folds and rucks of its coast were not enough to make me feel as though I was traversing great tracts of land. I was always aware that I was only a matter of hours from London, though the differences in landscape and manners were so vast it sometimes seemed a world away.

But the hinterland of Britain was not always the past. Sometimes it had the face of the future. That was certainly the case on this line at Windscale. Windscale was so much a part of the future it was not yet on the Ordnance Survey map. But there was something there. It had the simplicity and proportions of an enormous tomb and was the more frightening for its absence of identifiable features. Something so new, so huge, so heavily fenced-in, on so distant a beach *had* to be dangerous. On this old corrugated coast its size alone was disturbing, and its fresh red paint looked alarming against the grey landscape. Its cooling chimneys and its towers gave it the appearance of a Martian castle, but essentially this coastal monstrosity was no more than a tremendous box. There was nothing subtle about it. Its long flat planes made it grotesque. Even if you did not know what it was it would still have been fearsome; it was not that it was unfamiliar, but rather that it looked dangerously explosive.

It was of course another nuclear power station – the nuclear pile at Windscale.

New track was being laid for a line going in and out of the plant. It would connect to this branch line. That was certainly another sign of the times. The only new railway track I saw being laid in Britain, this little spur to the nuclear power station, was for radioactive material, not passengers.

'They say they're not dangerous,' a man next to me said. His name was Cutbill, but he pronounced it 'Cootbill'. 'That's what they say – they're safe as houses.'

'Do you think they're right?' I had no idea who he meant by 'they'.

Mr Cutbill said, 'Know something? You can't insure them.' And he grinned. 'That's encouraging, isn't it? I mean to say, if they're so bloody safe, why can't you insure them?' Then he laughed: he knew the answer to that question.

It was low tide: great empty beaches of black rocks and black sand, and rock pools that looked greasy in the poor light. I had expected something different, greener, higher, fresher, perhaps Wordsworthian. That was the trouble with England – it was imaginary. 'The West Cumbria Line' called up images of deserted woodland and steep fells and pikes, not a nuclear time-bomb of incomparable ugliness on a black coast.

It was at that point that Cutbill told me about the coal mines. They had been running for hundreds of years. ('Whitehaven,' Defoe wrote in 1725, 'now the most eminent port in England for the shipping of coals.') One of the pits had been sunk in 1780, but it had closed in the 1940s when an explosion killed 147 men. Cutbill knew all the dates and all the casualty statistics. An explosion at Wellington Pit in 1910 had killed, he said, 'a hundred and fifty men and boys'. Haig Pit was still working.

'And the interesting thing,' Cutbill said, 'is that the mineshafts are under the sea – they go straight out, some of them for miles. But they're never flooded, and the water that leaks in is fresh not salty.'

A green headland loomed, and the train slowed down. This was St Bees. I liked the look of it – villagey, with a handsome school on the right and cliffs on the left; I even liked its funny name. And this was a good time of day – the sun breaking beneath late-afternoon clouds for a long well-lighted evening.

'I think I'll get off here,' I said.

'I've got things to do in Corkickle,' Cutbill said. 'I'm not like you blokes with your rooksacks,' and he smiled. 'I've got to fill the unforgiving minute.'

Kipling, the great standby in the English oral tradition. The English often quoted with approval writers they hadn't read, just as they damned as vulgar or dull, places they hadn't been.

I walked around St Bees ('named from St Bega, a seventh-century Irish maiden') and then, because Cutbill had aroused my curiosity with his talk of submarine coal mines, I walked on to Rottington and Whitehaven.

I could smell the coal and the potash before I saw the town. Whitehaven was old and moribund and like many another bad place in England its only hotel was dreary and expensive – fifteen pounds for a narrow room and a damp bath mat. Writing my diary that night I generalized on this, concluding that every large hotel at which I had stayed in England was run down or badly managed, overpriced, understaffed and dirty, the staff overworked and slow; and all the smaller places were preferable, the smallest always the best. The English were great craftsmen but poor mass-producers of goods. They were brilliant at running corner shops, but were failures when they tried their hands at supermarkets. Perhaps this had something to do with their sense of anonymity? Person to person, I had found them truthful and efficient and humane. But anonymity made them lazy, dishonest and aggressive. Hidden in his car the Englishman was often impatient to the point of being murderous; over the phone they were unhelpful and frequently rude. They were not timid, but shy; shyness made them tolerant, but it also gave them a grudge against foreigners, whom they regarded as boomers and show-offs. It was hard to distinguish hotels in England from prisons or hospitals. Most of them were run with the same indifference or cruelty and were equally uncomfortable. The larger an English industry was, the more likely it was to go bankrupt, because the English were not naturally corporate people; they disliked working for others and they seemed to resent taking orders. On the whole, directors were treated absurdly well, and workers badly, and most industries were weakened by class suspicion and false economies and cynicism. But the same qualities that made English people seem stubborn and secretive made them, face to face, reliable and true to their word. I thought: The English do small things well and big things badly.

I called the Haig Pit the next day and asked whether I could go down the mine. I thought it would make a good story, another Orwell footnote, and with an underground railway as well, 'The Railway Under The Sea', sweating Cumbrians toiling at the coal-face by the light of flaring lamps, here in the bowels of the earth, the sewer of the Lake District; all of it strange news – and you thought you knew something about England!

'Because it's more than my job's worth,' Jack Smale was saying in a discouraging way. 'If I let you go down there and something happens I'll be in dead trouble. How do I know you're not going to throw a fit or something.'

'I promise not to throw a fit,' I said

'You can bloody promise anything you like, but if you've never been down a mine before how do you know what's going to happen? You might come all over queer.'

'I suppose I can't promise that I won't come all over queer,' I said.

'I don't make the rules,' Mr Smale said. 'It's just that our insurance people are always on at us.'

'I only wanted to have a look,' I said.

Mr Smale said, 'I don't want to be rude, mate. But –'

It was one of the rudest expressions in English; it was certainly the tetchiest.

We were of course speaking on the phone. If I had asked Mr Smale the question in the Collier's Arms on Whitehaven harbour one evening while he was smiling into his pint of beer ('Aye, it's brain damage, but it's loovely stoof –'), he would probably have said, 'I'm supposed to say no, but I don't see the harm in it'; the English working-man enjoyed a conspiratorial posture: 'Pop round in the morning and I'll sort you out,' he would wink, 'I'll see you right.'

I decided to leave Whitehaven. It was partly because four different people told me that George Washington's grandmother was buried in the local churchyard. It was a disappointing town – hundreds of small dark houses pitched across a bare hillside, and an air of doom about it. Coalmining towns always seemed to wear an expression of fatigue, and they had a scattered volcanic look, the itch of coal dust, the atmosphere of eruption.

The rest of the coast, from the window of the train, was low and disfigured. There were small bleak towns like Parton and Harrington, and huge horrible ones like Workington, with its steelworks – another insolvent industry. And Maryport was just sad; it had once been an important coal and iron port, and great sailing ships had been built there in Victorian times. Now it was forgotten. Today there was so little shipbuilding on the British coast it could be said not to exist at all. But that was not so odd as the fact that I saw very few vessels in these harbours and ports at all: a rusty freighter, a battered trawler, some plastic sailboats, little else where once there had been hundreds of sea-going vessels.

I watched for more. What I saw was ugly and interesting, but before I knew what was happening the line cut inland, passing bramble hedges, and crows in fields of silage, and small huddled-together farm buildings, and church steeples in distant villages. We had left the violated coast and now the mild countryside reasserted itself. It was green farms all the way to Carlisle – pretty and extremely dull.

'*Keswick Punks*', a scrawl said in Carlisle, blending Coleridge and Wordsworth with Johnny Rotten. But that was not so surprising. It was always in the fine old provincial towns and county seats that one saw the wildest-looking youths, the pink-haired boys and the girls in leopard-skin tights, the nose-jewels and tattooed earlobes. I had seen green hair and swastikas in little Llanelli. I no longer felt that place-names like Taunton or Exeter or Bristol were evocative of anything but graffiti-covered walls, like those of noble Carlisle, crowned with a castle and with enough battlements and city walls to satisfy the most energetic vandal. *Violent Revolution*, they said, and *The Exploited* and *Anarchy* and *Social Scum*. Perhaps they were pop groups? *The Rejects*, *The Defects*, *The Outcasts*, *The Damned*, and some bright new swastikas and *The Barmy Army*. And on the ancient walls, *Skinheads Rule!*

Some of it was hyperbole, I supposed, but it was worth spending a day or so to examine it. It fascinated me as much as did the motorcycle gangs, who raced out of the oak forests and country lanes to terrorize villagers, or simply to sit in a thatch-roofed pub, averting their sullen dirty faces. I did not take it personally when they refused to talk to me. They would not talk to anyone. They were English, they were country folk, they were shy. They were only dangerous by the dozen; individually they were rather sweet and seemed embarrassed to be walking down the high road of dear old Haltwhistle in leather jackets inscribed *Hell's Angels* or *The Damned*.

The graffiti suggested that England – perhaps the whole of Britain – was changing into a poorer, more violent place. And it was easier to see this deterioration on the coast and in the provincial towns than in a large city. The messages were intended to be shocking, but England was practically unshockable and so the graffiti seemed merely a nuisance, an insult. And that was how I began to think of the whole country; if I had only one word to describe the expression of England's face I would have said: insulted.

15

The Boat Train to Ulster

There was a gloomy irritable air about the passengers on the boat train to Ulster. It was not only that they had been on board for five hours and had three more to go before the ferry. It was worse than tiredness. It was resentment – as if they were being exiled, or forced back to school, or jailed after a period of freedom. But in fact they were homeward-bound.

I had joined the train at Carlisle. I expected to see either drunks or sleepers – it was mid-afternoon. But the passengers sat silently, holding their sallow faces in their hands, and they became gloomier as we progressed through the long Scottish hills of the border – Dumfries and Galloway. They were the sad-faced people in the wind at grey Stranraer.

By then the Scots had got off the train – the men who sat six to a table with a bottle of vodka and twenty cans of Tartan Ale; the families sitting in a nest of newspapers and sandwich wrappers and plastic bags; the poor stinking trampled terriers and their defiant owners; and the children screeching, 'How much farva!' and 'I can hear funda!' No trains got more befouled than the ones to Scotland, but this boat train was mostly empty by the time it reached Kilmarnock, and so on the last stage of its journey, along the Firth of Clyde, it looked wrecked and abandoned, the beer cans clanking and the bottles rolling on the floor, and an atmosphere of sour mayonnaise and stale cigarette smoke.

But I liked the hills and I was relieved once again to be near the shore. It was green countryside on a granite sea. Some of the coast was bare; in places there were forests, and hidden in deep lovely valleys there were baronial houses. The grey town of Girvan, with stone houses and squinting windows, had its back turned to the water and wind. At Glenwhilly there were crimson poppies beside the track.

It was here, just before arriving, that the returning Ulster people became very irritable.

'Go and sit *dine*!'

'I'm tullying ya fer the last time!'

'I says go and find your suster!'

'Don't look so surpraised!'

The Ulster accent is disliked in England, where it is regarded as a harsh, bastard, lowland Scots with a Glaswegian glottal stop. It is a blustering accent, and just as Welsh people seem permanently conciliatory in the way they speak, so the gabbling Ulster folk seem forever on the boil, trying to swallow and be cruel at the same time. The accent seems full of strain and greed, and yet the people are relaxed and friendly. A linguistic quirk makes them seem angry; it is as odd and as fascinating as the national lisp in Spain. Each time I heard an Ulsterman open his mouth I reached for my pen, like a missionary learning a tribal language and imagining a vernacular Bible or a dictionary.

Stranraer, in Loch Ryan, on the sea, was the main town on a peninsula shaped like a hammerhead. The ferry *Galloway Princess* was at the quayside, waiting for the arrival of the boat-train passengers to Larne. There were not many of us, but everyone was searched including the children – and the officers even groped in the infants' clothes. I was frisked, and then my knapsack was sifted through. They found my sheaf of maps, my binoculars, my notebook, my switchblade knife.

'And what's your purpose in going to Northern Ireland?' the policeman asked. This was Constable Wallace. Crumbs, the things he'd seen!

'Just looking around,' I said. 'A little business, a little pleasure. I might do a spot of bird-watching.'

'Carry on then,' Officer Wallace said, and handing me my knife he turned to his mate and said, 'A spot of bird-watching.'

There was a sign at the ferry entrance listing the various people who would not be allowed on board the *Galloway Princess* – rowdy people, drunks, and 'Football supporters ... displaying their club "favours" in any shape or form.'

Over dinner, Jack Mehaffy said, 'It's because the football clubs are one religion or another, and if you wear a certain colour scarf you're a Catholic or you're a Protestant. It causes friction. They don't want trouble on this boat.'

We met by chance: we were each dining alone and so were asked to sit at the same table. The conversation got off to a slow start. Later, Mehaffy said, 'You don't talk too much unless you know who you're talking to. No one in Northern Ireland expresses opinions of any kind to strangers until he's very sure his listeners will be sumpathetic. If not, they'll puck a fight.'

Perhaps our conversation was typical. It took us forty-five minutes to get to religion and another hour before Mehaffy volunteered that he was a Protestant. By then it would have been too late to quarrel about Irish politics. We were friends.

He had not stated his religion. He had said in a challenging way, 'I'm British.' But that meant the same thing as Protestant. He was in the tailoring business and he told me how, very soon, most tailoring would be done automatically by sewing machines operated by microchips. This was bad news for Ulster, where shirt factories employed large numbers of people. Mehaffy said many were being closed down – he had shut a number of them himself.

He had grown up in a neighbourhood in County Down with Protestants and Catholics. 'We didn't have much money, and when we were short it was the Catholics who helped us out, not the Loyalists who were always running the Union Jack up the flagpole. We're still friendly with those Catholic families.'

He told me about his being a scoutmaster and how he always had Catholic boys in his troop. He asked the local priest's permission to include those boys and the priest said, 'Yes, me only regret is that you're doing something I wish I were doing meself.'

'I liked him for saying that,' Mehaffy said.

We talked about tailoring, about unemployment, about strife, and that was when he said, 'I'm British. But I'm also Irish. I mean, culturally I'm British, but I was born in Ireland, so I'm Irish too.'

'Do you feel an affinity with the Republic?'

'No, no. The south is different. They have a different tradition

there. Funnily enough, at one time I could actually see union
with the Republic – a united Ireland. But now it's less and less
a possibility.'

He was reluctant to explain why, but then said, 'The influence
of the church is too strong there. Do you think any Ulsterman
would accept the infallibility of the Pope?'

I said, 'But they accept the infallibility of the Queen.'

He laughed. He said, 'And contraceptives on prescription!
We'd never accept it.'

Whenever the issue of union was raised Ulstermen mentioned
contraceptives.

'And there's the tribalism,' Mehaffy said. 'The tribalism starts
in July, with the Orange parades. The Catholic parades are in
August. And then, people who are the best of friends all year
won't speak to each other. There's a lot of suspicion in the
summer – a lot of tribal feeling – between Catholic and Protestant.'

I said, 'Is it possible to tell them apart?'

'There are people who say it is,' Mehaffy said, and pointing
to his eyes he went on, 'For one thing, a Catholic's eyes are closer
together.'

We went out on deck and watched the cluster of lights at Larne
drawing near. The mist liquefied the lights and made the harbour
entrance dramatic. Mehaffy said that Ulstermen worked hard and
had pride in their country. They hated people who tried to make
jokes out of bombings and killings. This was while the ferry was
making its way into Larne harbour, and the lights were piercing
the mist and illuminating the dark brown waterfront, the gleaming slates on the roofs, the oily lough to port. The wind groaned
among the dockside cranes. Mehaffy said it never stopped raining
here. The returning Ulster people who had been on the boat-train
stood silently at the rail, gazing upon Larne like mourners.
Mehaffy said the trouble was, there was only one bloody topic of
conversation, and who was really interested in that? The ferry
horn echoed all over the harbour and lough, as if from a thousand
empty holes in the night.

'I'm thinking of moving to England,' Mehaffy finally said.

His tone was confessional, his voice a whisper. I was still staring
at Larne and did not know what to say.

'I've got two kids,' he said. 'They're still young. They'll have a better chance there.'

I expected formalities – customs and immigration – Larne was so foreign-seeming, so dark and dripping; but there was not even a security check, just a gangway and the wet town beyond it. I wandered the streets for an hour, feeling like Billy Bones, and then rang the bell at a heavy-looking house displaying a window-card saying *Vacancies*. I had counted ten others, but this one I could tell had big rooms and big armchairs.

'Just off the ferry?' It was Mrs Fraser Wheeney, plucking at her dress, hair in a bun, face like a seal pup – pouty mouth, soulful eyes, sixty-five years old; she had been sitting under her own pokerwork *Rejoice in the Lord Alway* waiting for the doorbell to ring. 'Twenty-one fifteen it came in – been looking around town?'

Mrs Wheeney knew everything, and her guest house was of the in-law sort, oppression and comfort blended – like being smothered with a pillow. But business was terrible – only one other room was taken. Why, she could remember when, just after the ferry came in, she would have been turning people away! That was before the recent troubles, and what a lot of harm they'd done! But Mrs Wheeney was dead tired and had things on her mind, like the wild storm last night.

'Thonder!' she thundered. 'It opened up me hud!'

We were walking upstairs under a large motto – *For God So Loved the World*, and so forth.

'It gave me huddicks!'

The house was full of furniture, and how many floors? Four or five anyway, and pianos on some of them, and there was an ottoman, and a wing-chair, and pokerwork scenes from the Old Testament, Noah possibly, and was that Abraham and Isaac? The whole house was dark and varnished and gleaming – the smell of varnish still powerful, with the sizzle of a coal fire. It was June in Northern Ireland, so only one room had a fire trembling in the grate.

'And it went through me neighbour's roof,' she said, still talking about the storm, the thunder and lightning.

Another flight of stairs, heavy carpet, more Bible mottoes, an armchair on the landing.

'Just one more,' Mrs Wheeney said. 'This is how I get me exercise. Oh, it was turrible. One of me people was crying –'

Mirrors and antlers and more mottoes and wood panelling, and now I noticed that Mrs Wheeney had a moustache. She was talking about the *reeyun* – how hard it was; about breakfast at *eeyut* – but she would be up at *sux*; and what a dangerous *suttee* Belfast was.

Christ Jesus Came Into The World To Save Sinners was the motto over my bedstead, in this enormous draughty room, and the bed was a great slumping trampoline. Mrs Wheeney was saying that she had not slept a wink all the previous night. It was the thunder and the poor soul in number eight, who was scared to death.

'It's funny how tired you get when you miss a night's sleep,' she said. 'Now me, I'm looking forward to going to bed. Don't worry about the money. You can give me the five pounds tomorrow.'

The rain had started again and was hitting the window with a swish like sleet. It was like being among the Jumblies, on a dark and rainy coast. They were glad to see aliens here, and I was happy among these strangers.

That first morning in Larne I discovered everything there was to know about Ulster rain – how it bucketed down from a sky no higher than a two-storey house; how it was never the quicksilver of the Channel rain but always dark, striking at such a merciless slant that it penetrated everything; how it was cold and noisy, and how it could be sharp enough to sting; how it never cleansed but rather blackened everything it struck. And no matter how often it ̄ained, it was always so surprisingly cruel that everyone mentioned it. It was impossible to ignore. In this solemn, rain-darkened place people regarded the rain as unfair.

It was the setting that was solemn, not the people. (Though solemn was an understatement; Ulster looked black and deva-stated.) The people were curious – they stared, they smiled, they talked loudly and still managed to be polite. The women, most of all, seemed to me remarkable – just the way they stood and spoke, their decisive gestures, their spirit. It was true of girls, as well.

They seemed bold and friendly and able to take care of themselves.

These were judgements I made on the train from Larne to Belfast. It was a warm and rattly branch-line train, with bushes on the embankment beating against the door-handles, and bog ferns sliding across the wet windows.

I was talking to Dick Flattery. 'It's not a civil war,' he was saying. 'The Catholics and Protestants kill each other, but they haven't actually fought each other –'

Now who would have thought you could make such useful distinctions between 'fight' and 'kill'?

'– they kill each other singly,' he went on, 'but they fight the army and the police.'

Flattery seemed intelligent and detached. He had left Belfast seven years before, for good; he was only returning now because his father was ill. He wasn't planning to stay. He was frightened by the violence.

'It started as a civil rights issue, ten or eleven years ago' – he meant the marches, the first one in Londonderry in 1969 – 'and then it got violent. No one talks about civil rights anymore.'

He swiftly referred to Catholics as 'they' and I knew he must be a Protestant. I asked him whether he could tell a Catholic from a Protestant.

'The Protestants are from Scottish stock,' Flattery said. 'They look Scottish.'

We were travelling along Larne Lough – dark water, dark banks and the dark rain falling fast. We were talking about poverty.

'There's always been unemployment here,' he said. 'There's not the same stigma attached to it that you find in England. People here aren't lost when they're on the dole. It's really a kind of chronic condition – groups of men, standing on the street, doing nothing.' He looked out of the window. 'God, I hate this place.'

Now we were smack on the coast, leaving Whitehead and swaying towards Carrickfergus on a narrow shelf just above the sea, and then,

The little boats beneath the Norman castle
The pier shining with lumps of crystal salt;

The Scotch Quarter was a line of residential houses
But the Irish Quarter was a slum for the blind and the halt.

Louis MacNeice grew up in Carrickfergus, but it was not only
his poem about that town that seemed to me clear-sighted – all
his Ulster poems were vivid and true. And he wrote so well about
the sea, sometimes as a tumultuous thing ('Upon this beach the
falling wall of the sea . . .') and sometimes as a fuss-budget ("That
never-satisfied old maid, the sea/Rehangs her white lace curtains
ceaselessly'), and ultimately in its cosmic and thalassic sense: 'By
a high star our course is set,/Our end is life. Put out to sea.'

He had looked out to sea here, beyond Belfast Lough into
North Channel, and he had certainly been on this train, or else
he could not have written, 'Like crucifixes the gantries stand',
seeing the shipyard at Belfast.

I knew at once that Belfast was an awful city. It had a bad
face – mouldering buildings, tough-looking people, a visible
smell, too many fences. Every building that was worth blowing
up was guarded by a man with a metal detector, who frisked
people entering and checked their bags. It happened everywhere,
even at dingy entrances, at buildings that were not worth blowing
up, and again and again, at the bus station, the railway station.
Like the bombs themselves, the routine was frightening, then
fascinating, then maddening, and then a bore – but it went on
and became a part of the great waste-motion of Ulster life. And
security looked like parody, because the whole place was already
scorched and broken with bomb blasts.

It was so awful I wanted to stay. It was one of those cities
which was so demented and sick some aliens mistook its desperate
frenzy for a sign of health, never knowing it was a death agony.
It had always been a hated city. 'There is no aristocracy – no
culture – no grace – no leisure worthy of the name,' Sean
O'Faoláin wrote in his *Irish Journey*. 'It all boils down to mixed
grills, double whiskies, dividends, movies, and these strolling,
homeless, hate-driven poor.' But if what people said was true,
that it really was one of the nastiest cities in the world, surely
then it was worth spending some time in, for horror-interest?

I lingered a few days marvelling at its decrepitude and then
vowed to come back the following week. I had never seen any-

thing like it. There was a high steel fence around the city centre, and that part of Belfast was intact because, to enter it, one had to pass through a checkpoint – a turnstile for people, a barrier for cars and buses. More metal detectors, bag searches and questions: lines of people waited to be examined, so that they could shop, play bingo, or go to a movie.

There were still bombs. Just that week a new type of bomb had started to appear, a fire-bomb made of explosive fluid and a small detonator; it exploded and the fiery fluid spread. And it was very easily disguised. These bombs had turned up in boxes of soap flakes and breakfast cereal and pounds of chocolates. One in a tiny bag had been left on a bus, and ten passengers had been burned and the bus destroyed. That was my first day in Belfast – *Driver Steers Through Blaze Hell to Save Lives* displaced the Falklands news.

Threats, was a headline in every newspaper, with this message: *If you know anything about terrorist activities – threats, murders or explosions – please speak now to the Confidential Telephone – Belfast 652155.*

I called the number, just to inquire how busy they were. But it was an answering machine, asking me for information about bombs and murder. I said, 'Have a nice day,' and hung up. On the way to Coleraine and the coast I was in a train with about ten other people, two in each car – and some got out at Botanic Station, a mile from Central. I had never imagined Europe could look so threadbare – such empty trains, such blackened buildings, such recent ruins: *Dangerous Building – Keep Clear.* And bellicose religion, and dirt, and poverty, and narrow-mindedness, and sneaky defiance, trickery and murder, and little brick terraces, and drink shops, and empty stores, and barricades, and boarded windows, and starved dogs, and dirty-faced children – it looked like the past in an old picture. And a crucifix like a dagger in one brute's lapel, and an *Orange Lodge Widows' Fund* badge in another's. They said that Ulster people were reticent. It seemed to me they did nothing but advertise. *God Save the Pope* painted on one ruin, and on another, *God Save the Queen.* And at Lisburn a large sign by the tracks said *Welcome to Provoland.* Everyone advertised, even urban guerrillas.

Fifteen minutes outside Belfast we were in open country:

pleasant pastures, narrow lanes, cracked farmhouses. But in such a place as Ulster the countryside could seem sinister and more dangerous than a crowded city, since every person on the move was exposed in a meadow or a road. The old houses all stuck up like targets, and it was hard to see a tree or a stone wall and not think of an ambush.

No Surrender, it said on the bridge at Crumlin. That town was a low wet rabbit-warren set amid cow parsley and wet fields. And then Lough Neagh, one of Ulster's great lakes, and the town of Antrim. Now the train had a few more sullen skinny faces on board. The towns were no more than labour depots, factory sites surrounded by the small houses of workers. But the factories were shut, the markets were empty, and the farmland looked flooded and useless. We came to Ballymena. I asked a man in the car if it was true that in Slemish near here ('where St Patrick herded his sheep') children used to be kept in barrels to prevent them fighting.

He said he did not know about that. His name was Desmond Corkery and he guessed I was from the United States. He wished he were there himself, he did. He was after coming from Belfast, he was, and was there a more bloody miserable place in the whole of creation? And dangerous? Policemen and soldiers everywhere – and they talked about Lebanon and the flaming Falklands!

I guessed that Corkery was a Catholic. I asked him my usual question: How do you tell a Protestant from a Catholic? He said it was easy – it was the way a Protestant talked, he was better educated. 'If he's using fancy words you can be sure –'

And then Corkery became reflective and said, 'Ah, but you're never really safe. You go into a bar, and you don't know whether it's a Protestant or Catholic bar. It can be frightening, it can, sure. You don't say anything. You call for your beer and you keep your mouth shut, and then you go.'

But I began to think that it was an advantage to be a stranger here, not English, not Irish; and it was a great advantage to be an American. I never felt the Ulster people to be reticent or suspicious – on the contrary, it was hard to shut them up.

'And it was around here,' Desmond Corkery was saying – we were past Ballymoney and headed into Coleraine; I had been encouraging him to tell me a story of religious persecution – 'just about here, that a bloody great team of footballers started to walk up and down the train. They were drinking and shouting. "Bloody Fenian bastards!" Up and down the train. "Bloody Fenian bastards!" Looking for Catholics, they were. One comes up to me and says straight out, "You're a bloody Fenian bastard!"'

I shook my head. I said it was terrible. I asked him what he did then.

'I said no,' Corkery looked grim.

'You told him you weren't a Catholic?'

'Sure I had to.'

'Did he believe you?'

'I suppose he did,' Corkery said. 'He slammed the door and went roaring off.'

We travelled in silence along the River Bann, and I thought how that denial must have hurt his pride, and it seemed to me that it was this sort of humiliation that made the troubles in Ulster a routine of bullying cowardice. It was all old grievances, and vengeance in the dark. That was why the ambush was popular, and the car bomb, and the exploding soap box, and the letter bomb. The idea was to deny what you stood for and then wait until dark to get even with the bugger who made you deny it.

It was drizzling at Coleraine, where I boarded a two-coach train to Portrush, a small seaside resort, emptier than any I had so far seen in Britain. But emptiness had given the place its dignity back.

Portrush was rainswept and poor, and part of it was on a narrow peninsula with waves breaking on three sides. The rain intimidated me for an hour or so. I had lunch with a man named Tubby Graham – there were only the two of us in the restaurant. Tubby was seventy and from Bangor. He liked motoring around, he said. 'But I stay out of those ghetto places. Bushmills, for example – that's a completely Protestant town. And Derry's a Catholic one.' He recommended Magilligan Point. Did I want a lift?

I said I had other plans and when he was gone I sneaked down the beach and started walking towards Bushmills, to see what a Protestant ghetto looked like. It was still raining, but I thought that if I kept walking it might stop; and so it did, by the time

I reached Dunluce Castle, three miles away. I walked along the sandy beach – not a soul in sight. And the cliffs were like battlements, made of white chalk with flint embedded in it. The only sounds were the gulls and the wind.

Further on I climbed the cliff and walked through the wet grass to Bushmills. The more prosperous a place was in Ulster, the sterner and more forbidding it looked. Bushmills, rich on whiskey, was made of flat rocks and black slates and cemented to the edges of straight roads. And now I saw what Tubby meant: the Orange Hall was large enough to hold every man in town.

I began to develop a habit of asking directions, for the pleasure of listening to them.

'Just a munnut,' a man in Bushmills said. His name was Emmett, about sixty-odd, and he wore an old coat. He had a pound of bacon in his hand, and pressing the bacon to the side of his head in a reflective way, he went on.

'Der's a wee wudden brudge under the car park. And der's a bug one farder on – a brudge for trums. Aw, der used to be trums up and down! Aw, but they is sore on money and unded it. Ussun, ye kyan poss along da strond if the tide is dine. But walk on the odder side whar der's graws.' He moved the bacon to his cheek. 'But it might be weyat!'

'What might be wet?'

'The graws,' Mr Emmett said.

'Long grass?'

'In its notral styat.'

This baffled me for a while – *notral styat* – and then I thought: Of course, in its natural state!

Kicking through bracken, I pushed on and decided to head for the Giant's Causeway.

> *Boswell*: Is not the Giant's Causeway worth seeing?
> *Johnson*: Worth seeing? Yes; but not worth going to see.

I stayed on the coastal cliffs and then took a short cut behind a coastal cottage, where I was startled by a big square-faced dog. The hairy thing growled at me and I leaped to get away, but I tripped and fell forward into a bed of nettles. My hands stung for six hours.

The Giant's Causeway was a spectacular set of headlands made of petrified boilings and natural columns and upright pipe-shaped rocks. Every crack and boulder and contour had a fanciful name. This massive coastal oddity had been caused by the cooling of lava when this part of Ireland had oozed during a period of volcanic activity. I walked along it, to and from Dunseverick Castle – 'once the home of a man who saw the Crucifixion' (supposed to be Conal Cearnach, a roving Irish wrestler, who happened to be in a wrestling match in Jerusalem the day Christ was crucified).

The basalt cliffs were covered with black slugs and jackdaws, and at seven in the evening the sun broke through the clouds as powerfully as a sunrise, striping the sea in pink. It was very quiet. The wind had dropped. No insects, no cars, no planes – only a flock of sheep baaing in a meadow on a nearby hilltop. The coves and bays were crowded with diving gulls and fulmars, but the cliffs were so deep they contained the birds' squawks. The sun gleamed on the still sea and in the west above Inishowen Head I could spy the blue heights of Crocknasmug. Yes, the Giant's Causeway was worth going to see.

It had been a tourist attraction for hundreds of years. Every traveller to Britain had come here to size it up. There had been tramlines out to it, as Mr Emmett had told me in Bushmills. But the troubles had put an end to this and now the coast had regained a rough primeval look – just one stall selling postcards, where there had been throngs of noisy shops.

This landscape had shaped the Irish mind and influenced Irish beliefs. It was easy to see these headlands and believe in giants. And now with people too afraid to travel much, the landscape had become monumental once again in its emptiness.

In pagan Ireland cromlechs had been regarded as giants' graves, and people looked closely at the land, never finding it neutral but either a worry or a reassurance. Hereabouts, there were caves that had been the homes of troglodytes. And it seemed to me that there was something in the present desolation that had made the landscape important again. So the Irish had been returned to themselves in this interval, and their fears restored to them, for how could they stand amid all this towering beauty and not feel puny?

Enough of these natural wonders, I thought, and at the hotel that night I button-holed Mr McClune from Ballywalter. 'Oh, I like Ballywalter! Oh, yes, Ballywalter's pleasant, it is! We only get the odd bomb in Ballywalter!'

But he was worried about his sister.

'My suster is going down to Cavan this weekend. I don't unvy her. She's a Protestant girl, you see.'

'Where is Cavan exactly?'

'In the Free State,' Mr McClune said.

I smiled; it was like calling Thailand 'Siam', or Iran 'Persia'.

'A pig farm,' he explained. 'I mean to say, that's where my suster's staying. Now at this piggery there's a foreman. He is a member of the IRA.'

'I see why you're worried,' I said.

'But that could be a good thing, couldn't it?' he said. 'It could keep her safe.'

He meant that no one from the IRA would murder his sister, because a man from the IRA was employed by his sister's friends.

'We'll see what hoppens,' he said.

We were having coffee at the Causeway Hotel, sitting in front of the fire. We were the only two guests. An Ulster conversation could be very restful. I was never asked personal questions. People talked in general, on harmless subjects, unless I took the plunge. Mr McClune, who was seventy-three and very wealthy – he had a Jaguar out front – said he had been to Australia and Canada and California.

'But I've never set futt on the continent of Europe,' he said. 'And I've got no desire to.'

I said I was going to Londonderry.

'I haven't been to Derry for thirty-three years.'

The next morning I walked back to Portrush. I passed a signboard indicating the way to Blagh. It was eight-fifteen and there were no cars on the road, and very quiet except for the birds – crows and finches. I kept walking, towards the train. It was green as far as I could see, and I could see twenty miles up the lovely coast.

16

The 10.24 to Londonderry

The 'troubles' – that quaint Ulstonian word for murder and mayhem – had something to do with the Irish differences between men and women here, I was sure. Why, look at this train to Derry. Nearly all the passengers were women, talking in normal voices. The few men on board were either shouting or whispering. The women were neither demure nor brassy; they were plain, frank and a bit careworn. The men by contrast looked both jaunty and evasive, and they seemed to have nothing whatever to do. Women and men; duty and dereliction. Usually, though, there were only women around, and it seemed all the men had gone away to war – which in a sense was true.

There were always women and girls waiting for buses at cross-roads. They were early risers – they walked, they even hitch-hiked. I saw them along the coast of Londonderry, the shore of Lough Foyle, from Ballyrena to Waterside. It was a country of active women, going shopping, or to work, shovelling manure, driving tractors, riding trains.

People in Ulster only travelled when absolutely necessary, so it was significant that women travelled much more than men. Very often the only man on an Ulster bus was the driver. The wife was frequently the breadwinner – particularly in Derry: she was cheaper to employ and more dependable. I was never frightened in a train or a bus. They were seldom attacked, because they were full of women and children. The children could seem almost demented – nowhere in my life had I seen such excitable rowdy kids – but the women were noticeably friendly.

Women had assumed so many domestic and social duties here that a situation had arisen in which the men had no responsibilities. It was idleness more than religion that made Ulstermen fighting mad. The proof that they were demoralized was the self-hatred in Ulster aggression. What was more self-destructive than a hunger strike? And wasn't it peculiar that the hunger strikers, far from being pacifists, were often very violent men who ought to have known that their captors were eager to be rid of them?

Let Them Die was scrawled on the bricks all over Orange Antrim, and ten hunger strikers had recently fasted until death in the Maze Prison. Then there was the so-called 'Dirty Protest'. I could not imagine a preoccupied and overworked Irish woman dreaming up this loony tactic. But it was easy to see how a maddened and self-hating Irishman might decide to act out his frustration by smearing the walls of his prison cell with his own shit, and refusing to wear clothes, or have a bath or a haircut. 'Take that!' they cried, and pigged it in those cells for months, innocently believing they were getting even with the British government by stinking to heaven.

I thought: This behaviour is so strange and stupid there's probably no name for it. But surely it was in a way profoundly childlike? This was how small children behaved when they felt angry and abandoned, when they wanted to be pitied.

At home these men were treated by their overworked women-folk as if they were forever boys and burdens. The shame or guilt this dependency inspired made the men aggressive; but they had all the time in the world to ventilate their aggression. Religion was hardly a restraining force. Irish Catholicism was one long litany of mother-imagery and mother-worship, which only bolstered the odd family pattern; and Irish Protestantism seemed mainly to be based on a tribal memory of bloody battles, remembered with special relish in the all-male Orange Lodges.

I did not believe that it was religion as Christian doctrine that was at the bottom of it all. Ulster was a collection of secret societies, to which only men were admitted. The men dressed up, made rules, beat drums, swore oaths, invented handshakes and passwords, and crept into the dark and killed people. When they were done they returned home to their women, like small children to their mothers.

Anyway, this was how it seemed to me in Londonderry.

*

From a distance, Derry was lovely and familiar. It looked like a mill-town in Massachusetts – churches and factories piled up on both banks of a river, the same sort of tenements, the same sleepy air of bankruptcy. But up close, Derry was frightful.

Some Ulster towns inspired fear the way a man with an ugly face frightens a stranger – their scars implied violence. Derry was a scarred city of broken windows and barricades; it was patterned with danger zones, and every few blocks there was a frontier: the Waterside, the Bogside, the Creggan, and all the disputed territories among them. And it was possible to tell, from the damage and the slogans, that this was the principal killing ground of Ulster. *Fuck the Pope* was scrawled at the Protestant end of the Craigavon Bridge, and at the Catholic end, *Fuck the Queen*, and now and then corpses were found bobbing in the pretty River Foyle that ran beneath the bridge. Derry was also the headquarters of the most violent of the nationalist factions, the Irish National Liberation Army. They made the IRA seem a party of dear old Paddys, twinkling and fiddling in the Celtic twilight. By contrast the INLA was heartless and unsentimental – eager to establish a reputation for cruel tenacity. It was always easy to spot an INLA slogan on a Derry wall: *Peace Through Superior Firepower*.

The geniality and filth of Derry, and its state of siege, made the city an interesting muddle. Here were old geezers being shifty and jaunty in an Irish way, and over there the British soldiers were tense and watchful and stiff with starch. They crouched in doorways, peering, rifles poised, while the women gathered at Foyle's Pork Store (nothing but sausages and hams) and the men strolled into the betting shop. The soldiers meant business. They wore helmets and face masks and they travelled in armoured cars; they moved singly, covering each other; all their vehicles had wire skirts beneath the chassis so that fire bombs could not be rolled under them.

While I was in Derry the annual Foyle Festival was on. It was one of the paradoxes of Ulster that for many life continued as usual, and that everything happened at once – the festival concert and talent show and bicycle race and cooking exhibit, along with mass frisking, soldier patrols, bomb threats and arrests. There was the traditional football game, and a festival art exhibition; and on the opening day there was a grotesque killing.

It was a typical Derry murder, the Derry men said: a phone-call reported a cache of stolen goods; the policemen arrived and examined the stuff – a television, a fur coat, clocks, radios. One man lifted the television, and it blew up. It had been booby-trapped – the policeman was torn apart. 'They was pieces of the bugger all over the place.' Two other policemen were badly injured, one blinded. Then a mob gathered. The mob was hostile. They howled at the injured men, they jeered at the corpse. They obstructed the ambulance and booed when it broke through. And while the men were put into stretchers the screams were, 'Let the bastards die!'

Two men described this to me with approval – it was not an atrocity story to them, it was a success story. Their attitude was: 'Look at the horrible things they make us do to them – sure, it's tragic, but it's their fault. Won't they ever learn?'

Those same men, Tim Cronin and Denny McGaw, urged me to go to Donegal.

'Ah, Donegal's a lovely place, like,' Cronin said. He was seventy-five years old, as white-faced as Yeats and with the same black-rimmed glasses. And he boasted, 'Sure, I've been there almost a dozen times.'

He was speaking of County Donegal, four miles from where we stood.

'So it's not violent like Derry?' I said. Call it Londonderry and they thump you for being English.

'Derry's not violent,' Mr McGaw said. 'Belfast – that's the violent place. They fight each other there. Aw, Derry's a lovely old town. Have you seen the fine walls?'

'But the police,' I started to say.

McGaw pointed behind me. 'A policeman was killed as he stood right there, not two weeks ago. Two men in a van came up that hill, and shot him and rode on.'

'So people do get killed?'

'Policemen and soldiers get shot, no doubt about it,' Cronin said. 'But we don't shoot each other. Ah, sure, stay out of Belfast – that's a bad place!'

Most people called Eire 'the Free State', but they were not

particularly sentimental about it. The IRA was of course banned in Eire, and Irish soldiers at the border post had a reputation for harassing Ulstermen, getting them to empty their pockets and turn out their suitcases. But that was not the main grievance Ulstermen had with Eire – the main grievance was money.

In a high-pitched voice of complaint, Paddy Dineen said, 'Do you know what a beer costs in the Free State? Twenty-two shillings in the old money. Twenty-two shillings for a pint of beer!'

I said, 'Is that an argument for staying British?'

'It is!' he said. 'You can get a beer for half of that in Derry.'

So much for Irish unity. But the notion of unity was very blurred by all the contending groups. In fact, the most nationalistic ones like the IRA and the INLA seemed to want to sweep both the British Government and the Irish Government away, and start all over again with the People's Republic of Ireland.

The hatred for British soldiers in Derry was extraordinary. Soldiers raided houses and, searching for guns, tore up floors and broke cupboards – they were vandals. Soldiers took money and personal effects, and did not give them back – they were thieves. Soldiers drove through the streets in Land-rovers, shouting abuse at women and children – they were brutes. Soldiers timed their visits to Catholic areas to coincide with children getting out of school, in order to coax them into starting riots – they were criminal-minded. Soldiers shot innocent men – they were murderers.

This was how the *Derry Journal* portrayed the soldiers. And one day the paper announced, 'The Army are now adopting Cromwellian tactics – destroying Catholic homes.'

I stayed in a boarding house in Derry that was the Catholic counterpart to Mrs Fraser Wheeney's pokerwork paradise in Larne. Instead of Bible mottos, Mrs McCreadie had portraits of the Blessed Virgin Mary, and statuettes, too, the shape and size of Oscars. 'Mothera God,' Mrs McCreadie was always saying, while Joe her only other lodger told her what terrible things he had seen the night before in the Bogside.

They were great readers of the newspaper, these two. It was not the Falklands news. They were ignorant of the fact that British soldiers seemed about to recapture Port Stanley; but they knew every bit of the Ulster news because the Ulster newspapers printed everything – rumours, hearsay, gossip, 'witnesses saw', 'it is believed', and sentences such as, 'He alleged that the soldiers called him a "Fenian bastard".'

The most popular page at Mrs McCreadie's was the one – or sometimes two – that contained the *In Memoriams*. It made me think that there was a sort of cult of death in Ulster. There certainly was one in Derry. It was not merely a list of obituaries saying 'So-and-so died yesterday' – it was a sheaf of tributes to people who had died years ago. '11th Anniversary', one read, and another '15th Anniversary', and I saw one that commemorated the twenty-second anniversary of a parent's death. And with each tribute was a poem:

> The mother is someone special, patient, kind and true,
> No other friend in all the world will be the same as you.

Or,

> Sweet are those memories, silently kept,
> Of a mother I loved and will never forget.

Or,

> We never fail to think of you
> We never cease to care
> We only wish we could go home
> And find you sitting there.

There were hundreds of these in the paper every day, often a dozen or so to the same person, invoking the prayers of St Columba – the sixth-century Irish missionary – and 'Mary, Queen of Ireland'. The Virgin Mary had been elevated to the Irish throne. Mothera God, as Mrs McCreadie said.

There were always tributes to men who had been killed in the Irish cause. This one was typical:

> 4th Anniversary
> Vol. Dennis Heaney
> *Shot dead by S.A.S. on 10th June, 1978*
> 'Life springs from death; and from the graves
> of patriot men and women spring living nations '

Proudly remembered by [a long list of names]
Sacred Heart of Jesus, have mercy on him
St Columba, pray for him
Mary Queen of Ireland, pray for us.

One day I left Mrs McCreadie's and kept walking. It was a lovely morning – clear skies and warm sunshine. I walked on a boggy path along the River Mourne, which was the border between Eire and Ulster – though you would never have known it. The grass was just as spectacularly green on this bank as on that one. I walked ten miles and the weather changed. The rain came down, flattening the buttercups in the fields. So I caught a bus into Strabane.

Strabane was said to be the poorest town in Europe – it had the highest murder rate, for its size, and the highest unemployment rate, and the fewest pigs and the dimmest prospects. It was smack on the border and it had the curiously unfinished look of a frontier town – like a house with one wall missing. It was sorry-looking, with men propped against shopfronts, whistling, and a number of cracked windows. But it was not noticeably more decrepit than other towns I had seen in Ulster. I considered staying the night, but the Control Zone and all the soldiers and police complicated the mildest stroll. And when I thought it over I decided that I had seen few places on earth more depressing than Strabane in the rain.

The day after I left Strabane a man walked out of a motor accessory shop where he worked. He was thirty-nine, a member of the Ulster Defence Regiment – a hated paramilitary force that had come into existence when the Protestant 'B-Specials' were disbanded. A car drew up, the man was shot four times, the car sped away. The man died immediately. He was the 123rd UDR man to be gunned down since the regiment was formed, ten years before.

Every town and village was deserted by six or six-thirty and it was eerie, because the summer evenings were often sunlit and long, and the desertion was obvious.

'There's a dread of trouble,' Sean McLaughlin said. He lived in Omagh, where I had gone after Strabane. Omagh was also funereal. But Sean's solution was to get out of town on a bus to

Belcoo, on the border of Eire. There was a *fleadhceoil* being held there that weekend – a 'flah' he called it – a festival of fiddles and flutes and concertinas. Sean got on the bus, with only his fiddle for baggage. He said that three days of drinking and singing in Belcoo would put him right.

That was the real paradox of Ireland. The dimple-chinned fiddler heading down the road to the 'flah' at Belcoo – as warm-hearted and unsuspicious an Irishman as ever plucked a sham-rock; and on the same bus as Sean (though I did not speak to him until we got to Enniskillen), the grey-browed Morris Grady Smith, who also knew Belcoo.

'I was driving out of Belcoo towards Garrison in the van' – Morris worked for the Public Works Department in Enniskillen – 'there were eight of us in the van and I was at the wheel as usual. Suddenly there was a blue flash right in front of me. The wind-screen burst open and all the glass fell on me. It was an explosion, and then there was shots! I kept driving, though I felt some pain in my arm. I was shot seven times, but the bullets just passed through my arm – not one of them struck a bone!'

He offered to show me his scars, but I said that I believed his story. He kept talking.

'Three of my men were dead – hit with small slugs from an M60 rifle. One of the men was a Catholic. See, they were shooting across the border – that Belcoo to Garrison road passes right along the border. They must have mistook our van for an army vehicle and thought we were soldiers. We were just men with shovels, fixing the pot-holes in the road.'

One day all cities will look like this, I had thought in Belfast; and the same thought occurred to me in Derry and now in Enniskillen. The centre of these places was a Control Zone, with an entrance and exit. All cars and all people were examined for weapons or bombs, and the tight security meant that inside the Control Zone life was fairly peaceful and the buildings generally undamaged. It was possible to control the flow of traffic and even to prevent too many people entering. It was conceivable that this system would in time be adapted to cities that were otherwise uncontrollable. It was not hard to imagine Manhattan island as one large Control Zone, with various entrances and exits; Ulster suggested to me the likely eventuality of sealed cities in the future.

In Enniskillen each car in the Control Zone was required to have at least one person in it. If a car was left empty or unattended, a warning siren was sounded and the town centre cleared. If the driver was found he was given a stiff fine; if no driver claimed the car the Bomb Squad moved in. This system had greatly reduced the number of car bombs in Enniskillen (only ten miles from the border). The last car bomb had gone off two years ago. The nicer part of Church Street was blown to smithereens, but it was a pardonable lapse, the soldiers said. That wired-up car *seemed* to have a person in it: how were they to recognize the difference between an Ulsterman and a dummy?

Willie McComiskey, who described himself as a fruiterer, told me that Enniskillen had been pretty quiet lately – no bombs, not many fires, only a few ambushed cars.

'What they do, see, is they go to isolated farms near the border. They take the farmer and stand him up and shoot him.'

He seemed rather emotionless as he spoke, and he described how the men were sometimes murdered in front of their families – the wife and children watching.

I asked him how he felt about it.

He said in the same even voice, 'Why, you wouldn't do it to a dog.'

'So what do you think of these gunmen?'

'I hate them,' he said. He began to smile. What absurd questions I was asking! But he was uncomfortable stating the obvious. Here, such attitudes were taken for granted.

He said, 'We're eight per cent British here. We couldn't have union with southern Ireland. A Protestant would have no chance. He wouldn't get a job' –

So McComiskey was a Protestant; that was his emphasis.

'– but I don't think the IRA want union now. They don't know what they do want.'

From Enniskillen I walked south to Upper Lough Erne, one of the two enormous lakes here in County Fermanagh. The sun came out as I walked, and a milkman I met said, 'The weather's being kind to us.' There was no sound on these country lanes except the odd squawk of a crow. I found a hotel near the village of Bellanaleck, and now the sun was shining on the green woods and the lake. It was a sixty-room hotel. I thought I was the only guest, but the next day at breakfast I saw two Frenchmen in rubber waders – fishermen.

'I have to check you for bombs,' Alice, the room-girl, said.

She followed me to my room and then peered uneasily into my knapsack.

'I'm not sure what a bomb looks like,' she said.

'You won't find one in there,' I said. 'It's just old clothes –'

'And books,' she said. 'And letters.'

'No letter bombs.'

She said, 'I have to check all the same.'

I went for a walk. This was deep country. The pair of lakes went half-way across this part of Ulster. People spent weeks on cabin cruisers, Germans mostly. There were no English tourists here any more.

'The English started to believe what they saw on television,' Bob Ewart said. 'They actually thought all that stuff about bombs and murders was true!'

He himself was from Nottingham.

'I've lived here fourteen years and I've yet to see an angry man.'

That night the movie on television was *The Invasion of the Body-Snatchers*. I watched it with the Irish hotel workers. It was a horror movie about the world being taken over by alien germs. The Irishmen said it was frightening and of course went to bed happy. Then it struck me that a horror movie could only enjoy a great popular success if its frights were preposterous – like someone saying, 'Boo!' The ultimate horror was really what was happening in many Ulster towns: bombs, murders, people's hands being hack-sawed off, or men having their knee-caps shot off as a punishment for disloyalty, or the tarring-and-feathering of young girls for socializing with soldiers. Because this was the truth, unlike the Hollywood monster movie. It was worse than frightening: it was unbearable.

And the next day a man named Guilfoyle told me there was quite a bit of rural crime in the border areas – cattle-maiming. I had no idea what he was talking about. He explained that to take revenge on farmers, some of the republican country-folk sneaked into the pastures at night and knifed off the cows' udders.

*

On my map of Lough Erne I saw there was a hotel at Carrybridge about four miles away by water. The man who let me have a rowing-boat said, 'It's a fair old pull. Your arms are going to be screaming.' This was John Joseph Skerry, who hadn't rented out a boat for years. He waved to me as I rowed away, down the narrow lake, to have lunch at Carrybridge. I saw herons and terns and curlews, and a circling flock of swans. My boat was a shallow dinghy – two hours it took me to row the four miles, and I arrived at the hotel at about three o'clock. 'We've just closed,' the girl at the bar said as I entered. 'I can't sell you anything.' But I was glad to have a chair. I went into the lounge where a television was on – a tennis match. 'You can't sit here if you're not a resident,' a young man said. 'You'll have to leave.' I went outside and saw that the hotel was the whole of Carrybridge. This was the middle of nowhere, on the lake! It was beautiful, but I was hungry. Then it started to rain. And there among the yellow irises and the cows, on the bridge at Carrybridge it said NO SURRENDER – 1690 and on a pillar NO POPE HERE. I cast off and rowed four miles back, thinking: This is just a row on an Irish lake for me, but it's their whole life.

There was an army checkpoint down the road at Derrylin. On the way to see it I stopped in local inns, in villages so small they were not on any map. The inns were full of men and boys and on summer evenings places like Crocknacreevy looked and smelled like Rhodesia, a tough and beautiful colony in the dust.

'They're not farmers,' an innkeeper told me. 'They're all on the dole. They're not bad, but they've been brought up to behave like cretins. They chuck their cigarette ends on the carpet and grind them in with their boot-heels. Farmers don't stay up until all hours drinking. They work hard for their money, so they save it.'

The army checkpoint was just a barrier manned by six soldiers, but this road went straight to the border. The soldiers would not talk to me.

Don't talk politics, don't talk religion, people said; but I thought: Ridiculous! What was the point in travelling around Ulster if you avoided those two subjects?

A Protestant named Mortimer gave me a lift and said, 'The army are very rough when they first arrive in an area. Those men you saw are paratroopers. They've just got here – that's why they look so nasty. After three or four weeks they'll be a bit more polite.'

I asked him whether they harassed people, as the papers reported.

'Aye. They do. Especially if you have some connection with Irish politics – or if they think you have. They come to your house at six in the morning. They don't knock you up – they kick your door off its hinges. Sometimes they tear the place apart.'

I said it sounded fairly severe.

He smiled. 'It's worse when they take you in. There are lots of stories. Even if they're half-true they're very bad.'

'Have you been arrested?' I asked.

'They don't have to arrest you,' Mortimer said. 'They take you in.'

'And then?'

'Beat you up.'

I said, 'Maybe you'd be better off without the army?'

'I wouldn't say that. But it can be pretty rough with them.' He thought a moment and said, 'We get more trouble from the UDR than the army.'

'Who's "we"?'

He said, 'Everyone.'

I took a bus in an easterly direction to Dungannon. The hills were steep and green and very close together in this part of Tyrone, and in the small town of Clogher they were like green wrinkles on the face on the earth, the ridges of hills, one after another.

Every town looked as though it was expecting trouble at any moment. All the police, the Royal Ulster Constabulary, were armed and alert and seemed nervous. They knew that the suddenness of violence was peculiar to this sort of piecemeal siege: everything happened in seconds.

I made the mistake in Dungannon of going repeatedly through the same checkpoint turnstile. 'You again,' the policeman's expression said. 'Make up your mind – stay in or stay out.' He seemed irritated, like a man who has to keep getting up to unlock a door. The town centre was completely sealed off, and surrounded by police marksmen, with automatic rifles.

On the way to Portadown in North Armagh I sat in a bus filled with women and children, as always. The children were hyperactive, jumping on the seats and yelling. One kicked at the window.

'Missus,' the driver kept saying, 'take that chayld awee from that wunder.'

The villages all followed the same pattern: a church, a post-office, a manor house, an Orange Hall, a cluster of tiny cottages. There were no strangers here, no city slickers moving in and fixing up the cottages, as they did in Dorset and Devon; and no people who had come here to retire, and grow roses, as they did in Sussex and Kent. The old people in Ulster villages had been born in those same villages. They did not move to the coast. They did not move at all. This was a society in which everyone stayed put.

Where was the railway station? I asked people in Portadown. They said: Over there, over there. But there was no station; I couldn't see it. Over there, they said. Then Mr Cleary said, 'It's right here.'

I could not see it, I said.

'Aye,' he said. 'It got blew up four months ago. But this is where it used to be.'

It had been bombed on Sunday night. Mr Cleary had heard the explosion himself in his kitchen. He asked where I was going.

'Newry,' I said.

'Ah, that's all right then. The train doesn't go to Newry.'

He meant I need not have troubled myself. Anyway, the train was gone. It went to Dundalk in the Republic: it didn't stop for twenty-five miles.

Why didn't the train stop anywhere? I asked.

'No necessity. No one goes to Newry.'

Sean O'Faoláin had written of being in Portadown in the 1940s and asking a man, 'What is the outstanding characteristic of this town – a typical Ulster town – compared with any typical southern town?' And the man had replied, 'I'll tull ye. No Jew ever made a living here or in Ballymena.'

I told this to Mr Cleary and he said, 'Aye. That's true, right enough.'

There was no quick way out of Portadown, and it was a dreary place. I wanted to go to Newry and then Kilkeel and continue up the coast. People said: Don't go to Newry – it's bandit country there, sure it is. I'm after coming there meself and I'm surprised I'm still alive, like.

'Aw, if they'd listened to Joe Gibson we'd still have a railway station,' a man named McGrane told me. 'But they didn't believe him. He's daft, see. "I seen the kyar!" he says. He was trying to warn them. But he's sort of screwy. They just laughed and then *bang*!'

'Who did it?' I said.

'No one took credit for it. Could have been anyone,' McGrane said. 'Take your pick. We've got the IRA, the Provos, the INLA and Provisional Sinn Fein. There's the UDA, the UVF, the UFF, the Tartan Army and Paisley's Third Force. There's also common criminals. There's people cashing in on the violence. There's bloody kids. There's too many, if you ask me.'

McGrane was against union with the Republic: 'If a woman don't want any more kids, the priest will come round and tell her not to take any conthra-conthra-conthrathep –' He winced, trying to say the word.

I said, 'I get the point.'

Thomas B. Mules was very fat and had small close-set eyes. He had stopped smoking only a few months before, because he could no longer afford it. He had gained forty pounds and now weighed two hundred and thirty.

Mr Mules said, 'Don't go to Newry.'

'Why not?'

'''Tis a Provo town,' he whispered, edging nearer.

'So?'

'Talking English,' he said. 'Asking questions,' he said. 'Dey'll take ye for an SAS man,' he said. 'Dey'll cull ye.'

'Cull' seemed somehow worse than 'kill'. It was like being noiselessly dispatched forever.

Mr Mules said, 'Go to Newcastle.'

So I went to Newcastle, via Gilford and Banbridge, on more country buses ('Missus, please take yer chayld . . .').

All municipal buildings were protected in an unusual way. They were not merely fenced in – they were enclosed in cages that occasionally rose over the top of the building. They had elaborate gates and barbed wire, and the mesh was very fine. They made the police stations and telephone exchanges and all the other likely targets bomb-proof. It was strange to see such heavy security in what were otherwise sleepy country towns, and also strange – in the face of such ugly fortifications – to be told: 'Aye, but it's very quiet here, really.'

In Banbridge I wrote in my diary: *Over a week in N. Ireland pestering people with questions and I still haven't met a real bigot.*

Because Banbridge was on the main road from Eire to Belfast there were a number of checkpoints just south of the town. Some were manned by the jug-eared volunteers of the Ulster Defence Regiment ('Open yer boot –') and some by the Royal Ulster Constabulary ('Have you ever been in the North before?'), and some by British soldiers ('Carrying a gun?').

On the country bus to Newcastle I kept glimpsing the Mourne mountains. They were sudden and unusual in the gentle land-scape. Farther east the land was stony, and the mountains which had looked blue from Katesbridge were pale green and bare, smooth, bulging and undulant, like a naked giantess lying in a green sleeping bag.

Newcastle lay beneath the high peak of Slieve Donard, and it was empty. In pretty places like this I got the full flavour of Ulster desolation: no one at the beach or in the park, no one promenading on the promenade; no parked cars, because there was a bomb-law against it; no one in the shops, and only one couple in the Chinese restaurant. Bright and bleak, the sunlit ghost towns of the Ulster coast!

Scrawled on a building in Newcastle was the slogan VIVA ARGENTINA. It was the first time in my travelling that I had seen any graffiti in support of Argentina in the Falklands war. The irony was that the day I saw it was the day the British Army entered Port Stanley, forcing the Argentines to surrender. The next morning's newspapers all had the same headline: VICTORY!

17

The 15.53 to Belfast

The British victory in the Falklands was not celebrated in County Down. The people I spoke to were perplexed and bitter. 'Too many men had to die for that,' Mr Hackett told me in Newcastle. 'Yes, I saw the papers,' Constance Kelly said in Castlewellan, 'but we're too busy with our own troubles to take an interest in that pile of rocks in the South Atlantic.' And a man named Flannagan in Downpatrick said, 'What about the lads getting killed here? There was a bomb in town not long ago, but none of the English papers printed a story saying, "Tim Flannagan took a light head and is far from well at the moment."'

I caught the school bus – it was the only one at that early hour – and went to Castlewellan with the yelling boys and the womanly girls of St Malachy's. I was hardly thirty miles from Belfast, but instead of heading straight there I took a roundabout route on the coastal side of the Ards Peninsula. I was making for Bangor, and the train to Belfast. It was a June day of suffocating dampness, the brown sky like a mass of ravelled wool, threatening rain.

Walking out of Downpatrick, where I had just met Tim Flannagan, I was thinking about the Falklands and the attitude here. *What about us?* the Ulstermen said. Catholic and Protestant alike objected to the attention given to the far-off Falklands and their 1700 inhabitants (who, at that time, were not even full citizens of Britain). I came to a war memorial on the outskirts of the town, with a slab inscribed with the lines,

> They shall not grow old, as we that are left grow old:
> Age shall not weary them, nor the years condemn.
> At the going down of the sun and in the morning
> We will remember them.

What fascinated me was that the verse portrayed the advantage of dying young – being spared the fatigue and weakness of old age. The poet, Laurence Binyon, was English, but this was a very Irish sentiment. It seemed to me that the real problem in Ulster – and the reason there were so many bloody killings – was that everyone believed in an after-life.

It was nine miles to Strangford. I walked to Milestone Seven and then the rain started. I did not mind the rain, but the thunder-growl worried me. I was on an open road between flat fields – no village, no trees, no shelter. I decided to hitch-hike.

This was Ulster, and hitch-hikers here often hijacked the car and kicked the driver into the road (the bombers and gunmen nearly always used stolen cars), and yet I got a ride from the second car that passed.

Mr Hurley was a Strangford man. It was a mixed community, he said, and he was proud to say they all worked together.

'Of course, there's extremist groups operating in the area,' Mr Hurley said. 'And there's political parties. And there's clubs and lodges. Now out of all that lot you'd think one of them would reflect my thinking, wouldn't you? But none of them does. I think if we had better leadership we'd get somewhere.'

He said he had worked in London as a plumber's mate.

'Three years in London and for the whole of that time no one asked me my religion. That's what I liked about London.'

Strangford was about five streets – fifty families, no more – and a ferry landing. I crossed the harbour-mouth on a ferry to the neat and rather formal village of Portaferry. It was unusual in Ulster to find a village with no graffiti, no bomb damage, no broken windows, no blasted buildings; and Portaferry was almost like that – the only sign of fanaticism was a blasted church.

'It's a wee pretty little town,' a man said to me. 'You should see it with the sun shining in the square.'

It was still raining very hard. He said Portaferry was famous for its offshore whirlpools.

I said I was not staying here but was going on to Portavogie.

'I'm after coming from Portavogie meself,' he said. 'And how are ye getting there?'

I said I would either walk or hitch-hike.

'I'll take ye,' he said. 'I have to go home for me lunch.'

His name was Cosmo Shields and he said his bus was just around the corner. I was surprised to see that this was no euphemism: a big empty bus was parked on the next road. This was his bus, he said. He had done his morning run from Newtownards and now he was going to lunch. He took the bus home, because he had an afternoon run up to Kirkcubbin and Belfast. Not long ago there had been sixteen buses on this peninsula, but as the drivers had died – 'Most of them took heart attacks' – the buses were phased out.

It was not that people had cars nowadays, Cosmo Shields said. It was that they did not have any money and it was not safe to travel.

He had been lucky, he said. He had been driving for thirty-three years – driven double deckers down these country lanes. But in all that time, making two trips a day into Belfast, he had had trouble only twice – both times he was stoned and the windows broken in the Short Strand district.

'Aye, but it wasn't me they was throwing stones at. They'd have thrown stones at the bus if you'd been driving it. It's the bus, see. Government property.' He drove with his elbows on the wheel. He was a stocky man, in his late fifties. He had not collected any fare from me. This was not a service run, he said. 'Mind you, I've had plenty of trouble with drunks. And children.'

I said, 'The kids seem very jumpy.'

'They're more destructful than ever they were!' Mr Shields said. 'They've got destruction in their heads. Aye, there's talk. People are worried about Ulster children nowadays.' Mr Shields swung his whole body over, and taking his eyes off the road for five dramatic seconds, he said, 'Aye, the wee kids see what's going on.'

We were just then entering Portavogie. It was attractive in the same way as Portaferry – no bomb-craters, no hysteria, and an air of normality. High-sided trawlers were moored at the docks, discharging cratefuls of herrings and prawns.

Cosmo Shields was still grunting darkly. I guessed he was thinking about the destructive kids.

He said, 'Aye, the way things are going, it'll hoppon soon, like.'

'Pardon?'

'The end of the world.' He was nodding with certainty now.
'Aye, I reckon the end of the world is not far off' –

And in the same breath:

'– shall I take you up to Ballywalter?'

It was my walking and hitching up that coast to Bangor that
made me modify my opinion of Ulster. Part of the society was
wild, and religious mania only made that wildness worse –
martyr-mad and eager to chant, 'Anti-Christ! Anti-Christ!' (as
Doctor Paisley's congregation had done to the Pope in England
just a few weeks before). It was an old society, with a long memory,
and no nose at all for the future – 1690 was considered just
yesterday by people who were not sure whether they had their bus
fare home tonight.

I had no idea where the cruelty came from. Tennyson said that
Irish cruelty was due to a lack of imagination, but other writers
had put it down to a strain of anarchy and an evasion of moral
worries. The Irish could be glad about the idea of Ireland, but
Ulster was a nebulous thing – and wasn't it really nine counties
and not six? The people of Ulster, neither Irish nor British, felt
lonely and left behind.

It was a society of hard workers who were unemployed. It was
a beautiful country that was impossible to live in. It was a society
which still had real peasants and real skinflint duchesses, pig-
farmers and dowager countesses. And, amazingly in a country
where roots went very deep it had the highest rate of emigration
in the world – especially lately: almost 140,000 people had left
Ulster in the ten years between 1971 and 1981. It was, most of all,
a society with tribal instincts – tribal warfare, tribal kinships, and
(common among tribal people) a sense of isolation that inspired
both suspicion and generosity, particularly towards strangers.
They said, 'Fuss is better than loneliness.'

When I hitch-hiked I was picked up. When I asked questions
they were nearly always answered. I saw signs of violence but I
never felt I was in physical danger. I liked the Ulster curiosity – so
different from the English narrowness and fear. I was dressed like
a tramp or a bandit, but I was made to feel welcome. 'Come home
with me and have some lunch!' It was not until I visited Ulster
that I received that invitation. I made my way up the bouldery

coast to Millisle, and walked to Donaghadee, which was rainswept and empty. 'You should have been here three weeks ago,' I was told in Donaghadee. 'The sun was shining. It was lovely and warm. Still. Not to worry. Come in and get your feet up. I'll put the kettle on.'

Most of these coastal places were only incidentally seaside resorts. They were small towns with the Irish Sea splashing against them and taking the sewage away and drowning the odd cat. Down there was an empty amusement arcade, an empty café, a fish-and-chip shop, a few broken benches and a rocky foreshore covered with black seaweed – maybe kelp, maybe tar: it made no difference, no one swam.

'Come back in a few weeks,' I was told.

'Is that when the season starts?'

'No. Just the one day. Orange Day.'

'I'll make a note in my diary,' I said.

'The twalth.'

I walked via Groomsport to Bangor. Bangor resembled a certain kind of English coastal town. It was a a little like Bexhill and a little like Dawlish; it was elderly and respectable and cliffy, and in a tawdry-genteel way it had a comic air of pretension that was rare in Ulster. But that was at the better end of Bangor. At the other end it was just as desolate and friendly as everywhere else. Some of Bangor served as a refuge for the fairly well-off, the businessmen and professional people who worked in Belfast but could not bear to live there. So Bangor was safer but a great deal duller than any other town its size in Ulster, including Newcastle, which did no more than gape like an oyster.

It was a sign of Bangor's relative quietness that there was no security check at the railway station. I took the 15.53 one day – all the trains went west, Bangor was the end of the line – and after a few miles it was like any suburb in England with old and new semi-detached houses, rose gardens and high hostile fences. Now I was passing along the southern part of Belfast Lough, and at Carnalea I could see the towns of Carrickfergus and Whitehead across the bay. I had almost completed my circular tour of Ulster.

The rain came down. In places there were meadows to the sea. Helen's Bay railway station was designed by Lord Dufferin as a mock-fortification, with arrow slits in the towers and castellated walls – the Irish aristocracy seemed to me more foolish and artless than the peasantry. It was here in Helen's Bay and further on at Cultra and Marino that people said, 'I've never seen a riot nor heard a bomb, and I don't think I ever shall.'

We passed Holywood and the large army depot, and then the gantries and cranes of the shipyard, which meant we were near Belfast, the old horror.

It was a city of drunks, of lurkers, of late-risers. It smelled of wet bricks and burning coal. It stank. It had a sort of nightmare charm. When the rain came down in Belfast it splashed through the roof and spattered through the window glass and poured into your soul. It was the blackest city in Britain, and the most damaged.

Belfast had a tourist bureau. Don't be afraid, was their message. I liked the blarney in their brochure:

> No coward soul is mine
> No trembler in the world's
> storm-troubled sphere

> These lines by Emily Brontë (daughter of an
> Ulsterman) are often quoted to describe the spirit
> of Belfast. Visitors, having heard only news of the
> city's political troubles, are invariably surprised
> when they see the citizens' 'business as usual' brisk-
> ness and the positive signs of achievement ...

But the Brontë poem ('Last Lines') was about the love of God and 'Heaven's glories' and faith 'arming me from fear'. Trust in God and you'll be safe in Belfast!

The achievement, I supposed, was that after such a battering the city still stood; after so many streets had been torn up, and so many bombs thrown, there were still buses running; after so many windows broken there were still windows intact. Life went on, how could it not? Forty per cent of the Ulster population lived in this city and most of the remaining industry was here. But the outlook was grim. The shipyard, Belfast's largest employer, was said to be laying off 4,000 men. 'That's when the real trouble will start,' a hard-faced man named Muncaster said to me. 'The

British Government's been protecting their "workers". But what happens when they don't have any more workers?'

Muncaster – 'call me Jack' – was a real Belfast toughie. The city either destroyed a person or else it made him merciless. The people of Belfast – most of them – suffered from what journalists had begun calling 'compassion fatigue'. They had seen so much misery and heard so many explosions and cries for help they hardly blinked.

'What do I think of the bombers?' Muncaster said. 'I think they're boring. When I hear a bomb go off I just look at my watch. I look at the time – I don't know why – and then I walk away. And I feel a little safer after a bomb, because there probably won't be another one that day. But God, it's boring!'

It was true – a dangerous society was frightening, and then inconvenient, and then annoying, and then maddening, and ultimately a bore. All the security checks! All the metal detectors! All the body searches and friskings and questions! I was being put through a security check one day and the police officer, a woman, shrieked and jumped away from my knapsack crying, 'Feathers! Feathers!' and shaking her hands. 'Get them away from me!'

They were the hackles of a dead pheasant I had found down at Dundrum Bay.

In Belfast I stayed in a dirty hotel with a damp interior and wallpaper that smelled of tobacco smoke and beer and the breakfast grease. But there was no security check here. I had been searched in Enniskillen, a town that hadn't had a bomb in years; and I would have been searched at the grand Europa Hotel in Belfast – it was surrounded by a high barbed-wire fence and had sentries and guard dogs. The tourists and journalists stayed at the Europa – it was a good target for bombs. But no one of any importance stayed at Mooney's Hotel.

I called it Mooney's because it greatly resembled Mrs Mooney's flophouse in James Joyce's story, 'The Boarding House'. Our Mrs Mooney also had an enormous florid face and fat arms and red hands, and she catered to travelling salesmen and drifters. The carpets were ragged, the wallpaper was peeling, there were nicks all over the woodwork. But I was free there, and I would not have been free in an expensive hotel; and I also thought that in this grubby place I was out of danger. It was Belfast logic, but it was also a pattern of life that I was sure would become more common in the cities of the future.

The bar at Mooney's was busy all night, filling the whole building with smoke and chatter.

'What time does the bar close?' I asked on my first night.

'October,' a drinker told me, and laughed.

One day in Belfast I saw a poster advertising 'the world première' of a play called *The Interrogation of Ambrose Fogarty*. It sounded political – that was promising; and the author, Martin Lynch, was a local man. It was being staged at the Lyric Players Theatre near the Botanical Gardens and Queens University. I splashed through the rain to buy a ticket – my shoes had been wet for three days! Rain was general all over Ireland, falling on every part of the dark central plain, softening the Bog of Allen and blackening Belfast still more.

It was still raining the night of the world première. But the play drew a good crowd and I thought afterwards I could not have seen a better play. It summed up the mood I had detected in Ulster – farce and tragedy, one turning into the other, one sometimes indistinguishable from the other.

Ambrose Fogarty, a Catholic from the Falls Road, is picked up on suspicion by a British soldier and taken to a police station for questioning. He is kept for three days and given the third degree. Fogarty is innocent; the British soldier is a lecherous, toffee-nosed brute who is contemptuous of Ulster and Ulstermen; two of the policemen are ineffectual; the rest are sadists and bigots. There is another suspect, Willy Lagan, but he is a fool – drunken, feeble-minded, and plucking a guitar; he is as comic as Fogarty is pious.

It was a play about persecution and torture. In places it was crudely written, but it seemed to confirm all the stories I had heard about the intimidation of suspects. Ambrose is asked to sign a confession admitting that he is a member of the IRA and that he has taken part in an armed bank robbery. He refuses to sign – he denies everything. So he is threatened. He still refuses. At last, he is savagely beaten, kicked, choked and his arm nearly twisted out of its socket. But all the police have succeeded in doing is giving a rather pleasant young man a grievance. The play ends with Fogarty political in a platitudinous way.

The violence was eased somewhat by the presence of the second suspect, Willy, who provided the comic relief by singing off-key, appearing to co-operate and then collapsing, pulling faces and saying everything twice. And he looked ridiculous: he was dressed in a zoot suit and a loud tie and had slicked down hair – straight out of the American fifties. But he was too ridiculous, and really wasn't it all preposterous – Ambrose too innocent, Willy too bizarre?

'What do you think?' I was asked afterwards by a lady in the foyer, as I was having a pint of Guinness.

I thought: It's loaded. And why were such plays always about innocent people? Why not make Fogarty an IRA man? After all, there were enough of them around, shooting people in the back and muttering *Sinn Fein*, 'Ourselves Alone'.

I said, 'Very interesting. But I'm an alien, so naturally I have a few questions.'

'Why don't you ask them? The author's standing right behind you.'

Martin Lynch was about thirty. I was immediately struck by his physical resemblance to his main character, Fogarty. I said that I had heard about such interrogations, but how true was his play?

'It's about me,' he said. 'I was arrested and held for three days. They beat me up. They tried to make me sign a confession. All that in the play – it's true.'

'The Willy character is dramatically right, I think,' I said; but I meant he was too convenient and preposterous.

'Want to meet him?' Lynch said. He called a man over.

This one was older and uglier than Willy Lagan but there was no doubting that he was the original. He pulled a face, he winked at me and started to sing. He wore a white satin necktie and a black shirt, and a flashy zoot suit. He got on to his knees and made monkey noises; he snatched at my hand.

'We were in prison together,' Lynch said smiling at the man's antics. 'Well, it's just like in the play. If he hadn't been there it would have been unbearable. I'm really grateful to him.'

The man made affectionate monkey noises, and rolled his eyes;

and now it was impossible to tell at what point the play ended and the lives of these men began.

It seemed to me a healthy sign that there were such plays being produced, but it was a play about a deranged society. I kept wishing that it had been a play about a real bomber, because it was a society in which everyone talked about persecution but no one took any blame.

No one admitted to crime in Ulster. The most they said was, 'Look what they make us do!' It was as if all the street violence was imaginary or else rigged by soldiers who (so it was said in Derry) coaxed children into starting riots. It was slippery, shadowy, tribal; it was all stealth. It was a folk tradition of flag-waving and the most petty expression of religious bigotry west of Jerusalem. Apart from the bombing it was not public crime anymore. It was sneaking ambushes and doorstep murders ('I've got something for your father') and land mines in the country lanes. Some of the worst crimes took place in the prettiest rural places – the shootings and house-burnings and the cattle-maiming – in the green hills, with the birds singing.

People said, 'There is no solution ... Ireland's always had troubles ... Maybe it'll die out ... I suppose we could emigrate ...'

I kept thinking: This is Britain!

It was like being shut in with a quarrelling family and listening to cries of 'You started it!' and 'He hit me!' And I felt about Ulster as I had felt about some south coast boarding houses on rainy days – I wanted to tiptoe to the front door and leave quietly and keep walking.

But I was grateful, too. No one had imposed on me. I had done nothing but ask questions, and I always received interesting answers. I had met hospitable and decent people. No one had ever asked me what I did for a living. Perhaps this was tact – it was an impolite question in a place where so many people were on the dole.

I had been asked the question in England and Wales. 'I'm in publishing,' I always said. Publishing was respectable, harmless and undiscussable. The conversation moved on to other matters. 'I'm a writer' was a fatal admission, and certainly one of the great conversation-stoppers. Anyway, in my wet shoes and scratched leather jacket and bruised knapsack would anyone have believed I was a writer? But no one knew what publishers looked like.

On my last night in Belfast I was asked. I was at Mooney's talking to Mr Doran, and I had asked too many questions about his upbringing, his mother, his ambitions, the crime rate, his job –

'And what do you do?' Doran asked, risking the question no one else had dared.

Obviously I did something. I was an alien.

'I'm in publishing,' I said.

Doran's face lit up. No one, in seven weeks of my saying this, had responded so brightly. But this was Ireland.

'I'm working on a wee novel,' Doran said, and ordered me another pint. 'I've got about four hundred pages done – it's right in me room upstairs. Let's meet tomorrow and have another jar. I'll bring me novel with me. You'll love it. It's all about the troubles.'

The next day I tiptoed past Doran's room. I heard the flutter-blast of his snoring. I slipped out of Mooney's and shut the door on Ulster.

18

The Train to Mallaig

After my days of being menaced by Belfast's ugly face I went by boat and train to Glasgow and found it peaceful, even pretty. It had a bad name. 'Gleska', people said, and mocked the toothless population and spoke of razor fights in the Gorbals, and made haggis jokes. Yet Glasgow was pleasant – not broken but eroded. The slums were gone, the buildings washed of their soot; the city looked dignified – no barricades, no scorchings. Well, I had just struggled ashore from that island of antiquated passions. In Ireland I had felt as though I had been walking blindly into the dark. But Scotland made me hopeful. This sunny day stretched all the way to Oban, where I was headed.

On my way from Glasgow Central to Queen Street Station, I fell in with two postmen. They asked me where I had come from. I told them Ulster. They said, 'Och!'

'It's full of broken windows,' I said.

'Aye. And broken *hids*!' one said.

The other man said, 'We got our Catholics. Ha' ye nae heard of the Rangers and Celtics fitba matches? They play each other a guid sux tames a year, but there's nae *always* a riot.'

No alphabet exists for the Glaswegian accent – phonetic symbols are no good either without a glottal stop, a snort, or a wheeze. I met rural-dwelling Scots who told me they could not understand anyone in Glasgow. The Ulster accent took a moment to turn from noise to language: I heard someone speak and then in the echo of the voice there was a meaning. But this did not always happen in Scotland: the echo was meaningless, and in Glasgow it was a strangled peevish hiccup, sudden and un-translatable.

I rode in an empty railway car up the Clyde, past tenements. I wondered about their age. They were striking in their size and their darkness – six storeys of stone, looking like prisons or lunatic asylums. Had the Scots originated the tenement? Their word for these old blocks was 'lands' and they had been using the word since the fifteenth century.

We went past Dumbarton (Dun Bretane, 'Hill of the Britons'), along the muddy rock-strewn shore, the Firth of Clyde. Across the firth was the busy port of Greenock ('birthplace of Captain Kidd, the pirate'). There were hills behind it. I always had trouble with hills. These were not so much risen loaves as smooth and sloping and lightly upholstered . . .

A big old man came through the connecting door, and though there was not another person in the whole railway car, he sat beside me. I put my notebook into my pocket.

'I hope you're not embarrassed,' he said.

Not embarrassed but something – perhaps startled.

'I'm going to Oban,' I said.

'Good,' he said. 'We can talk.' He was also going the hundred miles.

But he did most of the talking. He was very old and even sitting next to me he was a foot higher. He looked like a pope. He had a fat nose and big baggy-fleshed hands. He wore a long black overcoat and carried a small parcel of books tied with twine: detective stories. His name was John L. Davidson and he had been born in Lanarkshire in 1895. He said that occasionally he did feel 87 years old. How long had he lived in Dumbarton? 'Only fifty years,' he said. He lived in the Dumbarton Home for Aged Gentlefolks now. Everyone he had ever known was dead.

He said, 'I'm only seven years younger than John Logie Baird. Have you not heard of him? He invented the tellyvision. He was born here in Helensburgh.'

I looked out of the window.

'Over there somewhere,' Mr Davidson said. 'His teachers at school didnae think he was very bright. They thought he was a head case. One day he decided to invent a tellyphone. He put a wire across the road, a tellyphone instrument at either end, one in his house and one in his friend's. A man was riding a horse down the road, didnae see the wire – and strangled! Hanged himself on the wire of John Logie Baird's tellyphone! That's a true story.'

We came to Garelochhead, we travelled past Loch Long. The mountains above it were dark and rough, like enormous pieces of dusty coal. They were surrounded by pinewoods. The loch was blue-black and looked depthless.

'This loch is so long, so deep and so straight they test torpedoes in it,' Mr Davidson said. 'You can shoot a torpedo from one end to the other – thirteen miles or more. Want to see something interesting?'

He stood up and beckoned me to the window, and slid it down and said, 'Watch.'

We were coming to a junction, more tracks, and an isolated signal box. There were woods and hills all around. I expected the train to stop, but it did not even slow down. Mr Davidson stuck his parcel of books out of the window and dangled it. A railwayman was standing on a small raised platform near the signal box. He snatched the books and yelled, 'Thank you!'

'I've come this way before. The trains don't stop. I heard that the signalman here likes to read a good book. There's no shops here, no library, so I brought those books for him.'

Mr Davidson had no idea who the signalman was, nor did he know his name. He only knew that the man liked to read a good book.

'There used to be ever so many wee houses on this line, but now there's not many. It's out of touch. You see people on the train – after they've finished with their newspaper they throw it out the window to someone on the line to read.'

Then Mr Davidson screamed. He erupted in anger, just like that, without any warning.

'But some of them make me cross! People who travel through Scotland on the train, doing the crossword puzzle! Why do they bother to come!'

And, just as suddenly, he was calm: 'They call that mountain "The Cobbler". There's an open trough just behind it' – he pronounced it *troch*, to rhyme with loch.

At flat, mirror-still Loch Lomond, white as ice under a white sky, Mr Davidson began talking about printing unions. I had told him I was in publishing.

'You're not one of these bloody Fleet Street buggers!' he roared. It was another of his angry eruptions. 'The printing unions are bloody! They're just protecting their own interests. They show up drunk and they get paid! "Pay up!" "But he's drunk!" "Och, aye, but ye cannae bag Wully!" "I'll bag him!" "Bag him and we'll all go out!" It's bloody stupid!'

Mr Davidson was roaring at the window, at the creamy clouds reflected in the loch, not at me.

'I'm not a Queen Anne Tory,' he said. 'I'm a moderate Labour man. Aye, Jimmy, I was a trade unionist in 1912!'

He said he had been in the retail trade all his life – the grocery trade, another man's shop. He worked long hours. Eight in the morning until eight in the evening. A half hour for lunch, a half hour for tea.

The hills were bare from the mid-section upwards, and below this line were small pine trees. Mr Davidson was very silent and then he leaned towards me and whispered sadly, 'Everything you read's nae true.'

He exploded again.

'They went daft with afforestation! It takes forty years for a tree to be useful. You could have forty years of lambs here, and instead they have trees!'

But there were not many trees. Three hundred years ago this district was full of hardwood forests – oak and beech. They were cut down and made into charcoal for the iron smelters at Taynuilt, up the line, famous for its cannon balls – Lord Nelson had fired them at the Battle of Trafalgar. Now the trees were wispy pines, and the hills were rocky and bare and black-streaked with falling water. The dark clouds were like another range of mountains, another foreign land, and the sun on some stones gave them a pale bony gleam.

I suppressed a shiver and said that it seemed rather bleak around here.

'Aye,' Mr Davidson said. 'That's where its beauty comes from.'

And he went to sleep. His mouth dropped open and he slept so soundly I thought he had died.

Later, Mr Davidson awoke and gulped, seeming to swallow what remained of his fatigue. He recognized Kilchurn Castle. He said there had been a crazy old woman living in the ruin until very recently. She had thought she was the last of the Campbells. But he had also known hard times, he said. He had had 'three spells of poverty' – no work and nothing to eat.

'And I couldn't join the army. I wore spectacles, you see. If you wore spectacles a gas-mask was useless.'

Then he was talking about the Somme.

'This country has no friends' – he meant Britain – 'only enemies, and debts. We spent years paying off the Boer War debt. And we're still in debt.'

He hugged his heavy coat around himself and frowned. When he did this he looked shaggy and bearish. He was thinking.

'But there's nae debt for the Third World War. There'll be naebody left. Naebody can pay naebody! I blame' – he was erupting again – 'I blame the poultices in the House of Commons! They'll start the next war and then there'll be naebody!'

We came to Oban. The railway station was white, with a blue trim, and had a clock-tower showing the right time. There were seals in the harbour. On a hill above town was a full-sized replica of the Roman Colosseum, started in 1897 by a banker who thought something so ambitious would solve the unemployment problem. It was never finished; it was lovely and skeletal, symmetrical, purposeless. McCaig's Folly, they called it.

Even in Oban Mr Davidson stayed by my side as he had in the empty railway car. He said the folly had a window for every day of the year.

'I'm a bachelor,' he then explained. 'I never married.'

'No woman at all in eighty-seven years?'

'Nothing. And no drinking.'

'Never had a drink?'

'Maybe a toddy or two,' he said. 'And I never smoked.'

'A blameless life,' I said.

'I've been sick, though,' he said. 'But nothing as far as sexual, drinking or smoking.'

Oban was made of stone. It was Scottish and solid, no honky-tonk, no spivs. It was a town of cold bright rooms, with rosy-cheeked people in sweaters sitting inside and rubbing their hands; it had fresh air and freezing water. If you were cold you went for a walk and swung your arms to get the circulation up – no hearth fires until October. In Oban it struck me that most Scottish buildings looked as durable as banks. Here the dull clean town was on a coast of wild water and islands.

Some of these Scottish coastal towns looked as if they had been thrown out of the ground. They were fine polished versions of the same rocks they were on, but cut square and higher – not brought and built there by bricklayers but carved out of these granite cliffs.

I saw Mr Davidson my second day in Oban. He looked dead on a George Street bench, facing the harbour. His big hands were folded across his stomach, his mouth hung open. He had no suitcase – nothing but a rail ticket. Where had he slept? But I resisted asking questions, because I feared his answers.

He opened his yellow eyes on me.

I said, 'I'm thinking of going to Fort William.'

'There's a train in an hour,' he said. 'Where's your knapsack, Jimmy?'

He called everyone Jimmy.

I said, 'At the bus shelter. I'm taking a bus up the coast.'

He said, 'I wasn't planning to do that.'

'I'm sticking to the coast.'

'Aye, Jimmy, stick to the coast.' And he closed his eyes.

But there was a wild-eyed man on the bus. His name was Whitelaw, he chewed a pipe-stem, he watched the window and shouted.

There were cages in the sea.

He cried, 'Fish farm!'

There was dark and frothy water under the Connel Bridge.

He cried, 'Falls of Lora!'

I saw boggy fields.

He cried, 'That's where they cut peat!'

He was animated by the landscape. I wondered whether it was a Scottish trait. I had never seen an English person behave like this.

He cried, 'The tide's out!'

It was. Eventually he got off the bus, at Portnacroish, on the Sound of Shuna.

It was a complicated coastline of hills and bays, lochs and rushing burns. It could not have been anything but the Scottish coast – so much water, so much steepness, such rocks. Ballachulish was like an alpine valley that had been scoured of all its softness – the feathery trees and chalets and brown cows whirled off its slopes, and all the gentle angles scraped away, until it lay bare and rugged, a naked landscape awaiting turf and forest.

Most of this western coastline in Scotland looked elemental in that way – as if it had been whipped clean, and was waiting completion. It was hard and plain, most of it. It was very cold. I imagined sheep dying on it. Fort William was powerfully craggy. I began to think that this was the most spectacular coastline I had seen so far in Britain – huger than Cornwall, darker than Wales, wilder than Antrim. I stared at it and decided that it was ferocious rather than pretty, with a size and a texture that was surprisingly unfinished. It changed with the light as coastal cliffs always did; it was always massive, but in certain pale lights it seemed murderous.

I was anonymous in Fort William. The other visitors had knapsacks, too, and oily shoes and binoculars. With Ben Nevis above it, and all the campsites of the Highlands just behind it, Fort William was full of hikers and fresh-air fiends all frantically interrogating each other about footpaths. The town was crowded and unpleasant-looking, heaving with campers, so after lunch I wiped my mouth and walked north and west along the railway line to the coast. Once again I thought: Some travel is a fantasy of running away.

Three miles away I came to the lower end of the Caledonian Canal. I wanted to see a boat passing through, but there was nothing on it except ducks. It was a sunny day and I was glad to be alone in the empty glen.

Then a wheezing voice said, 'Hae ye got a match?' and I almost jumped out of my skin.

It was Jock MacDougall, with red eyes and a filthy face, trembling next to a tree. He had a scabby wound on his forehead and his clothes were rags.

'I just want a match,' he said. 'I'm nae being cheeky.

He was trying to reassure me: he knew he was filthy and dangerous-looking. I gave him my matches and he slowly lit an inch-long cigarette butt that was flat, as if it had been stepped on What an odd person to meet in a green glen

He said, 'I was never had up for assault or bodily harm or a breach of the peace in me whole life.'

I stared at him. I did not know what to say.

'Only for being drunk and incapable,' he said.

He had a little camp nearby – a nest of rags, some bottles, a smokey fire and two comrades. There was a frightened woman named Alice and a man named Crawford, who was even filthier than MacDougall. Crawford called himself Tex. He was from Aberdeen.

'But I'm a Glasgow man,' Jock said. 'A Glasgow man will stick by you.'

Alice looked wildly at him, but said nothing. She looked injured and was very silent.

Jock sang a song.

> Coom doon the stairs.
> Tie up your bonny hairs!

This seemed to frighten Alice even more.

He sang a song about a place called Fyvie. He said, 'At Fyvie there's a statue of a cow!'

'What's your trade?' Crawford said. He had a dewdrop at the end of his nose and smelled of dead leaves.

I told them I was in publishing.

'Ha!' Jock said. 'I'm a tramp! I'm a man of the road!'

Crawford said, 'Do much travelling?'

'A certain amount,' I said.

Crawford said, 'I've been everywhere in the world.'

'New Jersey? Argentina? Fiji?' I asked.

'Everywhere,' he said.

I asked him to describe for me some of the more colourful spots he had seen.

'That would be too hard. There were so many.'

Five feet away Jock was crouching with his arm around Alice. Then he thrust his hand under her green sweater and she squawked.

'I have three passports,' Crawford said. 'A woman in Perth once said to me, "I'd like to have twenty-four hours with you."'

This amazed me. He stank, his teeth were black, he had blades of grass in his beard.

'She said, "Know what you should do? You should write a travel book."'

'Why don't you?' I asked. Now I was sorry I had told him I was in publishing. But what would he write, under this tree?

'There's too many bloody travel books,' he said, and faced me, as if challenging me to deny it.

I did not deny it.

'Why are you here in Scotland?' Jock shouted to me. 'People in Scotland are rubbish!'

I said I had to go, but they stood on the path blocking my way.

'Give me some money,' Jock said.

'Which way to Corpach?' I asked, still walking.

'I'm not telling any secrets unless you pay me!'

'All right, I'll pay.'

He pointed. 'Down there on the road.'

I gave him a ten pence coin.

He said, 'Give me sixty or seventy.'

'That was only worth ten,' I said. 'Now step aside.'

The train was the 16.30 to Mallaig. I looked back and saw the hump of Ben Nevis, with streaks and splashes of snow in some of its hollows. It was a huge grey forehead of rock, with a green bare dome in front of it, and three more on the south side. All the mountains here had the contours of hogs.

Mrs Gordon in the next seat said, 'Taking the train, to me, is like going to the cinema.'

It was a splendid ride to Mallaig – one of the most scenic railway journeys in the world. But the train itself was dull and the passengers watchful and reverent, intimidated by all this scenery.

Scotland had a paradoxical beauty – its landscape was both lovely and severe; it was a monotonous extravaganza. The towns were as dull as any I had ever seen in my life, and the surrounding mountains very wild. I liked what I saw but I kept wanting to leave. And the Scots had a nervous way with a joke. Their wit was aggressive and unsmiling. I kept wondering: Was that meant to be funny? When they were forthright they could become personal, especially on the subject of money. A Scot I met in Oban had accused me of wasting money when I told him that I had been planning to take a first-class sleeper to London – regarded it as wasteful and selfish that I should want to be alone. And here on this Mallaig train a man wanted to know why, if there was no Youth Hostel in Mallaig, I planned to stay the night there? And why hadn't I bought a round-trip ticket – didn't I know it was cheaper than the one-way fare on a weekend? This was Mr Buckie, who saved rubber bands – he had fourteen on his wrist – and had been wearing the same tweed cap since 1953, Coronation Year. He was not trying to be helpful. Penny-pinching had made him abusive, obstructive and cross. He ended up by disliking me, as if I was wasting *his* money.

But I thought: In travel you meet people who try to lay hold of you, who take charge like parents, and criticize. Another of travel's pleasures was turning your back on them and leaving and never having to explain.

I changed my seat as we passed along the shore of Loch Eil. There were high mountains rising in the west, and more lochs. Some of the mountains were 3,000 feet high and some lochs 1,000 feet deep (Loch Morar a few miles away was even deeper). We crossed the Glenfinnan Viaduct – it was curved and long and had romanesque arches, and it stood at the north end of the shiny black water of Loch Shiel, which lay beneath more rugged mountains.

There was great emptiness here. The train stayed high on the hillsides and did not descend into the valleys. There were ferns and bracken in the foreground, and some trees growing in narrow sheltered gullies out of the wind, but no human beings. The westerly gales had torn the soil from most hillsides. It was hard and lovely. The beauty was only part of it; you had to be tough to live here.

The landscape widened after Loch Ailort Station, and we were heading west where the bright sun was setting, making the water blaze on Loch Nan Uamh, which was also the sea, and making the green grass luminous and vibrant, as if the pasture were trembling a foot from the ground. The light was perfect, because there was nothing in the way: the mountains stood separate and all the sea lochs were long and stretched westward, so that the last of the sun shone uninterruptedly down their length.

The train bucked and turned north at Arisaig. The bays were like crater crusts filled with water. The offshore islands – Rhum, Eigg, Muck and Canna – had names like items from a misspelt menu. The Scour of Eigg was a hatchet shape against the sky. And now beneath the train there was a basin of green fields for three miles to the Sound of Sleat – and above the train were mountains of cracked rock, and swatches of purple heather. Suddenly a horse was silhouetted in the sun, cropping grass beside the sea.

The train stopped at the level crossing at Morar – the opening and closing of gates, the latching and unlatching, clunk, clunk; and then chugged into Mallaig, where people were swimming in the freezing water, the foaming waves making lace caps for their bobbing heads.

That night I stared out of the window at the freakish mountains on Skye. They were sharp-pointed, fantastic and high like peaks in dragon stories. They were the Cuillins, and their strange shape made them look unclimbable. Although it was after eleven there was enough light for me to see them, and then near midnight they were ghostlier still: it was like winter light, a February afternoon in Boston, with the greyness of a gathering shadow.

In all my coastal travel I never met a fisherman who said he was satisfied. They hated the life, they said. The price. were bad, the competition was tough, the waters were overfished. Foreign fishermen were to blame – the Russians, the Japanese, the Danes. Foreigners scooped up everything – sprats, fry, undersized fish – and beat them into fishmeal on their factory ships.

Captain Cameron on his fishing boat *Lord Roberts* at Mallaig said, 'Anyone here would sell his boat if he could get a fair price for it. The fishing business is dead. I should have sold mine when I could, a few years ago. Now I'm fifty-seven, and I have to work as long as I can. I won't be able to retire – haven't got the money. I'll work until I'm too weak to go on and then my kids will be cursed with this bloody boat.'

He was taking seventeen crates of prawns' tails ashore, about a thousand pounds' worth, but his fuel bill for this trip was five hundred and he had a crew of five. There was hardly any profit in it. They had been at sea for nearly a week.

'Some day there'll be no fishing at all,' Captain Cameron said. 'It'll pass into ancient history.'

On my second morning at Mallaig, Mrs Fleming's daughter

served me my breakfast and said, 'Princess Diana's had a baby boy.'

Everyone was pleased: an heir to the throne. It was another national event in an eventful period. The Falklands war had started and finished as I had been travelling. The pope had come and gone. The Royal Baby was born – Prince William. A railway strike was threatened. Three million people were unemployed – 13 per cent of the workforce – and one person out of six in Scotland was without a job. There was a deranged murderer loose in Yorkshire. They were public events and they had the effect of making people unusually talkative. 'This Falklands business –' And then the American president visited and went horseback riding with the Queen. He made a speech. People smiled a little when they heard my accent. 'I just saw your president on television –' It was supposed to be a kingdom of tight-lipped people, but the war and the strife and the pope and now the birth of a future king had brought about a relentless garrulity. I needed a little air.

I took the road north out of the town. The road ended; a track began. It was a rough stony path which circled a grey hill above the sea. I walked along the shore of Loch Nevis. Just over the hill at Loch Morar people sometimes searched for underwater monsters. I walked to Inverie, which was a house on a road that went nowhere. I wondered how much farther I should go. The coast was in-and-out for hundreds of miles. I liked walking, but I was no snorting rambler with plus-fours and a pick-axe. If I saw a sheep on the path I stopped and stared at it. I sat down and sketched a tall thistle at Inverie – the Scottish thistles seemed to me magical, and as complicated as crystals. I looked at birds. I tried to think of descriptions for these unusual islands – they were less like islands than old bare mountains in the sea. I was distracted by all the water and rock, the great heights of cloud, the ruined stone cottages along the coastal paths, the lived-in cottages in remote places which looked as though they were growing more remote – places only reachable in small boats.

It would have taken more than a week to walk from Mallaig to the Kyle of Lochalsh, up the coast. So I sailed there in the ferry *Lochmorar*, twenty-three miles along the Sound of Sleat. The boat passed more of these remote cottages. It said something about Scottish self-reliance and toughness that people willingly lived in such difficult places. In the whole of Britain there could not have been houses more inaccessible than these scattered over the shores of the Western Isles. The Scots here chose a distant ledge or a remote shore, and put up a stone house, and slammed their door on the world.

The coast had deep inlets and high cliffs, and it was so steep it had the effect of concentrating travellers in specific places. On this boat, for example. Or on certain valley roads. In Fort William and Oban and Mallaig. In England and Wales people were quickly absorbed by the countryside, and the coastal towns could seem very empty. But here in Scotland the countryside and the coastal steepness was forbidding, and so everyone travelled on a few routes; and they had always travelled on those routes. The traveller to Mull had to go to Oban, just like Doctor Johnson and Boswell in 1773.

At the Kyle of Lochalsh I crossed to Skye, on the ferry to Kyleakin ('from Hakon, King of Norway, who sailed through here in 1263') and walked the empty roads to Broadford, eight miles. I stayed and climbed part way up a red mountain merely to have another glimpse at the Cuillins. I did not go any closer. I wanted to save them for another time. I had seen so much on the British coast that I never wanted to see again that it was a surprise and a pleasure to find a place I wished to return to. It gave me hope, because I knew I would not come back alone. I wanted to come here again with someone I loved and say, 'Look.'

The sun on Skye warmed the pines and the flowers and gave it the fragrance of Nantucket.

The way between the huge simple mountains and cold lochs, from the Kyle of Lochalsh to Dingwall, was one of the great railway routes of Britain. It took me off the coast, but what else could I do? The northerly shore was broken and labyrinthine. It would only be a stunt to follow every mile of it, just to report on Loch Snizort and Trotternish. And the train was a greater temptation. Anyway, many of these lochs were also notches on the coast. Loch Carron, for example: the south bank, on which this train was travelling, was sixteen miles of coast.

Nothing looked to me colder than a Scottish loch, and they

seemed to become colder still as the clouds piled up and night deepened. But these were short nights – a few cloudy hours of wintry light, and then morning. It was eight o'clock and every landscape feature was clearly visible: the water, the hills, the trees and farms, the long valley floor of Glen Carron that seemed to be covered with grassy mounds – tombs and tumuli.

'Ach, some of these villages have been here since the year dot,' a man named Macnab said to me. Yes, they had a mossy, buried look. But many looked bleakly exposed, plopped down and untidy with no hedges, no bushes. The bushiest thing in Achnasheen was the stationmaster's beard.

We were delayed at Garve. I thought: I'll give it an hour and if we're still here I'll get off and walk up the Black Water or hitch to Ullapool. (Delays always sent me to my map for an escape route.)

Malcolm Biles asked for a look at my map. He was twenty-three, a post office clerk from Inverness, who was on a cheap day-return. I had wanted to meet a post office worker, I told him. British post office workers did much more than sell stamps. They processed car licences, television licences, Family Allowances, pensions, Inland Telegrams, Postal Orders, all the tasks required by the Post Office Savings Bank, and a hundred other things. They had seven weeks' training and the rest had to be learned on the job, in full view of the impatient public. It was Malcolm who spoke of the impatience. People were much ruder than they used to be and some of them stood there and ticked you off!

'What about dog licences?' I asked.

Dog licences! It was Malcolm Biles's favourite subject. The price of a dog licence was 37½ pence, because in 1880 it had been fixed at seven shillings and sixpence. The fee had never been changed. Wasn't that silly? I agreed it was. There were six million dogs in Britain, and only half of them were licensed. But the amazing thing was that it cost four pounds (almost seven dollars) to collect the dog licence – the time, paperwork, and so forth.

'Why not abolish the fee?' I asked.

Malcolm said, 'That would be giving up.'

'Why not increase it to something realistic – say, five quid?'

'That would be unpopular,' he said. 'No government would dare try it.'

'How long do you figure you'll be staying in the post office?'

'For the rest of my life, I hope,' he said. The train jolted. 'Ah, we're away.'

I tried to imagine a whole lifetime in a post office. I could not imagine it. I got to the end of a few years and then nothing would come – a blur, fatigue, bewilderment, indifference. It was easier to imagine the life of that crofter talking gently to his dog at Strathpeffer.

Still, we discussed the post office and debated the issue of dog licences until we came to Dingwall ('birthplace of Macbeth').

19

The Flyer to Cape Wrath

My Blue Guide's description of the north-west coast of Scotland suggested a setting that was straight out of *Dracula* or *The Mountains of Madness*. 'The road crosses a strange and forbidding mountain wilderness,' it began, 'of sombre rock-strewn glens, perched glacial boulders, and black lochs.' And then, 'after 8 m. of lonely moor and dark bog . . . the road from the ferry's w. end to Cape Wrath crosses a bleak moor called *The Parph*, once notorious for its wolves,' and at last, 'the road rises across a desolate moor . . .'

It made me want to set off at once. It seemed the perfect antidote to the presbyterian monotony of Dingwall. If the guidebook's description were accurate it would be like travelling to the end of the world – in any case, the British world. Cape Wrath was not merely remote – the ultimate coastline – it was also such a neglected place and reputedly so empty that the method for getting there had not changed for eighty years or more. Baedeker's *Great Britain* for 1906 said, 'From Lairg, mail-cart routes diverge in various directions, by means of which the highly picturesque country to the W. and N.W. . . . may be conveniently explored . . .'

At Dingwall Station I asked the best way to Cape Wrath.

'Get the post bus at Lairg,' Mr MacNichols said.

In other words, the mail cart. There was no train, there was no bus, there was hardly a road – it was paved the width of a wagon for fifty-six miles. There were people who still called the post bus 'the flyer', as they called tenant farms 'crofts' and porridge 'crowdie'.

The train to Lairg left Dingwall and passed along the edge of Cromarty Firth, which at this state of the tide was shallow water seeping into the mudflats. Not long before, the railway line was to have been shut down; but it had been reprieved. It passed through the bleakest boggiest part of Caithness, where the roads were often bad, and in winter it was an essential service. But Mr MacNichols had confided to me that in the off-season there were sometimes only three or four people on board.

To save money on the line some of the stations had been closed. The ruined, boarded-up station building at Alness resembled many I had seen in Ulster. A large aluminium smelter had just closed at Invergordon – 900 more people out of work and another building left to rot. Decrepitude was decrepitude – the fury of terrorists was indistinguishable from the wilfulness of budget-cutters and accountants.

Beyond the village of Fearn there were farms and fields of a classic kind – long vistas over the low hills, quiet houses and smooth fields of fat sheep. There were steeples under the soft grey sky at Tain – the Tolbooth, with a conical spire and turrets, and a church spire like a pepper-mill. Pink and purple lupins shook on the station platform.

People used this train for shopping, travelling to a place like Tain from miles up the line. Two ladies were sitting next to me. They were Mrs Allchin and Mrs MacFee. They were discussing the butcher.

'Duncan is very obliging,' Mrs Allchin said. 'We often give him a lift on stormy days.'

'I think it's an ideal place, Tain,' Mrs MacFee said.

Mrs MacFee had two large bags of groceries, and she had also managed to find a packet of 'toe-spacers' at the chemist's shop. It eased her mind to know that she had these for pedicures and nail varnishing. Kenneth had mentioned a dinner-dance at the Lodge and she did not want to fuss at the last minute.

Mrs Allchin had been very lucky in Tain. Ian's lad, wee Colum, was having a birthday, and she had found a box of something called 'indoor fireworks'. Apparently, you just cleared a space on the table and set them off. Apparently, they were perfectly safe. Chinese.

'What won't they think of next?' Mrs MacFee said.

But Mrs Allchin's mind was elsewhere. The indoor fireworks reminded her that she was chain-smoking again. She often chain-smoked in trains. It worried her, like nail-biting.

'I dinna drink, at any rate,' Mrs Allchin said.

We travelled inland, towards the hills at Culrain, which had a ruined look. And the roof was off the station at Invershin. Some other stations had clearly been sold off to be turned into common bungalows or holiday homes. There were cabbages growing where the platform had been.

We went through Acharry Glen – the River Shin on the left. I had settled down to watch the mountains passing, but soon we came to Lairg and I had to get out.

There was something very disconcerting about leaving a train in the middle of nowhere. It was all activity and warm upholstery and then the clang of a carriage door and the train pulled out and left me in a sort of pine-scented silence. Lairg Station was two miles from Lairg, but even Lairg was nowhere.

I saw a man throwing mailbags and bundles of newspapers into the back of an old-fashioned vehicle. It was a cut-down version of a bus, about the size of a hearse. Still the man went on loading it with the bags and bundles the train had left.

I cleared my throat. He looked up. I said I was going to Durness on the post bus.

'This is the post bus,' he said. 'We can leave as soon as I get these bags loaded.'

His name was Michael Mathers. He pronounced it 'Maithers'. His accent was not Scottish. It was fairly Gaelic and very Scandinavian, a soft Norse whirr in every syllable. Later, I discovered that everyone in his part of Sutherland had the same accent, a legacy of the Vikings. This accent was all that remained of their language, Norn.

We set off for Lairg and picked up more mail and an old couple on their way to Scourie. Michael said that this was a Bedford bus, only ten years old. It had gone 400,000 miles.

'When I took over,' he said, 'we had an Albion. Made in Glasgow. That one went 650,000 miles in fifteen years.'

He had been driving for twenty-one years. He was forty-four and had the solemn kindly face of a fisherman. He had once tried working on a fishing boat. He said, 'You need a strong stomach for that.' It was cold, it was hard, there wasn't much money. At midnight on a pitching boat, struggling with nets, he would look into the distance and see the lights of Durness: the lucky people indoors. So he had chucked it.

We headed out of Lairg and were almost immediately in a bog. It was a wide dark landscape, with rocks and grass and heather close by, and mountains ahead.

There was no better glimpse into the life of remote Sutherland than through the smeared windows of this eight-seater. The post bus was a life-line and Mr Mathers much more than a driver. He not only picked up mail and dropped it off, and ran with it to houses in the rain, and carried scribbled messages from house to house, he also drove along a single track road for the whole of the way north, which meant he had to stop when a car approached from the opposite direction – eighty or ninety times in a single trip, because the road was only wide enough for one car. He carried milk. He carried newspapers. He carried shapeless bundles labelled 'For Graham'.

He stopped the bus at 'The Reeks', in the middle of a peat field, and with the mist flying sideways he hurried to the door with a pint of milk, the *TV Times*, today's *Scotsman* and a birthday card for Mrs Campbell. Farther down the road at 'Fernside' it was two pints and a *Mirror*, and then a five-minute trot up a muddy path to deliver a junk-mail Sunglasses Special Offer from the Automobile Association (though Mr Innes was expecting a long overdue letter from his daughter in Australia), and then a copy of the *Sun* to 'Hope Cottage' and another favour – fifteen pounds of wet fish in a plastic shopping bag for a householder who had asked for it over at Kinloch. And more newspapers. Such effort and expense to bring people copies of the gutter press! But that was Mr Mathers' job. And he was never abrupt. Whenever he handed something over he exchanged a greeting. 'How's your mother feeling?' and 'The sheep are looking well' and 'It feels like rain'.

We came to an unearthly, gigantic landscape along Loch More in the Reay Forest. The fields looked bitter and brown, and the loch very cold, and the mountains were vast shrouds of rock. One of these silver mountains was the most beautiful I had so far seen in Britain – a great bulge glittering with cataracts of scree. It looked as if it had just frozen in that carbuncular shape the day before.

'That's Arkle,' Mrs MacGusty said. She wasn't local. Her accent was amused and tentative, like someone nibbling short-bread, the tones of Morningside – the genteel landlady accent of Edinburgh. 'It's Icelandic, you see.'

What did that mean?

'It's all turned over. These high mountains' – she seemed to be describing babies, her voice was so affectionately savouring the words – 'Ben Stack and Arkle – what should be on the bottom is on the top, they reckon, the geologists. You look at them and you think, "They all look duffrent!"'

Mr MacGusty said, 'They're also very beg.'

This was Achfary – 'the Duke of Westminster's estate,' Mrs MacGusty said.

'Does he farm here?' I asked.

'Oh, no. It's an estate. He keeps it for the shooting and the fishing. Prince Charles comes here in a helicopter sometimes, for the shooting. Och! I expect you're a republican!'

We were sitting by the roadside in the post bus as the rain came down. Mr Mathers was bringing a copy of yesterday's *Express* to a cottage behind a high wall.

I said, 'So it's all gamekeepers here?'

'Aye,' Mr MacGusty said. 'The Duke owns a good butt of Sutherland.' He thought a moment. 'It's the old way of life.' He thought again. 'It's very unfair, in a way.'

It was more a shrug than a protest. But he was resigned. After all, we were talking about feudalism.

The past was accessible here as a present fact. Not only in ducal estates and private game reserves, but also in ancient names. The MacGustys got off the bus at Laxford Bridge. It was a Norse name – *lax* meant salmon (and of course the Yiddish *lox* for smoked salmon was a cognate). Then Mr Mathers told me how his parents had both been fluent Gaelic speakers and that he spoke it fairly well. And peat-cutting was part of the past, too. The peat was free, but cutting it was back-breaking work. They were cut and left to dry in stacks, so everything depended on good weather. Even present-day crime sounded somewhat outdated – sheep rustlers, and squatters and poachers.

We drove up the narrow track to Rhiconich. This was actually the coast, a muddled maze of islands and lochs. We went to

Kinlochbervie, which was a busy fishing port on a sea loch, dealing in white fish and lobsters.

We stopped twenty more times. Mr Mathers did this twice a day on this small windy corner of Scotland. When he stopped and parked, the wind shook the bus and rattled the cottage gates and moaned against the telegraph wires. A pint of milk, a *Scotsman* and a printed postcard saying, *This is to acknowledge your communication of the 13th inst.* to Mrs Massey at 'Drumbeg'.

'Cape Wrath doesn't mean "angry",' Mr Mathers said. 'It's from a Norse word that means "turning-point". This is where the ships turned south. Sutherland is another Norse name – it was south for them.'

Then he smiled. 'Don't be disillusioned,' he said. 'The weather can be hellish here. In 1952, when I was still at school, we had a January storm. The winds were a hundred and twenty miles an hour – roofs were torn off houses. The Irish ferry was lost that night. It's often bad weather – horrible weather. I pity the lads in those wee fishing boats.'

We came to Durness. He said, 'This is it. There aren't more than three hundred people here. It's the work problem, you see. There's no employment.'

The village was empty, but the wind was a presence – wild gusts flew in from the direction of the Faroes.

I walked back through the sandy cliffs, among the rabbit holes, to Keoldale and the Cape Wrath Hotel, and had my first good meal for days. There were a number of English anglers at the hotel. They blustered when the national news came on. They were all Tories. They called the Prime Minister 'Maggie'. Her nonsense suited their nonsense. One said he wanted to shoot the man being interviewed, who claimed he had known all along that the Falklands were going to be invaded. 'Too many bloody people giving advice!' Another said that half the Labour Party should be shot for treason. One thing about anglers, though. They went to bed early.

The next day I crossed the Kyle of Durness and walked seven miles to Kearvaig, which was like the end of the earth. But this was Cape Wrath proper and had peaty soil – it was crumbling cliffs and sand at Durness.

I saw a seal take a salmon. People told me that seals did not really eat them – that they just took bites of the fish's shoulders and threw the rest away. But this seal lay on his back with the eight pound salmon in his mouth, and he tossed his head and snapped his jaws and ate the whole thing.

Then on my way back I saw a flock of sheep crossing a sandbar in the Kyle of Durness. The tide was coming in. The sheep started moving. Soon they were swimming, the big horned sheep in front, the lambs behind with their noses out of the water. They were North Highland Cheviots. They moved very slowly, for the tide was still rising and they were still far from the bank. Fifteen minutes later the Kyle was filled, there were fewer sheep visible; and then there were none. They had all drowned, about nine of them, under the grey torn sky.

Some fantasies prepare us for reality. The sharp steep Cuillins were like mountains from a story-book – they had a dramatic, fairy-tale strangeness. But Cape Wrath was unimaginable. It was one of those places where, I guessed, every traveller felt like a discoverer who was seeing it for the first time. There are not many such places in the world. I felt I had penetrated a fastness of mountains and moors, after two months of searching; and I had found something new. So even this old, over-scrutinized kingdom had a secret patch of coast! I was very happy at Cape Wrath. I even liked its ambiguous name. I did not want to leave.

There were other people in the area: a hard-pressed settlement of sheep farmers and fishermen, and a community of drop-outs making pots and jewellery and quilts at the edge of Balnakiel. There were anglers and campers, too, and every so often a brown plane flew overhead and dropped bombs on one of the Cape Wrath beaches, where the army had a firing range. But the size of the place easily absorbed these people. They were lost in it, and as with all people in a special place they were secretive and a little suspicious of strangers.

Only the real natives were friendly. They were the toughest highlanders and did not match any Scottish stereotype I knew. They did not even have a recognizably Scottish accent. They were like white crows. They were courteous, hospitable, hard-working, and funny. They epitomized what was best in Scotland, the strong cultural pride that was separate from political nationalism. That took confidence. They were independent, too – 'thrawn' was the Lowlands word for their stubborn character. I admired their sense of equality, their disregard for class, and the gentle way they treated their children and animals. They were tolerant and reliable, and none of this was related to the flummery of bagpipes and tartans and tribalistic blood-and-thunder that Sir Walter Scott had turned into the Highland cult. What I liked most about them was that they were self-sufficient. They were the only people I had seen on the whole coast who were looking after themselves.

It was a shire full of mountains, with spaces between – some valleys and some moors – and each mountain was separate. To describe the landscape it was necessary to describe each mountain, because each one was unique. But the soil was not very good, the sheep were small, the grass thin, and I never walked very far without finding a corpse – loose wool blowing around bones, and the bared teeth of a skull.

'Look,' a shepherd named Stephen said to me on one of these hillsides.

A buzzard-sized bird was circling.

'It's a hooded crow,' Stephen said. 'They're desperate creatures. In a place like this – no shelter, no one around for miles – they find a lamb and peck its eyes out. It's lost, it can't get to its mother, it gets weak. Then the hooded crows – so patient up there – dive down and peck it to pieces. They're a terrible bird.'

He said that it was the predatory crows, not the weather, that killed the lambs. It was a cold place, but not excessively so. In winter there was little snow, though the winds were strong and the easterlies were usually freezing gales. There were always birds in the wind – crows and hawks, and comic squawking oyster-catchers with long orange bills, and singing larks and long-necked shags and stuttering stonechats.

It could be an eerie landscape, especially on a wet day, with all the scattered bones gleaming against the dun-coloured cliffs and the wind scraping against the heather. It surprised me that I was happy in a place where there were so few trees – there were none at all here. It was not picturesque and it was practically un-photographable. It was stunningly empty. It looked like a corner of another planet, and at times it seemed diabolical. But I liked it for all these reasons. And more important than these, my chief reason for being happy was that I felt safe here. The landscape was like a fierce-looking monster that offered me protection; being in Cape Wrath was like having a pet dragon.

On one of my walks I met a veterinarian, Doctor Pike, who was making the rounds of the Cape Wrath farms trying to persuade the farmers to dip their sheep. An ailment called 'sheep scab' had been brought over from Ireland and had endangered some of the flocks.

Doctor Pike was a fluent Gaelic speaker. He was self-assured and well-read, and though he did not boast he did imply a moral superiority in the highlander – and in the Scots in general – and he suggested that there was something lamentable and decadent in the English.

'Take the colonies,' he said. 'The Scots who went out were very hard-working and idealistic. But for a lot of the English families the colonies were the last resort. They sent the black sheep of the family – the rubbish, the drunkards, the layabouts.'

We were walking around Balnakiel Bay – he was heading for a farmhouse. We passed a shepherd driving a flock of sheep to be shorn.

Doctor Pike said, 'You might take that shepherd to be a fool or a rustic. But most of these shepherds are sensible men. I mean, they read. I go to many of these shepherds' wee cottages and – do you know? – I find lots of books in some of them. They take books with them out on the hillsides.'

We had a good view of the sea – the mouth of the bay was wide. There were no boats out there. I seldom saw boats, at any rate. It was one of the roughest areas on the British coast, and the scarcity of boats added to the feeling of emptiness I felt on shore. It was like the world after a catastrophic bomb.

Doctor Pike was still talking about shepherds. He said, 'There was a man here from Edinburgh. He saw a shepherd in the hills and said how wonderful it was to get so much fresh air and exercise. "But how does it feel to be so far from the centre of things?"

'The shepherd stared at him and smiled. "That depends what you mean by the centre of things." You see, he felt that it was just a matter of perspective. Who was this city man to say that the shepherd was not at the centre of things?'

I told Doctor Pike that I had seen nine sheep drown in the incoming tide at the Kyle of Durness. He said it was a pity but it sometimes happened. Although sheep could swim, the horns of a ram made it hard for the creature to keep its head up, and the lambs were too frail to swim very far. But he said that he loved sheep – he loved working with them.

'They have very keen instincts. They have a wonderful sense for forecasting the weather – they know when a gale is coming. They begin to leave the hills many days before it begins to snow.'

The next day I went with Doctor Pike to Loch Eriboll. It was a sea loch piercing ten miles of Sutherland, and it was deep enough to take the largest ships. In the storms for which this part of Scotland was notorious, ships found a quiet anchorage here.

'I want you to see something,' Doctor Pike said.

We rounded a bend, turning south towards Laid, along the shore of the huge loch.

'Look at this hillside,' he said.

It was a rough, steep slope, covered with small white boulders. Patches of the slope had been ploughed, but most of it was covered with glacial rubble and humps, and the grass was blackish and sparse. Some sheep stood on it and looked at us with their characteristic expression of indifference and curiosity. This grazing land was very bad.

'Now look over there, across the loch,' he said.

It was like a different country, a different climate. It was not bouldery – it was soft and green. There were grassy meadows and gentle slopes over there. It was sheltered by the mountains behind it, and pleasant streams ran through it. There were trees over there! There were no houses, there were no sheep.

But this windswept side of the loch – the western shore on which we stood – was lined with tiny whitewashed cottages. They were surrounded by broken walls and fences and some bushes. There were gnarled trees, none higher than the cottage eaves. The roofs fitted the cottages in an irregular way like lopsided caps and made the cottages pathetic.

'These people once lived over there, on the good side of the loch. They were cleared off that land and moved here. They were crofters then – they're crofters still. They were given the worst land.'

He was talking about the Clearances, the evictions by the chiefs and landlords who wanted to cash in on the land. It had taken years, but the Highlands were eventually emptied – the fertile parts, that is. Enormous sheep farms replaced some crofts, and others were turned into playgrounds, grouse moors and baronial estates. This was a major reason for the tremendous number of Scottish emigrants, dispersed across the world between 1780 and 1860. So what had seemed to me no more than an early chapter in a history of Scotland, or a melodramatic painting by Landseer, was a lingering injustice. The cruelty of the Clearances was still remembered, because many people who had been made poor still remained where they had been dumped.

'Is it any wonder that some of them are poachers?' Doctor Pike said.

He was fairly passionate on the subject. He said the land ought to be nationalized and divided into smaller units. The land could be made productive – people would have jobs.

I said he was the first left-wing veterinarian I had ever met. He denied that he was left-wing. He said most radicals were devils. Then he said, 'Want to meet one of the victims of the Clearances?'

We stopped at a small white cottage near the edge of the loch and were greeted by an old man. This was Davey McKenzie. He wore a tweed hat and a threadbare jacket and loose trousers. His shoes were cracked and broken. He had a healthy face, good colour, and he was sinewy. He was about seventy or a bit more. He raised some sheep and he grew vegetables and he was always followed by a black terrier with a pleading face which lay down and snored whenever Mr McKenzie sat down.

'We can't stay,' Doctor Pike said.

'You'll have a cup of tea,' Mr McKenzie replied. He had the same Norse whirr in his accent that I had been hearing for days.

We entered the cottage and were introduced to Jessie Stewart, Mr McKenzie's sister. She was perhaps a year or two younger than he, but she was pale and rather feeble. Doctor Pike whispered to me that she had recently had an operation and he added, 'She's far from well.'

'Sit down in front of the fire,' she said. 'I'll put the tea on.'

It was the end of June – a few days from July – and yet a fire burned in the cottage hearth, and the wind made the rose bushes scratch at the window.

Doctor Pike said, 'Don't trouble yourself, Mrs Stewart.'

'It's no trouble,' she said. 'And don't call me Mrs Stewart. No one calls me that. I'm Jessie.'

The cottage was comfortable but austere – a few potted plants, pictures of children and grandchildren, a calendar from Thurso and some Scottish souvenirs, a glass paperweight showing Arthur's Seat, and a little doll in a tartan kilt.

Doctor Pike said his piece about sheep scab and then turned to me. 'You know you're in the Highlands when people make you welcome like this. No one is sent away. If you come to the door of a Highlander he lets you in.'

'That's very true,' Davey McKenzie said softly.

'I know a rune about that in Gaelic,' Doctor Pike said. 'Translated, it goes like this –

> 'I saw a stranger yest'reen.
> I put food in the eating place,
> Drink in the drinking place,
> Music in the listening place –
> And the lark in its song sang!
>
> Often, often, often, often,
> Comes the Christ in the stranger's guise.'

'That's very beautiful,' Davey said.

'Some people come,' Jessie said. 'But these days there are vandals about. We never locked our doors before, but now we lock them. People come – they look so strange, some of these hikers and campers, and the women are worse than the men.'

She went for the tea. Doctor Pike said, 'I was telling Paul about the crofters here, how they were moved from the other side – from that good land.'

He did not say that it was over a century ago.

'It was unfair, aye,' Davey said He blinked at me. He had wet red-rimmed eyes. 'There's so much good land lying idle. Aye, it's hard land where we are.'

He was a quiet man. He said no more. It seemed to me terrible that he had spent his whole life trying to feed his family by digging this stony ground, and always in sight of the green fields under Ben Arnaboll across the loch.

But the bad land had turned many people into emigrants or wanderers. Jessie Stewart's life was proof of that.

'So you come from America,' she said to me. 'I've been to America myself. I spent eighteen years there.'

I asked her where exactly.

She said, 'In Long Island and Virginia. New York City. Bar Harbor, Maine.'

'The best places.'

'I was in service,' she said. 'The people were wealthy you see.'

Her employers had moved from house to house, according to the season, and she had moved with them. Perhaps she had been a cook. Her scones were wonderful – she had brought out a whole tray of scones and shortbread and sandwiches with the tea.

Why had she left America?

'I got very ill. For a while I couldn't work, and then I started getting doctors' bills. You know how expensive hospitals are in the United States. There's no National Health Service –'

And she had no insurance; and the family she worked for wouldn't pay; and she needed major surgery.

'I could never have afforded it there,' she said. 'It would have taken all my savings. I came back home here and had my operation on the National Health. I'm feeling a wee bit better now.'

So she had left the poverty trap in the Highlands and emigrated to the United States, and become a servant, and fallen into the American poverty trap. And now she was dying on the croft where she had been born. Most of the crofters here were old people whose children had moved away.

I continued to Caithness alone. The farther east I went the greener it was, the more fertile the land. There were high mountains near the sea. The sheep were fat. They winced from the ditches where they crouched to get out of the wind. I went on to Coldbackie, Bettyhill and Swordly. They were small cold places. I went to Brawl and Bighouse. The grass was better here.

Caithness was a milder, more sheltered place, with sweet-smelling grass. But I liked it much less than Sutherland – its mountains streaming with pale scree, its black valleys of peat, its miles of moorland and bog, its narrow roads and surfy coast and its caves. It was like a world apart, an unknown place in this the best-known country in the world. No sooner had I left it than I wanted to go back.

20

The 14.40 to Aberdeen

From Thurso I walked ten miles to Dunnet Head ('the most northerly point of mainland Britain'). On this sunny day its cliffs were a rich bronze-orange and the foam on the violent currents of the Pentland Firth was being whipped into peaks by the wind. The rest of the countryside was as flat and tame as the flagstones it had once produced. Only the place-names were exciting – not just Buldoo and John O'Groats, but Hunspow and Ham, and Thrumster, Scrabster, Shebster and Lybster. And who or what were the Hacklemakers of Buckies?

People had babies in Thurso and round about. That was unusual. It was a noticeable fact that in most places on the coast there were few small children being towed by parents – not even on the sands. I saw big idle youths and middle-aged people and the very old. The very old, especially. They lived in the poorer, sorrier places. But Thurso had become prosperous from the off-shore oil, and in the three or four towns on the British coast where there were jobs there were also young families.

After a day and a night in Thurso I took the branch line down to Helmsdale on the east coast. The summer brightness of the Scottish evenings made the flat brown moorland shimmer, and even the fissured bogs and sandpits did not seem so bad. We went along, stopping at ruined stations. *This is the Age of the Train*, the British Rail posters said, showing a celebrity who was noted for his work on behalf of handicapped people and incurables. He had been hired to promote British Rail. This branch line was certainly on its last legs. It was slow and dirty. But I liked it for being derelict and still stubbornly running across the moors. This was a little like being in Turkey.

The heather was in bloom at Helmsdale, and among the low

twisted trees there were thorn bushes and yellow flowers on the gorse. Large boulders stood on the strand here, where the North Sea lapped the coast, filling the rock pools. The sea was over-looked by small isolated farms and hills coifed with thick ferns. Sheep nosed around old gun emplacements and crumbling pill-boxes.

I had High Tea – kippers, a poached egg and scones with fresh cream – and took a later train south. It was sandy beaches to Brora and beyond. At Brora I saw a sheep-shearer. He was kneeling against a fat sheep and clipping her with hand shears, just beside the railway line. He did not look up. There were smears of sheep grease on his arms. He was clipping the creature gently, and the sheep was not struggling much. It was as if the shearer was giving his big child a haircut.

It was a long zigzag through Easter Ross to Inverness, where I was planning to head for Aberdeen. I walked through this slow branch-line train. In the guard's van there was a crate with a label saying, *Pathological Specimens – Do Not Freeze*, and in the next coach a girl was writing a letter that began, 'Dearest Budgie'. There were campers returning from the Orkneys, and cyclists winding up their coastal tour. A Polish couple (the Zmudskys) were gnawing bread rolls, and their laps were spangled with crust crumbs. A man with unforgiving eyes named Wockerfuss, and his middle-aged-looking child, a boy of ten, sat sharing a book titled *Schottland*.

Mr Zmudsky smiled at a group of six men.

'Pgitty tgees,' Mr Zmudsky said, nodding at the trees out of the window.

'Yews,' one of the men said, and realizing that Mr Zmudsky was a foreigner, he raised his voice, crying, 'Yews!'

At this Mr Wockerfuss stiffened, seeming to understand but refusing to look.

The group of men were railway buffs. They were always a sure sign that a branch line was doomed. The railway buffs were attracted to the clapped-out trains, like flies to the carcass of an old nag. They had stop-watches and time-tables and maps. They sat by the windows, ticking off the stations as we went by. Ardgay (*tick!*), Tain (*tick!*), Invergordon (*tick!*), Alness (*tick!*), Muir of Ord (*tick!*), and then a bewildered little ticker named Neville twitched his big lips crossly and complained, 'Hey, what happened to Dingwall?'

In a bed-and-breakfast place ('Balfour Lodge') in Inverness I pondered the question as to whether Inverness could be regarded as on my coastal route. It was a matter of perspective. The map was not much help. Everything seemed to depend on how one described the Moray Firth. Was that part of the North Sea?

And then I was too bored to do anything but set off immediately for Aberdeen. Balfour Lodge was operated by a quarrelsome couple named Alec and June Catchpenny. It was a cold house. The bathmat was damp. The Catchpennys sulked. Their dog looked diseased and I wanted to tell them it ought to be put down. I hated Alec's bowling trophies. Nor did either Catchpenny speak to me. 'Six pounds,' were the only words spoken to me in my twenty hours at Balfour Lodge. But what they bellowed at each other made me suspect that if I were to go fossicking in their bedroom drawers I would find what the dirty shops called 'marital aids'.

I went, via Elgin and Insch, to Aberdeen on the 14.40. A new railway strike was threatened and most of the passengers were talking angrily about the strikers.

'They won't have jobs to come back to,' said one man. This was Ivor Perry-Pratt who described himself as being in an oil-related industry. He supplied the off-shore rigs with non-slip rubber treads for ladders and walkways. It seemed they wore out very quickly or else perished in the wet and cold conditions. Business was good, but Ivor Perry-Pratt always wondered, *Will it last?* He sympathized somewhat with the railwaymen.

His friend Eric Husker said, 'They ought to sack the whole lot of them.'

Husker was in earth-moving equipment. Aberdeen was the fastest-growing city in Britain.

'That's too drastic,' Mr Perry-Pratt said.

'Rubbish. It's not drastic at all,' Mr Husker said. 'And it will come – you'll see! This will either be a fully-automated railway or else it won't exist at all. Ivor, be reasonable. A few years ago there were twenty-five farm labourers on every farm. Now, how many are there?'

Mr Perry-Pratt pleaded, 'But look at unemployment!'

Mr Husker was implacable. He said, 'We'll have to have a lot more unemployment before this country begins to run properly.'

Of course, he had a job.

We reached the coast. Offshore, a four-legged oil-rig looked like a mechanical sea monster defecating in shallow water. It was like a symbol of this part of Scotland. Aberdeen was the most prosperous city on the British coast. It had the healthiest finances, the brightest future, the cleanest buildings, the briskest traders. But that was not the whole of it. I came to hate Aberdeen more than any other place I saw. Yes, yes, the streets were clean; but it was an awful city.

Perhaps it had been made awful and was not naturally that way. It had certainly been affected by the influx of money and foreigners. I guessed that in the face of such an onslaught the Aberdonians had found protection and solace by retreating into the most unbearable Scottish stereotypes. It was only in Aberdeen that I saw kilts and eightsome reels and the sort of tartan tight-fistedness that made me think of the average Aberdonian as a person who would gladly pick a halfpenny out of a dunghill with his teeth.

Most British cities were plagued by unemployed people. Aberdeen was plagued by workers. It made me think that work created more stress in a city than unemployment. At any rate, this sort of work. The oil industry had the peculiar social disadvantage of being almost entirely manned by young single men with no hobbies. The city was swamped with them. They were lonely. They prowled twilit streets in groups, miserably looking for something to do. They were far away from home. They were like soldiers in a strange place. There was nothing for them to do in Aberdeen but drink. I had the impression that the Aberdonians hated and feared them.

These men had seen worse places. Was there in the whole world an oil-producing country that was easy-going and economical? 'You should see Kuwait,' a welder told me, 'you should see Qatar.' For such a man Aberdeen was civilization. It was better than suffering on an oil-rig a hundred miles offshore. And anyone who had been in the Persian Gulf had presumably learned to do without a red-light district. Apart from drinking and dancing

Scottish reels there was not a single healthy vice available in Aberdeen.

It had all the extortionate high prices of a boom town but none of the compensating vulgarity. It was a cold, stony-faced city. It did not even look prosperous. That was some measure of the city's mean spirit – its wealth remained hidden. It looked over-cautious, unwelcoming and smug, and a bit overweight like a rich uncle in dull sensible clothes, smelling of mildew and ledgers, who keeps his wealth in an iron chest in the basement. The windows and doors of Aberdeen were especially solid and un-yielding; it was a city of barred windows and burglar alarms, of hasps and padlocks and Scottish nightmares.

The boom town soon discovers that it is possible to make money out of nothing. It was true of the Klondike where, because women were scarce, hags came to regard themselves as great beauties and demanded gold dust for their grunting favours; in Saudi Arabia today a gallon of water costs more than a gallon of motor oil. In Aberdeen it was hotel rooms. The Station Hotel, a dreary place on the dockside road across from the railway station, charged £48 a night for a single room, which was more than its equivalent would have cost at The Plaza in New York City. Most of the other hotels charged between £25 and £35 a night, and the rooms did not have toilets. I went from place to place with a sense of mounting incredulity, for the amazing thing was not the high prices or their sleazy condition but rather the fact that there were no spare rooms.

For £25 I found a hotel room that was like a jail cell, narrow and dark, with a dim light fifteen feet high on the ceiling. There was no bathroom. The bed was the size of a camp cot. Perhaps if I had just spent three months on an oil-rig I would not have noticed how dismal it was. But I had been in other parts of Scotland, where they did things differently, and I knew I was being fleeced.

To cheer myself up I decided to go out on the town. I found a joint called 'Happy Valley' – loud music and screams. I thought: Just the ticket.

But the doorman blocked my path and said, 'Sorry, you can't go in.'

Behind him were jumping people and the occasional splash of breaking glass.

'You've not got a jacket and tie,' he said.

I could not believe this. I looked past him, into the pandemonium.

'There's a man in there with no shirt,' I said.

'You'll have to go, mate.'

I suspected that it was my oily hiker's shoes that he really objected to, and I hated him for it.

I said, 'At least I'm wearing a shirt.'

He made a monkey noise and shortened his neck. 'I'm telling you for the last time.'

'Okay, I'm going. I just want to say one thing,' I said. 'You're wearing one of the ugliest neckties I've ever seen in my life.'

Up the street another joint was advertising 'Country and Western Night'. I hurried up the stairs, towards the fiddling.

'Ye canna go in,' the doorman said. 'It's too full.'

'I see people going in,' I said. They were drifting past me.

'And we're closing in a wee munnit.'

I said, 'I don't mind.'

'And you're wearing blue jeans,' he said.

'And you're wearing a wrinkled jacket,' I said. 'And what's that, a gravy stain?'

'Ye canna wear blue jeans here. Regulations.'

'Are you serious? I can't wear blue jeans to an evening of country and western music?'

'Ye canna.'

I said, 'How do you know I'm not Willie Nelson?'

He jabbed me hard with his stubby finger and said, 'You're nae Wullie Nullson, now piss off!'

And so I began to think that Aberdeen was not my kind of place. But was it anyone's kind of place? It was fully-employed and tidy and virtuous, but it was just as bad as any of the poverty-stricken places I had seen – worse, really, because it had no excuses. The food was disgusting, the hotels over-priced and indifferent, the spit-and-sawdust pubs were full of drunken and bad-tempered men – well, who wouldn't be bad-tempered? And it was not merely that it was expensive and dull; much worse

was its selfishness. Again it was the boom town ego. Nothing
else mattered but its municipal affairs. The newspapers ignored
the Israeli invasion of Lebanon and the United Nations' initiative
on the Falklands and the new Space Shuttle. Instead, their headlines concentrated on the local money-making stuff – the new
industries, the North Sea Pipeline about to be laid, the latest
oil-rigs. The world hardly existed, but financial news, used cars
and property took up seven pages of the daily paper.

The *Aberdeen American*, a fortnightly paper, had the self-
conscious gusto of a church newsletter. It was a hotchpotch of
news about barbecues, schools, American primary elections and
features with an Anglo-American connection. It was a reminder
that the American community in Aberdeen was large. The
American School had three premises. I heard American voices
on the buses. And I was certain that it was the Americans who
patronized the new health clubs – weight-loss emporiums and
gymnasiums with wall-to-wall carpets. A lovely granite church
had been gutted and turned into 'The Nautilus Total Fitness
Centre'.

On a quiet street in the western part of the city was the
American Foodstore. I went there out of curiosity, wondering
what sort of food Americans viewed as essential to their well-
being on this savage shore. My findings were: Crisco, Thousand
Island Dressing, Skippy Peanut Butter, Cheerios, Pepperidge
Farm Frozen Blueberry Muffins, Bama Brand Grape Jelly,
Mama's Frozen Pizza, Swanson's Frozen Turkey TV Dinner,
Chef Boyardee Spaghetti Sauce, El Paso Taco Sauce and
Vermont Pancake Syrup. I also noted stacks of Charmin Toilet
Paper, Budweiser Beer and twenty-five-pound bags of Purina
Dog Chow.

None of it was good food, and it was all vastly inferior to the
food obtainable locally, which cost less than half as much. But
my experience of Aberdeen had shown me that foreigners were
treated with suspicion, and it was quite understandable that there
was a sense of solidarity to be had from being brand-loyal. Crisco
and Skippy were part of being an American – and, in the end,
so was Charmin Toilet Paper. I imagined that, to an American
in Aberdeen, imported frozen pizza was more than cultural
necessity – it was also a form of revenge.

'Isn't there *anything* you like about Aberdeen?' Mr Muir asked imploringly, as we waited on the platform at Guild Street Station for the train to Dundee. I had spent ten minutes enumerating my objections, and I had finished by saying that I never wanted to see another boom town again. What about the Cathedral, the University, the Museum – hadn't I thought the world of them?

'No,' I said.

He looked appalled.

I said, 'But I liked the bakeries. The fresh fish. The cheese.'

'The bakeries,' Mr Muir said sadly.

I did not go on. He thought there was something wrong with me. But what I liked in Aberdeen was what I liked generally in Britain: the bread, the fish, the cheese, the flower gardens, the apples, the clouds, the newspapers, the beer, the woollen cloth, the radio programmes, the parks, the Indian restaurants and amateur dramatics, the postal service, the fresh vegetables, the trains, and the modesty and truthfulness of people. And I liked the way Aberdeen's streets were frequently full of seagulls.

21

The 9.51 to Leuchars Junction

It was a mild meadowy coast for seventy miles, from the mouth of the Dee to the mouth of the Tay – Aberdeen to Dundee. I had hoped to walk part of it, keeping to the cliff-tops and avoiding the deep cuts and gullies and the dark promontories. I liked the way the shaggy grass hung into the coves from the cliff edge. Today that grass was streaming and even the sea was flattened by the falling rain. The storm brightened the stone on the snug coastal cottages and gave it the colour of snail shells.

Stonehaven was visibly prosperous, which was odd, because most well-off Scottish towns tried to hide their prosperity. Our train skirted the town's pretty bay, turned inland for perhaps twenty miles, and then returned to the coast at Montrose, which lay on a landspit in front of a large tidal lagoon, Montrose Basin. Slouching cows searched for grass near the apartment houses at Montrose, and farther south at Lunan Bay a hundred hogs in the field were suddenly illuminated by a gleam of sunshine through the draperies of the downpour. The light also reddened a nearby castle ruin and briefly warmed the sands of the bay.

The gale surged again, with mares' tails off Arbroath, and it swept across the front. But I imagined it to be a joyless place even in full sunshine. The coast had turned duney. In Scotland it was either black cliffs or grey links, and sometimes for miles it was bleak attenuated golf courses, end to end in the sand. Scottish golf courses were never pretty things; they were windy and lacking topsoil, they were oddly lumpy, scattered with rabbit holes and bomb craters; they looked like minefields. Carnoustie was that way – battle-scarred – and so was Barry. And then we came to Monifieth, where three tall swans were swimming in the sea.

I chose to stop at Dundee because it had a reputation for dullness ('possesses little of interest for the tourist'). Such places were usually worth seeing. I had found that in Britain less was revealed by the lovely old town than the ugly new one. Old Dundee had been destroyed and new Dundee was an interesting monstrosity. It was certainly an excellent example of a hard-edged horror – the prison-like city of stony-faced order – that I associated with the future. Just the word 'futuristic' brought to my mind the most depressing images of idle crowds and ugly buildings, unfriendly streets, steel fences, barred windows and defoliation; and it was bound up with the concept of organized leisure – the intimidating symmetry of group fun. Public swimming pools were futuristic.

There had always seemed to me something uncomfortable and dangerous about public swimming pools. Their tiles had a particularly frightening way of turning a shout into a scream, and this noise and the water and the cold showers and the nakedness could make a swimming pool seem like Auschwitz. Rowdy gangs loved to swim – the atmosphere of a pool brought out a bullying streak in them.

The 'Dundee Swimming and Leisure Centre' had the look of a Russian interrogation headquarters, a vast drab Lubyanka in rain-streaked concrete. Inside were three crowded pools, and one was Olympic-sized. They contained a stew of thousands of screaming kids. The building smelled of human flesh and disinfectant; it steamed like a changing-room; it was damp in a sickening way. It had a dark cafeteria and a 'Therapy Suite' containing sunlamps and sauna baths ('O A Ps' Sauna – 80 pence'). There were a number of ping-pong tables in one room, but no one was playing. In the lobby there were four electric games being frantically played – boys feeding money into 'Space Invaders' and 'Frogger' and 'Moon Landing', while the single parents and the pensioners and the unemployed came and went. It was in the metropolitan plan, in a world where there was no work and no money but plenty of time; it was part of the process of life in the years to come.

Leuchars Junction was no longer a junction, though the name had stuck. It lay across the Firth of Tay, in Fife. It was as near as I could get by rail to St Andrews ('perhaps the most fashionable watering place in the country'), and I began walking as soon as I arrived at the station.

After a mile or so I came to Guard Bridge. Some men were standing in front of the paper mill there. They said they were waiting for a funeral to go past – a man who had worked his whole life at the paper mill was being buried today. The hearse was overdue.

'And I'll tell you something,' one of the men said. His name was Gordon Hastie and he was fairly agitated, twisting his cloth cap in his hands as he peered up the St Andrews Road. 'Do you see those flags?'

There were three on the flagpoles in front of the factory – a Union Jack, the Scottish national flag and what I took to be the paper mill's own flag – all flying at half-mast.

'What a morning it's been,' Mr Hastie said. 'A couple of hours ago we had to raise those flags for Queenie. Then after she went by we had to lower them again for Donald.'

Donald was the dead man, obviously, but who was Queenie?

'The Queen herself,' Mr Hastie said. 'Aye.'

'You mean the Queen's here?'

'In St Andrews,' Mr Hastie said. 'Hurry up, you might see her.'

Just as I started to run, Donald's hearse went by. I froze. The paper mill men doffed their caps. And then the funeral cars continued down the wet road, and the men went back to work.

It was four miles more to St Andrews. I walked fast and after a few miles I cut across a field, continuing along the estuary of the River Eden, ending up in the middle of a golf course. There were four golf courses here, but the one I found myself in belonged to the Royal and Ancient Golf Club of St Andrews, the capital of the golfing world. The course was just as rough and desolate as every other one I had seen in Scotland – perhaps that was the point of golf?

But there was not a town its size in Britain to compare with St Andrews, and it was one of the most beautiful towns on the coast, the white stone ruins and the brown stone buildings perched on the rocky cliffs of a wide bay. The golf courses ran into the seafront and the seafront was part of the playing fields of the university, which was a third of the town; but it was impossible to tell where one ended and the other began. The whole effect was somewhat ecclesiastical, but with fresh air, like a lively cloister with the roof off.

Today the streets were scrubbed, flags flew, the whole town gleamed with flowers and bunting. And there was a heightened hum, a vibration racing in the air, the equivalent in sound of twinkling light, something electric and almost visible. It was genuine. I felt it as soon as I entered the cobbled streets. It was as if the town had been refreshed with a blessing. In a way it had, for that atmosphere was the spirit left by the progress of the royal visit. The Queen of England had left just a moment ago.

'What a pity you missed her,' Freda Robertson said. She was the buyer in the largest bookshop in St Andrews and she looked dignified and indestructible in her Scottish way, her voice half-inquiry and half-reprimand and full of the precise ironies of a headmistress. She loved books. She recognized me. Did I want a cup of tea?

With her finger tracing upon the sharp panes of her mullioned window, Mrs Robertson described how Her Majesty rode up here in her Rolls-Royce, and got out there, and walked over there near the barriers.

'I hung out of the window with a pair of binoculars and my camera,' Mrs Robertson said. 'I didn't know which one to look through. I'm sure my pictures will have fingers and thumbs on them. But you should have heard the cheers!'

Was this Falklands feeling, I wondered? No, Freda Robertson said, it was for the Queen's being a grandmother. The child had been born when I was in Mallaig and now he had a name: Prince William. One of the largest St Andrews signs had said, *Health to Prince William*.

'What brings you to St Andrews?' Mrs Robertson asked.

I said that I was making my way around the British coast, clockwise.

'Aye, so we're on your itinerary.'

'And a man in Guard Bridge told me that the Queen was here.'

It was then that Mrs Robertson said what a pity it was that I had missed her. 'Her Majesty just left for Anstruther.'

That was only eight miles away and also on the coast.

I said, 'I think I'll go to Anstruther and see her.'

'I hope you do see her,' Mrs Robertson said. 'This is a great occasion. Do you know that this is the first time the Queen and Prince Philip have ever come to St Andrews?'

'Ever?'

'Aye,' Mrs Robertson said. 'Now I want you to do me one favour, if you will.'

'Gladly,' I said.

She went on, 'As you're travelling around the British coast, so you say, you are seeing a great many places. I have never been to half those places and I don't suppose I shall. What I want you to do is write me a non-fiction book about travelling around the British coast. I think it would do very well in my shop, but that's not the important thing. I mean to say, I want to read it.'

I said I would do my best and started towards Anstruther thinking: That was a page, and here's another page, and there's probably a page in Anstruther.

I tried to hitch-hike in order to get to Anstruther in time to see the Queen, but no one picked me up. I fell in with a farm labourer on the road. He was coming from St Andrews. He had gone there for the Royal Visit.

'I saw the Queen,' he said, and he winced, remembering.

'How did she look?'

He winced again. His name was Dougie. He wore gumboots. He said, 'She were deep in thought.'

Dougie had seen something no one else had.

'She were preoccupied. Her face were grey. She weren't happy.'

I said, 'I thought she was happy about her new grandson.'

Dougie disagreed. 'I think she were worried about something. They do worry, you know. Aye, it's a terrible job.'

He began to walk slowly, as if in sympathy for the hard-pressed Queen.

I said, 'Being Queen of England has its compensations.'

'Some compensations and some disadvantages,' Dougie said. 'I say it's half a dream world and half a nightmare. It's a gold-fish bowl. No privacy! She can't pick her nose without someone seeing her.'

Dougie said this in an anguished way, and I thought it was

curious, though I did not say so, that he was pained because the monarch could not pick her nose without being observed.

He then began to talk about television programmes. He said his favourite programme was *The Dukes of Hazzard*, which concerned high jinks in a town in the American south. This Scottish farm labourer in Fife said that he liked it because of the way the character Roscoe talked to his boss. That was very funny. American humour was hard to understand at times, he said, but every farm labourer in Scotland would find Roscoe funny for his attitude.

At last a bus came. I flagged it down. It was empty. I said I wanted to go to Anstruther, to see the Queen.

'Aye. She's having lunch there,' the driver said.

I wondered where.

The driver knew. 'At the Craw's Nest. It's a small hotel on the Pittenweem Road.'

He dropped me further down the road and I followed the bunting into Anstruther, sensing that same vibrant glow that I had felt at St Andrews – the royal buzz. It was a holiday atmosphere. The schools were out. The shops were closed. The pubs were open. Some men were wearing kilts. People were talking in groups, seeming to remind each other of what had just happened – the Queen had already gone by, to the Craw's Nest.

I cut across the harbour sands and went up the road to what seemed a very ordinary hotel, but freshly painted and draped in lines of plastic Union Jacks. There were more men in kilts here. They had such wonderfully upright posture, the men in kilts: they never slouched and hardly ever sat down.

'She just left,' one said. His name was Hector Hay McKay.

But there was something of her still here, like perfume which is strongest when a woman leaves suddenly. In the Queen's case it was like something overhead – still up there, an echo.

Mr McKay turned to his friends and said, 'They had two detectives in the kitchen –'

'Do you want to see the flowers?' Mrs Hamilton said.

Everyone was whispering excitedly.

It seemed to me that if the Queen and Prince Philip had eaten here the food might be good. I had seldom had a good meal in my travelling, not that it mattered much: food was one of the dullest subjects. I decided to stay the night at the Craw's Nest. And this hotel which had just received the blessing of a royal visit was a great deal cheaper than any hotel in Aberdeen.

'She never had a starter,' the waitress Eira said. 'She had the fish course, haddock mornay. Then roast beef, broccoli and carrots. And fresh strawberries and cream for dessert. Our own chef did it. It was a simple meal – it was good. The menu was printed and had bits of gold foil around it.'

Much was made of the good plain food. It was English food – a fish course, a roast, two boiled veg. and fruit for the sweet course. The middle-class families in Anstruther – and everywhere else – had that every Sunday for lunch. *She's just like us*, people said of the Queen; *of course, she works a jolly sight harder!*

What was difficult for an alien to see was that this was essentially a middle-class monarchy. Decent philistines, the royal couple liked animals and country-house sports and variety shows. They never mentioned books at all, but they were famous for preferring certain television programmes. Newspapers had published photographs of the Royal Television Set: it had a big screen and a sort of shawl on the top, but it was just like one you could hire for two quid a week up the high street. Over the years the Queen had become shrewder-seeming, an even-tempered mother-in-law and a kindly gran. Prince Philip was loved for being irascible. He was noted for his grouchy remarks. He used the word 'bloody' in public and after that it was hard for anyone to find fault with him. The Queen was his opposite, growing smaller and squashier as he seemed to lengthen and grow spiky – the illusion had sprung out of his having become vocal. The Queen and the Prince were well-matched, but it was less the sovereign and her consort than the double-act that all successful middle-class marriages are.

In the lobby they were selling souvenirs of the Royal Visit. How had they had time to prepare these paperweights and medallions and letter openers and postcards saying *Craw's Nest Hotel – Souvenir of the Royal Visit*?

'We knew about it in January, but we had to keep it a secret until May,' Eira said. 'We kept praying that nothing would go wrong. We thought the Falklands might finish it.'

So they had been putting the place in order and running up

souvenirs for almost seven months. The royal lunch had lasted an hour.

That night they held a celebration party in the hotel car park. It was a way of giving thanks. The hotel invited the whole town, or rather two – Easter Anstruther and Wester Anstruther. They had a rock band and eight pipers and some drummers. The racket was tremendous and continued until two o'clock in the morning, hundreds of people drinking and dancing. They sold sausages, and fish and chips, and there were bales of hay for people to sit on. The band was bad but no one seemed to mind. There were old people, families, drunks and dogs. Small boys smoked cigarettes in a delighted way and sneaked beer from the hotel. Girls danced with each other because the village boys, too embarrassed to be seen dancing, congregated in small groups and pretended to be tough. There was a good feeling in the air, hilarity and joy, something festive, but also grateful and exhausted. It wasn't faked; it was like the atmosphere of an African village enjoying itself.

At eleven I took a walk down to the beach. I passed a man in rubber waders standing alone and looking puzzled on the road. A girl and her grandmother were eating ice-cream cones in the half dark. I passed a cottage; inside, a family of five was singing out loud. I saw more children smoking behind a wall. In another house a man and woman seemed to be proposing a toast. There was moonlight on the water, and this moon-glow had settled on the waves and made them stand out like the ribs of a washboard. I walked towards this light and on the stony beach, just below the sea-wall where I was standing, a boy was clumsily fucking a girl, his buttocks plum-blue under the bright moon and her upraised legs almost luminous and seeming to steady him. It was chilly, he was having a little trouble, but he was so eager he did not see me. They made me feel invisible, but I left them there. I thought of the band and the dancing and beer and the haybales and the moonlight and the smell of seaweed and the young couple fucking where the Queen had just been – it was like a mural, an allegorical painting, but a funny one, a Gully Jimson or a Stanley Spencer.

The cleaning ladies were buzzing early the next morning.

'I couldn't believe it,' Mrs Ross said. 'It didn't seem real. It was like a dream.'

I said, 'What will Willie Hamilton think?'

Willie Hamilton was their member of parliament and noted for being in favour of abolishing the monarchy.

'Willie Hamilton can get stuffed.'

After breakfast, I set off for Leven. It was a grey morning, and rather chilly. After I had walked a few miles it began to rain. I kept walking and heard a throstle, as they were called here. Then the rain was too much for me. I hurried to a village and waited for the bus to Leven. The villages on the coast of Fife had a quiet beauty, and the farmhouses and barns were built like fortresses in flat stone.

On the way to Leven we stopped at Largo. 'Alexander Selkirk, the original of Robinson Crusoe, was born here in 1676.' There was a statue of Selkirk in front of his birthplace, a cottage in Lower Largo.

'Its proper name is the Seatoun of Largo,' a man next to me said. He had just boarded the bus, and we began talking about Largo and Selkirk. The man said, 'Alexander Selkirk was a rogue! He was no good at all!'

I said that I had read somewhere that Selkirk had once kicked his mother and father downstairs.

'Aye, a rogue,' the man said. 'And I'm a direct descendant of him, on my mother's side of the family.'

The man's name was David Gillis. He was ninety years old It seemed my fate to be quite often encountering very old men But it was these buses and trains — the old men didn't drive, didn't own cars, and I ran into them travelling. I was glad of it. David Gillis was bright-eyed and his hearing was fine. He could have been seventy or so. He was going to Leven to do a little shopping.

I was always interested to know what work these people had done. What had Gillis done seventy-five years ago at the age of fifteen?

'I was apprenticed to a plumber in Largo and earned half a crown a week. But it wasn't just plumbing I had to learn — all plumbers were tin-smiths and bell-hangers. I got my first job in 1906. I was offered a pound a week by a man in Largo, but I turned it down. I went to Glasgow and got two pounds. You see, the country employers used to take advantage of us.'

He stayed in Glasgow for some years, and eventually went to London, where his skills were in demand.

'Nowadays, plumbing is easy. You put in the pipes and the pump does all the work. But in those days we didn't have pumps. That made it very tricky work, because the flow had to be just right. And bell-hanging was a delicate thing. There was a bell in every room in the big houses. They worked on wires – no electrics at all. *Bing* went the bell and it would register on a panel downstairs, where the servants were. Bell-hanging was quite an art. No one does it now.'

In 1941, Mr Gillis's doctor in London said, 'If you want your wife to live you'll get her out of here.' Her nerves were bad, and the German bombs were tearing into the city. People asked him why he had come back to Largo, but he always said that if they had spent two nights together in London with those bombs they wouldn't ask.

In the mid-sixties the railway to Largo closed. It was the worst thing that had ever happened in this part of Fife. The end of the railway was the end of the village.

'It was a terrible thing,' Mr Gillis said. 'Now we're twelve miles from a railway station, and the bus is awful. Some days it doesn't come at all. And it's getting worse. If I miss the bus I have to wait hours in Leven. And there's nothing to do there – Leven is more dead than alive.'

There had been a railway through Largo and all the way to Crail and St Andrews, Mr Gillis said. The buses had not replaced it, and who had the money to run a car?

Mr Gillis, at ninety, was surprised at how slow and difficult it was for anyone to get from place to place these days. Years ago it had been very easy.

He confirmed my feeling that great parts of Britain were turning into what they were before the railway age. Villages were becoming crabbed and shrunken, and businesses were closing, and the people who stayed in rural areas became more and more tied to their houses. The urban areas were growing in population and becoming poorer, like Leven, the last stop. Areas of high unemployment like this had a distinctively sooty look and woeful air – not much traffic but plenty of people on the sidewalks. In these poor towns the people walked rather slowly.

In a report on Kirkcaldy, eight miles down the coast, half the sample of unemployed people described 'wandering along the High Street' as a regular activity. They did not leave Kirkcaldy ('birthplace of Adam Smith, author of *The Wealth of Nations*') because bus fares were too high. They could not afford to look for jobs elsewhere. I had bought a copy of this report. It was called *Biding Time* and subtitled 'Reflections of unemployed young people in Kirkcaldy, 1982'. Reflections was the wrong word. They were not particularly alarmed by the lack of work available. Unemployment was so common there was no stigma attached to it; it was accepted as a permanent condition. The report noted that few of the young people expressed a 'desperate willingness to do "anything"'. There was always the dole and, for pleasure, the High Street to wander along. And while several were angry at their inability to find jobs, others had their own solutions: 'One person was thinking about emigrating; one expected a prison sentence soon . . .'

I had passed East and West Wemyss ('so called because of the numerous large "weems" or caves . . . along this coast') and some defunct coalfields. I would have stayed in Kirkcaldy if it had seemed a desperate place, but it was more dull than desperate. I made a tour of the town and then continued past the small windy resort at Burntisland and along canyons of junk and discarded cars near the cliffs at Inverkeithing. But this junkyard was also part of the embankment of the Firth of Forth, and if you turned your back on this ramshackle shore, which was like a mortal wound in Scotland's side, there was a grand view of ships and water and the Forth Bridge.

Edinburgh was the next stop, but it was not on my coastal itinerary. It was, in atmosphere, an inland city, and now that the port of Leith was moribund it hardly counted as important to shipping. But it was a handsome place still, a city of black crags and old solemn tenements of slate rising to a castle that looked like a dark drum on a cliff. Wind gusted up its steep alleys. What was now grass and railway tracks in a ravine beside Princes Street had once been a loch. It was the most beautiful city in Britain and one of the most beautiful in Europe. It looked as if it was the setting of great intrigues and passionate vice, but

I knew it to be a quiet indoor city inhabited by private souls who lived in narrow seclusion.

In Edinburgh I was told that a railway strike was looming and that in three or four days there would not be a single train running in Britain. This event was not viewed with much passion by the general public. The sort of punishing strike that created misery in other countries was met in Britain with either excitement — a kind of community thrill at the drama of it – or else indifference. The British were fatalistic; it was the origin of their cynicism, but it also made them good sharers of misfortune. 'Oh, well, mustn't grumble!'

I hurried to North Berwick, which lay on a corner of land between the Firth of Forth and the North Sea; and from here I walked to Dunbar, spending a whole day making detours. I had seen Dunbar from the train as it sped by, and I had liked the look of it, so I took this chance to stop there. The harbour was on a bleak and rocky bay, faced by rotting ramparts and collapsing red stone walls. The old buildings in Dunbar were also made of this red stone and the main street was fifty yards wide. But it was a lifeless place and a little sad on this cold day in July. I debated whether to stay the night or head for the border. On these long summer evenings there was always plenty of time to decide.

I was reluctant to leave Scotland; I had liked nearly everyone I had met. But, then, in Dunbar I met a loud-mouth named Billy Crombie. He was travelling south and had stopped to drink three pints of beer. He was a Glaswegian, with a moustache as large as a ferret, and a cowering wife. His face was purple, he drove a Jaguar.

'I'm going to a foreign country!' he declared. 'Aye, England – it's a foreign land! Scotland's ruled by the bloody English. They dropped Exchange Controls so that they could spend our money abroad – they don't spend it in Scotland, though they stole it from us in the first place by stealing our oil resairves. And you bloody Yanks have atomic bombs a few miles from Glasgow, and nuclear subs in Holy Loch! Why don't you put them in London, that's what I want to know. Don't mention politicians. They're beyond a joke. David Steel is a Unionist! Tam Dalyell is a carpetbagger! Jenkins is a Tory – it was an Orange seat and they ran a Catholic to oppose him – how could he lose? I'm a freedom fighter – don't let these tweeds fool you. You can ask my wife if you don't believe I'm a freedom fighter. Now, listen, go home and tell them we don't want your bombs!'

I headed south on the train, with his voice still ringing in my ears. Scotland ended at the tiny coastal village of Lamberton, the Northumbrian border, below Lammermuir and the hills of black-faced sheep.

22

The Last Train to Whitby

'It wunt rain, lad,' Mr Yeaver the joiner said to me at Berwick-upon-Tweed. 'The clouds is too high. The swallows is flying too high.'

I had decided to walk to Lindisfarne – Holy Island – at low tide. The Venerable Bede had called it a 'semi-isle' twelve hundred years ago. It was still a semi-isle – 'accessible at low water, but it is necessary to be acquainted with the quicksands which are dangerous.'

Mr Yeaver said, 'I used to work there. I had a joinery. But I lived in Spittal.'

That was right across the Tweed. Spittal was an old word for hospital. There were seven Spittals in Britain.

'How did you get out to the island?'

'Pony and trap.' It sounded as medieval as the word spittal, but Yeaver was my own age.

He said I could take a bus to a certain public house, and then it was a seven-mile walk. When I started away he spoke up again.

'They're strange people out there,' Mr Yeaver said. 'They're like people with their own different language. And they hate outsiders.'

I thanked him for this information and caught the bus to the public house, and then walked down a country lane to the shore. I faced an expanse of bubbling mudflats, some of it marked with poles showing the Pilgrims' Way; to the left of this was a narrow causeway. There was a bridge some distance out with a sign on it saying *This Bridge is Totally Submerged at High Tide*. It was a sunny day, with a light breeze off the North Sea. (Seventy years ago it was called the German Ocean.) I started across the Pilgrims' Way, looking back every so often to see my footprints

fill with water. The imprint sank, as if in quicksand, so I made
for the causeway. Ahead, Lindisfarne was an island of low
straggling dunes, with white houses and red stone ruins at its
extreme end. It was banked by sand and it lay in a tide of mud;
for half the day it was a village in the sea.

This offshore stroll to the island was one of the most pleasant
walks I made on the coast – a memorable mile. The ruins that
had been painted by Turner and William Daniell still stood. The
sand gleamed. The Priory ruins in shadow were silver-black like
charcoal, with the same frail sculpted look of burned wood, but
where the daylight struck them they were as red and porous as
cake. The surface colour of the island was the yellow grey of
human skin, and further off there was a castle wrapped around
a solitary high rock. It was exciting to walk across the silty sea
bed with nothing but this island in view under a towering sky.

Most offshore islands have an atmosphere of shipboard
isolation, with the sea all around. But on Holy Island I felt a
sense of being on board a ship that was moored on a long hawser,
occasionally drifting to sea and occasionally bumping the shore.
The village was small but had a number of cosy hotels. I had
no trouble finding a bed or a good meal. I sketched pictures of
the strange Lindisfarne boat sheds – hulls of boats cut crosswise
and turned over. They were storehouses, but they looked like
beached whales or sea monsters. There was a path just above
the high water mark which went entirely around the island, passing the Links, full of darting rabbits and carrying on to a sandy
promontory called the Snook. It was a restful island and even
seemed to have an air of sanctity – something about its flatness
and the way the wind murmured softly across the dunes.

The islanders were watchful, but not unfriendly. Yet Yeaver
had been right on one score. Their accent was incomprehensible
to me, a mixture of Scottish and Geordie, with a kind of Gaelic
gargle. They did some fishing but their income was derived from
the people who visited the island. They sold postcards and ice-
cream cones and offered tours of the ruins. Most people raced
to the island in cars at low tide, and raced back to the mainland
again before the causeway was flooded. Few people stayed the
night, though it was a peaceful place to sleep.

*

There was a good view of Holy Island from the train, on the east coast line. It appeared about ten miles south of Berwick and because it was such a long island it stayed in view for a number of minutes. More castles and ruins emerged on the low shore of ancient meadows. This part of Northumberland was flat and today it had a great dome of clouds – an amphitheatre with a ceiling of detached cirrus filaments tufting high over a whitish veil of undulant fluff and, below that, decomposing quilts of loose cumulus. This country was cloudland.

I was on the train because the strike was nigh. Soon, people said, there would be no trains. They seemed to like this doomsday drama. They whispered about it at Widdrington and Morpeth ('scanty ruins ... and a curious clock-tower'). I had missed Amble-by-the-Sea – which sounded like a book title – and the Scars; but I did not have time to walk today. In any case, the speed of the train intensified the stains on the landscape and showed how quickly grassy pastures vanished into strange industrial cubism – rising chimneys and towers and the steel stick-figures of pylons which made it almost zoo-like, for the wires were criss-crossed against the sky, creating the impression of an enormous cage. This geometric clutter also suggested that we were rushing towards a populous place, and of course we were It was the beginning of the great sad sprawl of the north-east of England, and even the riverine name of this poor county was like a laborious and demoralized sigh, Tyne and Wear. Newcastle was inland. I made for the coast.

This part of England had the highest rate of unemployment, and today in the sudden shower of rain at Jarrow ('whose name recalls unemployment and the hunger marches of the twenties') it had the poisoned and dispirited look of a place that had just lost a war. It was an area of complex ugliness – not just the dumps full of gulls and crows, and the weak defiance in the faces of the teenagers I saw at Boldon Colliery; it was also the doomed attempts at survival: the farmer ploughing a small strip of field behind an abandoned factory, and the garden allotments of shacks and overgrown enclosures, cabbages and beans, geese and pigs, vegetables and animals alike dusted with fine smut and looking cancerous. It was like a sight of China – black factories and narrow, necessary gardens, and a kind of visible

hopelessness. It was one of the dreariest landscapes I had ever
seen.

It was hideous and fascinating. We crossed the River Wear
and instead of continuing I got off at Sunderland in order to
verify its desolation. People said business was terrible, the place
was dying on its feet. And Sunderland, because it was so
depressed, had a dangerous look: the unrepaired buildings and
the shabby streets, and the gangs of boys with spiky hair, and
long ragged coats, or else leather jackets painted over with fists
and swastikas.

A man named Begbie who was a clerk at Binns Department
Store said, 'Some of the kids who left school six or seven years
ago have never had a job. There are jobs in the paper, but these
kids stay on the dole. They left school at sixteen and they
developed what I call a dole-queue mentality. They're unemployable! They don't want to work, and they've discovered they
don't really have to. They've learned how to do without it. That's
the main difference between the present and other times in
British industrial history. We've produced a whole generation of
kids who are unemployable!'

Begbie had a grudge, but whether there was any truth in what
he said or not, there really was no work here. I looked in the
local paper at the situations vacant ads. Very few jobs were listed
and most of them asked for people with experience.

But Sunderland was not a lively nightmare of poverty. It was
dark brown and depressed and enfeebled. It was threadbare, but
it was surviving in a marginal way. The real horror of it took
a while to sink in. It had stopped believing there would be any
end to this emptiness. Its hellish aspect was the hardest to see
and describe because it had a sick imprisoned atmosphere: there
was simply nothing to do there.

The weather made it worse. It was a summer afternoon but
so stormy and dark the street lamps were on, and so were the
lights in the train. I moved south again on the coastal line towards
Hartlepool. Even the sea was grim here – not rough but motionless and oily, a sort of offshore soup made of sewage and poison.
We passed the coal mining town of Seaham, with its pits next
to the sea and the shafts going under the sea floor. The house
roofs were like flights of steps on the sloping coast and the slag-

heaps had rivulets scored into them from the drizzling rain. It was a completely man-made landscape, a deliberate monstrosity of defilement. It was as different and strange as a coastal town could possibly be, with the sooty symmetry of a colliery grafted on to the shore. I had never seen anything like it in my life. Oddest of all were the people – small children laughing in a barren play-ground, and families picnicking on the foul-looking shore, and a glimpse between the crusted roofs of men playing cricket in spotless white flannels.

I wondered in Hartlepool how people could stand to live in such a place. Mine was not the breezy condescension of a traveller but a sense of puzzlement at the state of decay. For most people there was no choice, but I also guessed that what made it bearable was the English habit of living indoors most of the time. They loved squashy sofas and warm rooms and the prospect of tea. What difference did it make that the town's graveyard was squeezed between the cement works and the metal box factory, and that the steelworks that had disfigured half the town was now shut, and the rest of the place was just cranes and pipelines and Chinese allotments? Everyone agreed that it looked like a dog's dinner.

'You've got soup kitchens in the States,' a man named Witton said to me. Witton was a self-employed decorator. He hadn't worked since Easter. 'It's much worse in the States. I saw a programme about it on telly.'

But Richard Jellyman, a traveller for Morgan Crucibles, told me that when he came up north he always made a list of people to see. Inevitably, he said, half of them would have gone into liquidation between his trips. Recently he had made a list of nine places to go in Leeds – prospective clients or else people he had done business with in the past. He had found, on arriving in Leeds that week, that eight of them had gone bankrupt.

I came to Stockton. The railway station was very grand; this was understandable: the first public railway in the world steamed down this line in 1825. But Stockton seemed just as terrible as every other town I had seen in this area. At Middlesbrough I was told that if I was smart I would look at the auctions in the newspaper. Each time a company went bankrupt it auctioned everything – machinery, chairs, lights, desks, everything. I could

get them at a good price and sell them in London. Out of
curiosity I checked the newspaper and found it to be full of
bankruptcy auctions.

'It's the blacks, see,' a respectable-looking man named Strawby
told me. 'We whites are the original inhabitants of this coontry,
but they make all the laws in favour of the blacks. That's why
it's all gone bad.'

Mr Strawby saw me making notes. He was not alarmed. He
gave me a little lecture on racial characteristics and offered me
tea.

'You can get a soobstantial tea here,' Mr Strawby said at a
Middlesbrough café, and handed me the tattered menu.

Chip butty: a bread sandwich filled with fried potatoes. *Pease
pudding*: green oatmeal. *Black pudding*: dark knotted entrails fat
with pig's blood. *Faggots*: hard shrivelled sausages that looked
like mummified slugs.

I said I wasn't hungry.

This made Mr Strawby smile. 'Soom people don't know what's
good for them.'

'And some people do,' I said.

'Aye. That's true, right enough,' Mr Strawby said, and ordered
a chip butty.

Strike Night, the Middlesbrough newspaper said, and in
another story, *Mad Killer Loose in Yorkshire*.

The mad killer overshadowed the railway strike. He was
crazy and had a gun. He had already murdered three people,
two of them policemen. There was particular anger directed
against armed criminals in Britain, and killers of policemen were
especially hated, because few policemen were armed. People said,
'Pretty soon it will be as bad as America, with all our policemen
carrying guns.' In Yorkshire the rural policemen carried truncheons and rode bicycles and wore helmets that looked like old
fire buckets. When they suspected foul play they took out a little
whistle and blew hard on it.

Barry Prudom, the killer, was a psychopath. He hated the
police. It was said that he planned to wipe out the Yorkshire
police force. He had been a commando. He knew how to live
off the land. 'Do not approach strangers,' the police said in public

warnings. They published Prudom's picture – he was unshaven, jug-eared, rather wolf-like and dark. *Have You Seen This Man?* the posters said. Four hundred people reported that they had. Every day there were fresh sightings. No one said his name. They said, 'Haven't they caught that bloke yet?' People were giddy and talkative, excited by the danger. It was a classic example of the mad killer on the loose – a form of public theatre.

Because of it, no one around here talked about the strike. This was very odd, because the entire railway network in Britain was shutting down tonight. I wanted to say, *But what about my trip?*

Mr Swales, the conductor on the 17.53 Middlesbrough to Whitby train, said, 'They want to close this branch line. They've been trying to for years.'

I thought: You might have guessed! It was a beautiful line. But the opponents of these branch lines said that so few people used them it would be cheaper to give the passengers the taxi fare to their destination.

'This is the last train to Whitby,' Mr Swales said. 'This is probably the last train to anywhere.'

That was very British. The strike was not actually supposed to start until tomorrow, but the British impatience to wind a thing up – they characteristically left work early and always shooed the customers out of a store well before closing time – meant the strike would start this evening.

A fat lady named June Bagshawe said to Mr Swales, 'I don't know what I'm going to do without you!' She also shouted it into the guard's van and then out of the window, at every railway employee she saw. 'I don't know what I'm going to do without you!' She used the train every day to get to her job at a knitting mill in Acklam.

But when she saw me, Mrs Bagshawe hurried away heavily, pulling her legs along. And then I realized that, unshaven and square-faced and rather dark, I somewhat resembled Barry Prudom. I even had a knapsack like the former commando, and I wore commando-type oily shoes. She had taken me for the mad killer.

I sat alone. Ten minutes out of the grey trough of Middlesbrough and this lovely train was passing through the green valleys of the Cleveland Hills in North Yorkshire. It was a bright evening, sunshine as soon as we were out of the city: it was like stepping out of a tent. All around the train were woods and fields and scarred hills, with trees blowing, and earth the colour of fudge. And at the rural station of Battersby (*what's a train doing here?* you think – but it was once a railway junction!) the wind was making the dog-roses wag.

There is an English dream of a warm summer evening on a branch-line train. Just that sentence can make an English person over forty fall silent with the memory of what has now become a golden fantasy of an idealized England: the comfortable dusty coaches rolling through the low woods, the sun gilding the green leaves and striking through the carriage windows; the breeze tickling the hot flowers in the fields, birdsong and the thump of the powerful locomotive; the pleasant creak of the wood-panelling on the coach; the mingled smells of fresh grass and coal smoke; and the expectation of being met by someone very dear on the platform of a country station.

It was like this tonight at Kildale and Commondale. The train halted in the depths of the countryside, the platform surrounded by daisies and buttercups, and the birds singing, and the leaves fluttering in the sunlight. A few people got out; no one got on. When the train pulled out of Castleton a small girl on the platform in a white dress put her fingers in her ears and stared with round eyes at the loud thing leaving.

There was great pride in the stations. At Glaisdale well-tended rose bushes rambled around the platform, and there were more at Egton and again at Sleights, and the train that had seemed miserable at Middlesbrough Station had been transformed, changing as it progressed up the line, growing emptier, brighter, more peaceful and more powerful, until, where the River Esk widened just above Whitby, it seemed – the locomotive moving majestically through the dale – like the highest stage of civilization.

In Whitby, on its pair of steep cliffs, there was a sign saying *Vacancies* in every guest house and every hotel. And yet the Horswills, Rose and Sid, were reluctant to give me a room in their hotel.

'My daughter said, "If a single man comes for a room, don't

let him in, Mum,"' Mrs Horswill said nervously, still holding the door against me.

Mr Horswill said, 'There's this killer,' and stared at my commando rucksack.

'You won't have any trouble finding a room in Whitby,' Mrs Horswill said. 'Ordinarily, we'd be glad to put you up. It's just that –'

'I'm an American,' I said.

'Come in,' Mr Horswill said, and forced the door out of his wife's hand. 'We had Americans here in the war. They used to give us gum, lumps of steak, chops – they handed them out of the windows of their barracks. We went by and took them. Cigarettes – Lucky Strikes and that.'

I asked him what the Americans had been doing in Whitby.

'Towing targets over the sea,' Mrs Horswill said, 'and shooting at them from the cliffs.'

Soon we were having cups of tea and reminiscing about the war and watching the news. The hunt for the mad killer was still on. *Police wish to interview Barry Prudom. They think he may be able to assist them with their inquiries.*

'Wish to interview!' I said.

'Wish to kick in the goolies,' Mr Horswill said, and winked.

Mrs Horswill said, 'I hope he's not cummin garound to see us.'

That was how she talked, slowly and methodically fracturing her words. 'If you nee dennything, just say so,' she said, and, 'toffees – do you wan tenny?' She said she cooked 'everthin gon that menu' and that Sid helped with 'the washin gup'. She said I could settle my bill on the 'morny gov departure' and that I could take my room key with me if I was 'goin gout'.

I was the only guest in their twenty-room hotel. 'A lot of people left yesterday,' Mr Horswill said. 'If it's not the strike it's the killer. They were getting nervy.' But I peeked into the register. Only one couple had been there in the past five days, the Hallwarks from Darlington. So Sid was just trying to put up a good front. *Things will pick up next month*, these hotel people always said. But it did not seem likely, and it could be creepy having a meal alone in a dining room with nineteen empty tables. It was like Lahore at Ramadan.

The Horswills had given me the smallest room in the place. I had asked for a single. This was a literal-minded country and not given to the expansive gesture. I was three flights up, in the back, one of the few five-pounders, and every other room was empty.

The weather turned bad on my second day. Whitby people claimed that the weather was always much worse north of here – in Newcastle and Berwick. Mrs Horswill told me how, a month ago, a woman had been walking along the breakwater extension of the harbour, and a gale sprang up and swept the woman into the sea.

'They spen tevver so much time looking for her, and when they found her she were naked. The sea were so rough it strip toff all her clothes.'

Mrs Horswill was a little morbid on this subject. She kept track of the Whitby lifeboat, its comings and goings, its rescues and disasters, how many saved, how many drowned, and whether they were British. She sat at the window of her hotel on the cliff, always watching and usually knitting.

'Lifeboat's goin gout,' she said.

It returned empty, she reported.

'Lifeboat's goin gout again,' she said an hour later, and in the same breath, '*A Tribute to Frank Sinatra*,' and smiled at the television screen.

They loved him in England, the older folk. In places like Ugglebarnby they knew all the words to 'Chicago'. American crooners were very popular: Bing Crosby, Perry Como, and singers I had never heard of, and of the most obscure they would say, 'of course, his grandmother was English'. And dancers – Fred Astaire, Ginger Rogers; and figure skaters – they knew the names of the American ones ('Bert and Betty Woofter – ever so graceful – they won a gold at Husqvarna'). And corny American musicals, and *Dallas*, and Dixieland jazz, and in the depths of the English countryside country-and-western music was popular, the farm labourers had sideburns and sometimes one saw – as I did in Whitby – a man of forty with a tattoo on his arm reading *Elvis the King - R.I.P.*

The day before I left Whitby I was sitting on a bench staring in the direction of the beautiful ruined abbey, and a woman of about fifty, with a bow-legged dog, sat down and we started talking. Her name was Mrs Lettsom and she had a boarding house in Whitby, but her real ambition was to move to Sandsend, a mile up the coast.

'The houses there are smashing,' Mrs Lettsom said. 'They say the people are posh,' she added sadly, 'but I don't mind.'

A three-bedroom house in Whitby cost about £22,000, and in Sandsend £34,000.

'But it's a dream,' Mrs Lettsom said. 'I'll never have that kind of money.' She was looking in the direction of Sandsend. Then she turned to me and said, 'So what do you think about this bloke, going around killing people?'

I decided to walk to Scarborough, about twenty miles down the coast on a footpath called the Cleveland Way. I slipped out of Horswill Heights, crossed the harbour and climbed the stairs up East Cliff where in *Dracula* Lucy Westenra ('I was waked by a flapping at the window') went sleep-walking and got the horrors. Now instead of a vampire there was a tent and caravan site there at Saltwick Nab. It was not messy but it was very ugly and it occurred to me that such places were a reduplication in canvas and tin of the neighbourhoods the people had left, little canvas Smethwicks and tin Pudseys jammed together, with a pub, a shop and a video shed in the centre.

The coast was littered with black wrecks and stoved-in hulks, and this path had cracks in it – parts of it had already fallen into the sea, a hundred feet down.

There was a young woman ahead of me, walking alone, but moving briskly. When I came abreast of her she asked me the time, and I took this to mean that she would not mind talking to me. Her name was Hazel, she was thirty and she was walking to Robin Hood's Bay just for the hell of it. She had red cheeks and freckles, she was a jogger, her husband was in a fishing competition in Whitby. She was not interested in fishing (I never saw a woman in Britain holding either a fishing rod or a cricket bat). She had been married for two months.

'I live a strange life,' she said.

I was delighted to hear this, but when she explained, it did not seem so strange. Both she and her husband worked at night, eight-thirty in the evening until six-thirty in the morning, four ten-hour days and then a long weekend, Friday to Sunday. Henry worked in Maintenance and she was a cook in the staff cafeteria – head cook, actually – and she had been doing the job for six years.

The workers who ate in the cafeteria had a very tough union. Once they had threatened a strike over the food.

'I decided that we were wasting too much food,' Hazel said. 'So I changed the menu – two main dishes and two sweets. The men moaned – "We'll go out on strike" – all that lark. The shop steward came to me and insisted that the night workers got the same four main dishes and four sweets – two hot sweets and two cold – that the day workers got. So that's what we have now, four main dishes, because the union says so. And we're back to wasting food. If one of the choices runs out they abuse me. They get a full breakfast, too. They're well looked after. It's an American company.'

Did she like working for an American company?

'In some ways they're just like the English,' she said. 'The management give themselves big fancy cars as perks. They don't need the cars for their work. They travel to work in them, same as we do. It makes me mad.'

She cooked for seventy men. Cooking for two people was easy. She didn't understand people who complained about it. But she wished she got outside more. She wanted to do more running, perhaps run a fast marathon – she could do four hours and ten minutes, but that wasn't good enough. Henry always wanted to play Scrabble, but they had terrible rows when they played.

'That is what I like,' she said, as we rounded the bluff called North Cheek. 'This is fun.'

However, the cliffs were falling into the sea and in places there were big bites out of the path, and a detour through a wheat-field or under a fence. On certain stretches, I thought: This path won't be here next year.

Hazel was silent for a while, and then she said, 'I wonder what's going to happen.'

What was she talking about?

She said, 'I read somewhere that they're closing down whole towns in Canada.'

At Robin Hood's Bay ('a quaint irregular fishing village on

a steep slope') I bought Hazel a drink and then set off alone along the bushy cliffs and lumpy green headlands. At Ravenscar there were shrieking schoolchildren. One said, 'They just shot that bloke!' I knew exactly who the dead man was. Sometimes it was not like a country at all, but rather a small parish.

23

Disused Railway Line

Hiking south on the teetering coastal path towards Scarborough I took a wrong turn and stumbled on to a gravelly lane. It led in a wide straight way through the woods. It was so impressively useless a thoroughfare I looked for it on my map. This sort of landscape feature was sometimes labelled *Roman road (course of)*, and indicated by a broken line. But just as often it was identified *Disused Railway Line*, and seemed just as ancient and just as derelict as a Roman road.

This thing had been part of the North Eastern Railway, between Whitby and Scarborough. 'The line skirts the coast, affording views of the sea to the right,' the old guidebooks had said. But now there were only two alternatives: the footpath that was falling into the sea, and the A171, a dangerous speedway of dinky cars and whining motorbikes. And the railway had been turned into a bridle path – a degenerate step, since the railway had itself replaced the mounted traveller, the coach and four, and the horse bus.

The railway had not been profitable, only useful. And now, after a century's interruption of technology, horses had repossessed the route. I had seen this all over Britain – defunct viaducts, abandoned cuttings, former railway stations, ruined railway bridges – and I thought of all the lost hopes and all the wasted effort. Then, small dismantled England seemed simple and underdeveloped – and too mean to save herself – deceived by her own frugality.

I continued down the Disused Railway Line, marvelling at the stupidity of it. They started by closing stations; then they cut the number of trains; then, with few trains and a reduced service, they could prove the line was losing money and not worth keeping; and then the line was closed for good and the tracks sold as scrap iron. And then it belonged to ramblers and hackers; it was where people took their dogs to shit.

It was like a ghastly parody of hard times. In what had been the greatest railway country in the world, and the easiest and cheapest to traverse, the traveller was now told with perfect seriousness, 'You can't get there from here.'

This was a wonderful thing for my circular tour, because parts of Britain which had been frequented by travellers for hundreds of years had now become inaccessible, and what had been villages well served by railway lines had become curiously anorexic-looking and tumble-down, somehow deserving an epitaph from Ozymandias. I had thought travelling around Britain would be a breeze; without a car it was often very difficult. It revealed to me long coastal stretches of unexpected decrepitude, which sometimes looked the reverse, yet it was decrepitude all the same. One such sight – one of the saddest and most irritating for me in Britain – was the railway station that had been auctioned off and sold to an up-and-comer who had turned it into a bijou bungalow. I found these maddening; the superbly solid Victorian railway architecture now the merest forcing-house for geraniums and cats – Nigel and Jenny Bankler ('We're planning to start a baby') presently hogging the whole premises that used to be the station building at Applecross. 'That was the waiting room, where Jenny has the breakfast nook, and do you see that funny little window thing, where there's that magnificent jar of muesli? Well, years ago, that was the –' Nigel wanted to call it 'Couplings' because the weekends they used it (their proper house was a semi in Cheadle) Jenny was practically insatiable. In the end they settled for 'The Sidings'. Most of the other stations had become second homes: 'Footplate Cottage' and 'Level Crossing' and 'Dunrailing' were right up the line, and one still had its original ticket window and grille (the Nordleys had trained some variegated ivy up it – looked smashing). 'We got this place for practically nothing,' they always said. 'Mind you, we've put a fair bit of money into it,' and then – with a jowly little grin – 'We've always liked trains. Haven't we, petal?'

I could not see one of these railway station bungalows and the owner-occupiers without thinking of *Planet of the Apes*. And now that the railway strike had started I could foresee a time when every railway line would be turned into a cinder track for dog owners and horse lovers; and all the stations into bungalows. Thousands of miles of railway had already gone that way – why not the rest of it? Many of these lines had been closed by the Beeching Report of 1963. While I was travelling around the coast in the spring and summer of 1982, a new report on British Railways was being written. This was the Serpell Report, offering several options. Option A, greatly favoured by the powerful road lobby, slashed the railway network from 11,000 to 1,600 miles, leaving a skeleton service on the rails, and creating a traffic jam on the roads that extended from John O'Groats to Land's End.

This trackless railway line took me to Scarborough.

Scarborough was the most complete seaside resort I had seen so far in Britain. It was a big full-blooded place, three hundred feet up on a part of the coast that was a geological freak. A buckling during the Jurassic age had given Scarborough a front like a human face – two bays like eye-sockets and the bluff between like a great nose of oolite. (It was a fact that people tended to settle those parts of the coast that had huge and recognizably human features – and the settlers even gave those features anatomical names.) Scarborough had theatres and concert halls and department stores; its ledges and steeps were lined with boarding houses. The town had the same ample contours as its landladies, and the same sense of life in which even platitudes were delivered with gusto. 'The biggest fool to a working man these days is hisself!' The butchers wore straw boaters and blood-stained smocks and among their sausages and black puddings were braces of pigeons still wearing feathers. On a coast in which one place was turned into a holiday camp, and another was declared bankrupt, and a third was sliding into the sea, Scarborough seemed – if not eternal – at least busy, prosperous, and alive.

When a British coastal place was modernized it seemed to strangle itself on its own novelty. Scarborough had sensibly remained unchanged, and even its entertainments were antique. It was praised for having good theatre, notably Alan Ayckbourn's playhouse – Mr Ayckbourn was a local resident. But live plays were nothing new in a seaside resort – they were as old a virtue as the music halls and the bandstand concerts, and the end-of-the-pier shows.

At the Floral Hall on the cliff-top above North Bay I went to see 'An Evening of Viennese Operetta', put on by the Scarborough Light Opera Society. The English were such brave and unembarrassed amateurs! They loved graceful waltzers, the ladies in ballgowns, the men in tuxedos; perfumed tits, violins and gliding feet.

'The year is 1850 – and Vienna is the city of dreams,' John Beagle said as the curtain rose, and the violins swelled under the baton of Gordon Truefitt.

It was 'The Blue Danube'! Two pairs of dancers, Maureen Bosomworth and Albert Marston, and the Pobgees – Elizabeth and Malcolm – swept across the floor. *Die Fledermaus* was next, Eunice Cockburn singing 'The Laughing Song'. And there was more: gypsy songs, polkas, more violins. 'My Hero', 'The Gold and Silver Waltz', 'Girls Were Made to Love and Kiss (and who am I to interfere with this?)' and Maureen Bosomworth changed her gown for every new number. They ran through Franz Lehar and then we had Sigmund Romberg's 'Golden Days', and selections from *The Dancing Years* by Ivor Novello. The hall was full. 'You Are My Heart's Delight' brought forth grateful applause, and the selections from *Bittersweet*, especially 'I'll See You Again (Whenever spring breaks through again)' had people wiping tears away.

It was old hat and corny, but it was done with such attention and energy that it was effective. It was the essence of the place itself: Scarborough was a success because it had stayed old-fashioned.

No one swam at such places. 'Let's look round the shops,' people said. They milled around until four and then treated themselves to 'a meat tea'. Or they roamed the gardens at the Spa. They chased their children on the sand and encouraged each other to buy ice-cream cones, which they called 'cornets'. They went to the matinees and saw in the flesh their favourite television stars – that fat comedian, that cockney magician, that man who sang 'There'll Always Be An England' so beautifully; the drag-artist who did 'Mother Goose'.

But, mostly, the seaside resort was for sitting in the sunshine reading something really lurid in the gutter press. Today it was the shooting of the Mad Killer. He had been tracked to Malton, only twenty miles away; he was found crouching in a shed near the tennis club; he was heading for Malton police station – it was going to be part of what the papers called his 'murder spree'. He was asked to surrender and when he refused, he was shot as he lay in the shed.

An elderly clay-pigeon champion had been watching the police close in. This was John Blades. 'I just hoped he would go on to the tennis courts,' Mr Blades said. 'I could have shot him between the eyes from 200 yards, and that's just what I wanted to do.' Chris Burr was putting milk bottles out when he heard shots. He said, 'It was just like the Alamo out there. Really frightening. When it was all over, one policeman said to me, "He had a ton of lead inside him."'

This I gathered from a *Daily Mail* handed to me by Phyllis Barmby, who shared a bench overlooking Clarence Gardens. She was glad the Mad Killer had been gunned down. If they had arrested him he probably would have got a flipping suspended sentence. Ordinarily she didn't believe in capital punishment, but this lad was a nasty piece of work and deserved everything he got. She was not angry. You could tell she was pleased. The Mad Killer business, and its satisfying conclusion, was just the thing for a breezy day on the front at Scarborough. Barry Prudom in fact shot himself at the same time as the police got him.

Though Yorkshire was always associated with factories and mines, four-fifths of it was open country, and the whole of its coast was countrified. I walked to Osgodby and then to Filey. On the way I passed through some woods and saw a man shouting at a small owl. This was Edgar Overend, a local naturalist. He explained that it was an owlet. 'A foolish woman gave it to me to feed. I've been going mad trying to catch mice for it. If she'd left it alone, its mother would have looked after it. But no, she had to meddle! Now the little chap doesn't want to fly away.'

The owlet sat on the ground, staring sadly at Edgar Overend.

'Off you go,' Mr Overend said.

The owlet was uncomprehending. Then it twisted its head upward. A bird had just flown by.

'That's it – *you* fly,' Mr Overend said. 'Shoo!'

The owlet didn't move.

Mr Overend clapped his hands sharply.

The owlet jumped into the air and made for a tree-top.

'At last!' Mr Overend said. 'He'll be all right.'

At Filey I saw a holiday camp ahead and hurried to the road. I caught a bus and climbed to the top deck. It was like being in a boat riding the swells of a sea that was running high. I became seasick – nauseated anyway – and descended to the lower deck. If there hadn't been a railway strike I could have taken a train from Scarborough. At Bridlington, I took another bus to Flamborough Head, a headland and chalk stack so huge I had seen it from twenty miles away, as I had walked towards Scarborough. This, unfortunately, was one of the Yorkshire sights – a popular outing – and so I did not stay, but instead took a bus south to Beverley, all the while cursing the buses.

It was another area of Disused Railway Lines. There was one from Hornsea to Hull, and another back to the coast from Hull to Withernsea. Further south there had been a train from Louth to Saltfleetby and on to Sutton, Willoughby and Skegness; and to Spalding, and to King's Lynn. And now there were only straight paths in the woods and a dot-dot-dot on the map – sometimes not even that. And if you wanted to get to Catwick, Newbald, Swine, Warter, Sigglesthorne, Great Limber, Rise, Thorngumbald or Burstwick, you tried to find a bus, but probably you walked.

Trains are different from country to country, but buses are pretty much the same the world over. I stood in a long line of people at the bus shelter – no one knew when the bus was due – and waited for an hour or more on a windy road, and then I saw the bus moving slowly down a road five hills away, and I crowded in, and jounced for another hour to go fifteen miles; and I thought: Afghanistan. It was like travelling in a Third World country – the sort of country that was always promising that as soon as it achieved a modest prosperity it would build itself a railway. Buses were slow and sickening and unpredictable, and it was dreadful having to depend on them in Britain. Of course, there were long-distance coaches – but I was not going long distances; and there were city buses – but they were not much good to me. With the rain coming down and the railway strike in full swing, I needed a way of moving down the coast. But there was no reliable way. It took me almost an entire day to get from Bridlington to Hull, where I had a two-hour wait for the next bus out. I would have stayed, but Hull was not on the coast. It was all slow progress, and it got so that the very expression 'Take a bus' began to sound as mocking to me as 'Fly a kite'.

In the end, the bus did not take me where I wanted to go. I was headed straight across the Humber to Barrow, but the bus only went as far as Barton. So I spent part of the afternoon walking to Barrow. Yet the prospect of finding the place excited me. I knew someone who lived here. Just that morning I had seen how near I was to it, and I thought: Why not pay the old boy a visit?

Ten years before, I had met Mr Duffill on the Orient Express, going from Paris to Istanbul. His frailty and his shabby clothes had made him seem a little mysterious. He smelled of breadcrusts. He carried paper parcels tied with string. He avoided questions. I took him to be an embezzler or someone in the midst of a strange fugue, bound for Turkey in a mouse-grey gabardine coat.

We had shared a compartment. One morning at Domodossola, on the Italian frontier, Mr Duffill got off the train to buy some food – there was no dining car – and while he was still on the platform, the Orient Express began moving. Mr Duffill went rigid, biting on his pipe. And then we were speeding to Milan without him. His name became a verb for me. To be duffilled was to be abandoned by one's own train. You got off at a sleepy place to buy some gum or a newspaper and, before you could get back on, the train pulled away, taking your suitcase, your clothes, your money and your passport with it. The point was not merely that you were left behind, but that you were left behind in a strange country, figuratively naked.

I never saw Mr Duffill again. I had left his suitcase and his paper bags at Venice with a note, and I had wondered whether he caught up with them and continued to Istanbul. Once, I had tried to call him, but he did not have a telephone. One of the few things he had told me was that he lived in Barrow-upon-Humber, in Lincolnshire – here.

It was a tiny place – a church, a narrow high street, a manor

house and a few shops. It had an air of rural monotony that was
like the drone of a bee, as it bumped slowly from flower to flower.
No one ever came here; people just went away from it and never
returned.

I walked down the street and saw a man.

'Excuse me, do you know a Mr Duffill?'

He nodded. 'The corner shop.'

The corner shop had a small sign that said *Duffill's Hardware*.
But it was locked. A square of cardboard in the window was
lettered *Gone on Holiday*. I said out loud, 'God damn it.'

A lady was passing. This was Mrs Marden. She saw that I
was exasperated. She wondered if I needed directions. I said I
was looking for Mr Duffill.

'He won't be back for another week,' she said.

'Where has he gone this time?' I asked. 'Not Istanbul, I hope.'

She said, 'Are you looking for *Richard* Duffill?'

'Yes,' I said.

Her hand went to her face and I knew before she spoke that
he was dead.

'His name was Richard Cuthbert Duffill. He was a most
unusual man,' said his sister-in-law, Mrs Jack Duffill. She lived
at 'Glyndebourne', a bungalow just beyond the churchyard. She
did not ask who I was. It seemed only natural to her that someone
should be inquiring about the life of this strange man, who had
died two years before, at the age of seventy-nine. He had been
as old as the century – seventy-three the year he had stepped
off the Orient Express at Domodossola. Mrs Jack said, 'Do you
know about his adventurous life?'

I said, 'I don't know anything about him.' All I knew was his
name and his village.

'He was born right here in Barrow, in the Hall cottages. The
Hall was one of the grand houses. Richard's father was the
gardener and his mother was a housemaid. Those were the days
of servants. The Hall was the manor – Mr Uppleby was the Lord
of the Manor – and of course the Duffills were servants, and
rather poor ...'

But Richard Duffill was brilliant. At the age of eleven he was
encouraged by the headmaster of the village school to go to the

Technical College in Hull. He excelled at maths, but he was also a gifted linguist. He learned French, Latin, German, Russian and Spanish while still a teenager at Hull. But he had become somewhat introspective, for when he was twelve his father had died. Mr Uppleby took an interest, but the young boy usually just stayed inside and read and did his lessons, or else he went for long solitary walks.

His main recreation was swimming, and his skill in this resulted in his becoming a local hero. One summer day in 1917 he was on a swimming expedition with some friends at a quarry called the Brick Pits, near the Humber Bank. One of the boys, a certain Howson, began to struggle. He shouted, and then he disappeared beneath the murky water. Duffill dived repeatedly after him and finally surfaced with him and dragged him to shore, saving the boy's life. A few days later, the Hull newspaper reported the story under the headline *A Plucky Barrow Boy*.

For this, Duffill – a boy scout – was awarded the Silver Cross for Bravery. It was the first time this honour had ever come to a Lincolnshire scout. Some months afterwards, the Carnegie Heroes' Fund presented Duffill with a silver watch 'for gallantry', and they gave him a sum of money 'to help him in his education and future career'.

In 1919, still young, and fluent in half a dozen languages, he joined the Inter-Allied Plebiscite Commission and was sent to Allenstein, in what was then East Prussia, to deal with the aftermath of World War One – sorting out prisoners and helping at the Special Court of Justice. In the following few years he did the same in Klagenfurt and Oppeln (Opole, Upper Silesia – now Poland). Berlin was next. Duffill got a job with the celebrated firm of Price, Waterhouse, the international accountants. He stayed in Berlin for ten years, abruptly resigning in 1935 and leaving – fleeing, some people said – for England.

Politically, he was of the Left. His friends in Berlin thought he might be gathering information for the British secret service. ('One felt he would have made the ideal agent,' an old friend of Duffill's told me.) In any case, he left Germany so suddenly it was assumed that he was being pursued by Nazi agents or wolves from the *Sturm-Abteilung*. He made it safely home, and he was also able to get all his money out of Germany ('An

exceedingly clever and daring feat,' another friend told me. 'His
fortune was considerable.')

He may have had a nervous breakdown then; there was some
speculation. He sank for a year, re-emerging in 1936 as a chief
accountant for an American movie company. Two years later,
a letter of reference said that Duffill was 'thoroughly acquainted
with various sides of the film trade'. In 1939 there was another
gap, lasting until 1945: the war certainly – but where was Duffill?
No one could tell me. His brother said, 'Richard never discussed
his working life or his world-travelling with us.'

In the late forties, he apparently rejoined Price, Waterhouse
and travelled throughout Europe. He went to Egypt and Turkey;
he returned to Germany; he went to Sweden and Russia, 'for
whose leaders he had the greatest admiration'.

After his retirement he continued to travel. He had never
married. He was always alone. But the snapshots he kept showed
him to be a very stylish dresser – waistcoat, plus-fours, cashmere
overcoat, homburg, stick-pin. A characteristic of natty dressers
is that they wear too many clothes. Duffill's snapshots showed
this; and he always wore a hat.

He wore a rug-like wig, I was told – 'it stuck out at the back'.
He had had brain surgery. 'He once played tennis in Cairo.' He
had gone on socialist holidays to eastern Europe. He hated Hitler.
He was very 'spiritual', one of his old friends said. He became
interested in the philosophy of George Ivanovich Gurdjieff and
was a close friend of the great Gurdjieff scholar, John Godolphin
Bennett. 'And after a while, Richard got frightfully steamed up
about dervishes,' Bennett's widow told me. That was why Duffill
was on his way to Istanbul, she said – to renew his acquaintance
with some whirling dervishes!

But what I wanted to know was, what happened to him after
the Orient Express pulled out of Domodossola?

Mrs Jack said, 'He got out at a station. He didn't tell me where.
He had left his luggage on the train. Then the train pulled out.
He inquired when the next train was, and they told him the time
– five o'clock. Only a few hours, he thought. But he had got mixed
up. He thought they meant p.m. and they actually meant a.m. – five
the next morning. He had a very bad night, and the next day he
went to – where was it? Venice? Yes, he collected his luggage' –

The paper bags I had left with the *Controllare*.

– 'and eventually got to Istanbul.'

So he had made it!

I told Mrs Jack who I was and how I had met Mr Duffill.

She said, 'Oh, yes, I read your book! My neighbour's son is an avid reader. He told us about it. He said, "I think you should see this – I think this is our Mr Duffill." And then everyone in Barrow read it.'

I was eager to know whether Mr Duffill himself had read it.

'I wanted him to see it,' Mrs Jack said. 'I put a copy aside. But when he came over he wasn't too good. He didn't see it. The next time he came over I forgot about the book. That was the last time, really. He had his stroke and just deteriorated. And he died. So he never saw it –'

Thank God for that, I thought.

What an interesting man that stranger had been. He had seemed frail, elderly, a little crazy and suspicious on the Orient Express. Typical, I had thought. But now I knew how unusual he had been – brave, kind, secretive, resourceful, solitary, brilliant. He had slept and snored in the upper berth of my compartment. I had not known him at all, but the more I found out about him the more I missed him. It would have been a privilege to know him personally, and yet even in friendship he would never have confirmed what I strongly suspected – that he had almost certainly been a spy.

24

The North Norfolk Railway

At Grimsby I bought a London paper with the headline *Rail-Stricken Britain Rolls On!* But nothing was rolling in Grimsby, not even a train for the three miles to Cleethorpes. Nothing had been rolling in Scarborough, where I had walked, or Hull, where I had wasted a day on a bus that had taken Mexican-style detours (it was literally true that English country buses sometimes went backwards). Nothing was rolling at all: I never saw a train in motion during the long railway strike. The government kept claiming that a number of trains were operating and that the strike (the issue was drivers' work schedules) was half-hearted. London news always seemed shrill and untruthful up-country, but this situation-normal news was a damned lie in Grimsby and a cruel joke in poor starved Cleethorpes.

On the bus to Cleethorpes, the man in the next seat, Jim Popplewell, explained that he was a carpet-layer. 'But when times are bad, people stop buying carpets,' he said. He was earning fifty per cent less than he had two years ago.

'What do you think of the north?' he asked. He meant here.

'I don't think of this as the north,' I said. After all, I had been to Cape Wrath, four hundred miles north of this.

'But this *is* the north,' Mr Popplewell said. 'It's not half bad. Have a look at the Wolds.'

'What exactly are the Wolds?'

'Woods,' he said. 'Some hills. You'll see them as you head towards Lincoln.'

I said I would be sticking to the coast.

'Mablethorpe,' he said. 'Skeggy.'

'That kind of thing,' I said.

'I see. You just go from pillar to post.'

The Kingdom by the Sea

He said it in a kindly way. I was sure he meant 'from place to place'. But his statement was nonetheless accurate.

Was Cleethorpes a pillar or a post? It looked a terrible place. I wanted to go away. But how? The only way I could have left was on foot, in the rain, sinking in the mud of the Humber Bank. So I stayed the night in Cleethorpes and watched filthy children playing 'Tiggy'. It was a version of tag. Home was called 'the Hob'. 'If we tig the 'ob – before 'e gets to the 'ob – we say "on the 'ob".' They were twelve-year-olds and a little wary of me. 'It's okay,' one called to the others, ''e's not a copper!' I must have seemed a little strange to them – all my questions. But I was lonely, I was killing time, I wanted to leave Cleethorpes – to go anywhere. I mentioned Mablethorpe. The salesmen in the hotel laughed at this. Mablethorpe was anywhere.

The salesmen were that dying breed of hustlers that I had first seen on the Kent coast at Littlestone-on-Sea. They talked about places being 'shocking'. They talked about their territory, calling it 'my parish'. These gents stopping the night at the Dolphin in Cleethorpes sold everything – brushes, plastic basins, outsized garments, double glazing. One man told me he went a thousand miles a week in his car and made a hundred and eighty calls. He drove all over Lincolnshire and Yorkshire – automobile spares. A camera salesman told me that the profit on a hundred quid camera was a fiver for a retailer – hardly worth the effort, since he could make the same profit selling four rolls of film. This man, Jessel by name, said, 'We'll all be out of a job in a year or two. My job could be done by a computer. It wouldn't be the same – no human element, see – but it would be cheaper for my company.'

The next day I walked back to Grimsby. I asked the way and a lady said, 'You must be going to the docks.'

So I look like an Able Seaman? My coastal travelling had obviously taken its toll on my appearance. I was both flattered and appalled. Here I was, months after leaving Margate, still wearing my leather jacket, and my oily shoes, and my knapsack, and I suppose I was a little pigeon-toed from walking in a clockwise direction.

There had been stock-car racing, and wrestling, and bingo at Cleethorpes; but just next door in Grimsby there was the Caxton

Theatre and the fish docks and a sense that this had once been a bustling place and had only recently collapsed. The buildings and high-rise parking lots still stood; but they were empty. A sign at a Grimsby shop selling leathers and furs said, 'Coneys'. I had never seen this old word for rabbit in an advertisement before – and it was also a famous word for 'suckers'.

The railway station was still shut. Only one bus today was going down the coast – the 'Ron Appleby' coach to Mablethorpe. Well, that was my general direction. There were only five of us on board. I sat down and read the London papers again – more gloating, and what had already begun to be called 'the Falklands spirit'. Had these past months produced a national shift of mood? 'The travelling public are coping magnificently with the strike

.   Many people have found they can do quite well without British Rail,' the Tory papers said. More lies. My guess was that most people were coping with the strike by not travelling at all. That was the British way: inaction was a form of coping.

'Not a bad place is Grimsby,' an old man in the bus said to me. His name was Sam Dunball and he had worked at the fish docks. He was retired now, and a good thing, too, he said. 'The fish is gone and the docks is half-empty. It was the Cod War that finished Grimsby. We haven't been the same since. No, there's no fishing industry here any more.'

The so-called Cod War had been a legal dispute over Britain's traditional fishing grounds off the coast of Iceland. A two-hundred-mile fishing limit was declared by Iceland. There was a wrangle, which Britain lost. And the fishing industry in Britain was broken.

Mr Dunball wanted to know what I thought of London.

I told him that I thought London was more like a country than a city It was a sort of independent republic.

'I was in London once!' Mr Dunball said. 'It was before the war. Simpson's Hotel in the Caledonian Road, four-and-sixpence bed and breakfast. The doorknob, see, was in the middle of the door, and you pushed it and walked downstairs to the parlour. I was down there attending a course at Houndsditch Technical College. But it didn't do me a bit of good. I always wanted to go down for a Cup Final, but I never did. I just went that one time. I'll never forget it.'

We skirted the Wolds – they looked like low rolls of fog in the distance – and then we travelled through the spinach fields of Lincolnshire. It was an area of great flatness, land like sea, and a wide sky of white vacant light. There was something about this even landscape, and the four-square farmhouses, and the geometry of the fields, that hinted at moral probity and Bible reading and rectitude. It was clear in the angles of the hedges and all the way to the straight, ruled horizon. The highest object in the landscape was the church spire, and this solitary pencil point was a kind of sanctifying emphasis that could be seen ten miles away. But it was all illusion, like the apparent disorder that made jungles seem savage to missionaries. And yet it was true that people who lived in sight of a flat horizon tended to build square houses.

At North Somercoates we passed Locksley Hall. I should have known it from the way it overlooked the sandy tracts and the long hollow ocean ridges.

O the dreary, dreary moorland! O the barren, barren shore!

But was it really better, as the poem said, to have 'fifty years of Europe than a cycle of Cathay'? It did not seem so in Mablethorpe, a flat, sad place modelled on a holiday camp and thronged with shivering vacationers. It was cold, but that was not the reason these people were scowling. This was the coast of last resorts. In other years these people had had their fish and chips in Spain, but there was less work now, and all their dole-money got them this year was this place and Mumby and Hogsthorpe and Sutton-on-Sea. It was a dole-holiday, a cheapie, and no more fun than a day out on the prison farm, some enforced fresh air and then back to the classified ads and the Job Centre.

The caravan sites with their acres of tin boxes – whole caravan towns, in fact, tucked behind the duney shore – rivalled those I had seen on the coast of Wales. This was also a sort of miners' riviera, for as we neared Skegness we passed holiday camp hotels. They had the look of painted prisons, 'The Nottinghamshire Miners' Holiday Home' and the 'The Derbyshire Miners' Holiday Centre' and the huge wind-whipped Eastgate Holiday Centre at Ingoldmells. Fourteen applicants had expressed an eagerness to enter Eastgate's 'Miss Topless Competition' – a tit-show for amateurs – but the odd thing was that there were not enough vacationers to watch it, and so the date had been pushed ahead to late August.

And then Skeggy itself – it deserved its ragged-sounding nickname. It was a low, loud, faded seaside resort. It was utterly joyless. Its vulgarity was uninteresting. It was painfully ugly. It made the English seem dangerous. And, at last, it made me want to leave – to take long strides down its broad sands and walk all the way to Friskney Flats. But there was no walking here – too muddy, too many of the canals and ditches they called 'drains' here; and no path. There was no train, so I took a bus, or rather several of them, along the silty shore of The Wash, getting off at Butterwick and walking to Boston.

Boston's church – 'the Stump', they called it – was so tall and the land around it so flat, that I was able to see it for a whole afternoon as I rode and walked towards it. From a distance it looked like a water tower, and closer like a grey stone lantern, and in Boston itself it resembled a stone crown on a pillar. This corner of The Wash was all a landscape of ancient churches separated by flat fields. I could not see the shore until I was on top of it and it was impossible to walk there without getting wet feet. It was like the Netherlands – that white Dutch daylight and hard-packed sand and measured fields and plain old houses set in Calvinist clumps, with miles of vegetables between. The landscape was austere, but the placements were fantastic: Fishtoft, Breast Sand, Whaplode, Pode Hole and Quadring Eudike, and a very ordinary street would have a name like Belchmire Lane. But it was so flat you could see a mature poplar tree ten miles away.

After more than a week of the railway strike the management of British Rail said that they were breaking it. They said the drivers were showing up. They said the railways were being manned in a modest way. They said that all over the country people were travelling to work on trains – ten per cent of the trains were running.

London news had always sounded a little strange when I heard it in places like Enniskillen, Mallaig, Porlock or Grimsby. Now in King's Lynn it was perplexing to read of these running trains.

There were none running in King's Lynn. The station was empty. It was another lie, like 'Rail-stricken Britain rolls on'. No one I saw was going anywhere.

King's Lynn was dignified and dull, its stately centre so finely preserved it looked embalmed; and grafted to it was a shopping precinct. This rabbit warren was all discount stores and boutiques and hamburger joints; it would not have seemed out of place in Hyannis, Massachusetts. King's Lynn skinheads and motor-cyclists were particularly boisterous – these gangs seemed to me as much a part of the fine old market towns in provincial England as the period houses and the graceful windows, and they seemed especially to enjoy roaring down quaint cobblestone streets on their Japanese motorbikes. They called the bikes 'hogs' in their gentle rustic accents.

But King's Lynn was a habitable place, and patchily pretty, and it had hopes. The King's Lynn Festival would be starting soon. The brochures promised eight concerts, five orchestras, a jazz band, several plays, poetry readings, numerous movies and puppet shows. And although it was some miles from the coast – if The Wash could be called the coast – it had the air of a sea-port, and the same Dutchness I had sensed in Lincolnshire.

Five railway lines had met at King's Lynn, where there was now one – and it was strike-bound. It was marshy along the shore to Hunstanton. So I took the bus to the top of the Norfolk coast, Wells-next-the-Sea. It was such a tame landscape of meadows and thin woods that it looked like Wimbledon Common for forty miles. Wells and its neighbour Stiffkey were famous for their cockles. I walked at the edge of the Salt Marsh and had some cockles for lunch. They were salty and had the texture of under-done pasta. Stiffkey had once had a rector at its church who had scandalized – thrilled, was probably a more apt word – English society by trying to reform prostitutes. I stopped at a public house in Stiffkey to ask about this notorious clergyman, but before I could introduce the subject, the barman (Fred Watmough) began talking about trains. He said there was one at Weybourne that ran to Sheringham, and it was running.

'What about the strike?'

Mr Watmough said, 'This is a private line. They call it "the Poppy Line". Very pretty.'

I walked to Weybourne, almost ten miles. But Weybourne was no more than a hamlet – flinty cottages, a square-towered church and a lovely windmill. A small sign said *North Norfolk Railway* and pointed up a country lane. That was another mile, between pines and pastures, and then Weybourne Station.

'The last train – the last proper train – left here in 1964, travelling from Melton Constable to Great Yarmouth,' Mr Winch said. Mr Winch was a volunteer on the North Norfolk Railway. 'And now Melton Constable is just a little village in the middle of nowhere.'

'And if you said you wanted to take the train to Great Yarmouth people would probably laugh,' I said.

'In actual fact,' Mr Winch said, 'you can't get there from here.'

We sat on the platform, watching the poppies tossing in the wind.

Mr Winch said, 'All they'll have left in a few years will be the big inter-city routes. King's Lynn won't be on the map. Neither will Cromer or Great Yarmouth or Lowestoft.'

'How will people get around?'

He said, 'By car. And if they don't drive they'll live in cities.'

'Everyone can't live in the cities,' I said.

'Correct,' he said. 'How's that for a game of soldiers?'

Then he stood up.

'They'll be diddling. Fiddle-faddling,' he said. 'But they won't get anywhere.'

I said, 'Buses aren't the answer.'

Mr Winch was looking at the oncoming train. He said, 'Buses aren't even a good question. You go to a bus station and ask how to get to Swaffham. And they say, "Go to Fakenham. You'll probably get a connection there." They don't even have time-tables.'

I wanted to say, *Yes, it's like South America*, but I decided not to. And yet Mr Winch would probably have agreed with me. In a self-critical mood the English could be brutal.

And so I boarded the train. The North Norfolk Railway was a preserved line. It went three miles, to Sheringham, at a donkey trot. People snapped pictures of the engine and smiled admiringly at it. It was the railway buffs who were helping to dismantle British Railways. Their nostalgia was dangerous, since they hankered for the past and were never happier than when they were able to turn an old train into a toy. The commuter who spent two hours a day on the suburban train going to and from his place of work was very seldom a railway buff.

Rosalie and Hugh Mutton collected preserved railways. They had been on the Romney, Hythe and Dymchurch; the Raven-glass; all the Welsh lines, and more. They loved steam. They would drive hundreds of miles in their Ford Escort to take a steam train. They were members of a steam railway preservation society. They lived in Luton. This one reminded them of the line in Shepton Mallet.

Then Mrs Mutton said, 'Where's your casual top?'

'I don't have a casual top in brown, do I,' Mr Mutton said.

'Why are you wearing brown?'

Mr Mutton said, 'I can't wear blue all the time, can I.'

Rhoda Gauntlett was at the window. She said, 'That sea looks so lovely. And that grass. It's a golf course.'

We looked at the golf course – Sheringham, so soon.

'I'd get confused going round a golf course,' Mrs Mutton said. 'You walk bloody miles. How do you know which way to go?'

This was the only train in Britain today, the fifteen-minute ride from Weybourne.

It was sunny in Sheringham – a thousand people on the sandy beach, but only two people in the water. There were three old ladies walking along the promenade. They had strong country accents – probably Norfolk. I could never place these burrs and haws.

'I should have worn my blooming hat.'

'The air's fresh, but it's making my eyes water.'

'We can look round Woolworth's after we've had our tea.'

It was a day at the seaside, and then back to their cottages in Great Snoring. They were not like the others who had come to sit behind canvas windbreaks ('Eighty pence per day or any portion thereof') and read *Four Killed by Runaway Lorry* or *Wife Killer Given Three Years* (she had taunted him about money; he did not earn much; he bashed her brains out with a hammer; 'You've suffered enough,' the judge said) or *Blundeston Child Battered* (bruised tot with broken leg; 'He fell off a chair,' the mother said; one year, pending psychiatric report). They crouched on the groynes, smoking cigarettes. They lay in the bright sunshine wearing raincoats. They stood in their bathing suits. Their skin was the veiny white of raw sausage casings.

The tide was out, so I walked to Cromer along the sand. The crumbly yellow-dirt cliffs were like the banks of a quarry, high and scooped out and raked vertically by erosion. Halfway between Sheringham and Cromer there were no people because the English never strayed far from their cars; even the most crowded parts of the English coast were empty between the car parks. Only one man was here, Collie Wylie, a rock collector. He was hacking amber-coloured tubes out of the chalk slabs on the shore. 'Belamites,' he called them. 'Take that one,' he said. 'Now that one is between five and eight million years old.'

I saw a pillbox down the beach. It had once been on top of the cliff, and inside it the men from 'Dad's Army' had conned for Germans. 'Jerry would love to catch us on the hop.' But the soft cliffs were constantly falling, and the pillbox had slipped a hundred feet and was now sinking into the sand, a cute little artefact from the war, buried to its gunholes.

I came to Cromer. An old man in a greasy coat sat on a wooden groyne on the beach, reading a comic book about war in outer space.

'Seaside Special '82' was playing at the Pavilion Theatre at the end of the pier at Cromer. It was the summer show, July to September, every day except Sundays, and two matinees. I had not gone to any of these end-of-the-pier shows. I was nearing the end of my circular tour, so I decided to stay in Cromer and see the show. I found a hotel. Cromer was very empty. It had a sort of atrophied charm, a high round-shouldered Edwardian look, red brick terraces and red brick hotels and the loudest sea-gulls in Norfolk.

There were not more than thirty people in the audience that night at the Pavilion Theatre, which was pathetic, because there were nine people in the show. But seeing the show was like observing England's secret life – its anxiety in the dismal jokes, its sadness in the old songs.

'Hands up, all those who aren't working,' one comedian said.

A number of hands went up - eight or ten – but this was a

terrible admission, and down they went before I could count them properly.

The comedian was already laughing. 'Have some Beechams Pills,' he said. 'They'll get you "working" again!'

There were more jokes, awful ones like this, and then a lady singer came out and in a sweet voice sang 'The Russian Nightingale'. She encouraged the audience to join in the chorus of the next one, and they offered timid voices, singing,

> Let him go, let him tarry,
> Let him sink, or let him swim.
> He doesn't care for me
> And I don't care for him.

The comedians returned. They had changed their costumes. They had worn floppy hats the first time; now they wore bowler hats and squirting flowers.

'We used to put manure on our rhubarb.'

'We used to put custard on ours!'

No one laughed.

'Got any matches?'

'Yes, and they're good British ones.'

'How do you know?'

'Because they're all strikers!'

A child in the first row began to cry.

The dancers came on. They were pretty girls and they danced well. They were billed as 'Our Disco Dollies' on the poster. More singers appeared and 'A Tribute to Al Jolson' was announced: nine minstrel show numbers, done in black make-up. Entertainers in the United States were arrested for this sort of thing; in Cromer the audience applauded. Al Jolson was a fond memory and his rendition of 'Mammy' was a special favourite in musical revues. No one had ever tired of minstrel shows in England, and they persisted on British television well into the 1970s.

It had been less than a month since the end of the Falklands war, but in the second half of 'Seaside Special' there was a comedy routine in which an Argentine general appeared – goofy dago in ill-fitting khaki uniform – 'How dare you insult me!'

I could hear the surf sloshing against the iron struts of the pier.

'And you come and pour yourself on me,' a man was singing. It was a love song. The audience seemed embarrassed by it. They preferred 'California Here I Come' and 'When I Grow Too Old to Dream' sung by a man named Derick, from Johannesburg. The programme said that he had 'appeared in every night spot in South Africa and Rhodesia'. Say 'top night spots in Zimbabwe' and it does not sound the same – it brings to mind drums and thick foliage.

One of the comedians reappeared. I had come to dread this man. I had reason. Now he played 'The Warsaw Concerto' and cracked jokes as he played. 'It's going to be eighty tomorrow,' he said. 'Forty in the morning and forty in the afternoon!'

His jokes were flat, but the music was pleasant and the singers had excellent voices. In fact, most of the performers were talented, and they pretended to be playing to a full house – not the thirty of us who sat so silently in the echoing theatre. The show people conveyed the impression that they were enjoying themselves. But it can't have been much fun looking at all those empty seats. Cromer itself was very dull. And I imagined these performers were miserably paid. I wanted to know more about them. I played with the idea of sending a message backstage to one of the chorus girls. I'd get her name out of the programme. Millie Plackett, the one whose thighs jiggled. 'Millie, it's for you! Maybe it's your big break!' *Meet me after the show at the Hotel de Paris* ... That was actually the name of my hotel, an enjoyable pile of brick and plaster splendour. But I didn't look the part. In my scratched leather jacket and torn dungarees and oily hiking shoes I thought Millie Plackett might misunderstand my intentions.

I stayed until the end of the show, finally admitting that I was enjoying myself. One act was of a kind I found irresistible – the magician whose tricks go wrong, leaving him with broken eggs in his hat and the wrong deck of cards. There was always an elaborate build-up and then a sudden collapse. 'Presto,' he said, as the trick failed. And then the last trick, the one that looked dangerous, worked like a charm and was completely baffling.

They saved the saddest song for the end. It was a love song, but in the circumstances it sounded nationalistic. It was senti-mental hope, Ivor Novello gush, at the end of the pier that was trembling on the tide. I had heard it elsewhere on the coast. It was anything but new, but it was the most popular number on the seaside that year –

> We'll gather lilacs in the spring agine,
> And walk together down an English lane ...

25

Striking Southend

On my last long trudge, curving down the rump of England on the Norfolk coast and into Suffolk, I thought: Every British bulge is different and every mile has its own mood. I said Blackpool and people said, 'Naturally!' I said Worthing and they said, 'Of all places!' The character was fixed, and though few coastal places matched their reputation each one was unique. It made my circular tour a pleasure, because it was always worth setting off in the morning. It might be bad ahead, but at least it was different; and the dreariest and most defoliated harbour town might be five minutes from a green sweep of bay.

This was the reason 'typical' was regarded as such an unfair word in England. And yet there *was* such a thing as typical on the coast – but to an alien something typical could seem just as fascinating as the mosques of the Golden Horn.

There was always an Esplanade, and always a Bandstand on it; always a War Memorial and a Rose Garden and a bench bearing a small stained plaque that said, *To the Memory of Arthur Wetherup*. There was always a Lifeboat Station and a Lighthouse and a Pier; a Putting Green, a Bowling Green, a Cricket Pitch, a Boating Lake and a church the guidebook said was Perpendicular. The newsagent sold two *Greetings From ...* picture postcards, one with kittens and the other with two plump girls in surf, and he had a selection of cartoon postcards with mildly filthy captions; the souvenir stall sold rock candy and the local estate agent advertised a dismal cottage as 'chalet-bungalow, bags of character, on bus route, superb sea views, suit retired couple'. There was always a Funfair and it was never fun, and the video machines were always busier than the pin-ball machines or the one-armed bandits. There was always an Indian restaurant

and it was always called the Taj Mahal and the owners were
always from Bangladesh. Of the three fish-and-chip shops, two
were owned by Greeks and the third was always closed. The
Chinese restaurant, Hong Kong Gardens, was always empty;
Food to Take Away its sign said. There were four pubs, one was
the Red Lion, and the largest one was owned by a bad-tempered
Londoner: 'He's a real Cockney,' people said; he had been in
the army.

To Town Centre, said a sign on Marine Parade, where there
was a tub of geraniums. *Golf-links*, said another, and a third,
Public Conveniences. A man stood just inside the door of *Gents*
and tried to catch your eye as you entered, but he never said
a word. The man with the mop stood at the door of *Ladies*. Outside town was a housing estate called Happy Valley. Yanks had
camped there in the war. Beyond it was a caravan park called
Golden Sands. The best hotel was the Grand, the poorest The
Marine, and there was a guest house called 'Bellavista'. The best
place to stay was at a bed and breakfast called the Blodgetts.
Charles Dickens had spent a night in the Grand, Wordsworth
had hiked in the nearby hills, Tennyson had spent a summer
in a huge house near the sandy stretch that was called the Strand,
and an obscure politician had died at the Rookery. A famous
murderer (he had slowly poisoned his wife) had been arrested
on the front, where he had been strolling with his young mistress.

The muddy part of the shore was called the Flats, the marshy
part the Levels, the stony part the Shingles, the pebbly part
The Reach, and something a mile away was always called the
Crumbles. The Manor, once very grand, was now a children's
home. Every Easter two gangs from London fought on Marine
Parade. The town had a long history of smuggling, a bay called
Smugglers' Cove and a pub called the Smugglers' Inn.

Of the four headlands nearby, the first was part of a private
golf course; the second was owned by the National Trust and
had a muddy path and wooden steps on the steep bits; the third
– the really magnificent one – was owned by the Ministry of
Defence and used as a firing range and labelled *Danger Area* on
the Ordnance Survey maps; the fourth headland was all rocks
and called The Cobbler and His Dwarfs.

The pier had been condemned. It was threatened with

demolition. A society had been formed to save it, but it would be blown up next year just the same. There was now a car park where the Romans had landed. The discotheque was called 'Spangles'. The museum was shut that day, the swimming pool closed for repairs, the Baptist church was open, there were nine motor coaches parked in front of the broken boulders and ruined walls called the Castle. At the café near the entrance to the Castle a fourteen-year-old girl served tea in cracked mugs, and cellophane-wrapped cookies, stale fruitcake and cold pork pies. She said, 'We don't do sandwiches' and 'We're all out of spoons' and when you asked for potato crisps she said, 'What flavour?' and listed five, including prawn, Bovril, cheese and onion, and bacon. There was a film of sticky marmalade on the tables at the café and you left with a patch of it on your elbow.

The railway had been closed down in 1964, and the fishing industry folded five years ago. The art-deco cinema was now a bingo hall and what had been a ship's chandler was the Cinema Club, where Swedish pornographic films were shown all day ('Members Only'). There was an American radar station – or was it a missile base? No one knew – a few miles away; but the Americans had kept a low profile ever since one American soldier had raped a local lass in his car at the Reach (she had been hitch-hiking in her bathing suit after dark that summer night). A nuclear power station quaintly named Thorncliffe was planned for the near future a mile south of the Cobbler. Bill Haley and His Comets had once sung at the Lido. The new shopping precinct was a failure. The dog was a Jack Russell terrier named Andy. The new bus shelter had been vandalized. It was famous for its whelks. It was raining.

So I was prepared for certain things that lay between Cromer and Clacton-on-Sea; I could ignore what was typical and familiar, and I could concentrate on what was new. I moved on, towards Great Yarmouth and Lowestoft, sometimes walking and some-times taking a local bus. The buses were the same width as the country lanes – so narrow I had to dive into the hawthorn hedges when they passed me. There were poppies in the peaceful fields. At Scratby there were shallys, and at the village of California a caravan park.

The villages in East Anglia were all sorts – small stringy-rich places, ruined settlements, tiny hamlets with long memories, collapsing churches surrounded by desolation, shally cities, and coastal horrors on rotting docks. Caister-on-Sea had been a Roman camp, and now it was a caravan park, just squat dingy houses, and pup tents, and 'caravanettes', and a man in his under-wear lying on a small rug of grass by the roadside, sunning his spotty back as the traffic roared past. So much for the romance of Caesar's Caister. Place-names were always misleading. Fresh-fields was always the semi-slum, and Messing, Turdley and Swines always the pretty villages.

'Great Yarmouth, with its mile of cockneyfied sea-front and its overflow of nigger minstrelsy, now strikes the wrong note so continuously that I, for my part, became conscious on the spot, of a chill to the spirit of research' – thus Henry James, fluttering his hands and perspiring and easing his big bum into the next train south. He had hoped to sit on the front and sink into a reverie of David Copperfield and the Peggottys. But it was often a mistake in England to revisit fictional landscapes. Local people blamed the German bombing for Great Yarmouth's gappy, still-damaged look, but James's dismay was proof that the town had been just as raucous and profane a hundred years ago. Yet that was in itself interesting; aliens usually missed the point about England by investing its landscape with the passions of its great literature, and it had so seldom been seen plainly, without literary footnotes. Like England, Great Yarmouth's chief attraction was that it was no longer a place of reverential pilgrimage. It had long ago stopped being Dickensian.

There was a circus in town; there was all-in wrestling – Giant Haystacks was fighting a grudge match against Big Daddy. *Space in my Pyjamas* was playing at a theatre on the front: 'Miss Fiona Richmond, Live on Stage! A Non-Stop Nude Laughter Romp – the Ultimate Sexual Fantasy!'. There were now two miles of seafront: roller coasters, amusement arcades, shooting galleries. The town had swollen and burst long ago, but it had the English seaside characteristic of being self-destructive in its own way. The shows were popular and well attended, perhaps because they lacked the decent vulgarity of those at Cromer.

'That wally on the poster. I heard him on the flipping wireless.'

The accents of Great Yarmouth's visitors were the accents of London – a certain class, sticking to old-fashioned expressions and stubborn intonations.

'Let's nip over one of them caffys.'

And the two boys kicked at the traffic and hurried under the sign, *Frying for Dinner – Tea – Supper*.

The coast between here and Lowestoft was poor for walking: it was populous, bungalow-ridden and the only place to walk was on the main road. I hiked to Gorleston, a mile or so, and gave up. A new hospital had been built at Gorleston. It was flimsily made, and very ugly; it also looked temporary and unsafe. The national poverty was now evident in public buildings, some of them almost unbelievable eyesores. *She just let herself go*, people said of a woman who got fat and stopped combing her hair. Sometimes Britain seemed that way to me. And it was too bad a hospital looked so inadequate, because Britain had the best public health service in the world and certainly the fairest doctors.

At Lowestoft I began to understand East Anglia's modest prosperity. Lowestoft had large produce markets and on its seafront a frozen food plant as vast as a power station. East Anglia was intensively farmed, and all those vegetables I had seen ended up here in ice-bricks. After the failure of its automobile industry and its steel mills and its electronics factories, one of Britain's most notable post-war successes was in growing Birds Eye spinach.

The railway station at Lowestoft was open, but when I asked a group of men gathered there whether there were any trains they laughed.

'Come back September first,' Mr Fricker said.

They were all railwaymen. They were not picketing; they had just come to the station out of habit. They had nothing else to do.

'No trains at all,' Mr Beamish said. 'This station is one hundred per cent.'

Mr Holmesome, a driver said, 'Want to know the truth? The drivers here don't want to come out on strike. We're just doing it out of loyalty to the union. This isn't a busy station. It's only average. If the strike goes on, this will be one of the first stations to be axed, and then we'll lose our jobs, and we'll be in the shit with everyone else.'

It was an hour and twenty minutes from Lowestoft to Ipswich. By bus it was almost three hours – it took all morning It was a little over forty miles.

But I was headed down the coast for Southwold. I went to the bus station: Was there a bus? 'Left an hour ago, squire' – 'squire' because the news was bad, a further turn of the screw, sarcasm, not politeness. There was not another bus to Southwold today.

'I have to get to Southwold,' I said.

'I'd hitch-hike, if I were you,' he said. 'That's the only sure way.'

This was spoken to me in a town (pop. 52,000) on the coast of England in the summer of 1982. *Hitch-hike ... that's the only sure way.* Good God.

I walked a few miles to Kessingland and then stuck out my thumb.

'My mistake was stopping too long in my jobs. And this Jew-boy,' Mr Marwood said wearily, as we drove towards Southwold, '– though I didn't have anything against his religion – took advantage of me. I was earning five pounds, ten shillings in 1948. It was a good wage – I was sixteen. I was on commission. I started to sell cheese rolls – this was a grocery store, and we did a little bit of greengrocery. The profit on cheese rolls was five hundred per cent. My commission was sixpence in the pound. I worked very hard, but when my wages went up to seven pounds this Jewboy claimed he couldn't pay me. "I don't have that kind of money," he said. Imagine. So I left. I just told him what he could do with his job, and I found another one. There's always work for people who want it.'

Southwold was one of those coastal villages which had become remote with the closure of its railway. It was now emptier and more rural than it had been twenty years before. On a small house in the High Street there was a plaque saying, 'The Author George Orwell (E. A. Blair) Resided Here.' It was after he had been down and out in Paris and London; he had no money; he lived with his parents – this was their house. He got his pen name from a river some distance south of here on the Essex coast – the Orwell.

'I always pick up hitch-hikers,' Mr Grainer said. There was

no coast path to Dunwich, only marshes and an intrusive estuary. Mr Grainer picked up a silent man, and then a girl with a ruck-sack, all in the space of a few miles. He never passed a hitch-hiker if he had a spare seat.

'It's a lot of wear and tear on a car,' I said.

Mr Grainer laughed out loud. 'Not my car!' He was delivering it to a car dealer, he said. That was his job, delivering cars. He was so badly paid for doing it he took his revenge by picking up every hitch-hiker he saw. He laughed again. 'My guv'nor would do his nut if he saw me now.'

The girl said to call her 'Jerry'. She was on vacation. She taught school in Africa – the Sudan.

'We get a lot of spare parts from South Africa,' Mr Grainer said.

Jerry said that the Sudan was not anywhere near South Africa.

'All the same to me,' Mr Grainer said, cheerfully. 'Cannibals and communists!'

Dunwich ('once an important seaport, before the sea swept it away') was a disjointed village scattered thinly against a lumpy green shore. Everyone said how sad it was that it was no longer prosperous, but its prosperity had come in the Middle Ages, and by 1800 it was an impoverished fishing village. Its empty, de-populated atmosphere inspired ghost stories, tales of sinking spells that travelled through Dunwich houses, and the legend of the Black Dog, a phantom hound that appeared at night in the village and caused acute depression. Dunwich was one of the strangest places on the coast – famous for no longer existing.

Many villages on this shore were associated with ghosts. It was the low boggy land, the marshes, the fogs, the shifting sands, the long tides, and the medieval churches of cracked stone. Here were some of the oldest Christian graveyards in England, and they lay in a landscape which cast forth ghostly mirages. Some of this atmosphere had been invented by Montague Rhodes James in his powerful stories of the supernatural. But his topo-graphical descriptions could be very accurate, especially when (in 'A Warning to the Curious') he spoke of approaching a town and seeing 'a belt of old firs, wind-beaten, thick at the top, with the slope that old seaside trees have; seen on the skyline from the train they would tell you in an instant, if you did not know it, that you were approaching a windy coast.' That was Aldeburgh.

So some fictional landscapes were still worth revisiting. Aldeburgh, too, had lost its train, and from eighteen trains a day (nine in, nine out) it was now a car park lined with exquisite buildings, and with a shingly beach riding over its streets. The Moot Hall displayed a message from Buckingham Palace that had just been nailed up: 'We were both most touched by your very kind message on the birth of our son. We have been overwhelmed by the reaction to this exciting event. Best wishes.'

At the bottom edge of Suffolk, the coast collapsed in a mass of marshes and estuaries. There was no coastal path. Strictly speaking, there was no coast, but only forty miles of waterlogged land, and isolated towns at the end of long flat roads. It corresponded to the complexity of the Scottish coast at the opposite end of the country, except that this was sand, not rock, and instead of surf whipping into cliffs, this had a shallow sinking look. It was in and out to Felixstowe and Harwich and The Naze; I was fighting the strike, but also finding it funny that I now woke up in Walton-on-the-Naze and, packing my knapsack and oiling my shoes and putting an apple into my pocket and saying goodbye to Mrs Dumper at 'The Elms', set off like a man with a mission. I may have looked something like Robert Byron on the road to Oxiana, but in fact I was on my way to Frinton-on-Sea.

Frinton had its surprises. It was posh. Who would have guessed it from its name? There was a settlement of houses behind a fence with the sign 'Frinton Gates'; no trees – always an indication in an English suburb of a preference for rose gardens and herbaceous borders; large smug villas and a grassy esplanade and not a chip-shop in sight. It was a Tory stronghold, that was clear: you could tell by the tone of the golf club – by its forbidding gates. And Frinton was also sealed off from the rest of Britain. To get into the town it was necessary to go through a sort of valve, which was a level crossing on the railway line. It was a maddening bottleneck, but it had kept Frinton unviolated because it was the only way in or out of the place.

I walked on to Clacton, which was brash and noisy – holiday

people, a holiday camp, trippers and picknickers. I met a man named Arthur who said that if he had lived right, saved his money instead of losing it on the dogs, used his loaf instead of trusting people who had said they'd see him right, he would have ended up in Frinton in a detached house instead of a semi-detached in Clacton. That was an English characteristic: they did not allude to distant places on the coast when they were making comparisons. They would play with a mile or two and compare their lot in Bournemouth with what it might have been in Poole; they compared Brighton with Hove, Whitby with Sandsend, Exmouth with Budleigh Salterton. They did not reach far when they tried to imagine how their lives might have been different. And, really, Clacton wasn't so bad, Arthur said, when you compared it to Jaywick Sands.

'Jaywick's a shanty town,' Arthur said.

It was. There was sand in the streets. People slept in the shallys. Most houses were shacks the size of one-car garages. Jaywick was crowded and cheap. It looked as though it had taken a terrific thumping – war or weather – and was awfully battered, like a seaside slum in Argentina or Mexico. It had the same grubby geniality, the same broken fences. The beach was empty. This was a Sunday in late July. Two women stood facing the murky sea. They were holding hands. I was especially fascinated by their affection, because the smaller one was pregnant. They were Roberta and Mandy; they had been living together in a borrowed bungalow at Jaywick for five months as a couple. Roberta had left her husband in Dagenham after she had met Mandy and realized she was a lesbian. She had been two months pregnant then. Mandy had been a tower of strength, and tonight they were going to a pre-natal class of the National Childbirth Trust up in Clacton – breathing exercises and general awareness. Mandy said, 'I'm her labour support.' They were planning to raise the child themselves.

At last I took a bus to Southend, an inland detour, because there was no direct way across the flats and sand of the Essex coast. There were no trains running, the bus went over the hills with a natural bounce, and to the east it was impossible to tell the brown land from the brown sea; one ran into the other. Here, the sea was the River Thames at its widest part. I met Brenda

Priestley on the bus. She had worked at Harvey Nichols Department Store in London. She had served Mahatma Gandhi one day. Handkerchiefs – a box of three, Irish linen, lovely they were. He seemed an odd one, though – wearing a sort of nappy. I looked out of the window, trying to imagine it, and saw sliding gulls, and a boy behind me muttered, 'Sowfen'.

Even Southend had a respectable district – the higher, leafier ledge called Westcliff. The seedy part of Southend was down the hill, below the crumbling white wedding cake of the Palace Hotel, and the 'Kursaal' amusement park. This was where the gangs fought at Easter – and not only then but on every Bank Holiday. Just a few months ago two thousand Skinheads had battled two thousand Mods. But they had not destroyed buildings, they had not broken windows or set fires. They had not even made much noise, people said. They had broken each other's heads on the promenade along the seafront. To slow them down, the police had confiscated their bootlaces as soon as the boys had got off the train at Southend Central.

This was high summer, but Southend was as empty as it had been in March. It was the effect of the strike in this railway resort. Without trains it was hard to get in or out. Traditionally, it was for day-trippers, Londoners. Its atmosphere wasn't briny and coastal, it was riverbank sag, the greasy Thames, London toughness. In many senses Southend was a part of London. The river was its spiritual link, but the river was not put to any practical use. The physical link, the railway, had been severed by the strike, and now Southend was revealed in this empty condition as a mixture of river rawness and sleazy elegance. The few people here were not vacationers. They were between jobs, between lives, waiting for something to open up. Other places could do without the railway, but Southend was expiring, because this seaside place was not on the way to anywhere except Foulness, which was one of the very few aptly-named places in the country.

'That little geezer with the piggy eyes,' a toothless young man named Ron Woodbag said. The isolation made people irritable He was amazingly tattooed – his neck, his face, the backs of his hands. So was the fellow he was now addressing – spider webs on his forearms, Britannia on his chest, skulls on his knuckles. 'I'm going to kill that geezer '

But Ron Woodbag did not do anything. This was in the Foresters' Arms. The juke box was deafening, playing the hits of Britain's most popular music groups – Raw Sewage ('Kick it to Death'), Nupkins ('Yellow Pain'), Slag ('What You Like to Eat'), Gender-Bender ('Getting it Behind You'); and then a live group, Spurm, got up on the little stage and howled. They looked like ferrets, they had spiky hair and claws. But they were harmless – pale skinny English faces and bad teeth. The bikers and punks in the bar were well-behaved. Like many other places I had seen in Britain it looked much worse than it was. It was not vicious, it just had that dirty desecrated look that I thought of as English. There was no vice that I had seen, no red light district, nothing wicked, nothing stirring after midnight, on the whole of the British coast.

Southend's pier, the longest one in the world, stretched for a mile and a half. It showed on route maps as a distinct feature, like Portland Bill. The end of the pier was as far as I wished to go in Britain.

On my second morning I strolled through Southend, past the dog-walkers ('Come here, Princess! Leave the man alone, Princess! Stop, girl! Princess, don't – oh, I am so sorry –') and down to the front and to the pier. It was muddy underneath for more than a mile. The gulls were rasping in annoyance – mewing, barking, yapping, shrieking. I kept walking. The pier was so long and the air so polluted that Southend dissolved in the heat haze yonder. It was a fitting end to my trip. I had walked into the sea. But the tide was out. It was a sea of the filthiest mud.

Once the English shore had been fabulous, and parts of it so hidden that the rock pools had never been touched by man. The magic had lasted for a long time. The creatures at the tide-line had floated and swayed for eons – 'since the creation of the world', Edmund Gosse wrote in *Father and Son*. He had seen it perfect in the 1850s and he compared the coast to Keats's Grecian urn, 'a still unravished bride of quietness'.

'All this is over and done with,' he went on. 'The ring of living beauty drawn about our shores was a very thin and fragile one. It had existed all those centuries solely in consequence of the indifference, the blissful ignorance of man ... No one will see again on the shore of England what I saw in my early childhood.'

Every British person who knew the coast said that, and every single one of them was right. The rock pools of Devon and Cornwall had been violated, and Dunwich had sunk into the sea, and Prestatyn was littered and Sunderland was unemployed. Oddest of all, there were hardly any ships on a coast that had once been crammed with them. 'Once a great port', it always said of the seaside towns in the guidebook. And shipbuilding was finished, too – places like Maryport and Nefyn which had made great ships for the world were nothing now, and perhaps Clydeside and Belfast would follow them into obscurity. So much had withered and gone, and reckless people had done damage with their schemes; and didn't the hungry ocean also perpetually gain advantage on the kingdom of the shore?

One of the few boasts the British risked was that their country was changeless. In some trivial ways it was, but to an alien it seemed entirely irregular and unpredictable, changing from day to day. It was not a question of seismic shocks, but rather a steadier kind of erosion – like the seemingly changeless and consoling tide in which there was always, in its push and pull, slightly more loss than gain. The endless mutation of the British coast wonderfully symbolized the state of the nation. In a quiet way the British were hopeful and, because in the cycle of ruin and renewal there had been so much ruin, they were glad to be still holding on – that was the national mood – but they were hard put to explain their survival. The British seemed to me to be people forever standing on a crumbling coast and scanning the horizon. So I had done the right thing in travelling the coast, and instead of looking out to sea I had looked inland.

And the paradox was that Britain was changing constantly in unalterable ways. Perhaps that was another way of saying it was ageing – 'the same, only older', as people said of themselves in Bexhill-on-Sea, where it was bad manners – un-English – to mention death. I knew that the things I had seen would be changed, like Gosse's pretty pools of corallines and silken anemones. For example, a pressurized water reactor, like the one that had cracked and leaked at Three Mile Island, was planned for the Suffolk coast at Sizewell. And yet it is every traveller's conceit that no one will see what he has seen: his trip displaces the landscape and his version of events is all that matters. He is certainly kidding himself in this, but if he didn't kid himself a little he would never go anywhere.

Today I was done; I had no plans. Over there, across the Thames estuary at Margate, I had set out almost three months ago. It was not far across the river mouth, less than thirty miles. So I had made a connection. I had found a way of joining one end of this kingdom to the other, giving it a beginning and an end. I would not have done it differently in Africa. I felt I knew the world much better for having seen Britain – and I knew Britain so well and had been in its pockets so long I felt impatient to leave; I had my usual bad dream that I would be forced to stay longer.

The tide came in. I was still at the end of the pier. I had never seen a tide rise so fast, from so far away. I could see it flowing across the foreshore as if it was being poured. It became a rippling flood. Now, after a few minutes, it was a foot deep. It was moving the boats, buoying them, rocking them on their keels. I saw a shallow dinghy, just like the one I had rowed across Lough Erne from Bellanaleck to Carrybridge, past people standing in wet fields, who were living their lives there. I had rowed back and forth, and then gone away. Every day on the coast I had gone away, leaving people staring out at the ocean's crowded chop: 'Our end is Life – put out to sea.'

The rising tide took the smell away. Then the gulls flew off – and that was another thing about travel: these flights, these disappearances. It was no different in Britain than in any other foreign place, except that a country could sound sad if you spoke the language.

Fish were jumping where there had been coils of rope sinking in the mud and bubble-holes. The boats were straightening and creaking. Now the sea was splashing against the pier. I sat there until all the boats were upright – even those big peeling motor launches. One hulk had been holed and did not rise – the water lapped at the roof of its wheelhouse. I did not want to think of a name for it. The tide was high. I started down the long pier towards the shore, trying to figure out a way of getting home.

FOR THE BEST IN PAPERBACKS, LOOK FOR THE

In every corner of the world, on every subject under the sun, Penguin represents quality and variety – the very best in publishing today.

For complete information about books available from Penguin – including Pelicans, Puffins, Peregrines and Penguin Classics – and how to order them, write to us at the appropriate address below. Please note that for copyright reasons the selection of books varies from country to country.

In the United Kingdom: For a complete list of books available from Penguin in the U.K., please write to *Dept E.P., Penguin Books Ltd, Harmondsworth, Middlesex, UB7 0DA*

In the United States: For a complete list of books available from Penguin in the U.S., please write to *Dept BA, Penguin, 299 Murray Hill Parkway, East Rutherford, New Jersey 07073*

In Canada: For a complete list of books available from Penguin in Canada, please write to *Penguin Books Canada Ltd, 2801 John Street, Markham, Ontario L3R 1B4*

In Australia: For a complete list of books available from Penguin in Australia, please write to the *Marketing Department, Penguin Books Australia Ltd, P.O. Box 257, Ringwood, Victoria 3134*

In New Zealand: For a complete list of books available from Penguin in New Zealand, please write to the *Marketing Department, Penguin Books (NZ) Ltd, Private Bag, Takapuna, Auckland 9*

In India: For a complete list of books available from Penguin, please write to *Penguin Overseas Ltd, 706 Eros Apartments, 56 Nehru Place, New Delhi, 110019*

In Holland: For a complete list of books available from Penguin in Holland, please write to *Penguin Books Nederland B.V., Postbus 195, NL–1380 AD Weesp, Netherlands*

In Germany: For a complete list of books available from Penguin, please write to *Penguin Books Ltd, Friedrichstrasse 10 – 12, D–6000 Frankfurt Main 1, Federal Republic of Germany*

In Spain: For a complete list of books available from Penguin in Spain, please write to *Longman Penguin España, Calle San Nicolas 15, E–28013 Madrid, Spain*

Paul Theroux in Penguin

The Mosquito Coast

'Stunning ... an adventure story of classic quality' – *Sunday Times*

'An epic of paranoid obsession that swirls the reader head-long to deposit him on a mudbank of horror' – *Guardian*

'As oppressive and powerful as its central character. It bursts with inventiveness' – *The Times*

The London Embassy

'Fiendishly entertaining' – *Guardian*

'An alert, elegant, cunning book' – *Observer*

'Paul Theroux is a Somerset Maugham at heart: telling a story, conveying an atmosphere, getting an emotion dead right' – *Sunday Express*

The Family Arsenal

'One of the most brilliantly evocative novels of London that has appeared for years ... very disturbing indeed' – *The Times*

'This is a thriller, tightly plotted, terribly evocative' – *Daily Telegraph*

'Mr Theroux has the ability to turn the familiar into the fabulous' – *Sunday Telegraph*

Picture Palace

'Maude's voice, harsh, coarse and yet surprisingly inno-cent, remains in the ear long after the book has been put down' – *The Times*

'Startlingly original, very funny' – *Daily Telegraph*

'Too good to miss' – Auberon Waugh

and

Doctor Slaughter
Girls at Play
The Consul's File

Monsignor Quixote   Graham Greene

Now filmed for television, Graham Greene's novel, like Cervantes' seventeenth-century classic, is a brilliant fable for its times. 'A deliciously funny novel' – *The Times*

The Dearest and the Best   Leslie Thomas

In the spring of 1940 the spectre of war turned into grim reality – and for all the inhabitants of the historic villages of the New Forest it was the beginning of the most bizarre, funny and tragic episode of their lives. 'Excellent' – *Sunday Times*

Earthly Powers   Anthony Burgess

Anthony Burgess's magnificent masterpiece, an enthralling, epic narrative spanning six decades and spotlighting some of the most vivid events and characters of our times. 'Enormous imagination and vitality . . . a huge book in every way' – Bernard Levin in the *Sunday Times*

The Penitent   Isaac Bashevis Singer

From the Nobel Prize-winning author comes a powerful story of a man who has material wealth but feels spiritually impoverished. 'Singer restates with dignity the spiritual aspirations and the cultural complexities of a lifetime, and it must be said that in doing so he gives the Evil One no quarter and precious little advantage' – Anita Brookner in the *Sunday Times*

Paradise Postponed   John Mortimer

'Hats off to John Mortimer. He's done it again' – *Spectator*. A rumbustious, hilarious new novel from the creator of Rumpole, *Paradise Postponed* is now a major Thames Television series.

Animal Farm   George Orwell

The classic political fable of the twentieth century.

FOR THE BEST IN PAPERBACKS, LOOK FOR THE

A CHOICE OF PENGUIN FICTION

Other Women   Lisa Alther

From the bestselling author of *Kinflicks* comes this compelling novel of today's woman – and a heroine with whom millions of women will identify.

Your Lover Just Called   John Updike

Stories of Joan and Richard Maple – a couple multiplied by love and divided by lovers. Here is the portrait of a modern American marriage in all its mundane moments and highs and lows of love as only John Updike could draw it.

Mr Love and Justice   Colin MacInnes

Frankie Love took up his career as a ponce about the same time as Edward Justice became vice-squad detective. Except that neither man was particularly suited for his job, all they had in common was an interest in crime. But, as any ponce or copper will tell you, appearances are not always what they seem. Provocative and honest and acidly funny, *Mr Love and Justice* is the final volume of Colin MacInnes's famous London trilogy.

An Ice-Cream War   William Boyd

As millions are slaughtered on the Western Front, a ridiculous and little-reported campaign is being waged in East Africa – a war they continued after the Armistice because no one told them to stop. 'A towering achievement' – John Carey, Chairman of the Judges of the 1982 Booker Prize, for which this novel was nominated.

Every Day is Mother's Day   Hilary Mantel

An outrageous story of lust, adultery, madness, death and the social services. 'Strange . . . rather mad . . . extremely funny . . . she sometimes reminded me of the early Muriel Spark' – Auberon Waugh

1982 Janine   Alasdair Gray

Set inside the head of an ageing, divorced, alcoholic, insomniac supervisor of security installations who is tippling in the bedroom of a small Scottish hotel – this is a most brilliant and controversial novel.

Family Myths and Legends Patricia Ferguson

Gareth was just beginning to believe that he really enjoyed his relatives these days. And then Gareth's grandmother turns up in Gareth's hospital – and he is up to his upwardly-mobile neck in family once more. 'Great funniness and perception, and stunning originality' – *Daily Telegraph*

The Beans of Egypt, Maine Carolyn Chute

Out of the hidden heart of America comes this uncompromising novel of what life is like for people who have nothing left to them except their own pain, humiliation and rage. 'It's loving, terrible and funny and written as deftly as stitching on a quilt . . . a lovely, truthful book' – *Observer*

City of Spades Colin MacInnes

'A splendid novel, sparklingly written, warm, wise and funny' – *Daily Mail*. *City of Spades*, *Absolute Beginners* and *Mr Love and Justice* make up Colin MacInnes's trilogy on London street life from the inside out.

The Anatomy Lesson Philip Roth

The hilarious story of Nathan Zuckerman, the famous forty-year-old writer who decides to give it all up and become a doctor – and a pornographer – instead. 'The finest, boldest and funniest piece of fiction which Philip Roth has yet produced' – *Spectator*

The Rachel Papers Martin Amis

A stylish, sexy and ribaldly funny novel by the author of *Money*. 'Remarkable' – *Listener*. 'Irreverent' – *Daily Telegraph*. 'Very funny indeed' – *Spectator*

Scandal A. N. Wilson

Sexual peccadilloes, treason and blackmail are all ingredients on the boil in A. N. Wilson's new, *cordon noir* comedy. 'Drily witty, deliciously nasty' – *Sunday Telegraph*